Rob Eisenberg and
Christopher Bennage

Sams **Teach Yourself**

WPF

in **24** Hours

SAMS   800 East 96th Street, Indianapolis, Indiana, 46240 USA

Sams Teach Yourself WPF in 24 Hours

ISBN-13: 978-0-672-32985-2
ISBN-10: 0-672-32985-9

Library of Congress Cataloging-in-Publication Data

Eisenberg, Robert (Robert Harold)

  Sams teach yourself WPF in 24 hours / Robert Eisenberg and Christopher Bennage.

    p. cm.

  ISBN-13: 978-0-672-32985-2

  ISBN-10: 0-672-32985-9

 1. Windows presentation foundation. 2. Application software. 3. Windows (Computer programs)—Standards. 4. Microsoft .NET. I. Bennage, Christopher. II. Title. III. Title: Teach yourself WPF in 24 hours.

  QA76.76.A65E39 2009

  006.7'882—dc22

                        2008020014

Printed in the United States of America

Second Printing July 2008

Trademarks

All terms mentioned in this book that are known to be trademarks or service marks have been appropriately capitalized. Sams Publishing cannot attest to the accuracy of this information. Use of a term in this book should not be regarded as affecting the validity of any trademark or service mark.

Warning and Disclaimer

Every effort has been made to make this book as complete and accurate as possible, but no warranty or fitness is implied. The information provided is on an "as is" basis. The authors and the publisher shall have neither liability nor responsibility to any person or entity with respect to any loss or damages arising from the information contained in this book or from the use of the programs accompanying it.

Bulk Sales

Sams Publishing offers excellent discounts on this book when ordered in quantity for bulk purchases or special sales. For more information, please contact

U.S. Corporate and Government Sales
1-800-382-3419
corpsales@pearsontechgroup.com

For sales outside the U.S., please contact

International Sales
international@pearson.com

Editor-in-Chief
Karen Gettman

Executive Editor
Neil Rowe

Development Editor
Mark Renfrow

Managing Editor
Kristy Hart

Project Editor
Betsy Harris

Copy Editor
Barbara Hacha

Indexer
Brad Herriman

Proofreader
Debbie Williams

Technical Editor
J. Boyd Nolan

Publishing Coordinator
Cindy Teeters

Book Designer
Gary Adair

Composition
Nonie Ratcliff

This Book Is Safari Enabled

The Safari® Enabled icon on the cover of your favorite technology book means the book is available through Safari Bookshelf. When you buy this book, you get free access to the online edition for 45 days.

Safari Bookshelf is an electronic reference library that lets you easily search thousands of technical books, find code samples, download chapters, and access technical information whenever and wherever you need it.

To gain 45-day Safari Enabled access to this book

 ▶ Go to www.informit.com/onlineedition.

 ▶ Complete the brief registration form.

 ▶ Enter the coupon code F613-Z84G-8HWN-PHGQ-1G5E.

If you have difficulty registering on Safari Bookshelf or accessing the online edition, please email customer-service@safaribooksonline.com.

Contents at a Glance

WITHDRAWN

Part IV: Creating Rich Experiences

Part V: Appendixes

Table of Contents

Sams Teach Yourself WPF in 24 Hours

About the Authors

Rob Eisenberg is vice president and cofounder of Blue Spire Consulting, Inc. (www.blue-spire.com). He is a frequent blogger in the Devlicio.us (www.devlicio.us) blogging community and speaks at various community events on the subjects of WPF, Agile, and TDD. His career began in music composition, which very naturally led him into interactive media. He was drawn to the .NET Framework by the persistent recommendations of his present business partner and soon after discovered WPF. Rob has been working with WPF since the pre-beta days and was among the top 20 finalists in Microsoft's Code Master Challenge in 2006. In his spare time, he enjoys playing and teaching drums, making artisan cheese, reading, and swing dancing with his lovely wife, Anna.

Christopher Bennage is the president and cofounder of Blue Spire Consulting, Inc., a Florida-based software consulting firm specializing in .NET technologies and emphasizing personal interactions with the customer. Christopher began programming on his Texas Instrument in elementary school but fell in love with computers with the advent of the Commodore Amiga. His career has brought him through various technologies beginning with Lotus Notes, VBA, and classic ASP before eventually landing him in the marvelous world of C# and the .NET Framework. His early interest in Flash, rich user experiences, and usability led him to be an early adopter of both WPF and Silverlight.

Christopher embraces the values of the Agile Software Manifesto and has been heavily influenced by Extreme Programming, Domain Driven Design, and other related practices.

In his free time, Christopher is usually very distracted by a dozen different, competing creative ideas. Aside from that he can sometimes be found playing Frisbee golf, guitar, or video games. He lives in Tallahassee, Florida, with his wife, Sandra, and their two children, Adah and Ranen (soon to be three children).

Dedication

This book is dedicated to our wives, Anna Eisenberg and Sandra Bennage.
Without their patience, love, and support we would not
have been able to make this happen.

Acknowledgments

Rob and Christopher would like to thank the following: Mark Loy, Kevin Crumley, and Bryan Gertonson for help in reviewing the book, the Monday Night gang for perpetual support and friendship, and our parents for encouraging us to play with computers. Christopher would also like to thank the high school seniors at Canopy Roads (class of 2008). You guys rock!

We also benefited a great deal from many bloggers: John Gossman, Dan Crevier, Charles Petzold, Beatriz Costa, Josh Smith, Lee Brimelow, Kevin Hoffman, Karsten Januszewski, Daniel Lehenbauer, Jeremy Miller, and Paul Stovell.

We'd also like to give a shout out to our friends at CodeBetter.com and Devlicio.us. A special thanks goes to Mark James at famfamfam.com for his excellent open source icon library.

Finally, we would like to thank God for his grace and mercy, and for allowing us to combine our passion with our profession.

We Want to Hear from You!

As the reader of this book, *you* are our most important critic and commentator. We value your opinion, and we want to know what we're doing right, what we could do better, what areas you'd like to see us publish in, and any other words of wisdom you're willing to pass our way.

You can email or write me directly to let me know what you did or didn't like about this book—as well as what we can do to make our books stronger.

Please note that I cannot help you with technical problems related to the topic of this book, and that due to the high volume of mail I receive, I might not be able to reply to every message.

When you write, please be sure to include this book's title and author as well as your name and phone number or email address. I will carefully review your comments and share them with the authors and editors who worked on the book.

Email: feedback@samspublishing.com

Mail: Neil Rowe
            Executive Editor
            Sams Publishing
            800 East 96th Street
            Indianapolis, IN 46240 USA

Reader Services

Visit our website and register this book at www.informit.com/register for convenient access to any updates, downloads, or errata that might be available for this book.

Introduction

Windows Presentation Foundation, or WPF, is Microsoft's latest framework for building sophisticated and rich user interfaces for desktop applications. WPF differs significantly from its predecessor, and yet draws on many of the concepts found existing in frameworks for both desktops and the web.

WPF enables developers to easily and quickly handle tasks that were either very difficult or impossible to accomplish in previous frameworks.

Audience and Organization

This book is intended for those who have at least some experience with general .NET development. If you have worked with WinForms or ASP.NET, you should feel comfortable with this book. The code examples provided are written in C#, but we've been careful to keep them readable for those whose primary language is Visual Basic.

Because WPF is both a broad and a deep topic, it can easily become overwhelming. Our approach in this book is to stay broad. We cover the essential concepts of the framework. Our goal is for you to feel confident building a WPF application when you are done with the book, as well as equipping you to dig deeper into any areas of the framework that interest you.

The book is organized into five parts. In each of the first four parts, we build a sample application that demonstrates the features of WPF covered in that part. Although the applications are simplified, they are designed to reflect real-world scenarios that you are likely to encounter. Each of the parts builds on its predecessor, and we recommend reading them in order. Part V concludes with information designed to help you move forward after the book.

▶ **Part I, "Getting Started"**—We build a utility for browsing the fonts installed on your system. You'll learn about the new markup language XAML that is an integral part of WPF. We also introduce you to most of the basic controls, including those that handle layout. You'll also learn about basic data binding in WPF.

▶ **Part II, "Reaching the User"**—You'll create your own rich text editor. You'll learn about the powerful new event and command systems. We also introduce you to a few more controls and show you how you can deploy your WPF applications. You also discover how to print from WPF.

- ▶ **Part III, "Visualizing Data"**—This part teaches you how to style an application, as well as how to use WPF's powerful graphics capabilities for visualizing the data in your applications. We also dig further into data binding and show you some options for architecting your WPF applications.

- ▶ **Part IV, "Creating Rich Experiences"**—You'll learn how to easily embed media in your applications. You'll see how WPF's drawing and templating APIs make it easy to create unique and visually attractive interfaces. You'll also get started with animation.

- ▶ **Part V, "Appendices"**—This includes a brief introduction to 3D and a list of tools, frameworks, and other resources that aid in WPF development.

Throughout the book, we use code-continuation characters: When a line of code is too long to fit on the printed page, we wrap it to the next line and precede it with a code-continuation character, like this:

```
public object ConvertBack(object value, Type targetType, object parameter,
➥CultureInfo culture)
```

Farther Up and Further In

Learning WPF is really a lot of fun. We've discovered a new joy in building user interfaces since we've begun using this technology. We believe that you'll have the same experience working through this book. Although it may take some time to become a master of WPF, it's actually quite easy to get up and running quickly. By the time you are done here, you'll be ready to start using WPF on your next project.

Now, let's get started!

PART I

Getting Started

HOUR 1

What WPF Is and Isn't

What Is WPF?

WPF is big. In fact, it can be overwhelming because it has lots of moving parts that all interconnect. The shortest answer to the question, though, is that WPF is an API for building graphical user interfaces (UI) for desktop applications with the .NET Framework.

Now for the longer answer.

To begin with, WPF is an abbreviation for *Windows Presentation Foundation*. Physically, it's a set of .NET assemblies and supporting tools. It's intended to provide a unified API for creating rich, sophisticated user interfaces on Windows XP and Windows Vista.

WPF combines the good things from web development, such as style sheets and a markup language for declarative UI, with good things from Rich Internet Applications, such as scalable vector graphics, animation, and media support. These good things are wrapped up with the good things from traditional Windows development—things like strong integration with the OS and data binding. In WPF, these concepts are strengthened and unified. Even all that does not capture the full extent of WPF. It has other facets, such as support for 3D drawing, advanced typography, and portable documents similar to PDF.

WPF is also a *unified* API. Many of the things you are able to do in WPF, you could do before. However, doing them all in one application was extremely difficult. Not only does WPF enable you to bring these disparate features together, but it provides you with a consistent API for doing so.

WPF is just one part of a larger picture. Three additional libraries were also released as part of .NET 3.0. All four of these libraries have the same intent of providing a consistent, unified API for their domain. Additionally, combining any of these four libraries in an application can yield some very impressive results. The three sibling libraries of WPF are shown in Table 1.1.

TABLE 1.1   The Sibling Libraries of WPF

WCF	Windows Communication Foundation is focused on messaging. This API greatly simplifies all sorts of networking and communication tasks. It covers everything from web services to remoting to P2P and more.
WF	A powerful library for building workflow enabled applications. It utilizes a markup language for declaring workflows in an application, and thus prevents workflow from becoming hard-coded. It also makes it very easy for developers to create custom workflow tasks.
CardSpace	The least famous of the four libraries, CardSpace provides a common identification system that can be used by desktop applications, web sites, and more.

The immediate predecessor to WPF is Windows Forms, the graphical API available to developers in .NET 2.0 and earlier. Windows Forms provides a managed wrapper for accessing the graphical functions of the traditional Windows API. WPF differs fundamentally in that it builds on top of DirectX. The DirectX API was originally focused on multimedia and game programming in particular. As such, you are able to do some nifty visual tricks in WPF that were practically impossible with Windows Forms. It also means that WPF will take advantage of hardware acceleration when it is available.

WPF still has some similarities to Windows Forms (and even ASP.NET Web Forms). Microsoft provides a library of basic controls such as text boxes and buttons. You'll also encounter familiar concepts such as data binding and code-behind files. All these concepts have been refined and improved for WPF.

Getting to Know the Features of WPF

Let's take a moment to review the major features of WPF. We'll cover each of these with more depth in later hours.

Declarative UI

WPF allows you to construct your interface using a markup language called XAML (pronounced *zammel*, rhymes with *camel*). We'll dig into XAML in Hour 2, "Understanding XAML," but if you have ever worked with HTML, you are already familiar with the concepts. XAML is a much richer markup language than HTML, and it has less ambiguity. Visual Studio, as well as some members of the Expression family of products are able to generate XAML natively.

XAML provides a common medium for interacting with designers.

Intelligent Layout

Arranging the various components of an application onscreen can be complicated, and it's further complicated by the myriad display possibilities that users might have. WPF provides an extensible layout system for visually arranging the elements of a user interface. It can intelligently resize and adjust, depending on how you define the layout. We'll cover this in some detail when we discuss panels in Hour 4, "Handling Application Layout."

Scalable Graphics

Graphics in WPF are vector based, in contrast to raster based. Vector graphics are inherently scalable and typically require less storage than a comparable raster image. WPF still has plenty of support for raster graphics, but vectors are an excellent fit for constructing user interfaces.

Vector graphics have already become popular on the web, primarily because of Adobe Flash and to a lesser extent the Scalable Vector Graphics specification (SVG).

The net result for developers with WPF is that applications scale nicely without a loss in visual quality.

Vector Versus Raster

A raster graphic is an image that is stored as rectangle grid of pixels, and each pixel is assigned a color. Most graphic file formats that you are familiar with are just variations to this method. This includes formats such as GIF, JPEG, BMP, and PNG.

Raster graphics are also called *bitmaps*. (Don't let the the BMP file format confuse you. The term *bitmap* is a general term describing a particular way to store image data.)

Suppose that you have a raster image of a blue circle on a white background that is 100×100 pixels. The computer loads those 10,000 pixels into memory and displays them on the screen. That's a lot of data for such a simple image. Imagine that we need the same image but two or three times larger. The number of pixels increases exponentially. If we could simply provide the computer with the dimensions, position, and color of the shapes, then we would have much less data to worry about. In this way, raster graphics are inefficient.

Another problem with raster images is that they do not resize well. There's a noticeable loss of quality, especially when you are enlarging an image. Suppose that you wanted to double the size of a 100×100 image of yourself. To increase the size to 200×200, you would need 390,000 more pixels. These missing pixels would need to be interpolated from the existing ones.

Vector graphics, however, are stored as geometries. The data structure for a vector image contains just enough information for the computer to draw the image. A vector image of a blue circle on a white background would contain the x and y position of the circle, its radius, and metadata indicating the circle was blue and the background white. When a computer renders this image, it figures out the actual pixels on-the-fly. This means that there is no difference in quality between the 100×100 vector image and the 200×200 image, and that the size of the data needed to draw the image is substantially less.

A general rule of thumb is that vector graphics are good for geometrical or cartoonish images and that raster is better for photographs and realistic images.

Templates

WPF makes it very easy to create reusable elements for your user interfaces. There are two types of templates in WPF: control templates and data templates. Control templates enable you to redefine the way a control looks. (For ASP.NET developers, they are conceptually similar to control adapters.) For example, if your application needs to have all its list boxes with a blue background and a red border, you could use a control template to redefine the visual appearance of list boxes. Control templates also make it easier for designers. They are able to provide a "look" for a list box through a control template, with little to no impact on the actual development process.

Data templates are similar, except that instead of defining the way a control looks, they define the way certain types of data are rendered. Imagine that you have an application dealing with people, such as a contact manager, and that you represent people in code with instances of a `Person` class. You can create a data template that defines how an instance of a `Person` is rendered in the UI. For example, an instance of `Person` might be visualized as a business card with a picture, first name, last name, and telephone number. If you use such a data template, whenever a `Person` instance is bound to some UI element, such as a list box, WPF will use the corresponding data templates. In practice you will find that data templates are really handy when dealing with lists or other collections of data.

Binding

When we talk about binding in WPF, you probably jump immediately to the concept of *data binding*. Data binding has already been made popular with Windows Forms and ASP.NET Web Forms, and has demonstrated its usefulness there. Although WPF has significant data binding features—significant in that it greatly outclasses its predecessors—it also allows you to declaratively bind other things such as commands, key bindings, animation, and events. For example, you can declaratively bind a button control to a command for pasting.

Styling

WPF really shines when it comes to making an application look pretty. It allows you to do such things as make the background of a text box red or surround a button with a thick blue border. Styles in WPF are similar to cascading style sheets for HTML. Though again, WPF styles are richer and have less ambiguity. They encompass all the visual characteristics you would expect, such as padding, margin, position, color, and so on. But you can also use styles to declare nonvisual properties.

Styles are also easy to reuse, and when you combine them with templates, you are able to do some amazing things.

Triggers

Both templates and styles in WPF support the notion of triggers. A trigger enables you to tell WPF something like this: "When the mouse is over the button, make the background purple." In other words, triggers enable you to declaratively handle changes of state. You will also find them useful for kicking off animations.

Animation

The animation framework in WPF is very impressive, and a great deal more useful than you might think. Most properties in WPF can be animated, and support exists for timelines, key frames, and interpolation. Animations are easily integrated with templates and styles. For example, you might define a style for a button that animates the button when you move the mouse over it. Flash developers and designers will be impressed with the available features.

3D

Finally, WPF allows for some basic 3D modeling and animation. I say basic because WPF is not intended for building high-performance 3D applications. You won't be constructing a first person shooter in WPF. (If that is what you are interested in, be sure to give Microsoft's XNA platform a look.) Nevertheless, the 3D features are powerful and easily integrated into any user interface. We won't be covering the 3D features of WPF in this book; however, a very basic tutorial is available in the appendixes.

Why Use WPF?

WPF, as well as its sister libraries released with .NET 3.0, are well-factored and consistent APIs. They unify many programming concepts and, on the whole, make a lot of complicated development tasks easier. However, WPF is not necessarily the right choice for every project. Some desktop applications would be easier to build and maintain in Windows Forms. But, you'll find many benefits when you work with WPF. Any Windows developer should begin learning WPF because it will eventually mature to a point where it completely replaces Windows Forms.

Many of the key benefits are apparent by reading the list of features in the "Getting to Know the Features of WPF" section. The following are some scenarios where WPF will really shine:

▶ Your project requires collaboration with designers. The use of XAML and its supporting tools can really help out here. After the developers and the designers become familiar with the tools, your team can experience tremendous gains in efficiency.

▶ Your application is media aware. If you need to integrate video and audio into your product, you'll definitely want to consider WPF.

▶ The anticipated hardware for your application has support for DirectX 9 or greater. WPF is built on top of DirectX, and your applications will benefit from the hardware acceleration.

▶ Your application needs support for advanced typography. WPF has support for OpenType and many other features that are not available with Windows Forms.

Finally, you as a developer can get more done in less time. Even if you are not concerned with many of the bells and whistles of WPF, you will be able to produce quality software with less effort. In Part I, "Getting Started," we'll demonstrate this principle by building a simple but useful utility using just markup language.

Comparing WPF to Other Options

If you are solely a .NET developer, you really have only two other options to consider: Windows Forms and ASP.NET. We've already compared WPF to Windows Forms throughout the course of this hour. The only real advantages that Windows Forms has are its mature library of controls and significant third-party support. WPF is still the new kid on the block, and the mass of supporting tools and materials has not had time to build up yet.

Comparing WPF to ASP.NET is a little more involved. The question here really centers on deployment and distribution. WPF is currently limited to the Windows platform, and there's obviously no such limitation with a web application. WPF requires the .NET Framework 3.0 or later, as well as a means of deploying the application. If your application is centralized, requiring one or more server components, you are likely to reduce the complexity significantly by choosing to develop a web application.

Outside of the .NET world, some of the same features are available with Adobe Flash, primarily when it comes to media and animation. Historically, Flash has really only been useful in a Web context. However, the Adobe AIR platform utilizes Flash for developing cross-platform, desktop applications. Nevertheless, Flash still has some notable drawbacks. The development environment is not as robust as .NET although, admittedly, Flash does tend to be more designer friendly. Control libraries for Flash are much more limited and cumbersome to use. It is possible that AIR will provide some healthy competition for WPF.

The Pieces of .NET Framework

Unfortunately, a lot of terms and version numbers are floating around in the .NET world right now, and sorting them out can be particularly difficult. Let's take a moment and step through the various pieces of the .NET Framework and how they relate to all the version numbers.

It is easiest to think of the .NET Framework as a family of products including the runtime, the compilers, and the common code libraries.

The runtime is the common language runtime, or CLR. It is the virtual machine that hosts .NET applications. It provides many of the core services such as memory management, garbage collection, and security. It's outside the scope of this book to discuss the CLR in depth, but you should know that the CLR is the .NET runtime and its version numbers differ from those of the .NET Framework in general. The current CLR is 2.0.

The two dominant languages in the .NET world are C# and Visual Basic .NET. Both of these languages have their own version numbers and those numbers differ from the .NET Framework as a whole. The current version of C# is 3.0, and Visual Basic is 9.0.

You'll also hear about the Base Class Library (BCL) and the Framework Class Library (FCL). The BCL is a set of classes available to any language in the .NET family. These classes mostly live in the System namespace. The FCL is a term that includes both the BCL and the common libraries in the Microsoft namespace. Distinguishing between the two sometimes results in hair splitting, and many people use the terms interchangeably.

Figure 1.1 shows how these "products" have changed with each release of the .NET Framework beginning with 2.0.

Some interesting points to clarify are the following:

▶ The CLR has not changed since the release of 2.0. Thus, the core features of the .NET Framework are the same.

▶ C# 3.0 and VB .NET 9.0 both compile to bytecode (or IL) that is compiled "just in time" on the CLR 2.0. The new language features with .NET 3.5 are essentially enhancements to the respective compilers.

▶ WPF is a class library; nothing changed the underlying CLR. This means that unlike .NET 2.0, version 3.0 of the Framework was just the addition of new libraries.

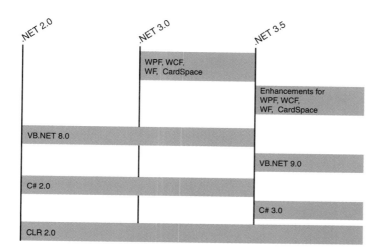

FIGURE 1.1
The version history of the .NET Framework.

Tools for WPF

In this book we work primarily with Visual Studio 2008. Specifically, we use the Express Edition, which Microsoft provides free of charge. Visual Studio 2008 has native support for WPF applications.

> The Express Edition of Visual Studio 2008 is available at www.microsoft.com/express/, along with many other resources.

By the Way

It is possible to build WPF applications with Visual Studio 2005; however, you need to install the WPF extensions for Visual Studio that never made their way to a final release. I strongly advise to move to 2008 if at all possible.

You can also use SharpDevelop (also known as #develop). It is an open-source IDE for .NET, and it has support for building WPF applications in .NET 3.0. It is a solid IDE, but it is hard to beat the level of support for WPF in Visual Studio.

The second primary tool for creating WPF applications from Microsoft is Expression Blend. Blend targets designers rather than developers. It works with the same files as Visual Studio, so a designer using Blend and a developer using Visual Studio can both work on the same projects, solution, and files. Blend is somewhat comparable to the IDE for Adobe Flash. You will find drawing tools, animation timelines, palettes, and other designer-centric features. Despite its focus, I recommend that developers become familiar with Blend. Blend is also one of the first Microsoft products to be written with WPF.

A third-party product exists for designing WPF interfaces—Aurora, by Mobiform Software. It provides a similar set of features as Expression Blend. One notable feature is that Aurora designer can be embedded in another WPF application. So if you have a need for providing a built-in XAML editor in your application, be sure to check it out.

Expression Design is another Microsoft product. It is for authoring vector-based graphical content, similar to Adobe Illustrator or Inkscape. Expression Design can be used to create logos, icons, and illustrations for use with WPF. It can natively output graphics as XAML, which can then be directly incorporated into WPF. Expression Design differs from Blend, in that Blend's focus is purely on authoring user interfaces.

Many other applications for producing 2D and 3D art now have plug-ins available for exporting assets in XAML. (Remember, XAML is the native tongue of WPF.) Some of the applications that have plug-ins available are Adobe Fireworks, Adobe Illustrator, Inkscape, Maya, Blender, and Lightwave.

Aside from the 3D tools just mentioned, at least one WPF-specific 3D content editor is available—ZAM 3D by Electric Rain. ZAM 3D is very similar to the Swift 3D product for Flash. It's more approachable than most 3D editors and is probably the best place to start for WPF developers interested in 3D.

One final tool worth mentioning is Kaxaml. It is a lightweight XAML editor featuring a live preview. That is, you can see how WPF will render your markup as you are typing. It is a very handy utility to have around, and at the time of this writing it is free.

> Visit www.kaxaml.com/ to download Kaxaml. Even though the tutorials in this book focus on Visual Studio, you might find it useful to test some of the markup in Kaxaml. Unlike the preview in Visual Studio, Kaxaml is truly what-you-see-is-what-you-get (WYSIWYG).

Many other tools, utilities, control libraries, and so on become available every day. Some are third-party commercial products, and others are community-driven and free. Be sure to check in the appendixes for additional resources. For the sake of simplicity, we use only Visual Studio 2008 Express Edition in this book.

Constrasting WPF with Silverlight

Silverlight is a platform for developing Rich Internet Applications (RIA), whereas WPF is primarily intended for desktop applications. Silverlight is a direct competitor to Adobe Flash and it has a strong focus on media, cross-platform compatibility, as well as a small download and install footprint. Like Flash, Silverlight applications are hosted in a browser.

Microsoft has intentionally designed Silverlight to be very similar to WPF, although the two are separate products. In fact, an early name for Silverlight was WPF/E or Windows Presentation Foundation/Everywhere. Developers familiar with one technology will have a head start with the other.

Like WPF, Silverlight uses XAML for declaring user interfaces. In version 1.0, a Silverlight application consists only of text files containing JavaScript and XAML. Silverlight 2.0, however, will support a more robust runtime and a base class library similar to the standard .NET BCL. You will be able to write Silverlight applications in your favorite .NET language and compile them to assemblies for distribution. Silverlight 2.0 will look a lot more like WPF, but you should be aware that significant differences exist. It is almost certain that Silverlight will not support all the features in WPF. Likewise, code written for Silverlight may need significant changes before it will compile for a standard .NET application. Always keep in mind that the runtime for Silverlight is different from the CLR.

Summary

Windows Presentation Foundation is the future of software development for desktop applications. The API is very large, and the features are numerous. Becoming an expert in WPF can take some time. However, a basic understanding of the core features can greatly increase a developer's productivity. WPF is also a leap forward in promoting collaboration between designers and developers.

Q&A

Q. *Are there any good reasons for not using WPF to build your application?*

A. A WPF application is generally more resource intensive than a Windows Forms application. If you are building applications for low-end hardware, you might want to do some performance testing before you commit to using WPF. Additionally, .NET 3.0 and 3.5 are not yet widely installed and they are prerequisites for a WPF application. (.NET 3.0 is included with Vista and Windows Server 2008.)

Q. *There seems to be a lot to understanding WPF; do I really need to master all of these concepts to use it?*

A. No, you don't. As we've emphasized, WPF is big. However, by the end of Part I, you can begin building useful applications and realizing the benefits of WPF.

Workshop

Quiz

1. What is the benefit of using a markup language for designing a user interface?

2. What operating systems does WPF currently support?

3. How does WPF differ from Silverlight, and in what ways are they similar?

4. Aside from Visual Studio 2008, what is another tool from Microsoft that WPF developers should become familiar with?

Answers

1. Using a markup language such as XAML, or even HTML, is beneficial because it provides a common medium for both designers and developers. Additionally, the markup language allows for a declarative approach for building applications, which is often easier to construct and maintain.

2. WPF is currently available on Windows XP and Windows Vista.

3. WPF is part of the .NET Framework, and it is intended for building graphical user interfaces for desktop applications. Silverlight targets Rich Internet Applications that are hosted in a web browser. Silverlight's runtime is different from the standard .NET runtime. Both Silverlight and WPF use XAML for defining interfaces. Microsoft has intentionally made Silverlight as close to WPF as possible to lower the barrier for developers and designers.

4. WPF developers should be at least somewhat familiar with Microsoft's Expression Blend. The application is primarily intended for designers, but can often be useful for developers as well. It uses the same file formats as Visual Studio, so that solutions and projects are interchangeable between the two applications.

HOUR 2

Understanding XAML

What You'll Learn in This Hour:

► What is XAML?
► The basic syntax of XAML
► How properties can be represented as elements
► Namespaces
► Markup extensions

XAML, or Extensible Application Markup Language, is an XML-based language created by Microsoft. It's as fundamental to WPF as HTML is to web development.

What Is XAML?

XAML (pronounced *zammel*) is the language used for creating user interfaces in WPF. It's an XML-based markup language similar to HTML, MXML, or XUL. XAML has applicability well beyond defining user interfaces. In fact, it's even possible to represent data with XAML, such as an array of strings or an instance of object. XAML is also used by Windows Workflow Foundation (WF) for defining workflows. In the most general sense, XAML is a language for serializing .NET object instances into a human readable format.

Even though Visual Studio 2008 provides a WYSIWYG editor with drag-and-drop support for producing and manipulating XAML, you will often need to edit your markup directly. We'll be writing our XAML by hand for most of the book. The default file extension is .xaml.

XAML can be either compiled or interpreted, depending on how it is used. Some features, such as embedding C# or VB code in XAML, work only when the XAML is compiled. When you create a WPF application with Visual Studio, the XAML used in the application is compiled into the resulting executable. However, you can create .xaml files that are meant to be interpreted on-the-fly (no compilation is involved). These XAML files are usually hosted in a web browser.

Let's create a simple "hello world" XAML application. You'll need to have the .NET Framework 3.5 installed to do this exercise. It's installed as part of Visual Studio 2008.

1. Open your favorite text editor, such as Notepad.

2. Create a plain text document and enter the following:

```
<Page xmlns="http://schemas.microsoft.com/winfx/2006/xaml/presentation"
      xmlns:x="http://schemas.microsoft.com/winfx/2006/xaml">
  <TextBlock Text="Hello World!" />
</Page>
```

3. Save the text file and name it **HelloWorld.xaml**.

4. Double-click the newly created file, and it should open in a web browser. If another application has been mapped to .xaml, you will need to launch the browser first (either Internet Explorer 7 or Firefox will do) and drag the file into the browser.

Congratulations, you've just created your first WPF application using XAML. HelloWorld.xaml is an example of interpreted XAML because we never compiled the application to an executable. XAML-only applications are rather limited, and in real life you're much more likely to use XAML in concert with C# or VB.

In HelloWorld.xaml, notice that the root element is a Page tag. Some other possibilities exist, most frequently the Window tag, but we'll get to that shortly. When authoring XAML, your root element always defines two namespaces. The default namespace is specifically mapped to WPF, whereas the prefix x: is for XAML's more generic features. Remember, XAML can be used to represent all kinds of data; we used the default namespace to say that we are representing data about WPF. The x namespace is representing a broader context. That may sound a little backward, but you'll quickly find that you don't use the x namespace as much as the default one. If this doesn't make sense, don't worry about it for the moment. It won't stop you from using XAML, and we'll review it again later. Just know that these namespace aliases are the convention adopted by Microsoft, and you'll see it in all the examples and documentation.

Namespaces in XML are often confusing if you have not worked with them before. Namespaces in XML serve the same function as namespaces in .NET; they provide a scope for unique names.

It's similar to the idea of having two people named John Smith. To distinguish between them, you might call one John Smith from Surrey and the other John Smith of Boston. Including the place where they are from is analogous to the namespace. When two things are named the same, and we can't tell them apart, it is called a naming collision.

The xmlns attribute is used to map a local name (or alias), such as x, to the actual namespace, which is specified as a URI. Individual elements or tags that reside in the namespace use the local name as a prefix in their tags.

The namespace tells the XML parser how the elements in the document should be interpreted.

By the Way

The Syntax of XAML

As a general rule, an element in XAML is an instance of an object and attributes are properties on that object. The markup in Listing 2.1 is for a simple button on a page.

LISTING 2.1   A Simple Button in XAML

```
<Page xmlns="http://schemas.microsoft.com/winfx/2006/xaml/presentation"
      xmlns:x="http://schemas.microsoft.com/winfx/2006/xaml">
  <Button x:Name="blueButton"
          Width="100"
          Height="40"
          Background="Blue"
          Content="Click Me" />
</Page>
```

The root element corresponds to an instance of Page, more specifically System.Windows.Controls.Page. Page, and everything else in the System.Windows.Controls namespace, is a WPF control.

The Button element corresponds to an instance of the class System.Windows.Controls.Button. In turn, the attributes on the Button element represent properties on an object instance. Thus, we are setting the values for the properties of Width, Height, Background, and Content.

There is also the x:Name attribute, which breaks the rule here. x:Name is not a property on the Button class. Instead, it's a special attribute that provides a unique identifier for the object for accessing it in code. It is the same as creating a variable of type Button with the name blueButton. The Button element in the preceding XAML is equivalent to the following C#:

```
Button blueButton = new Button();
blueButton.Width = 100;
blueButton.Height = 40;
blueButton.Content = "Click Me";
blueButton.Background = new SolidColorBrush(Colors.Blue);
```

The Background property is a little more complex than the others. We'll talk about that in a second. It is important to understand that any XAML element you want to reference, in code or elsewhere in the XAML, must have a unique value for x:Name. Providing a value from x:Name is like creating a variable and then setting the variable to the instance of the object.

> The Button class has a Name property, and interestingly enough, setting a value for x:Name also sets the same value for Name. In fact, for any object that has a Name property, the two attributes can be used interchangeably. This was very confusing for us when we first started working with XAML.
>
> It's pretty easy to get into trouble using the Name property, though, and unless you have a specific need, we recommend sticking with x:Name. It's the convention that is generally adopted.

Setting Properties That Aren't Simple Types

On the Button class, Width and Height are simple value types. WPF converts the string value 100 to a double implicitly. However, many properties on controls are not simple value types. Some properties are objects that have lots of properties themselves, which could also be complex types. In our example, the Background property on Button is of type SolidColorBrush. In the XAML, we are able to simply say Blue and it works.

There are many places in XAML where commonly used types, such as SolidColorBrush, can be represented by a simple string value that WPF *just knows* how to handle. In the case of SolidColorBrush, you can provide any named color, as found on the System.Windows.Media.Colors class, or you can provide a hexadecimal representation of the color similar to those you would use in HTML or CSS. Both of the following XAML snippets are equivalent:

```
<Button Background="#FF0000FF" />
<Button Background="Blue" />
```

In some situations, however, this shorthand is not sufficient for telling WPF what you want. In those cases we can use *property element syntax*. Property element syntax is an alternative syntax used for providing values for complex types. Instead of setting the `Background` property using an attribute, we can use a child element. The following snippet demonstrates using this alternative syntax for setting the background to blue:

```
<Button>
    <Button.Background>
        <SolidColorBrush Color="Blue" />
    </Button.Background>
</Button>
```

The child element is referred to as a *property element*. Property elements take the form of `<ClassName.PropertyName />`. That is, the first part of the element's name is the class name, followed by a dot, followed by the property's name. The content of the child element is the value we want to set. When using a property element, we need to be more explicit and tell WPF that we want the value to be an instance of `SolidColorBrush` with the `Color` property set to blue. This syntax can become very verbose, but in many situations it is the only way to provide the exact value that you desire.

It's preferable to use the shorthand when possible. Succinct markup is easier to read and it makes the intention of the XAML clearer.

The Content Property

Many of the WPF controls that you will encounter have a property named `Content`. `Content` is a special property. In Listing 2.1, we set the `Content` of a `Button` to a string value, `Click Me`. However, you can also set the Content property implicitly using a child element. For example, the following XAML elements are equivalent:

```
<Button Content="Click Me" />
<Button>Click Me</Button>
```

Both buttons will be rendered the same in WPF. What's exciting is that `Content` is actually of type `object`. That means that we can make a button's content much more than just a simple string. For example, perhaps we want to draw a yellow circle inside our button. You could use the following XAML:

```
<Button>
    <Ellipse Width="24"
             Height="24"
             Fill="Yellow" />
</Button>
```

You can always set the `Content` property explicitly, too:

```
<Button>
    <Button.Content>
```

```
        <Ellipse Width="24"
                 Height="24"
                 Fill="Yellow" />
        </Button.Content>
    </Button>
```

However, doing so is more verbose and does nothing to improve the readability or maintainability of your code. Furthermore, the convention of setting the `Content` property implicitly is almost universally adopted.

If you go back to Listing 2.1 one more time, you will notice that our `Button` element is actually the value for the `Page.Content` property.

Markup Extensions

Sometimes we need to specify values in our markup that are either difficult to express in XAML or outside the scope of the XAML processor. XAML has a feature called *markup extensions* and it allows us to handle these awkward situations.

For example, suppose we have a specific color we want to use as the background for several buttons in a WPF application. We could set the `Background` property on each of the buttons to use the same color, but it would become tedious if we ever needed to change that color. With WPF, we can store the color with a lookup key in an application's resources. (We'll discuss this concept in depth in Hour 14, "Resources and Styles.") Now we can set the background of the buttons to the color we stored in the resources. If we want to change the color, we need do so in only one place. That's a lovely scenario, but how would we handle this in XAML? We would use a markup extension.

In the preceding scenario, the XAML with the markup extension might look like this:

```
        <Button Background="{StaticResource ResourceKey=myColor}"
                Content="Click Me" />
```

Markup extensions are indentified by the presence of curly brackets ({}). The first word in the markup extension tells WPF what kind of extension it is. The name of the extension is optionally followed by a set of named parameters. In this case, the extension is for retrieving a shared resource from a library of resources. The name of the extension is `StaticResource`, and we provide a value of `myColor` for the `ResourceKey` parameter. Many extensions have a default parameter. You don't have to explicitly reference a default parameter. You are allowed to omit the parameter name and the equal sign. For example, we could restate the snippet with `ResourceKey=`:

```
        <Button Background="{StaticResource myColor}"
                Content="Click Me" />
```

ResourceKey is the default parameter for StaticResource.

In some cases, you will have more than one parameter. If you do, you must separate name/value pairs with commas. The general pattern is this:

```
{ExtensionName Param1=Value1, Param2=Value2, Param3=Value3}
```

The most frequent mistake in dealing with markup extensions is to include quotation marks around the values. You are not allowed to have quotation marks between the curly brackets. This confuses the parser. It also means that parameter values cannot have whitespace.

Many markup extensions are built in to WPF, and you can even write your own (however, it is not common to do so).

We'll cover specific extensions as they become relevant throughout the book; however, Table 2.1 has a very brief summary of the most significant extensions. Don't be too concerned about understanding these extensions right now; they will make sense in context.

TABLE 2.1   Common Markup Extensions in WPF

Name	Description
Binding	The extension used for binding data. This is discussed in Hour 6, "Introducing Data Binding."
StaticResource	This is used for retrieving data from an application's resources. Static resources are not expected to change while the application is running. We cover this in Hour 14.
DynamicResource	Similar to StaticResource, except that the data in the resource might change during runtime. This is also in Hour 14.
x:Null	Used for specifying a null value in XAML. We'll show one way to use this in Hour 23, "Animation," although it has many uses.
x:Type	This extension is used for supplying a System.Type object. This is also in Hour 14.
X:Array	This allows you to define an array of objects in XAML. We'll demonstrate the use of this in Hour 15, "Digging Deeper into Data Binding."

Summary

Understanding XAML is essential to working with WPF. Although it is possible to write a WPF application without XAML, it is awkward and clumsy. XAML is very flexible, and a lot of traditional programming tasks can now be handled with XAML. Like WPF in general, you won't be able to master XAML overnight. Even developers who have worked with the language for some time often discover features they were unaware of.

The goal of this hour was to equip you with a foundational knowledge of XAML and how it is used. We will continue to build on that foundation in the remaining hours.

Q&A

Q. *Why are attributes in these examples often placed on new lines by themselves? Is that a requirement of XAML?*

A. No, it is not a requirement. For the most part, XAML is unconcerned about the whitespace. There is a growing trend of placing the secondary and following attributes on a new line, indenting to align with the first attribute. We adopted this convention for the book because it promotes the readability of the XAML.

Q. *I've heard about object element syntax in regard to XAML; how does that fit in with what we have discussed?*

A. Object element syntax is the name for declaring objects in XAML. Its name comes from the fact that an XML element in XAML corresponds to an instance of an object in .NET.

Q. *If powerful WYSIWYG editors exist for XAML, why should I bother learning all the details of the language?*

A. WYSIWYG editors are excellent tools for getting work done quickly; however, they don't always produce the most efficient XAML for your specific application. Additionally, there are many tasks that the editors do not support. You'll also find that some things are just easier to handle manually. Finally, a thorough understanding of XAML and how it relates to WPF provides a solid base for building efficient and effective WPF applications.

Workshop

Quiz

1. What is the purpose of the x:Name attribute in XAML?

2. What is a feature of XAML that is available when it is compiled rather than interpreted?

3. Can you identify the syntactical mistake in the following markup extension?

```
{StaticResource ResourceKey="myData"}
```

Answers

1. The x:Name attribute allows you to uniquely identify an instance of an object defined in XAML. The value of the x:Name attribute can be referenced in the associated C# or VB code.

2. When your XAML is compiled, you can embed procedural code such as C# or VB. For more information about this, look up the markup extension x:Code.

3. Quotation marks are not needed when specifying values in a markup extension. In fact, using quotation marks will confuse the XAML processor.

HOUR 3

Introducing the Font Viewer

What You'll Learn in This Hour:

▶ How to set up a new WPF project
▶ Some basics of Visual Studio
▶ The structure of a project
▶ XAML files
▶ Code-behind files

In this hour we'll begin developing our first WPF application, a small but useful utility for browsing the fonts currently installed on your system. We'll also learn the basics of setting up a WPF project in Visual Studio.

Building the Font Viewer

Let's begin by talking about the application we would like to build.

It would be convenient to have a lightweight utility that would allow us to see all the fonts currently installed on our system. Additionally, we could enter some sample text and see it rendered in the selected font.

To do this, we'll need the following:

▶ A list box displaying the names of the installed fonts

▶ A text box for entering the text that we'd like to preview

▶ A place for rendering the preview text in the selected font

Setting Up a New Project in Visual Studio 2008

We'll be working with the version of Visual Studio called *Microsoft Visual C# 2008 Express Edition* as shown in Figure 3.1. This is a special version of Visual Studio, released in conjunction with .NET 3.5. It has built-in support for WPF applications. If you have a different version of Visual Studio 2008, that's okay; however, the steps might differ slightly.

FIGURE 3.1
Microsoft Visual
C# 2008
Express Edition.

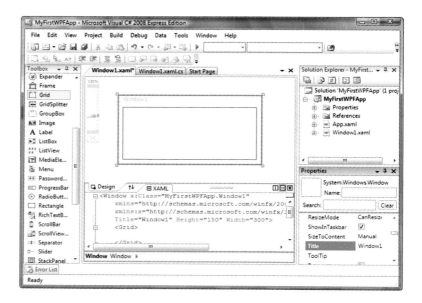

Here are the steps to creating a new WPF project:

1. Launch Visual Studio. It's named Microsoft Visual C# 2008 Express Edition on your start menu.

2. From the menu bar select File, New Project.

3. Select the template WPF Application, as shown in Figure 3.2.

4. Name your new application **FontViewer**, and then click OK.

> You may have noticed the project template WPF Browser Application. This is a special type of WPF application that we'll discuss in a later hour. It is used to build applications that behave like a web browser, using the metaphor of pages as well as forward and back buttons for navigation. If you are using a different version of Visual Studio, such as the Professional Edition, you will notice even more project templates relating to WPF.

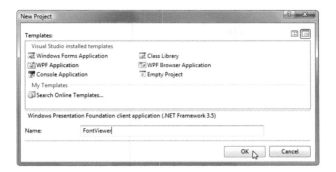

FIGURE 3.2
Creating a new
WPF Application
project.

Basic Project Files

Visual Studio will create App.xaml and Window1.xaml, along with the associated
code-behind files, and Window1.xaml will be open in your IDE.

The XAML files consist solely of the markup we discussed in Hour 2, "Understanding
XAML." The code-behind files contain the code supplementing the XAML (in this
case C#).

> One of the fantastic new features in Visual Studio 2008 is the split pane you can
> use when viewing a XAML file. By default, a live preview of your XAML is displayed
> in the upper (or Design) pane, and your markup is displayed in the lower (or XAML)
> pane. The two panes are synchronized so that typing markup in the XAML pane
> will be almost immediately reflected in the Design pane. Likewise, you can click
> elements in the Design pane and modify them in the property panel. You can even
> drag elements from the Toolbox and drop them on your window. We'll mostly keep
> to typing in the markup directly, because it is better for the learning process.

By the
Way

App.xaml represents the application itself. It is not visual, and it is primarily used to
store resources that will be used throughout an application. App.xaml also defines
which window opens when the application launches.

Window1.xaml is the main window for the application. Its markup contains all the
visual elements that represent the application on the screen, as well as declaring our
application's behavior.

What Are Code-Behind Files?

In a WPF Application project, every XAML file has an associated code-behind file.
The code-behind has the same name as its parent file with the .cs (or .vb) extension added. Thus, the code-behind file for window1.xaml is window1.xaml.cs.

In the Solution Explorer, code-behind files are children of the file that they are associated with. They will be nested underneath their parent.

You can toggle between the markup and the code by right-clicking a document in the editor and selecting View Designer or View Code, respectively. Note that Visual Studio will open a tab for both the XAML and the code-behind.

Separating Your Concerns

The intention of the code-behind model is to allow a developer to separate the visual rendering of an application from the behavior of the application. WPF supports this practice much better than either Windows Forms or ASP.NET Web Forms, although it is still very easy to muddy the waters.

For example, imagine a two-person team working on a WPF application that has a designer and a developer. The developer implements a feature that allows users to choose their favorite color from a list box. The designer would like to represent the list box as a palette displaying the colors as drops of paint. In this case, the designer can edit the XAML file and create a fancy list box, without disturbing the code written by the developer and without breaking the application.

This is only the beginning of what it means to separate concerns in your applications. We'll talk more about this concept throughout the book.

Partial Classes

The concept of partial classes was introduced with .NET 2.0. The essential idea is that a single class can be defined across multiple files. Each file contains a portion of the class. The files can even be of different file types; such as `.cs` and `.xaml`. The compiler is responsible for dynamically combining the code into a single class as it is compiled.

You can identify partial classes by the `partial` keyword in C#, and `Partial` in VB.

Partial classes are also helpful in scenarios where some of the source code is generated by a tool but needs to be extended manually by a developer. The generated code and handwritten code can be kept in separate files.

This technique is relevant when learning WPF because both the code-behind files and XAML files are partial classes.

Renaming a XAML File

Our newly created Font Viewer application is now open in Visual Studio. If we press F5, we'll see a functioning, but useless, WPF application running.

The default filenames provided by Visual Studio are not very meaningful. It's a good programming practice to name items such as files, classes, and methods with names that reflect their purpose. We're going to rename `Window1.xaml` to indicate that it is the main window of our application.

Renaming items in Visual Studio can break the code if we're not careful. To maintain the appropriate links between the files when renaming the window, do the following:

1. Select `Window1.xaml` in the Solution Explorer.

2. Press F2 on your keyboard. (Alternatively, you can right-click and select Rename.)

3. Change the filename to `MainWindow.xaml`. Note that Visual Studio renames the associated code-behind as well. However, Visual Studio does not correct references to the filename, nor does it change the name of the underlying class.

4. Double-click `App.xaml` in the Solution Explorer to open it in the editor.

5. The root tag in `App.xaml` is the `Application` tag, and it has an attribute `StartupUri`. `StartupUri` specifies the name of the primary window that is displayed when the application launches. It's still pointing to the old name; let's change it to point to `MainWindow.xaml`. `App.xaml` should now look like this:

```
<Application x:Class="FontViewer.App"
             xmlns="http://schemas.microsoft.com/winfx/2006/xaml/
             ➥presentation"
             xmlns:x="http://schemas.microsoft.com/winfx/2006/xaml"
             StartupUri="MainWindow.xaml">
    <Application.Resources>
    </Application.Resources>
</Application>
```

6. Open the code-behind for `MainWindow.xaml` in the editor; that's `MainWindow.xaml.cs`. Notice that the class is still named `Window1`. Renaming the XAML file did not change the name of the class.

7. To avoid confusion, we'll change the name of the class to match the name of the file. Right-click the name of the class, and select Refactor, Rename. Enter `MainWindow` for the new name, and click OK; then click Apply. You can also select Refactor, Rename from the menu bar as shown in Figure 3.3.

   You'll also notice that Visual Studio didn't change the class name in the comment just before the class. You'll want to change that as well; it's a best practice to always keep your comments up-to-date with the code.

8. Finally, in the markup for MainWindow.xaml, we need to correct the reference to the class. The root tag is Window, and it has an attribute x:Class. We need to change this to the full name of our class, including the namespace, which is FontViewer.MainWindow. MainWindow.xaml now looks like this:

```
<Window x:Class="FontViewer.MainWindow"
        xmlns="http://schemas.microsoft.com/winfx/2006/xaml/
        ➥presentation"
        xmlns:x="http://schemas.microsoft.com/winfx/2006/xaml"
        Title="Font Viewer"
        Height="300"
        Width="300">
    <Grid>
    </Grid>
</Window>
```

FIGURE 3.3
Choosing Rename from the Refactor menu.

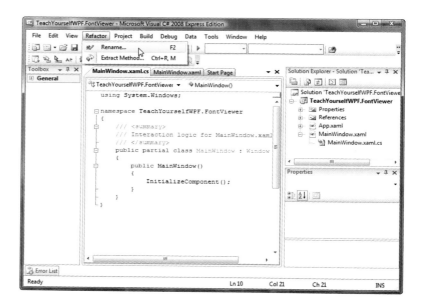

Have you heard the term *refactor* before? Refactoring code means that you improve the maintainability of the code without changing the behavior. The intent of refactoring is to make code more understandable, more explicit in its intent, and ultimately easier to maintain. Refactoring is a large subject, and there are many books on the topic. Visual Studio has a Refactor menu with some basic options that you should become familiar with. I also encourage you to investigate the topic on your own.

Developing the Application

We said at the beginning of the hour that we wanted our application to display a list of the fonts installed on our system. We also want to be able to select a font from that list, enter some text, and see it rendered in the font we chose.

It's also important to make an application easy to use, so we are going to add some helpful text and spacing around elements to improve usability.

Let's begin adding these features:

1. Open `MainWindow.xaml` in the editor. By default, Visual Studio displays the XAML file in a split window. The Design pane of the window is a near real-time preview of the XAML, and the XAML pane displays the actual markup.

2. First, let's give our application a meaningful title to display in its title bar. Change the `Title` attribute of the `Window` tag to **Font Viewer**.

3. The default size of the main window is pretty small. We can change the size with the `Height` and `Width` attributes of Window. Set the height to **480** and the width to **600**.

4. Now locate the `Grid` tag. Grid is one of several types of controls that enable you to visually arrange the elements of the UI. These layout controls are called Panels, and we'll cover them in more detail in Hour 4, "Handling Application Layout." Delete the `Grid` tag.

5. In the spot where the `Grid` was located, begin by typing **<DockPanel**.

   IntelliSense will kick in, and you can simply select DockPanel from the list. (Remember, to use IntelliSense for looking up XAML elements, always start by typing the < character for the opening tag.) DockPanel is another panel like Grid used for visually arranging elements of the UI. DockPanel is useful for the layout scenario in applications such as Visual Studio or Microsoft Outlook, when you want certain UI elements to be docked on the sides of the main window. The XAML should now look like this:

   ```
   <Window x:Class="FontViewer.MainWindow"
           xmlns="http://schemas.microsoft.com/winfx/2006/xaml/presentation"
           xmlns:x="http://schemas.microsoft.com/winfx/2006/xaml"
           Title="Font Viewer" Height="480" Width="600">
       <DockPanel></DockPanel>
   </Window>
   ```

6. Inside the `DockPanel`, enter the following:

   ```
   <Border DockPanel.Dock="Top"
           CornerRadius="6"
           BorderThickness="1"
   ```

```
      BorderBrush="Gray"
      Background="LightGray"
      Padding="8"
      Margin="0 0 0 8">
</Border>
```

Take a look in the Design pane; the application's main window is now filled with a light gray rectangle that has slightly rounded corners. Be sure to always keep an eye on the Design pane as you are editing the XAML. You'll gain a good understanding of what the markup does just by seeing the live preview.

7. It is always good to provide some guidance to your users. Let's add some instructional text. Place the following inside the newly added Border.

```
<TextBlock FontSize="14"
          TextWrapping="Wrap">
    Select a font to view from the list below.
    You can change the text by typing in the region at the bottom.
</TextBlock>
```

8. Now we will add a list box that will display all the currently installed fonts. Just outside the Border, but still inside the DockPanel, add the following:

```
<ListBox x:Name="FontList"
        DockPanel.Dock="Left"
        ItemsSource="{x:Static Fonts.SystemFontFamilies}"
        Width="160" />
```

The ItemsSource attribute tells the ListBox about the data that it should display. In this case, the data we want is the set of currently installed fonts. The .NET Framework provides us with a static property, SystemFontFamilies, on the class System.Windows.Media.Fonts. By default, the ListBox calls the ToString method on each of the FontFamily instances in the collection. Luckily for us, this returns the name of the font.

We'll dig into the rest of the details of all this in later hours.

The markup for MainWindow.xaml should now look like the following:

```
<Window x:Class="FontViewer.MainWindow"
       xmlns="http://schemas.microsoft.com/winfx/2006/xaml/presentation"
       xmlns:x="http://schemas.microsoft.com/winfx/2006/xaml"
       Title="Font Viewer"
       Height="480"
       Width="600">
    <DockPanel>
        <Border DockPanel.Dock="Top"
               CornerRadius="6"
               BorderThickness="1"
               BorderBrush="Gray"
```

```
        Background="LightGray"
        Padding="8"
        Margin="0 0 0 8">
            <TextBlock FontSize="14"
                       TextWrapping="Wrap">
            Select a font to view from the list below.
            You can change the text by typing in the region at the bottom.
            </TextBlock>
        </Border>
        <ListBox x:Name="FontList"
                DockPanel.Dock="Left"
                ItemsSource="{x:Static Fonts.SystemFontFamilies}"
                Width="160" />
    </DockPanel>
</Window>
```

9. Now we need a way to enter some sample text, as well as a way to display the preview text with the selected font.

   Add this markup just beneath the ListBox:

```
<TextBox x:Name="SampleText"
        DockPanel.Dock="Bottom"
        MinLines="4"
        Margin="8 0"
        TextWrapping="Wrap"
        ToolTip="Type here to change the preview text.">
    The quick brown fox jumps over the lazy dog.
</TextBox>
<TextBlock Text="{Binding ElementName=SampleText, Path=Text}"
        FontFamily="{Binding ElementName=FontList,Path=SelectedItem}"
        TextWrapping="Wrap"
        Margin="0 0 0 4" />
```

The TextBox accepts input from the user. We provide a default sentence to be helpful. The TextBlock is an element used for displaying text.

Note that the Text attribute of the TextBlock is binding to the Text property of our TextBox (we named it **SampleText**). This tells WPF to keep those two properties in sync. Whenever a user types in the TextBox, the TextBlock is automatically updated.

We also bound the FontFamily of the TextBlock to the currently selected item in our list box. The FontFamily property tells the TextBlock which font to use for rendering the text. If you review the markup, you'll notice that we gave our ListBox the name **FontList** and that our TextBlock is referencing this name.

10. Finally, run your application. Try changing a few things, and experiment.

> Everything that we did in XAML, we could have done in code. In fact, there may be times when it is easier to construct the UI programmatically, rather than declaratively. However, you may be surprised at what you can do declaratively. As a beginner in WPF, be sure to explore the options. In the end, you should base your decision on what is easier to maintain.

Polishing a Few Things

After playing with the Font Viewer for a few minutes, it became apparent that it would be useful to show the sample text in multiple sizes at the same time. Let's add some markup that will display the text in 10pt, 16pt, 24pt, and 32pt sizes.

We'll make the following changes to display the same text four times in different point sizes.

1. Replace the `TextBlock` that is bound to `SampleText` with the following markup:

```
<StackPanel Margin="8 0 8 8">
    <TextBlock Text="{Binding ElementName=SampleText, Path=Text}"
               FontFamily="{Binding ElementName=FontList,Path=SelectedItem}"
               FontSize="10"
               TextWrapping="Wrap"
               Margin="0 0 0 4" />
    <TextBlock Text="{Binding ElementName=SampleText, Path=Text}"
               FontFamily="{Binding ElementName=FontList,Path=SelectedItem}"
               FontSize="16"
               TextWrapping="Wrap"
               Margin="0 0 0 4" />
    <TextBlock Text="{Binding ElementName=SampleText, Path=Text}"
               FontFamily="{Binding ElementName=FontList,Path=SelectedItem}"
               FontSize="24"
               TextWrapping="Wrap"
               Margin="0 0 0 4" />
    <TextBlock Text="{Binding ElementName=SampleText, Path=Text}"
               FontFamily="{Binding ElementName=FontList,Path=SelectedItem}"
               FontSize="32"
               TextWrapping="Wrap" />
</StackPanel>
```

This adds a `StackPanel`, which is another type of layout control. The `StackPanel` stacks its children element on top of one another. In this case, the children are four `TextBlock` elements with various values for `FontSize`.

Notice that they are all bound to the same source—the `Text` property of the `TextBox` named `SampleText`.

2. Add an 8px margin to the DockPanel. It makes the UI a little less crowded, and improves the usability of the application:

```
<DockPanel Margin="8">
```

The complete markup for `MainWindow.xaml` is shown in Listing 3.1.

LISTING 3.1 MainWindow.xaml

```
<Window x:Class="FontViewer.MainWindow"
        xmlns="http://schemas.microsoft.com/winfx/2006/xaml/presentation"
        xmlns:x="http://schemas.microsoft.com/winfx/2006/xaml"
        Title="Font Viewer"
        Height="480"
        Width="640">
  <DockPanel Margin="8">
      <Border DockPanel.Dock="Top"
              CornerRadius="6"
              BorderThickness="1"
              BorderBrush="Gray"
              Background="LightGray"
              Padding="8"
              Margin="0 0 0 8">
          <TextBlock FontSize="14"
                     TextWrapping="Wrap">
          Select a font to view from the list below.
          You can change the text by typing in the region at the bottom.
      </TextBlock>
      </Border>
      <ListBox x:Name="FontList"
               DockPanel.Dock="Left"
               ItemsSource="{x:Static Fonts.SystemFontFamilies}"
               Width="160" />
      <TextBox x:Name="SampleText"
               DockPanel.Dock="Bottom"
               MinLines="4"
               Margin="8 0"
               TextWrapping="Wrap"
               ToolTip="Type here to change the preview text.">
          The quick brown fox jumps over the lazy dog.
      </TextBox>
      <StackPanel Margin="8 0 8 8">
          <TextBlock Text="{Binding ElementName=SampleText, Path=Text}"
                     FontFamily="{Binding
                     ➥ElementName=FontList,Path=SelectedItem}"
                     FontSize="10"
                     TextWrapping="Wrap"
                     Margin="0 0 0 4" />
          <TextBlock Text="{Binding ElementName=SampleText, Path=Text}"
                     FontFamily="{Binding
                     ➥ElementName=FontList,Path=SelectedItem}"
                     FontSize="16"
                     TextWrapping="Wrap"
                     Margin="0 0 0 4" />
          <TextBlock Text="{Binding ElementName=SampleText, Path=Text}"
                     FontFamily="{Binding
                     ➥ElementName=FontList,Path=SelectedItem}"
```

LISTING 3.1 Continued

```
                                FontSize="24"
                                TextWrapping="Wrap"
                                Margin="0 0 0 4" />
                <TextBlock Text="{Binding ElementName=SampleText, Path=Text}"
                                FontFamily="{Binding
                                ↪ElementName=FontList,Path=SelectedItem}"
                                FontSize="32"
                                TextWrapping="Wrap" />
            </StackPanel>
        </DockPanel>
</Window>
```

Figure 3.4 shows off our first WPF application!

FIGURE 3.4
The Font Viewer
application.

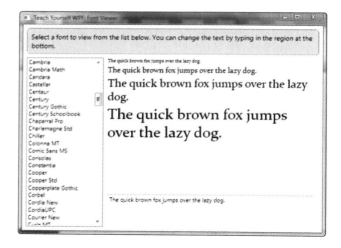

WPF makes UI development an order of magnitude easier. Developers are often criticized for building poor user interfaces. Although WPF makes it easier to improve the user experience, it will not do so by itself. In fact, WPF will allow developers to produce even worse user interfaces if they are not thoughtful about what they are building.

Did you notice that we have a functioning application, one with all the features we outlined at the beginning of the hour, and yet we did not write any code?

If we are able to do this, then what's the purpose of the code-behind files? We aren't writing any code!

We're intentionally starting out with a very simple application. You'll find that as the problems get more complex, you'll need to begin writing code. Nevertheless, this demonstrates one of the powerful features of WPF: You can do a lot without writing any code!

Summary

In this hour we covered how to set up a new WPF project, and we built our first functioning WPF application, the Font Viewer. We discussed the difference between XAML and code-behind files in your project. We demonstrated, at a very high level, some of the more impressive features of WPF, such as data binding, layout, and declarative programming.

Q&A

Q. Which files are automatically added to a new WPF Application project?

A. App.xaml and Window1.xaml, along with their associated code-behind files. The former represents the application as a whole, whereas the latter represents the primary window of the application.

Q. What is the difference between a XAML file and a code-behind file?

A. The XAML file contains the XAML markup, whereas the code-behind file is associated with a XAML file and contains code (such as C# or VB).

Q. When you rename a XAML file in Visual Studio, is the code-behind file affected?

A. Yes, the code-behind file is renamed as well; however, the class name is not altered and must be manually changed if you want to keep the filename and the class name in sync.

Workshop

Quiz

1. What type of controls are DockPanel and StackPanel?

2. What is the difference between a TextBlock and a TextBox?

Answers

1. DockPanel and StackPanel are both Panels. They are used to control the layout of UI elements.

2. A TextBlock is used for displaying read-only text. The TextBox can receive user input from the keyboard.

HOUR 4

Handling Application Layout

What You'll Learn in This Hour:

- ▶ Core layout concepts
- ▶ Panels
- ▶ Attached properties
- ▶ Decorators
- ▶ How to choose the right panel for the job

Deciding how to arrange pieces of an application on the screen can be a daunting task. Additionally, the challenge of this task can be amplified by the technical difficulties of supporting diverse screen resolutions, window size changes, and other real-world layout issues. One of the great advantages of building applications with WPF is that the framework has deep support for intelligently managing these types of situations.

In this hour, we take a look at the layout options available in WPF by digging deeper into the Font Viewer from Hour 3.

Understanding Layout

Before we discuss the Font Viewer layout, it's important to understand some basic concepts and terminology that will affect much of what you do.

Layout Panels and Decorators

Much of building a typical user interface in WPF consists of creating various types of *controls*, such as Button and TextBox. Panels are a special family of classes having the distinguishing capability of being able to arrange controls on the screen. For example, you might use a Grid to arrange a collection of Label and TextBox controls into a typical input form. In a different situation, you might use a DockPanel to "dock" your application's Menu at the top of the Window and fill the remaining area with your main UI. Sometimes, you don't need to arrange a control, but rather to extend its functionality or appearance. Another family of classes, related to panels, derives from the Decorator base class and fulfills this common need. The most common Decorator is Border, which draws a border around its enclosed control.

When it comes to panels and decorators, you can choose from a variety of options. We explore several of them in further detail later in this hour as well as discuss using nested panels for building more complex layouts.

By the Way

> The term *control* is used to speak generally of elements that derive from the System.Windows.Controls.Control base class. Controls have a rich set of functionality that includes features such as mouse and keyboard input, data binding, layout, styles, and animation.

By the Way

> An application developer can use other means to organize controls. It is common to use elements such as TabControl, GroupBox or Expander to aid in layout. These controls typically work in conjunction with panels or decorators to organize highly complex UIs. We discuss these in Hours 12, "Building a Contact Manager," and 13, "Presenters and Views."

FrameworkElement

Almost all the WPF elements that you will work with as you build interfaces derive from the System.Windows.FrameworkElement base class and inherit some common layout related properties. These properties serve to fine-tune the way the element is positioned within its parent. Let's work with the basic properties Margin, VerticalAlignment and HorizontalAlignment.

Using Alignment and Margin

In this section, we create a simple application with a Grid and one child control, a Button. As we progress, we'll change some of the basic properties that Button inherits from FrameworkElement to discover how the overall layout is affected.

   1. Open Visual Studio and create a new WPF Application project called
   AlignmentAndMargin.

2. Enter the following XAML in the `Window1.xaml` file:

```
<Window x:Class="AlignmentAndMargin.Window1"
        xmlns="http://schemas.microsoft.com/winfx/2006/xaml/presentation"
        xmlns:x="http://schemas.microsoft.com/winfx/2006/xaml"
        Title="Alignment and Margin"
        Height="300"
        Width="300">
    <Grid>
        <Button Height="35"
                Width="100" />
    </Grid>
</Window>
```

3. Run the application and notice that the `Button` is centered both horizontally and vertically within the `Window`.

4. Exit the application and make the following change to the `Button` element:

```
<Button Height="35"
        Width="100"
        HorizontalAlignment="Left" />
```

Notice how the designer updates the location of the button so that it is aligned to the left side of the window.

5. Now add a `VerticalAlignment`:

```
<Button Height="35"
        Width="100"
        HorizontalAlignment="Left"
        VerticalAlignment="Bottom" />
```

6. Try different combinations of horizontal (`Left`, `Right`, `Center`, `Stretch`) and vertical (`Top`, `Bottom`, `Center`, `Stretch`) alignment to see how they affect layout differently.

7. Now we will add some `Margin` to all the sides:

```
<Button Height="35"
        Width="100"
        HorizontalAlignment="Left"
        VerticalAlignment="Bottom"
        Margin="20" />
```

8. Using two numbers, you can specify left and right margins with the first and top and bottom margins with the second:

```
<Button Height="35"
        Width="100"
        HorizontalAlignment="Left"
        VerticalAlignment="Bottom"
        Margin="20 10" />
```

9. Use four numbers to specify left, top, right, and bottom margins, respectively:

```
<Button Margin="20 5 40 75" />
```

You can use spaces or commas to separate the parameters and double values for fine-grained control.

```
<Button Margin="20,5.75,40,75"/>
```

10. Continue to experiment with various combinations of these core layout properties.

After completing this task you should feel comfortable with some of the layout properties intrinsic to all FrameworkElements. These properties will be of great use in combination with various panels as you begin to master WPF.

Making Sense of Margin and Padding

Margin and Padding, as shown in Figure 4.1, are two similar layout concepts that are often confused. Margin, present on all FrameworkElements, represents the amount of space around the outside of the element. This space ensures that the FrameworkElement has room between it and neighboring elements. Padding functions differently. It is present on elements that inherit from Control (itself derived from FrameworkElement) and allows the control to specify an amount of space inside itself. This inner space separates the control from its own content. A Button control illustrates this most clearly. Picture the space inside the Button, around its text, that prevents the Button's border from shrinking to the size of its contents.

FIGURE 4.1
The relationship between Margin and Padding.

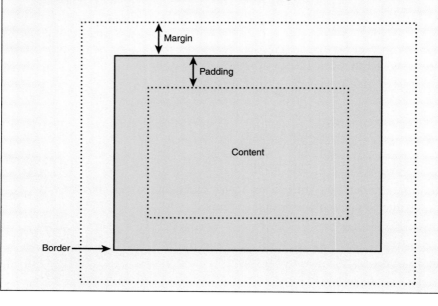

Using Panels to Create Dynamic Layouts

Panels, as mentioned previously, are the core means by which a WPF developer declares UI layout. Take another look at the MainWindow.xaml in the Font Viewer sample application. Two different panels are used in combination to create the general UI structure: DockPanel and StackPanel. Run the application and resize the window several times. Notice how the DockPanel keeps certain elements docked and the StackPanel keeps the TextBlock controls stacked vertically. The specified margins are also maintained.

> All layout described here is done using XAML, but the same layout can be accomplished by using code. Every Panel has a Children collection. This collection can be used to add or remove controls from the panel's layout at runtime.

By the Way

Keeping It Simple with StackPanel

StackPanel is the simplest and one of the most useful layout controls for WPF. By default, it organizes its child elements by stacking them one on top of the other, like a list. StackPanel also has an Orientation property that can be set to Horizontal, causing the panel to stack its children from left to right.

Using a StackPanel

Let's take a look at how StackPanel functions in the context of a real application. This shows us the variety of options that WPF provides, even for simple layout scenarios. We'll investigate how changing Orientation can drastically change layout and how other properties affect the Font Viewer in more minute ways.

1. Open the Font Viewer application and run it. Observe the layout of the four differently sized sample text regions.

2. Close the application and change the StackPanel's opening tag to this:

```
<StackPanel Margin="8 0 8 8"
            Orientation="Horizontal">
```

Notice the change in the designer. Run the application and resize the window horizontally. The contents of the StackPanel are stacked from left to right and clipped by the window boundaries.

3. Close the application and remove the StackPanel's Orientation attribute. This is obviously not what we want.

4. Now add a HorizontalAlignment of Right to one or more of the TextBlock elements that are inside the StackPanel. Notice how this changes layout. The elements are still stacked vertically but within the list, they align themselves to the right.

5. Try adding a VerticalAlignment of Bottom to the first TextBlock. Notice that the layout does not change. Now, change the StackPanel's Orientation back to Horizontal. The elements are now laid out from left to right, with the first element being vertically positioned near the bottom of the screen whereas the rest are at the top.

6. Experiment by changing the Margin on any of the TextBlock elements.

StackPanel is a good place to start when you need to lay out a list of elements. Though it is a simple option, StackPanel provides a diverse array of combinations when using its Orientation property in conjunction with the Alignment and Margin of its children.

> Interestingly, StackPanel is often used internally as the default layout for a number of other WPF controls. One example of such a control is ListBox, which we will look at in later hours.

Organize Your UI with DockPanel

WPF provides developers with a powerful layout option embodied in the DockPanel. This control is capable of attaching its children to any of its four sides and is often used as the root layout control of an application's UI. We have followed this pattern in developing the Font Viewer, but before we can discuss how DockPanel works in this environment, let's look at a very important related topic.

Attached Properties

It is common in layout scenarios for controls to specify additional information about their layout that is specific to the panel they are hosted in. For example, in the Font Viewer, the list of fonts needs to tell the DockPanel that it should be placed along the left side. To provide the DockPanel with this information, we use an *attached property*: DockPanel.Dock. Attached properties are simply a way of connecting additional information to an element. This data can then be used by another source. In the preceding example, DockPanel declares a Dock property that can be attached to any of its children. When the DockPanel lays out its child controls, it queries each one of them for this information and uses that to organize the view appropriately. Attached properties always follow the form Source.Property; where "Source" is the class that declares (and will use) the property and "Property" is the name of the property being set.

Mastering DockPanel

Now that we understand the basics of attached properties, we can use them in the context of our sample application. In this exercise we use attached properties to learn how Dock affects the children of a DockPanel.

1. Begin by examining the MainWindow.xaml in the Font Viewer. Notice that the root panel is a DockPanel with four child elements: Border, ListBox, TextBox, and StackPanel. All these elements, except the StackPanel, have a DockPanel.Dock value set. Run the application or view the designer to see how the panel has arranged the items. Notice that the StackPanel fills the leftover space in the DockPanel after all other controls are docked.

2. Rearrange the DockPanel's children so that the ListBox is declared above the Border. Notice how the docking remains the same but the layout is slightly altered, with the ListBox taking precedence over the Border for space.

3. Change the Border's Dock property to Bottom and the ListBox's Dock property to Right. Run the application and resize the window several times (see Figure 4.2).

4. Change the Border's Dock property to Right and set its Width to 160. Notice that both the ListBox and the Border are docked to the right. Whichever one is first in the list takes precedence, and any Margin that is applied still takes effect.

5. Revert all your changes so that you are back to the original layout. Reorder the last two elements in the list so that the StackPanel is above the TextBox. Remove the DockPanel.Dock="Bottom" from the TextBox and add it to the StackPanel. Notice that the TextBox now fills all the remaining space. Whichever element is last in the list will be used to fill the remaining space.

6. Change the DockPanel's start tag to this:

```
<DockPanel Margin="8"
           LastChildFill="False">
```

Notice that the TextBox no longer fills the remaining space in the DockPanel.

FIGURE 4.2
An alternative
layout with the
DockPanel.

Because attached properties do not actually live on the object they are being set on, they can be a little unintuitive to set in code. WPF follows a pattern of using "Get" and "Set" static methods on the defining class to fulfill this need. For example, this is how you would set the Dock on a Button in code:

```
DockPanel.SetDock(theButton, Dock.Right);
```

The DockPanel is a powerful option for laying out a user interface. It is more complex than the StackPanel, but offers a great deal more "intelligence" in its layout mechanism. A vast assortment of arrangements can be handled with the DockPanel and/or the StackPanel. But if you cannot accomplish what you are aiming for, it's likely the Grid will meet your needs.

Leveraging the Grid for Ultimate Layout Control

The Grid is WPF's all-purpose layout panel. It can achieve most of the same behavior as the previous controls and much more. This power comes with a price; the requirement of additional XAML and more attached properties. Let's see how the Grid works.

LISTING 4.1   Simple Grid Layout

```
<Grid ShowGridLines="True"
    TextBlock.FontSize="20">
  <Grid.RowDefinitions>
    <RowDefinition />
    <RowDefinition />
  </Grid.RowDefinitions>
```

LISTING 4.1   Continued

```
<Grid.ColumnDefinitions>
    <ColumnDefinition />
    <ColumnDefinition />
</Grid.ColumnDefinitions>

<Button Content="0,0" />

<Button Grid.Column="1"
        Content="0,1" />

<Button Grid.Row="1"
        Content="1,0" />

<Button Grid.Row="1"
        Grid.Column="1"
        Content="1,1" />
</Grid>
```

Using a Grid

1. Open Visual Studio and create a new WPF Application project called **UseAGrid**.

2. In Window1.xaml, replace the default Grid with the markup in Listing 4.1. Run the application and observe the layout behavior by resizing the window several times.

3. Note that the resulting Grid has two rows and two columns. This is a result of the RowDefinitions and ColumnDefinitions elements. Also, observe how the attached properties determine what row and column the buttons will be placed in. Row and column indexes begin at zero and default to this value if not specified. This is why the Button with no declared Grid.Row or Grid.Column appears in row and column zero. It is for the same reason that only one parameter needs to be specified on all but the last Button.

4. Change the RowDefinitions and ColumnDefinitions to match the following code:

```
<Grid.RowDefinitions>
    <RowDefinition Height="50" />
    <RowDefinition />
</Grid.RowDefinitions>
<Grid.ColumnDefinitions>
    <ColumnDefinition Width="*" />
    <ColumnDefinition Width="2*" />
</Grid.ColumnDefinitions>
```

5. Run the program and resize the window several times. Notice that the top row maintains a height of 50 device-independent pixels and that the second column is always twice as wide as the first. You can place exact heights and widths on rows and columns, respectively. You can also indicate proportional sizing using the "*" notation.

6. Change the first RowDefinition to this:

```
<RowDefinition Height="auto" />
```

7. Run the program. Notice that the first row is automatically sizing to the default size of its content—in this case Buttons.

8. Try adding additional rows and columns of buttons. Mix and match the different options for height and width. For example, you could define something like this:

```
<ColumnDefinition Width="34" />
<ColumnDefinition Width="1.5*" />
<ColumnDefinition Width="2*" />
<ColumnDefinition Width="auto" />
```

In this case, the first column would be 34 pixels wide, the last column would auto size to content and the middle columns would split the remaining space with the ratio 1.5:2.

9. Experiment by changing the vertical and horizontal alignment of the buttons as well as their Margin.

Hopefully this has given you a basic understanding of how to use a Grid to handle the layout of controls. You can do quite a lot more with a Grid. Take a look at Listing 4.2 and its depiction in Figure 4.3.

When using a Grid for layout, you may want to set the Grid's ShowGridLines property to True. This will draw the imaginary lines on the Grid so that you can be sure that your controls are being laid out properly. Before finishing the design of your UI, remember to remove this setting.

LISTING 4.2   **Advanced Grid Layout**

```
<Window x:Class="AdvancedGrid.Window1"
        xmlns="http://schemas.microsoft.com/winfx/2006/xaml/presentation"
        xmlns:x="http://schemas.microsoft.com/winfx/2006/xaml"
        Title="Window1"
        Height="480"
        Width="600">
```

LISTING 4.2 Continued

```
<Grid TextBlock.FontSize="48">
    <Grid.RowDefinitions>
        <RowDefinition />
        <RowDefinition Height="250" />
    </Grid.RowDefinitions>
    <Grid.ColumnDefinitions>
        <ColumnDefinition Width="2*" />
        <ColumnDefinition Width="auto" />
        <ColumnDefinition Width="*" />
        <ColumnDefinition Width="*" />
    </Grid.ColumnDefinitions>

    <Button Grid.RowSpan="2"
            Content="2 Rows" />

    <GridSplitter Grid.Row="0"
                  Grid.RowSpan="2"
                  Grid.Column="1"
                  Width="8"
                  Background="Black"
                  ResizeBehavior="PreviousAndNext"
                  ResizeDirection="Columns" />

    <Button Grid.Column="2"
            Grid.ColumnSpan="2"
            Content="2 Columns" />

    <Button Grid.Row="1"
            Grid.Column="2"
            Content="1,2" />
    <Button Grid.Row="1"
            Grid.Column="3"
            Content="1,3" />
</Grid>
</Window>
```

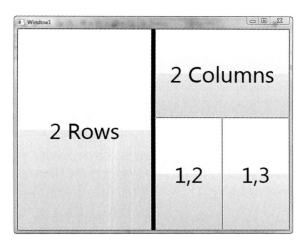

FIGURE 4.3
A more intricate Grid.

The AdvancedGrid code demonstrates some further features of the Grid. Notice that besides just specifying the row and column of a control, we can also make child controls *span* multiple rows or columns. With these additional attached properties, the layout possibilities of the Grid are virtually limitless.

GridSplitter

The GridSplitter is a special control capable of letting a user resize rows or columns of a Grid at runtime. You must place the control within a Grid, between the rows or columns you want to be resizable. Use the ResizeDirection property to indicate what the control will resize (rows or columns) and use ResizeBehavior to declare how the splitter will specifically interact with its own row/column as well as those around it. For example, will it resize its own column, or just the next one? A preferred practice is to place the GridSplitter in a row/column by itself and set the ResizeBehavior to PreviousAndNext. This makes the GridSplitter easier to manage and understand.

Often, building real-world applications involves complex UI layout. Even the versatile panels discussed so far are frequently incapable of expressing an entire layout on their own. For most scenarios you will need to combine multiple different panels. In fact, WPF was designed for building highly composited user interfaces by making it easy to nest controls and panels in one another.

Understanding How WrapPanel Works

The WrapPanel is used less often than StackPanel, DockPanel, and Grid, but offers useful functionality nonetheless. Essentially, a WrapPanel is like a StackPanel, but it has the ability to "wrap" what it is stacking to the next line or column if it runs out of space.

1. Open the Font Viewer application in Visual Studio.

2. Locate the opening and closing StackPanel tags. Change these tags to WrapPanel.

3. There is no change observed in the designer, so run the application.

4. Resize the window in the horizontal direction several times. Notice that the WrapPanel attempts to place the TextBlocks on the same line, but when there is not enough space, it *wraps* them to the next line.

5. WrapPanel, like StackPanel, has an Orientation property. Set the Orientation to Vertical. Run the application and try resizing the window in the vertical direction.

Exploit Canvas for Precision Layout

Canvas is different from all the Panels we have discussed so far. This difference lies in the fact that Canvas does not add any special dynamic layout behavior to its child controls. A canvas must have an exact Width and Height, and all its child elements must have an exact size and position as well. Canvas arranges controls at strict Left (x) and Top (y) positions using attached properties. Try out the XAML in Listing 4.3, visualized in Figure 4.4. Resize the window and try adding alignment; you'll notice that these things have no effect on layout. Margin, however, will offset the control from its location.

> As an alternative to using Top and Left on elements displayed in a Canvas, you can use Bottom and Right. Using these attached properties causes the Canvas to position elements from its bottom and right borders, measuring the distance to the right or bottom border of the element being arranged.

By the Way

> Occasionally, a Canvas (or any Panel) will contain elements that overlap, but that need to be drawn in a specific order. Use the special attached property, Panel.ZIndex, to specify the virtual Z coordinate of the element. Controls with higher ZIndex values are drawn on top of controls with lower values. If no ZIndex is specified, the child control will be rendered based on the order it was added to the panel's Children collection.

Did you Know?

> Although most panels will size to fit their children, if no size is declared for a Canvas it will collapse to zero.

Watch Out!

LISTING 4.3   Exact Positioning with Canvas

```
<Window x:Class="ExactPositionCanvas.Window1"
        xmlns="http://schemas.microsoft.com/winfx/2006/xaml/presentation"
        xmlns:x="http://schemas.microsoft.com/winfx/2006/xaml"
        Title="Window1"
        Height="300"
        Width="300">
    <Canvas Width="200"
            Height="200"
```

LISTING 4.3   Continued

```
            Background="LightBlue">
        <Button Canvas.Left="50"
                Canvas.Top="125"
                Panel.ZIndex="100"
                Width="100"
                Height="35" />
        <Button Canvas.Right="25"
                Height="200"
                Width="35" />
        <Button Canvas.Bottom="5"
                Height="20"
                Width="75" />
    </Canvas>
</Window>
```

FIGURE 4.4
Using a Canvas.

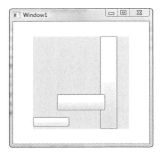

Watch Out!

> Avoid using Canvas for most Control layout scenarios. Using exact positioning and sizing undercuts the power of WPF's dynamic layout mechanisms. The Canvas was originally designed for the layout of Drawings and not Controls. It is best to stick to this practice when possible.

Enhancing a UI with Decorators

Decorators, as mentioned previously, add graphical decoration or behavior to other elements. A Decorator always has one Child that it decorates (although this child can be a Panel containing many other Controls).

Let's look at two of the most common Decorators that you will use or encounter in WPF programming: Border and Viewbox.

1. Begin by creating a new WPF Application called **UsingDecorators**. Enter the code from Listing 4.3 in Window1.xaml.

2. Surround the `Canvas` with a `Border`, like this:

```
<Border BorderThickness="2"
        BorderBrush="Red"
        CornerRadius="20">
    <Canvas ...>
</Border>
```

3. `BorderThickness` and `CornerRadius` can each accept four parameters, indicating how the properties should be applied on each side or corner of the border. Additionally, `BorderThickness` can be declared with two parameters, signifying the left and right in the first parameter and the top and bottom in the second. Try this:

```
<Border BorderThickness="10 5 20 3"
        BorderBrush="Red"
        CornerRadius="20 30 0 0">
    <Canvas ...>
</Border>
```

4. There are a lot of great uses for the `Border` control. Let's use it in conjunction with another `Decorator`, `Viewbox`. Change the code to this:

```
<Border BorderThickness="10 5 20 3"
        BorderBrush="Red"
        CornerRadius="20 30 0 0">
    <Viewbox Margin="10">
        <Canvas ...>
    </Viewbox>
</Border>
```

5. Adding the `Viewbox` causes the designer to stop displaying the layout preview. (This is a current limitation of the VS designer.) Run the application and resize the window several times to see the effect the `Viewbox` has on its content. Notice that it scales its child to fit all available space, as shown in Figure 4.5.

By now you should be familiar with the two most important decorators in WPF. Each of these decorators has a unique capability controlled by a specific set of properties. We have presented the most basic properties here. For another example of using a `Border`, take a look at the `Border` used for displaying instructions in the Font Viewer application. Experiment with the use of `BackgroundColor` and `Padding`. In the case of `Viewbox`, other properties allow further control of its behavior. Spend some time investigating properties like `StretchDirection` and `Stretch`. By altering these values, you can control exactly how the `Viewbox`'s content is scaled.

FIGURE 4.5
Combining
Border,
Viewbox, and
Canvas.

Building Up a Layout

Laying out a user interface can be a tricky task. WPF provides a variety of tools to help you succeed, but you can easily become overwhelmed by the sheer number of possibilities. More often than not, a typical user interface will combine multiple Panels together to create the desired effect. Even in our simple font utility, you can see how we combined a DockPanel and a StackPanel to achieve our goals. Following is a list of recommendations to help you in your interface design:

▶ Begin by using the simplest and most explicit Panel.

▶ Do not be afraid to combine multiple Panels to achieve the effect you desire.

▶ Pay close attention to the runtime behavior of your layout. You may need to change your strategy to accommodate window resizing.

▶ Try to choose layout options that allow for flexible sizing. Avoid setting hard-coded Height and Width properties when possible. Instead, if necessary, consider using MinHeight, MinWidth, MaxHeight, and MaxWidth. These properties give WPF's layout engine some flexible parameters by which it can work, rather than force it into a brittle layout strategy.

▶ If using a graphical UI tool such as the VS Designer or Expression Blend, keep a close eye on the Margin properties of your elements. Sometimes these tools get confused and alter these values in strange ways, resulting in unexpected layout behavior.

▶ Use Canvas only as a last resort. This panel was designed primarily for rendering Drawings, not UI. Using Canvas for ordinary layout scenarios can defeat the purpose of the WPF dynamic layout capabilities. If you want a similar effect, use a Grid control in combination with Margin set on its children. This creates a sort of *relative* canvas effect.

Summary

In this hour we explored many of the WPF layout options. We looked at several of these elements within the context of our first application, the Font Viewer. Hopefully you have taken the time to experiment with the variety of settings available through attached properties and the common layout properties of `FrameworkElement`. Using these properties with a combination of `Panels`, `Decorators`, and other elements will give your Windows application a rich and dynamic layout capable of displaying almost any user interface you can imagine.

Q&A

Q. *Are the* `Panels` *and* `Decorators` *listed in this hour the only options for WPF layout?*

A. No. Numerous ways of managing the layout of controls on a screen exist. One common way is by grouping items in tabs with a `TabControl`. You can also create your own custom panels by inheriting from `Panel` and overriding the proper methods, but that is outside of the scope of this book.

Q. *The* `Grid` *is such a powerful layout option. Why use any of the other panels when I can accomplish the same things with the* `Grid`*?*

A. In many cases, using the `Grid` to accomplish a similar design as another panel will result in more verbose markup. Often it is difficult to ascertain the intention of this markup. If you want docking behavior, be explicit and use a `DockPanel` rather than a `Grid`. The same goes for using other `Panels`. Always choose the simplest and most explicit means that will accomplish your design.

Workshop

Quiz

1. What are the three layout related properties present on all descendents of `FrameworkElement`?

2. What is an attached property?

3. What is the difference between a `Panel` and a `Decorator`?

Answers

1. VerticalAlignment, HorizontalAlignment, and Margin are layout affecting properties on all FrameworkElements. FrameworkElements also have a number of width and height related properties that indirectly affect layout.

2. An attached property is a property that is declared by one control and attached to another. It allows the inclusion of additional information with a control for later use by an external source.

3. A Panel has a collection of Children that it arranges according to various rules, based on the type of panel. A Decorator, on the other hand, has only one Child to which it applies some additional set of behavior.

Activities

1. Rebuild the Font Viewer with a different set of panels than were used in the original design.

2. Rebuild the Font Viewer using a single grid to lay out the entire application. Use one GridSplitter to allow dynamic resizing of the ListBox's width and a second GridSplitter to allow resizing of the TextBox's height.

3. Investigate the SDK to learn about BulletDecorator. This is a lesser-known decorator, but useful in some specific scenarios.

4. Using the search engine of your choice, look up "WPF Radial Panel" or "WPF Custom Panel" to learn about how to create your own custom panels or to see what others have already built.

HOUR 5

Using Basic Controls

What You'll Learn in This Hour:

- ▶ How to display rich flowing text
- ▶ How to accept keyboard input
- ▶ How to allow users to make decisions
- ▶ How to display dynamic feedback
- ▶ How to navigate a UI

In the previous hour you learned about Panels and Decorators; the basic elements of layout. But layout is useless without something to display. In the world of WPF, *controls* are the elements you will use most often in your layout. Controls allow an application to come to life and provide dynamic points of interaction with the user.

In Hour 5, you learn to use several of WPF's most important controls to enable interactive experiences.

Leveraging Controls

Most of the elements we discuss in this hour inherit from the common base class Control. This base derives from FrameworkElement and adds a large amount of additional and important functionality. Among the notable features are basic properties defining the control's colors, border, font, and accessibility characteristics. All controls also have some additional mouse events and enable *templating* (discussed in Hour 21, "Using Control Templates").

Working with Text

You can use several options for working with text in WPF. In this hour we look at the two most common options used for showing small amounts of text to the user: TextBlock and Label, as well as TextBox — the single most common control for receiving text input from the user. The differences between these controls are not immediately discernable to most WPF developers, but they each have important scenarios that they enable.

Displaying Rich Text with the TextBlock

The TextBlock was designed specifically for the purpose of showing small amounts of flowing rich text to the user. It is the perfect element for displaying instructions or summary information.

1. Open the Font Viewer application in Visual Studio and run it. Resize the application horizontally and notice how the instruction text at the top automatically reflows itself to fit the available space.

2. Exit the application and open the MainWindow.xaml file. Examine the TextBlock definition at the top of the markup:

```
<TextBlock FontSize="14"
           TextWrapping="Wrap">
    Select a font to view from the list below.
    You can change the text by typing in the region at the bottom.
</TextBlock>
```

The TextWrapping property is what enables this dynamic reflowing of the text. Removing it will cause the text to be truncated when resized. Also notice how the FontSize property affects the contained text.

3. Now, change the TextBlock element to be as follows:

```
<TextBlock FontSize="14"
           TextWrapping="Wrap">
    <Bold><Italic>Instructions:</Italic></Bold>
    <LineBreak />
    Select a <Underline>font</Underline> to view from the list
    <Italic>below</Italic>.
    <Span FontSize="10">
        You can change the text by typing in the region at the bottom.
    </Span>
</TextBlock>
```

4. Run the application to see the effects of the changes, depicted in Figure 5.1.

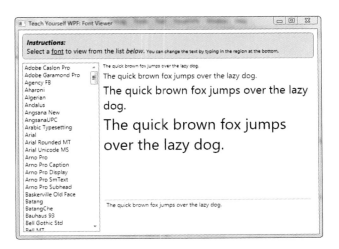

FIGURE 5.1
The Font Viewer
with fancy
instructions.

The TextBlock is quite versatile in its ability to display rich flowing text. The preceding example demonstrates a small sample of how you can enrich your applications with this functionality, but many more options are available for formatting text within a TextBlock. Table 5.1 shows Inline elements that can be used within the body of a TextBlock.

TABLE 5.1   Inline Elements Used in a TextBlock

Name	Description
Span	Groups Inline elements together.
Bold	Bolds the text.
Italic	Italicizes the text.
Underline	Underlines the text.
Hyperlink	Creates a web-style hyperlink in the text.
Run	A sequence of text.
LineBreak	Forces a new line in the text.
InlineUIContainer	Allows UIElements to exist in the text flow.
Figure	Allows text placement to vary from the main flow.
Floater	Displays content parallel to the main flow.

Gathering Text from the User

Perhaps the most common task among all Windows programs is gathering text input from a user. WPF supports this primarily with the TextBox control. You have already seen this control in action in the Font Viewer, where it was used in combination with TextBlock to input and display text with the currently selected font. Like TextBlock, TextBox has various font-related properties controlling size, color, style, and so on, but it differs with its capability to allow users to type in their own text.

Next, we'll use the markup in Listing 5.1 to build a simple form for entering basic information about customer contacts. We'll use TextBlock and TextBox together along with a Grid to accomplish this.

LISTING 5.1   Simple Contact Form XAML

```
<Window x:Class="SimpleContactForm.Window1"
        xmlns="http://schemas.microsoft.com/winfx/2006/xaml/presentation"
        xmlns:x="http://schemas.microsoft.com/winfx/2006/xaml"
        Title="Simple Contact Form"
        Height="300"
        Width="300"
        FocusManager.FocusedElement="{Binding ElementName=firstName}">
    <Grid>
        <Grid.RowDefinitions>
            <RowDefinition Height="auto" />
            <RowDefinition Height="auto" />
            <RowDefinition Height="auto" />
            <RowDefinition Height="auto" />
        </Grid.RowDefinitions>
        <Grid.ColumnDefinitions>
            <ColumnDefinition Width="auto" />
            <ColumnDefinition Width="*" />
        </Grid.ColumnDefinitions>

        <TextBlock Text="First Name:" />
        <TextBox x:Name="firstName"
                Grid.Column="1" />

        <TextBlock Grid.Row="1"
                Text="Last Name:" />
        <TextBox x:Name="lastName"
                Grid.Row="1"
                Grid.Column="1" />

        <TextBlock Grid.Row="2"
                Text="Sex:" />
        <TextBox x:Name="sex"
                Grid.Row="2"
                Grid.Column="1" />

        <TextBlock Grid.Row="3"
                Text="Additional Notes:" />
        <TextBox x:Name="additionalNotes"
                Grid.Row="3"
                Grid.Column="1"
                MinLines="5" />
    </Grid>
</Window>
```

1. Begin by opening Visual Studio and creating a new WPF Application called **SimpleContactForm**.

2. In the main window, type the code from Listing 5.1.

3. Run the application.

4. Use the Tab key to move to each of the TextBoxes and type in some information. Notice that you cannot use the Enter or Tab keys within any of the TextBox elements, and the multiline box never wraps to the next line. This is problematic for the "Additional Notes" section.

5. Change the last TextBox to this:

```
<TextBox x:Name="additionalNotes"
         Grid.Row="3"
         Grid.Column="1"
         MinLines="5"
         AcceptsReturn="True"
         AcceptsTab="True"
         TextWrapping="Wrap" />
```

6. Run the application again and notice the improved behavior of the last box. You can now format text with tabs and new lines as you see fit. The box has a minimum height of five lines but will grow to accommodate longer text.

7. Finally, change the last RowDefinition to have a Height of *. And alter the final TextBox to this:

```
<TextBox x:Name="additionalNotes"
         Grid.Row="3"
         Grid.Column="1"
         AcceptsReturn="True"
         AcceptsTab="True"
         TextWrapping="Wrap"
         VerticalAlignment="Stretch"
         SpellCheck.IsEnabled="True"
         ToolTip="Type additional notes here." />
```

8. As shown in Figure 5.2, notice that the TextBox now fills all the remaining space and that misspelled words are underlined with a squiggly red line. Type a word incorrectly and right-click it. A list of spelling fixes will appear. Hover over the TextBox and a ToolTip appears.

You should now be familiar with the basic capabilities of the TextBox. It is relatively simple, yet provides some nice functionality such as text wrapping, basic formatting, and spell checking.

FIGURE 5.2
A simple contact form.

By the Way

> `ToolTip` is a property on everything that inherits from `FrameworkElement`. Use this property to set pop-up text that appears when users place their mouse over an element.

Did you Know?

> Did you notice the use of `FocusManager.FocusedElement` on the `Window` in Listing 5.1? This is an attached property that lets the developer tell WPF which control in the `Window` should receive keyboard focus when first displayed. You should make a habit of setting this property on each UI that you build.

Accessing Controls with a Label

The contact form from the previous section is a nice start for a user interface. But a real-world form needs better keyboard navigation. To enable richer keyboard support, we'll swap out our `TextBlock` elements with `Label`s as shown in Listing 5.2.

LISTING 5.2   A More Navigable Contact Form

```
<Window x:Class="SimpleContactForm.Window1"
        xmlns="http://schemas.microsoft.com/winfx/2006/xaml/presentation"
        xmlns:x="http://schemas.microsoft.com/winfx/2006/xaml"
        Title="A Navigable Contact Form"
        Height="300"
        Width="300"
        FocusManager.FocusedElement="{Binding ElementName=firstName}">

    <Grid>
        <Grid.RowDefinitions>
            <RowDefinition Height="auto" />
            <RowDefinition Height="auto" />
```

LISTING 5.2   Continued

```xml
            <RowDefinition Height="auto" />
            <RowDefinition Height="*" />
        </Grid.RowDefinitions>
        <Grid.ColumnDefinitions>
            <ColumnDefinition Width="auto" />
            <ColumnDefinition Width="*" />
        </Grid.ColumnDefinitions>

        <Label Content="_First Name:"
               Target="{Binding ElementName=firstName}" />
        <TextBox x:Name="firstName"
                 Grid.Column="1" />

        <Label Grid.Row="1"
               Content="_Last Name:"
               Target="{Binding ElementName=lastName}" />
        <TextBox x:Name="lastName"
                 Grid.Row="1"
                 Grid.Column="1" />

        <Label Grid.Row="2"
               Content="Se_x:"
               Target="{Binding ElementName=sex}" />
        <TextBox x:Name="sex"
                 Grid.Row="2"
                 Grid.Column="1" />
        <Label Grid.Row="3"
               Content="Additional _Notes:"
               Target="{Binding ElementName=additionalNotes}" />

        <TextBox x:Name="additionalNotes"
                 Grid.Row="3"
                 Grid.Column="1"
                 AcceptsReturn="True"
                 AcceptsTab="True"
                 TextWrapping="Wrap"
                 VerticalAlignment="Stretch"
                 SpellCheck.IsEnabled="True"
                 ToolTip="Type additional notes here." />
    </Grid>
</Window>
```

1. Replace the markup of the previous contact form with what is found in Listing 5.2.

2. Run the application. Things should look very similar, with a few minor differences. Notice that the Label controls have some default Margin that makes the UI look a little nicer.

3. Press the `Alt` key on the keyboard and you will notice that certain letters in the `Label` text become underlined. These are called *access keys*. Pressing `Alt` in combination with the underlined letter will direct keyboard input to the corresponding `TextBox`. This makes it easy for users to quickly navigate between noncontiguous fields using only the keyboard. To define an access key, simply precede the character with an underscore. Setting the `Target` property of the `Label` tells WPF what control should be accessed when the key is pressed. We accomplished this by *binding* to the control with the given name (discussed more thoroughly in Hour 6, "Introducing Data Binding").

4. Replace the first `Label` with the following markup:

```
<Label Target="{Binding ElementName=firstName}">
    <Border BorderBrush="Blue"
            BorderThickness="2 0"
            CornerRadius="3"
            Padding="2">
        <AccessText>_First Name</AccessText>
    </Border>
</Label>
```

5. Run the application to see the new behavior. Step 4, depicted in Figure 5.3, demonstrates an important feature of `Label`. Its `Content` can be set to any type of `object`. Use of the `AccessText` element enables us to create rich content for the `Label` while maintaining its keyboard navigation characteristics.

FIGURE 5.3
A keyboard accessible contact form with custom `Label` content.

As you can see, the `Label` provides a different set of functionality from its cousin, the `TextBlock`. It is well suited for forms and other text scenarios that require keyboard navigation. It is also flexible enough to support a great variety of graphical and design possibilities.

> ### More on TextBlock Versus Label
>
> Although TextBlock and Label are both used to display text, they are quite different under the covers. Label inherits from ContentControl, a base class that enables the display of almost any UI imaginable. TextBlock, on the other hand, inherits directly from FrameworkElement, thus missing out on the behavior that is common to all elements inheriting from Control. The shallow inheritance hierarchy of TextBlock makes the control lighter weight than Label and better suited for simpler, noninteractive scenarios. However, if you want access keys to work or want a more flexible or graphical design, you'll need to use Label.

Using Buttons

Most applications involve clicking some type of button. Buttons are a fundamental part of the way we build applications today. To this end, WPF provides several types of buttons for various scenarios. Button, ToggleButton, RadioButton and CheckBox are all examples of controls that inherit from ButtonBase and provide common support for these situations.

Triggering Actions with a Button

Looking back at the contact form from the previous section, you'll see that a major feature is missing—the capability to save a contact. Let's add this.

1. Open the Visual Studio solution containing the project with the contact form.

2. Alter the RowDefinitions in the contact form's markup to match the following:

```
<Grid.RowDefinitions>
    <RowDefinition Height="auto" />
    <RowDefinition Height="auto" />
    <RowDefinition Height="auto" />
    <RowDefinition Height="*" />
    <RowDefinition Height="auto" />
</Grid.RowDefinitions>
```

3. Add the following to the bottom of the Grid definition:

```
<Button Grid.Row="4"
        Grid.Column="1"
        HorizontalAlignment="Right"
        Content="Save"
        Click="Button_Click" />
```

4. Add the following to the code-behind file:

```
private void Button_Click(object sender, RoutedEventArgs e)
{
    MessageBox.Show("Contact saved.", "Save");
}
```

5. Run the application and click the button. You should see a `MessageBox` appear.

Here we've created a `Button` for saving our contact and added it to the `Grid` in the bottom-right corner. We then attached an *event handler* to the button's `Click` event. When a user clicks the button, the code in the event handler is executed. In this case, we display a simple message to the user in place of actually saving any data. As you can see, adding a `Button` is quite straightforward.

Many controls in WPF expose events. Each event serves a different purpose and often has a different *signature* from other events. It's sometimes difficult to remember the signatures of individual events. Fortunately, if you are using the Visual Studio designer, you don't have to. In XAML, type the name of the event on the element, such as `Click`, and press the Equals key. The designer should give you the option <New Event Handler> and also display a list of existing handlers that match the signature. Choosing the New option will automatically generate the handler in the code behind.

Making Choices with ToggleButtons

We often need buttons to turn things on and off or to select one option over another. This is the job of `ToggleButton`. All implementations of `ToggleButton` have an `IsChecked` property indicating the state of the button. Let's spruce up our contact form a bit more by using two important descendents of `ToggleButton`: `RadioButton` and `CheckBox`. See Figure 5.4.

LISTING 5.3   A More Usable Contact Form

```
<Window x:Class="SimpleContactForm.Window1"
        xmlns="http://schemas.microsoft.com/winfx/2006/xaml/presentation"
        xmlns:x="http://schemas.microsoft.com/winfx/2006/xaml"
        Title="A Navigable Contact Form"
        Height="300"
        Width="300"
        FocusManager.FocusedElement="{Binding ElementName=firstName}">
    <Grid>
        <Grid.RowDefinitions>
            <RowDefinition Height="auto" />
```

LISTING 5.3 Continued

```xml
                <RowDefinition Height="auto" />
                <RowDefinition Height="auto" />
                <RowDefinition Height="auto" />
                <RowDefinition Height="*" />
                <RowDefinition Height="auto" />
        </Grid.RowDefinitions>
        <Grid.ColumnDefinitions>
                <ColumnDefinition Width="auto" />
                <ColumnDefinition Width="*" />
        </Grid.ColumnDefinitions>

        <Label Target="{Binding ElementName=firstName}"
               Content="_First Name:" />
        <TextBox x:Name="firstName"
                 Grid.Column="1" />

        <Label Grid.Row="1"
               Content="_Last Name:"
               Target="{Binding ElementName=lastName}" />
        <TextBox x:Name="lastName"
                 Grid.Row="1"
                 Grid.Column="1" />

        <Label Grid.Row="2"
               Content="Se_x:"
               Target="{Binding ElementName=male}" />
        <WrapPanel Grid.Row="2"
                   Grid.Column="1"
                   VerticalAlignment="Center">
            <RadioButton x:Name="male"
                         GroupName="sex"
                         Content="Male"
                         Margin="3" />
            <RadioButton GroupName="sex"
                         Content="Female"
                         Margin="3" />
        </WrapPanel>

        <Label Grid.Row="3"
               Content="_Education:"
               Target="{Binding ElementName=highSchool}" />
        <WrapPanel Grid.Row="3"
                   Grid.Column="1">
            <CheckBox x:Name="highSchool"
                      Content="High School"
                      Margin="2" />
            <CheckBox Content="Bachelor's"
                      Margin="2" />
            <CheckBox Content="Master's"
                      Margin="2" />
            <CheckBox Content="Doctorate"
                      Margin="2" />
        </WrapPanel>

        <Label Grid.Row="4"
               Content="Additional _Notes:"
```

LISTING 5.3   Continued

```
                Target="{Binding ElementName=additionalNotes}" />
        <TextBox x:Name="additionalNotes"
                Grid.Row="4"
                Grid.Column="1"
                AcceptsReturn="True"
                AcceptsTab="True"
                TextWrapping="Wrap"
                VerticalAlignment="Stretch"
                SpellCheck.IsEnabled="True" />

        <Button Grid.Row="5"
                Grid.Column="1"
                HorizontalAlignment="Right"
                Click="Button_Click">
            <AccessText>_Save</AccessText>
        </Button>
    </Grid>
</Window>
```

1. Replace the markup of the contact form with the new XAML found in Listing 5.3.

2. Run the application, navigate the UI, and input some data.

3. Notice that the RadioButton controls are mutually exclusive. This is accomplished by setting their GroupName property to the same value.

4. Notice that each of the CheckBoxes can be individually toggled.

5. Press Alt+S to execute the save Button. This is accomplished by the use of AccessText to cause the Click event to fire.

FIGURE 5.4
A usable contact form in action.

You should now be familiar with the basic usage of the most common button controls of WPF. Because of their ancestor ButtonBase, these controls have much in common. One property you may have noticed being used repeatedly is Content. ButtonBase, like Label, inherits from ContentControl, from which it receives its

Content property. If you investigate this property further, you will find out that it is of type object. This implies that a developer can set this property to any type of data, not just string values. Indeed, this is true, and this feature enables us to use AccessText with the Button. In future hours we discuss ContentControl further and dig deeper into the flexibility of its Content property.

MessageBox.Show

From time to time you need an application to display simple messages or gather yes/no responses from a user. The MessageBox class is the ideal solution for this problem. It is a static class with several method overloads called Show. As you might expect, calling any of these methods results in the appearance of a special kind of *modal dialog box*. Modal dialog boxes block interaction with other windows in the application, forcing the user to pay them attention until they are closed. Each of the overloads of Show let you choose different options affecting how it will be displayed. Some of these features include the capability to specify caption/ message text, icons, and types of buttons to show in the dialog.

Displaying a List with ListBox

If you're following along this hour, watching as we introduce each of the controls (and their cousins) used in the Font Viewer, you probably noticed one large and important control we haven't covered: ListBox. ListBox is a complex control, so I'm only going to mention it briefly here. We'll get much more in depth with this and similar controls in later hours.

1. Open the Font Viewer and run it.

2. Try interacting with the ListBox in multiple ways. You'll notice that you can use your mouse's scroll wheel, drag the slider, or click the arrow buttons to move through the list. Clicking any item in the list selects it and causes the sample text to be displayed in the selection font. You can also navigate the list using your keyboard.

3. Exit the application and examine the XAML. The list of items displayed in the ListBox is determined by the ItemsSource property. The ListBox also has a SelectedItem property to which the sample text is bound. Although it is not used in this example, there is also a SelectionChanged event on the ListBox, which gets fired whenever a new item is selected.

If you aren't quite comfortable with the ListBox, don't be concerned. We'll revisit this control later when you have some more experience—in particular, experience with the subject of the next hour: data binding.

Summary

In this hour we introduced some of the most important and commonly used controls in application building. These controls enable us to display text, both simple and rich, to the user. We have been able to enrich keyboard navigation and allow users to enter their own text into the UI. We have enabled basic decision making through various forms of buttons, such as RadioButton and CheckBox, and allowed the user to execute commands with the most widely used control: Button.

Q&A

Q. *Is there a way to manually control the tab order of controls?*

A. Yes. Everything that inherits from Control has a TabIndex property. Set this property on each Control with a number indicating the order in which the controls should be focused.

Q. *I like the functionality of* ToolTip, *but I'd like the tips to include formatted text or a graphic. Is there a way to accomplish this?*

A. Absolutely. ToolTip is a ContentControl so you can assign anything to its Content property. Try using this markup in the Font Viewer:

```
<TextBox x:Name="SampleText"
         DockPanel.Dock="Bottom"
         MinLines="4"
         Margin="8 0"
         TextWrapping="Wrap">
    <TextBox.ToolTip>
        <TextBlock>
                <Italic Foreground="Red">Instructions: </Italic>
                Type here to change the preview text.
        </TextBlock>
    </TextBox.ToolTip>
    The quick brown fox jumps over the lazy dog.
</TextBox>
```

Workshop

Quiz

1. List at least three types of `Inlines` that can be used in a `TextBlock`.

2. Give two examples of `ContentControl` mentioned in this hour.

3. What is the purpose of `AccessText`?

Answers

1. `Span, Bold, Italic, Underline, Hyperlink, Run, LineBreak, InlineUIContainer, Figure, Floater`.

2. `ButtonBase` and all its descendents and `Label`.

3. `AccessText` enables you to specify displayed text with an embedded keyboard shortcut used to access the corresponding control. Simply precede the desired letter of the text with an underscore.

Activities

1. Investigate the SDK (http://msdn2.microsoft.com/en-us/library/ms754130.aspx) and examine the inheritance hierarchy of the `ListBox`. See what other controls share its base class.

2. Take a closer look at `ButtonBase`. Determine what properties and events this class provides all buttons with. Also, investigate `ToggleButton`, the superclass of `CheckBox` and `RadioButton`, in the same way.

3. Rebuild the contact form from this hour with a different layout strategy or by using a different combination of controls to collect data.

HOUR 6

Introducing Data Binding

What You'll Learn in This Hour:

▶ The syntax used for binding data
▶ The different types and modes of data binding
▶ Dependency properties
▶ Data Context

In this hour we discuss how to bind data in your WPF application. Data binding is one of the most powerful and exciting features of WPF. Data binding enables you to declare, in a very simple manner, how data will interact with the controls and elements in your UI.

What Is Data Binding?

Data binding is a means of connecting the elements of a user interface with the underlying data that the application is interested in. Data binding is *declarative* rather than *imperative*. Declarative means that instead of writing a series of commands to be executed, you describe the relation that the data has to the elements in the UI.

For example, in the Font Viewer, we are interested in the collection of currently installed fonts. We would like to display that collection in a ListBox. If we took an imperative approach to the problem, we would write code that would retrieve the set of fonts and then populate the ListBox with items based on the collection. With data binding, we can simply describe the relationship between the set of fonts and the ListBox declaratively in the markup.

Understanding the Data Binding Syntax

The syntax that WPF uses for data binding can be confusing when you first encounter it. In fact, more than one way exists to declare a data binding in XAML. The most common method of declaring a binding uses a feature of XAML called *markup extensions*. We introduced markup extensions in Hour 2, "Understanding XAML," and you may remember that they enable you to concisely describe something that would be awkward or too verbose in plain XAML.

Markup extensions are identified by curly brackets ({}), and a data binding extension always begins with the word `Binding`.

Let's begin by examining the data bindings on one of the `TextBlock` elements in the Font Viewer. Consider the following markup:

```
<TextBlock Text="{Binding ElementName=SampleText, Path=Text}"
           FontFamily="{Binding ElementName=FontList,
                                Path=SelectedItem}"
           FontSize="10"
           TextWrapping="Wrap"
           Margin="0 0 0 4" />
```

We have two separate data bindings in this markup. The first binds the `Text` property of the `TextBlock` to the `Text` property of a `TextBox` named `SampleText`. Note that the `Text` attribute's value is a data binding markup extension. Again, it's important to emphasize that quotation marks are not allowed inside the markup extension. Markup extensions are not XML like the rest of XAML; rather, they are merely string values that are parsed when an application is compiled.

Our binding references two properties: `ElementName` and `Path`. The `ElementName` property tells the binding to look for an element named `SampleText` in the XAML and to use that as the source of the data. The `Path` property tells the binding where to find the specific data that interests us in relation to the data source. In this case, we are interested in the `Text` property on the source.

Examining the second binding on the `TextBlock`, we interpret the markup extension, `{Binding ElementName=FontList, Path=SelectedItem}`, to mean that we will use the `SelectedItem` property of an element named `FontList` as the data source.

Binding Two Controls Together

Wiring the properties of two controls together is one of the simplest forms of data binding. In the following steps, we bind the font size of a `TextBox` to a `Slider`.

1. Create a new WPF Application project in Visual Studio.

2. Open Window1.xaml in the designer.

3. Replace the Grid with a StackPanel using the following markup:

```
<StackPanel>
</StackPanel>
```

4. Inside the StackPanel, create a slider with the following markup:

```
<Slider x:Name="mySlider"
        Minimum="8"
        Maximum="64" />
```

The Maximum and Minimum attributes define the upper and lower bounds of the Slider. We want to restrict the font size to something meaningful. We also use the x:Name attribute to provide a unique name, mySlider, for the control.

5. Immediately before the Slider, create a TextBlock using the following markup:

```
<TextBlock Text="This is fun!"
           FontSize="{Binding ElementName=mySlider, Path=Value}"
           HorizontalAlignment="Center" />
```

We added an attribute to horizontally align the TextBlock in the center of the StackPanel. This causes the text to remain centered when the font size changes.

We bind the FontSize property of the TextBlock to the Value property of mySlider.

The complete markup is shown in Listing 6.1.

6. Run the application.

7. Move the thumb on the slider and observe how the size of the font changes automatically. You'll also notice that the slider is automatically repositioned as the font grows larger.

LISTING 6.1   Binding a Slider to a TextBlock

```
<StackPanel>
    <TextBlock Text="This is fun!"
               FontSize="{Binding ElementName=mySlider,Path=Value}"
               HorizontalAlignment="Center" />
    <Slider x:Name="mySlider"
            Minimum="8"
            Maximum="64" />
</StackPanel>
```

Two-Way Data Binding

In the preceding example, the data moves in only one direction, from the Slider to the FontSize property. What do we do when we want a user to input some data using either a TextBox or a Slider, and we'd like one to update the other? If the user moves the thumb on the Slider, we want the TextBox to display the Slider's new value, and if the user enters a value directly in the TextBox, we want the thumb to be repositioned on the Slider.

WPF makes this scenario very easy to implement. Let's walk through the steps for setting this up:

1. Create a new WPF Application project in Visual Studio.

2. Open Window1.xaml in the designer.

3. Again, replace the Grid with a StackPanel using the following markup:

   ```
   <StackPanel>
   </StackPanel>
   ```

4. Inside the StackPanel, create a TextBlock and a Slider with the following markup:

   ```
   <TextBox Text="{Binding ElementName=mySlider,Path=Value,Mode=TwoWay}" />
   <Slider x:Name="mySlider"
           Minimum="0"
           Maximum="100"/>
   ```

   This time we've made the range from 0 to 100.

5. Run the application.

6. Move the thumb back and forth and notice that the text changes immediately when the thumb is moved. You'll also notice that the number displayed has a lot of decimal places included. This is because Slider.Value is a double.

7. Now enter a number in TextBox between 0 and 100, and then press the Tab key.

8. Note that the slider did not update its position until the TextBox lost focus.

9. Enter some non-numeric text, like your name, into the text field and then press the Tab key.

10. Nothing happens; the thumb does not move and the text does not change. The data cannot be converted to the appropriate type and it's ignored.

11. Now enter a value greater than 100 and press the Tab key.

12. The thumb snaps all the way to the right, and the text is changed back to 100. The Slider cannot accept a value larger than its Maximum. When you enter a value that is larger, the Slider sets Value to the maximum. Because Slider.Value is changed to the maximum value, TextBox.Text is set to the new value.

The behavior in the last step can be confusing. Here is a breakdown of what is happening:

1. The value of TextBox.Text is changed by the user.

2. The data binding updates the value of Slider.Value.

3. The new value is both valid and greater than Slider.Maximum and so the Slider changes Value to the largest possible value allowed.

4. The data binding updates the value of TextBox.Text.

Take another look at the binding on TextBox.Text:

```
{Binding ElementName=mySlider, Path=Value, Mode=TwoWay}
```

We have introduced a new property, Mode. The value of Mode determines how the data will flow between the data source and the target. The possible values for Mode are listed in Table 6.1.

TABLE 6.1   Modes for Data Binding

Name	Description
OneWay	Changes to the source will update the target.
TwoWay	Changes to the source will update the target, and changes on the target will update the source.
OneTime	The target is set only when the application starts or when the data context is changed.
OneWayToSource	Changes to the target will update the source.

You are not required to set the Mode for a data binding. However it is a good practice to explicitly state the Mode. The default value for Mode is set by the target of the data binding, and different elements have different defaults. The default data binding mode for a TextBox is TwoWay, whereas the default for TextBlock is OneWay. The default values usually make sense, but it's always a good idea to make your intention clear.

Occasionally, you may run into a situation where a data binding does not appear to work. If a data binding cannot convert data to an appropriate type, it will fail silently. We demonstrated an example of this when we bound the TextBox.Text and the Slider.Value. The value of the first is a string, and the later is a double. When the data binding received a string value that it could not convert into a double, it did not complain—it just didn't work.

I have often encountered bugs in my WPF applications where a data source was unexpectedly null, and the application did not throw an exception. Be sure to keep an eye open for this.

Binding to the Collection of Fonts

In the Font Viewer, we bound a ListBox to the collection of currently installed fonts. The .NET Framework BCL provides this collection as a static property called SystemFontFamilies on the class System.Windows.Media.Fonts. This property returns an instance of type ICollection<FontFamily>. Anything that is enumerable can be bound to the ItemsSource property on the ListBox.

You may have noticed that we did not use the same syntax for binding the font collection to the ListBox as we did for binding the controls to one another. We used the following markup extension:

{x:Static Fonts.SystemFontFamilies}

This markup extension is used for referencing static value members on a class. Value members are fields, properties, constants, and enumeration values.

Technically, using x:Static is not a data binding, and WPF treats it a little bit different from standard data binding, but for a simple scenario such as this you can treat it the same.

If you would like to have additional information about a markup extension, you'll need to look for the extension by its class name. The class names are the identifier plus the word "Extension" (don't include the namespace alias).

For example, to find out more about x:Static you will need to search "StaticExtension".

Introducing DataContext

As we've mentioned before, all the controls in WPF inherit from FrameworkElement. FrameworkElement has a property called DataContext, and it is incredibly useful when it comes to binding data.

DataContext is the "context" or the "starting point" from which the data binding is taking place. In our earlier examples, we explicitly provide a context for the binding with the ElementName property. The Path property points to the location of source data within the given context.

Additionally, if you set the DataContext for a given FrameworkElement, all the children of that element will have the same DataContext. In other words, a control's DataContext is inherited from its parent.

Let's consider a new feature for the Font Viewer that will help us demonstrate how DataContext works. Perhaps we would like to display the number of fonts that are currently installed. We know that Fonts.SystemFontFamilies has a Count that returns the number of items in the collection. We can add a ToolTip to the ListBox that will display the count.

Let's modify the Font Viewer to add this new feature:

1. Open the Font Viewer project.

2. Locate the ListBox in MainWindow.xaml.

3. Replace the existing ListBox with the following markup:

```
<ListBox x:Name="FontList"
         DataContext="{x:Static Fonts.SystemFontFamilies}"
         DockPanel.Dock="Left"
         ItemsSource="{Binding}"
         ToolTip="{Binding Path=Count, Mode=OneTime}"
         Width="160" />
```

This places the collection of fonts in the DataContext for the ListBox. The ItemsSource is then bound to the DataContext itself. If you don't specify a Path, the binding points to the context itself. That's what we want in this case.

We also added a binding targeting the ToolTip property using the Count property of the font collection as the source. We told the binder to update just once because we don't expect the number of fonts to change while our application is running.

4. Run the application, and hover your mouse over the ListBox. Notice that it displays a number as shown in Figure 6.1. A number by itself could be confusing, so let's add a little explanatory text to the ToolTip to help out the user.

FIGURE 6.1
A very simple
ToolTip display-
ing the number
of fonts
installed.

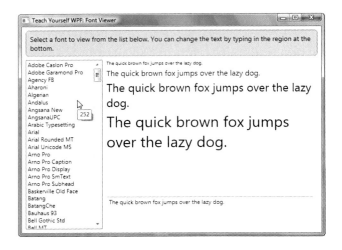

We'll change the markup to the following:

```
<ListBox x:Name="FontList"
         DataContext="{x:Static Fonts.SystemFontFamilies}"
         DockPanel.Dock="Left"
         ItemsSource="{Binding}"
         Width="160">
    <ListBox.ToolTip>
        <ToolTip>
            <StackPanel Orientation="Horizontal">
                <TextBlock Text="{Binding Path=Count,
                                          Mode=OneTime}"/>
                <TextBlock Text=" fonts are installed."/>
            </StackPanel>
        </ToolTip>
    </ListBox.ToolTip>
</ListBox>
```

We added a `StackPanel` because a `ToolTip` can have only one child and we
need the two bits of text. We use an `Orientation` of `Horizontal` because we
want the `TextBlock` elements to display next to each other (rather than being
on top of one another). The new ToolTip is shown in Figure 6.2.

The interesting part to note here is that the `DataContext` set on the `ListBox`
propogates all the way down through the `StackPanel` to the `TextBlock`.

5. Run the application. Listing 6.2 contains the complete markup for this
example.

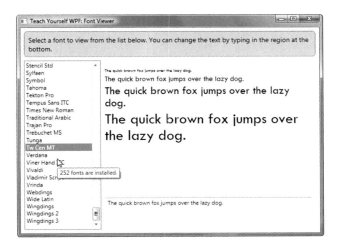

FIGURE 6.2
A slightly more
advanced
ToolTip display-
ing the number
of fonts
installed.

LISTING 6.2   Adding a ToolTip to the Font Viewer

```
<Window x:Class="TeachYourselfWPF.FontViewer.MainWindow"
        xmlns="http://schemas.microsoft.com/winfx/2006/xaml/presentation"
        xmlns:x="http://schemas.microsoft.com/winfx/2006/xaml"
        Title="Teach Yourself WPF: Font Viewer"
        Height="480"
        Width="640">
    <DockPanel Margin="8">
        <Border DockPanel.Dock="Top"
                CornerRadius="6"
                BorderThickness="1"
                BorderBrush="Gray"
                Background="LightGray"
                Padding="8"
                Margin="0 0 0 8">
            <TextBlock FontSize="14"
                       TextWrapping="Wrap">
            Select a font to view from the list below.
            You can change the text by typing in the region at the bottom.
            </TextBlock>
        </Border>
        <ListBox x:Name="FontList"
                DataContext="{x:Static Fonts.SystemFontFamilies}"
                DockPanel.Dock="Left"
                ItemsSource="{Binding}"
                ToolTip="{Binding Path=Count}"
                Width="160" />
        <TextBox x:Name="SampleText"
                DockPanel.Dock="Bottom"
                MinLines="4"
                Margin="8 0"
                TextWrapping="Wrap"
                ToolTip="Type here to change the preview text.">
            The quick brown fox jumps over the lazy dog.
```

LISTING 6.2   Continued

```
        </TextBox>
        <StackPanel Margin="8 0 8 8">
            <TextBlock Text="{Binding Path=Count}" />
            <TextBlock Text="{Binding ElementName=SampleText,
                                      Path=Text}"
                       FontFamily="{Binding ElementName=FontList,
                                            Path=SelectedItem}"
                       FontSize="10"
                       TextWrapping="Wrap"
                       Margin="0 0 0 4" />
            <TextBlock Text="{Binding ElementName=SampleText,
                                      Path=Text}"
                       FontFamily="{Binding ElementName=FontList,
                                            Path=SelectedItem}"
                       FontSize="16"
                       TextWrapping="Wrap"
                       Margin="0 0 0 4" />
            <TextBlock Text="{Binding ElementName=SampleText,
                                      Path=Text}"
                       FontFamily="{Binding ElementName=FontList,
                                            Path=SelectedItem}"
                       FontSize="24"
                       TextWrapping="Wrap"
                       Margin="0 0 0 4" />
            <TextBlock Text="{Binding ElementName=SampleText,
                                      Path=Text}"
                       FontFamily="{Binding ElementName=FontList,
                                            Path=SelectedItem}"
                       FontSize="32"
                       TextWrapping="Wrap" />
        </StackPanel>
    </DockPanel>
</Window>
```

What Makes Data Binding Work?

Part of the magic of data binding comes from the WPF property system. The WPF property system allows properties to participate in data binding, styling, animation, and several other exciting features. A property that is registered with the WPF property system is called a *dependency property*.

A property must be a dependency property to be the target of a data binding. If you are not certain as to whether a property on a control is a dependency property, just check the official documentation. Microsoft makes a note in the description indicating whether the property is a dependency property.

Dependency properties include metadata about the property, such as the default value for the property, the default binding mode, and other miscellaneous items.

Dependency properties also provide automatic *change notification.* In the example earlier this hour, when we bound `TextBox.Text` to `Slider.Value`, the `Slider. Value` was the data source and a dependency property. `Slider.Value` automatically notified the data binding target because it was a dependency property.

By the Way

Unlike the target of a data binding, data sources are not required to be dependency properties. However, if you want to use a binding mode other than `OneWay`, your properties need to implement some mechanism for change notification.

Other than dependency properties, WPF uses two methods for monitoring change notifications. The first is to raise an event in your property setter that is named after the property plus "Changed." For example, if your property is `FirstName`, the setter should raise `FirstNameChanged`. WPF automatically checks for this event and updates data bindings accordingly. We'll create a custom dependency property in Hour 11, "Output."

The second method is to implement `INotifyPropertyChanged` on the class that owns the property. We'll discuss that in detail in a later hour.

Demonstrating Automatic Change Notification

We are going to create a small application to demonstrate how WPF automatically wires events based on the name of the event. We will build an application that allows a user to enter a name in a text field and then store that name in a custom class. Whenever the user changes the name, we want to immediately display the name above the text field in a larger font. We will also see how to set the `DataContext` in the code-behind.

1. Create a new WPF Application in Visual Studio named **AutomaticChangeNotification**.

2. Right-click the project and add a class named `Person`.

3. Visual Studio will open the `Person` class in the editor. Add the following code to the class:

```
private string _firstName;
public string FirstName
{
    get { return _firstName;  }
    set { _firstName = value; }
}
```

4. In `Window1.xaml`, add some rows to the `Grid` element so that it looks like this:

```
<Grid>
    <Grid.RowDefinitions>
        <RowDefinition Height="auto" />
        <RowDefinition Height="auto" />
    </Grid.RowDefinitions>
</Grid>
```

5. Beneath the `RowDefinitions`, but inside the `Grid`, add the elements:

```
<TextBox Text="{Binding Path=FirstName,Mode=TwoWay}"
         Margin="4"/>
<Button Grid.Row="1"
        Height="40"
        Margin="4"/>
```

We are adding the `Button` right now because the `TextBox` does not change its data until it loses focus, so we need another control in the window that we can focus on. The data binding on the `TextBox` is implicitly referencing the data context of its container. After we set the data context to an instance of `Person`, the binding will point to the `FirstName` property.

6. To set the `DataContext` for the `Window` to a new instance of `Person`, open the code-behind for `Window1.xaml` and edit the constructor so that it reads as follows:

```
public Window1()
{
    InitializeComponent();
    DataContext = new Person();
}
```

7. Right-click the setter for the `FirstName` property, and select Breakpoint, Insert Breakpoint. Figure 6.3 shows the location of the breakpoint.

8. Run the application and enter some text in the `TextBox`, and then click the `Button`. When the TextBox changes, we hit our breakpoint.

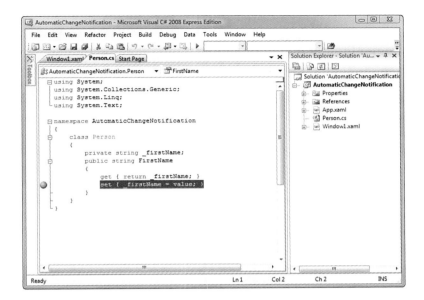

FIGURE 6.3
Breakpoint on
the setter for
FirstName.

9. Stop debugging, and open `Window1.xaml`. We're going to bind the content of the `Button` to `FirstName` as well. We're also going to add a handler for the `Click` event.

   Replace the existing `Button` markup with this:

   ```
   <Button Grid.Row="1"
           Height="40"
           Margin="4"
           Click="Button_Click"
           Content="{Binding Path=FirstName,Mode=TwoWay}" />
   ```

10. In the code-behind for `Window1.xaml`, add the event handler that changes the `FirstName` of our `Person` instance:

    ```
    private void Button_Click(object sender, RoutedEventArgs e)
    {
    ((Person)DataContext).FirstName = "My New Name";
    }
    ```

11. Run the application again and click the button. You'll notice that we still hit our breakpoint, but nothing is bound to the `Button`. This is because our `Person` class does not provide any notification when `FirstName` is changed.

Watch Out!

> If you enter some text in the TextBox, the Button updates when the TextBox loses focus. This happens even when we haven't implemented change notification for this class. WPF can do this because the change originates with the data binding system. Because TextBox is using two-way binding, it is initiating the change, and that's how WPF knows to update the Button. When we change the Person instance in the event handler, WPF doesn't know anything about it, and that's why we need to provide the change notification.

12. Stop debugging, and open Person.cs in the editor. We're going to raise an event when FirstName is changed; add the following code to the Person class:

```
public event EventHandler FirstNameChanged;
private void OnFirstNameChanged()
{
if (FirstNameChanged != null)
FirstNameChanged(this, EventArgs.Empty);
}
```

Remember, WPF automatically looks for an event based on the property's name.

13. Modify the setter for FirstName to raise the event:

```
set
{
_firstName = value;
OnFirstNameChanged();
}
```

14. Run the application again, and click the button. This time you will notice that the content of both the Button and the TextBox changes.

Watch Out!

> WPF will not look for these events on classes deriving from DependencyObject or on classes implementing INotifyPropertyChanged.
>
> I once created a property on a user control that I wanted to participate in data binding, and I was confused when WPF did not pick up the custom event I was raising when the property was changed. Then I realized that UserControl inherits from DependencyObject, and I implemented my property as a dependency property instead.

Another Data Binding Syntax

So far we have only used the markup extensions to declare data bindings; however, you can declare data binds without using markup extensions at all. Let's consider our example from the beginning of the hour:

```
<TextBlock Text="This is fun!"
           FontSize="{Binding ElementName=mySlider,Path=Value}"
           HorizontalAlignment="Center" />
```

To declare the same binding without using a markup extension, we would write the following:

```
<TextBlock Text="This is fun!"
           HorizontalAlignment="Center">
    <TextBlock.FontSize>
        <Binding Path="Value"
                 ElementName="mySlider" />
    </TextBlock.FontSize>
</TextBlock>
```

Notice that the `FontSize` attribute in the first example becomes the `TextBlock.FontSize` element in the second example. The markup extension becomes the `Binding` element, and the properties become attributes.

Even though it's easier to understand, this syntax is not used very often. It is much more verbose and adds a lot of noise to the markup. However, you may find it useful in situations where a data binding becomes very complicated.

Summary

In this hour we discussed the basics of using data binding in your WPF application. We demonstrated how you can easily wire controls together using only XAML. We examined how markup extensions are used to declare data bindings, as well as considering the alternative syntax using plain XAML.

We looked at how data context works, and implemented a custom class that was able to participate in data binding.

Q&A

Q. *What is the most common format for declaring a data binding in markup?*

A. Markup extensions are the most common means of declaring a data binding. They are identified by the use of curly brackets ({}).The less common format is XAML.

Q. *When a data binding uses the* `ElementName` *property, what sort of object will the data source be?*

A. The `ElementName` property is used to reference other elements in the XAML. We would then know that the data source would be an element whose name was specified by the value of the `ElementName` property.

Q. *Is* `x:Static` *the same as a data binding?*

A. `x:Static` is another markup extension that is different from the data binding markup extension. It is used to retrieve data from static value members on classes.

Workshop

Quiz

1. How would the following data binding be interpreted?

```
{Binding Path=Count}
```

2. Convert the following XAML snippet to use the markup extension for data binding.

```
<TextBox>
        <TextBox.Text>
            <Binding Path="FirstName"
                     Mode="TwoWay" />
        </TextBox.Text>
</TextBox>
```

Answers

1. WPF would examine the `DataContext` of the target of the binding and then attempt to locate the value of `Count` property on whatever object was found in the `DataContext`.

2. The XAML snippet is equivalent to the following:

```
<TextBox Text="{Binding Path=FirstName,Mode=TwoWay}" />
```

PART II

Reaching the User

HOUR 7

Designing an Application

What You'll Learn in This Hour:

▶ Application types (Windows, XBAP, Standalone XAML)

▶ Standard application versus navigation application

▶ User controls

In this hour we discuss the choices you will face when you first begin to design a WPF application. WPF offers several approaches to building an application that differ fundamentally and that are not easy to change after development has begun. We'll discuss the types of components that you can use to organize your applications.

Deployment Models in WPF

There are three ways to deploy a WPF application. Table 7.1 describes the ways you can deploy applications.

TABLE 7.1   File Formats for WPF Applications

Standard Executable	This is the format we've used so far. It is by far the most common. Your WPF application is compiled into a standard executable file. As you might expect, this uses an `.exe` extension.
XAML Browser Application	Sometime this is referred to as XBAP (pronounced "X-Bap"). This is a special WPF application that is intended to be hosted in a browser (Internet Explorer 6 and later and Firefox 2 have native support). Because an XBAP is hosted in the browser, there are lots of security restrictions, but this format can simplify deployment. This has an `.xbap` extension.

TABLE 7.1   Continued

XAML file	This is a text file with XAML markup. Running a `.xaml` file launches the application in a browser. The primary limitation is that you cannot have any code in the application. It's XAML only. This uses a `.xaml` extension.

Converting the Font Viewer to XAML Only

Not being able to include code with your application sounds like a rather severe limitation; however, XAML is surprisingly powerful. Our Font Viewer application from Part I did not use any code whatsoever. We can adapt the application to deploy as a XAML file.

Visual Studio doesn't offer a way to create a new standalone XAML file, but it will help us edit one.

Let's convert the Font Viewer to a simple XAML file.

1. Create a new text file on your desktop. Generally, you can right-click and select New, Text Document. Name the file **FontViewer.xaml**.

2. If you double-click `FontViewer.xaml`, the file launches in your default browser. We haven't added any markup, so the parsing fails and you receive an error message.

3. Launch Visual Studio and open `FontViewer.xaml` using File, Open File. This opens the empty file in the IDE.

4. We can reuse the bulk of the markup for the original Font Viewer application. Locate `MainWindow.xaml` from the original Font Viewer project and open it in Visual Studio as well. You can use File, Open File.

5. Copy the entire contents of `MainWindow.xaml` and paste it into `FontViewer.xaml`.

6. In `FontViewer.xaml`, locate the opening and closing `Window` tags at the very top and bottom of the file and replace them with corresponding `Page` tags. At this point, the application is executable.

7. This step is not required to run the application, but it is a good practice for usability. Change the `Title` attribute on the `Page` element to a `WindowTitle` attribute. The `WindowTitle` will be displayed in the title bar of the browser when the application runs.

8. Double-click `FontViewer.xaml` to launch the application. The complete code is available in Listing 7.1.

LISTING 7.1   Markup for `FontViewer.xaml`

```
<Page xmlns="http://schemas.microsoft.com/winfx/2006/xaml/presentation"
    xmlns:x="http://schemas.microsoft.com/winfx/2006/xaml"
    WindowTitle="Teach Yourself WPF: Font Viewer"
    Height="480"
    Width="640">
  <DockPanel Margin="8">
    <Border DockPanel.Dock="Top"
            CornerRadius="6"
            BorderThickness="1"
            BorderBrush="Gray"
            Background="LightGray"
            Padding="8"
            Margin="0 0 0 8">
      <TextBlock FontSize="14"
                 TextWrapping="Wrap">
        Select a font to view from the list below.
        You can change the text by typing in the region at the bottom.
      </TextBlock>
    </Border>
    <ListBox x:Name="FontList"
             DockPanel.Dock="Left"
             ItemsSource="{x:Static Fonts.SystemFontFamilies}"
             Width="160" />
    <TextBox x:Name="SampleText"
             DockPanel.Dock="Bottom"
             MinLines="4"
             Margin="8 0"
             TextWrapping="Wrap">
      <TextBox.ToolTip>
        <TextBlock>
          <Italic Foreground="Red">Instructions: </Italic>
          ➥ Type here to change the preview text.
        </TextBlock>
      </TextBox.ToolTip>
      The quick brown fox jumps over the lazy dog.
    </TextBox>
    <StackPanel Margin="8 0 8 8">
      <TextBlock Text="{Binding ElementName=SampleText,
                               Path=Text}"
                 FontFamily="{Binding ElementName=FontList,
                                     Path=SelectedItem}"
                 FontSize="10"
                 TextWrapping="Wrap"
                 Margin="0 0 0 4" />
      <TextBlock Text="{Binding ElementName=SampleText,
                               Path=Text}"
                 FontFamily="{Binding ElementName=FontList,
                                     Path=SelectedItem}"
                 FontSize="16"
```

LISTING 7.1   Continued

```
                        TextWrapping="Wrap"
                        Margin="0 0 0 4" />
            <TextBlock Text="{Binding ElementName=SampleText,
                                      Path=Text}"
                        FontFamily="{Binding ElementName=FontList,
                                             Path=SelectedItem}"
                        FontSize="24"
                        TextWrapping="Wrap"
                        Margin="0 0 0 4" />
            <TextBlock Text="{Binding ElementName=SampleText,
                                      Path=Text}"
                        FontFamily="{Binding ElementName=FontList,
                                             Path=SelectedItem}"
                        FontSize="32"
                        TextWrapping="Wrap" />
        </StackPanel>
    </DockPanel>
</Page>
```

Converting the Font Viewer to an XBAP

Deploying the Font Viewer application as an XBAP is very easy to do. Visual Studio provides a helpful mechanism for publishing your XBAP as well.

Let's create a new XBAP project and adapt the Font Viewer markup to it.

1. From inside Visual Studio, select File, New Project, and choose `WPF Browser Application`. Name the new project **FontViewerXBAP**.

2. After Visual Studio finishes creating the new project, take a moment to look over the files in the Solution Explorer. You will notice two differences. The first is that instead of `Window1.xaml`, you have `Page1.xaml`. Second, the file with the `.pfx` extension is a temporary key used for signing the ClickOnce manifest.

3. Open `Page1.xaml` in the editor and replace the contents of the file with the complete markup from Listing 7.1. Note that this is the same markup we used in the XAML-only version.

4. We need to make one adjustment before the XBAP is fully functioning. Add the following attribute to the Page element:

```
x:Class="FontViewerXBAP.Page1"
```

Press F5, and you can see the Font Viewer execute in the browser.

5. If you were not able to see the address bar in your browser, you would be hard pressed to know if this is a XAML file or an XBAP. Because this is an XBAP, we would like to prove to ourselves that we can add code and have it execute in the browser. Stop the application, and then double-click the `ListBox` in the design pane of `Page1.xaml`.

6. Visual Studio navigates to the code-behind file for `Page1.xaml` and adds an event handler for the `SelectionChanged` event on the `ListBox`.

7. We'll add some superfluous code, just to demonstrate to ourselves that it behaves as expected. Add the following code to the event handler:

```
MessageBox.Show("This is executed in code!");
```

8. Press F5 to run the application. It will launch in a browser. Click the list box and see your pop-up message. Figure 7.1 shows the Font Viewer running in Firefox.

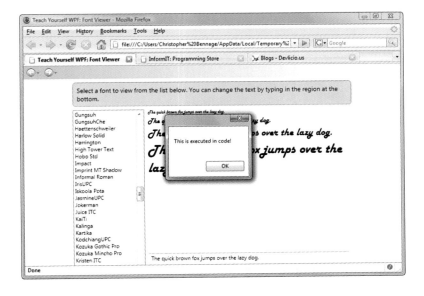

FIGURE 7.1
The Font Viewer
XBAP running
in Firefox.

Publishing an XBAP

Now that we have a functioning XBAP, what should we do with it? We want to publish it to a location where our intended users can access it.

Visual Studio will add a Publish option to the Build menu when working with a WPF Browser Application project. This option launches a wizard that assists you in publishing your XBAP to a website or some other known location.

Let's publish our application to a local folder to become familiar with the wizard.

1. Make sure that our FontViewXBAP project from the previous exercise is open in Visual Studio.

2. From the menu, select Build, Publish FontViewXBAP, as shown in Figure 7.2.

3. When the publish wizard launches, click the Browse button and select a folder where the application will be published.

4. Click Next.

5. You can continue to select the default options by clicking Next, or complete the wizard by clicking Finish.

6. The wizard opens the folder where the application was published. You will notice that there is a file named `FontViewerXBAP.xbap` as well as a directory named `Application Files`. `Application Files` contains files related to ClickOnce deployment.

FIGURE 7.2
Selecting the
Publishing
Wizard for
an XBAP.

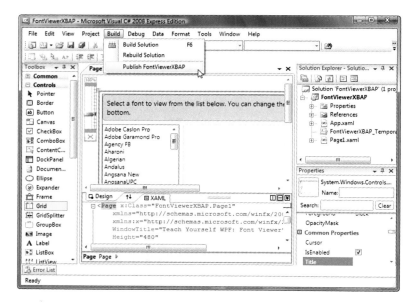

Navigation Models in WPF

You might have noticed something with the XBAP and XAML versions of the Font Viewer that differed slightly from our original standard executable. In the top-left corner of the application were two buttons, very similar to the back and forward buttons in a browser.

WPF has two built-in models for applications. The first is the conventional window-based model (recall that the root element of the first Font Viewer application was Window). Applications built on the second model are called *navigation applications*.

Navigation applications use the metaphor of a browser. They have pages instead of windows, and you can use the forward and back buttons to navigate through the application.

Navigation applications even have hyperlinks that allow you to reference other XAML pages in your application.

Let's create a simple navigation application so that we can see how these concepts work in WPF.

1. Launch Visual Studio and create a new WPF Application named **NavigationApp**.

2. In the Solution Explorer, right-click Window1.xaml and delete it.

3. Right-click the project in the Solution Explorer and select Add, Page. For this example, you can accept the default page name Page1.xaml.

4. Add a Page2.xaml the same way.

5. Open App.xaml in the editor, and in the XAML pane change the StartupUri to point to Page1.xaml.

6. Open Page1.xaml and replace the Grid element with the following markup:

```
<StackPanel>
    <TextBlock FontSize="24">Page 1</TextBlock>
    <TextBlock>
        <Hyperlink NavigateUri="Page2.xaml">Click Me</Hyperlink>
    </TextBlock>
</StackPanel>
```

We're adding some text to help us identify the page. Then add a HyperLink that will navigate to the other page. Note that the HyperLink is nested inside of a TextBlock.

7. Open Page2.xaml and replace the Grid element with the following markup:

```
<StackPanel>
    <TextBlock FontSize="24">The Second Page</TextBlock>
    <TextBlock>
            <Hyperlink Foreground="Green"
                     NavigateUri="http://www.sams.com">
                Go Online</Hyperlink>
    </TextBlock>
</StackPanel>
```

We've made the markup a little different so that we will notice the differences between the pages.

8. Launch the application. Notice that both navigation buttons are disabled.

9. Click the hyperlink on the first page. The back button is now enabled.

10. Click the hyperlink on the second page and now you are browsing the Web. (This will throw an error if you are not connected to the Internet or if your computer cannot resolve the URL!)

If you want to create a navigation application and have a portion of the interface that you want to be common across all the pages, you can use a control called Frame. This allows you to have a scenario very similar to a web page with frames.

Let's build a quick application that demonstrates how frames work:

1. Open the NavigationApp project we just created.

2. Right-click the Solution Explorer and select Add, Window. Name the new window **MainFrame.xaml**.

3. In MainFrame.xaml, replace the Grid with the following:

```
<DockPanel>
    <TextBlock DockPanel.Dock="Top">The Main Frame</TextBlock>
    <Frame Source="Page1.xaml" />
</DockPanel>
```

4. Open App.xaml and again change the StartupUri. This time point it to MainFrame.xaml.

5. Run the application again, and this time you will see that the navigation controls are placed inside the Frame element.

All the options available with WPF can be overwhelming. There's also a strong temptation to use something just because it is new. Think carefully about how your application is going to be used, and choose the type of application that best fits your needs. Often you will find that the conventional model is standard for a reason.

User Controls

User controls are similar to windows and pages. They allow you to easily define your own controls that can be reused throughout your application. They are generally used for creating some subset of the user interface, or perhaps a composite of other controls that are frequently used together.

User controls inherit from UserControl. They have a XAML file and a code-behind. Do not confuse them with *custom controls*. Custom controls are another way to create reusable elements for the UI, but I do not recommend them for a newcomer to WPF.

Unlike choosing a deployment or navigation model, breaking out your application into user controls is something you are likely to do when development is well under way. Organizing your source with user controls can be useful for promoting reuse, reducing complexity, or enabling team development.

Let's revisit our Font Viewer again and restructure the application to use a UserControl. We'll move both the TextBox and the TextBlock elements for previewing the font into a UserControl. We will also see another example of how DataContext operates.

1. Open the original Font Viewer project in Visual Studio.

2. Right-click the project in the Solution Explorer and select Add, User Control. Name the new control **TextPreviewControl.xaml**.

3. Visual Studio opens the new user control in the editor. Remove the Height and Width attributes because we'll want the control to stretch to fill the space we provide for it.

4. Replace the Grid element with a DockPanel.

5. Open the MainWindow.xaml, cut the TextBox and the StackPanel, and paste it inside the DockPanel we created in the previous step. The markup for TextPreviewControl.xaml should look like this:

```xml
<UserControl x:Class="TeachYourselfWPF.FontViewer.TextPreviewControl"
             xmlns="http://schemas.microsoft.com/winfx/2006/xaml/presentation"
             xmlns:x="http://schemas.microsoft.com/winfx/2006/xaml">
    <DockPanel>
        <TextBox x:Name="SampleText"
                 DockPanel.Dock="Bottom"
                 MinLines="4"
                 Margin="8 0"
                 TextWrapping="Wrap">
            <TextBox.ToolTip>
                <TextBlock>
                    <Italic Foreground="Red">Instructions: </Italic>
                    ➥ Type here to change the preview text.
                </TextBlock>
            </TextBox.ToolTip>
            The quick brown fox jumps over the lazy dog.
        </TextBox>
        <StackPanel Margin="8 0 8 8">
```

```xml
            <TextBlock Text="{Binding ElementName=SampleText,
                                      Path=Text}"
                    FontFamily="{Binding ElementName=FontList,
                                        Path=SelectedItem}"
                    FontSize="10"
                    TextWrapping="Wrap"
                    Margin="0 0 0 4" />
            <TextBlock Text="{Binding ElementName=SampleText,
                                      Path=Text}"
                    FontFamily="{Binding ElementName=FontList,
                                        Path=SelectedItem}"
                    FontSize="16"
                    TextWrapping="Wrap"
                    Margin="0 0 0 4" />
            <TextBlock Text="{Binding ElementName=SampleText,
                                      Path=Text}"
                    FontFamily="{Binding ElementName=FontList,
                                        Path=SelectedItem}"
                    FontSize="24"
                    TextWrapping="Wrap"
                    Margin="0 0 0 4" />
            <TextBlock Text="{Binding ElementName=SampleText,
                                      Path=Text}"
                    FontFamily="{Binding ElementName=FontList,
                                        Path=SelectedItem}"
                    FontSize="32"
                    TextWrapping="Wrap" />
        </StackPanel>
    </DockPanel>
</UserControl>
```

Note that we did not change the markup that docked the `TextBox` to the bottom, because we place this markup in a `DockPanel` in our `UserControl`.

6. The bindings for `TextBlock.FontSize` are no longer valid after moving the markup into the `UserControl`. To make this work again, we are going to make use of the `DataContext` for the `UserControl`. Change each of the four bindings to point to the `DataContext` by changing the `FontSize` attribute to the following:

```xml
FontFamily="{Binding Path=SelectedItem}"
```

When we add our new `UserControl` to `MainWindow`, we'll set its context to `FontList`.

7. To add the `UserControl` to the `MainWindow`, add the following markup immediately after the `ListBox`:

```xml
<local:TextPreviewControl DataContext="{Binding ElementName=FontList}" />
```

8. The `local` prefix is an alias that tells the compiler where to locate `TextPreviewControl`. We could use a name other than `local`. In this case, I

use local to indicate that the `TextPreviewControl` lives in the same assembly. We need to define `local` in the root node by adding the following attribute to the `Window` element:

```
xmlns:local="clr-namespace:TeachYourselfWPF.FontViewer"
```

This says that the prefix `local` refers to the namespace `TeachYourselfWPF.FontViewer`.

9. Run the application and you will see that it behaves exactly the way it did before we added the `UserControl`. The complete code for `MainWindow.xaml` is in Listing 7.2.

Notice in step 7 how we set the `DataContext` of the `UserControl` to `FontList`. This is the same as saying that by default any data binding inside the `UserControl` will use the `ListBox` called `FontList` as its source of data. Even though the `TextBlock` elements that need to reference `FontList` are nested several levels deep, the `DataContext` is automatically passed down.

LISTING 7.2   The Font Viewer with a User Control

```xaml
<Window x:Class="TeachYourselfWPF.FontViewer.MainWindow"
        xmlns="http://schemas.microsoft.com/winfx/2006/xaml/presentation"
        xmlns:x="http://schemas.microsoft.com/winfx/2006/xaml"
        xmlns:local="clr-namespace:TeachYourselfWPF.FontViewer"
        Title="Teach Yourself WPF: Font Viewer"
        Height="480"
        Width="640">
    <DockPanel Margin="8">
        <Border DockPanel.Dock="Top"
                CornerRadius="6"
                BorderThickness="1"
                BorderBrush="Gray"
                Background="LightGray"
                Padding="8"
                Margin="0 0 0 8">
            <TextBlock FontSize="14"
                       TextWrapping="Wrap">
            Select a font to view from the list below.
            You can change the text by typing in the region at the bottom.
            </TextBlock>
        </Border>
        <ListBox x:Name="FontList"
                 DockPanel.Dock="Left"
                 ItemsSource="{x:Static Fonts.SystemFontFamilies}"
                 Width="160" />
        <local:TextPreviewControl DataContext="{Binding
        ➥ElementName=FontList}" />
    </DockPanel>
</Window>
```

By the Way

User controls are a very useful feature of WPF. However, always ask yourself if using the feature will improve your code. When I first learned about user controls (in ASP.NET 1.1), I had a tendency to use them anytime I could. In retrospect, I realize that it was needless work and didn't provide any value.

Here are two scenarios (and there are certainly more than just two) where user controls are a great fit.

The first is when you have a portion of the interface that is being used in more than one location. We'll provide an example of this in Part IV, when we construct a media player. We'll have a user control that presents the controls for the media (play, pause, stop), and it will be used on both an audio screen and a video screen.

Another situation is when the intention of the interface is obscured by supporting elements. We'll see an example of this as we are building our text editor. Portions of the interfaces, such as a toolbar or menu, can get in the way of the real behavior we are interested in maintaining. These make good candidates for user controls.

Summary

In this hour we discussed the several ways to build WPF applications. We converted our Font Viewer application from Part I to be deployed as a simple XAML file and as an XBAP. We covered navigation application, the built-in support that WPF has for building applications using a web browser metaphor.

Finally, we examined user controls in WPF and how they can be used to help us build applications more effectively.

Q&A

Q. *How many ways are there to deploy WPF applications, and what are they?*

A. There are three ways to deploy WPF applications: as a simple XAML file, an XBAP, or a standard executable.

Q. *What is the prominent limitation of deploying an application as a XAML file only?*

A. XAML-only applications are not compiled and cannot contain code. You are limited to functionality that can be provided with XAML only.

Q. *What is the intended environment for WPF Browser Applications or XBAPs?*

A. An XBAP application is designed to be hosted in a browser, such as recent versions of Internet Explorer and Firefox.

Workshop

Quiz

1. How do navigation applications differ from standard WPF applications?

2. Imagine that you have a `UserControl` that has a `StackPanel` inside of it, and the `StackPanel` contains two `TextBlock` elements. If you set the `DataContext` of the `UserControl` to a collection of fonts, and set the `DataContext` of the `StackPanel` to the first instance in the collection, what will the `DataContext` of the `TextBlock` elements be?

Answers

1. Navigation applications are based on a web browser metaphor. They use pages instead of windows, and they include a forward and back button by default.

2. Child elements always inherit the `DataContext` of their parents, unless their `DataContext` is explicitly set. In our example, the `TextBlock` elements would inherit the same context as their parent, the `StackPanel`.

Building a Text Document Editor

What You'll Learn in This Hour:

▶ Design a new application

▶ Expand our control repertoire

▶ Discover new methods of handling interaction

▶ Componentize the UI with User Controls

With the foundation of preceding hours, we now have the tools we need to begin creating a more dynamic, real-world application. Over the course of the next few pages we'll begin building the foundations for a simple text document editor.

In this hour, we set up the core layout and controls for our Text Editor.

Designing a Text Editor

Building a text document editor is no trivial task. Think about the document editing you've done over the years and the myriad of features these tools support to help you get the job done. Our goal is to support a basic set of features that will leverage as much as possible the built-in capabilities of WPF without having to write too much custom code. To that end, we'll support the following features:

▶ New, Open, Save of .rtf documents.

▶ Basic text editing of .rtf documents.

▶ Common menu and toolbar options for editing .rtf.

▶ Common application and editing keyboard shortcuts.

▶ Spell checking.

▶ Basic printing.

▶ A look and feel consistent with similar applications.

Creating the Application Layout

One of the first things to do when building a new application is to create a quick prototype of the layout. This helps to kick start the process of thinking about application usability. Let's build a layout consistent with similar text editing applications:

1. Open Visual Studio and create a new WPF application. Call the application **TextEditor**.

2. Rename Window1.xaml to **MainWindow.xaml** and make the appropriate changes in the App.xaml file as well.

3. Open MainWindow.xaml for editing.

4. Add the following markup to create the basic application layout:

```
<Window x:Class="TextEditor.MainWindow"
        xmlns="http://schemas.microsoft.com/winfx/2006/xaml/presentation"
        xmlns:x="http://schemas.microsoft.com/winfx/2006/xaml"
        Title="Text Editor"
        Height="600"
        Width="800">
    <DockPanel>
        <Menu x:Name="menu"
              DockPanel.Dock="Top" />

        <ToolBarTray x:Name="toolbar"
                     DockPanel.Dock="Top" />

        <StatusBar DockPanel.Dock="Bottom">
            <TextBlock x:Name="status" />
        </StatusBar>

        <RichTextBox x:Name="body"
                     SpellCheck.IsEnabled="True"
                     AcceptsReturn="True"
                     AcceptsTab="True"
                     BorderThickness="0 2 0 0" />
    </DockPanel>
</Window>
```

5. Run the application and you should see something that looks pretty empty. Don't worry—when we're done, it will look like Figure 8.1.

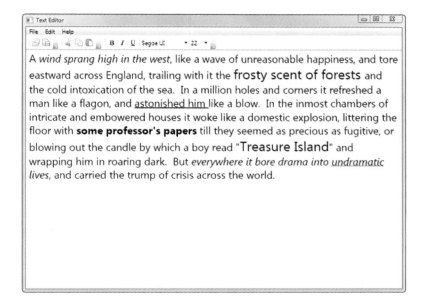

FIGURE 8.1
The Text Editor.

This is our basic application layout. It's not very interesting at the moment, mainly because we have no items in our menu or icons in our ToolBarTray. We'll remedy this shortly.

Adding Usability with ToolBars

A ToolBar is a simple and attractive way to make an application more user-friendly. The Text Editor should have several toolbars supporting the most common quick-access features. Let's expand our code in this way.

1. Open the MainWindow.xaml and locate the ToolBarTray.

2. Change the ToolBarTray to match the following markup.

```
<ToolBarTray>
    <ToolBar>
        <Button ToolTip="Open">
            <Image Source="Icons/folder_page.png" />
        </Button>
        <Button ToolTip="Save">
            <Image Source="Icons/page_save.png" />
        </Button>
    </ToolBar>
</ToolBarTray>
```

3. Right-click the project in Visual Studio and select Add, New Folder. Name the folder `Icons`.

4. Locate several `.png` icon files (or `.gif`, `.jpg`, `.bmp`, `.tif`, `.ico`) that you can use to represent the file operations `Open` and `Save`. For our sample, we are using icons licensed for use under the Creative Commons License 2.5. They can be found here: www.famfamfam.com/lab/icons/silk.

5. Copy the icons into the `Icons` folder.

6. Right-click the `Icons` folder in Visual Studio and select Add, Existing Item. Browse to the `Icons` folder and select all the icons to add them to the project.

7. Change the `Image` elements' `Source` properties to match the names of the icon files you have chosen.

8. Run the application to see the results.

So what is the preceding XAML doing for us? First, we have a `ToolBarTray` that provides a "home" for our toolbars to live in. It can host multiple `ToolBar` instances and allows the runtime to automatically arrange and size them. Inside the `ToolBarTray`, we have a single `ToolBar` hosting a collection of `Buttons`. Each button contains an `Image` element. You can point the `Source` property of an `Image` to almost any type of graphic and it can display it. We are taking advantage of the power of the `Content` property of the `Button` to display an image instead of static text.

Increasing Maintainability with User Controls

Looking back at the previous code sample, you might think: "If we add several more toolbars and a menu, there's going to be a massive amount of XAML crammed into one file." XAML like that seems as if it would be difficult to navigate, understand, and maintain over time. This is the perfect scenario for introducing a `UserControl` into our application.

1. Right-click the project file in Visual Studio and select Add, User Control. Name the file **TextEditorToolbar.xaml**.

2. Replace the generated XAML with the markup found in Listing 8.1.

3. Add the following code to the `TextEditorToolbar.xaml.cs` file:

```
private void UserControl_Loaded(object sender, RoutedEventArgs e)
{
    for (double i = 8; i < 48; i += 2)
```

```
            {
                fontSize.Items.Add(i);
            }
        }
    }
```

4. Add corresponding icons to the Icons folder and update their names in the markup.

5. Open MainWindow.xaml and add the following Xml Namespace declaration to the Window: **xmlns:local="clr-namespace:TextEditor"**.

6. In the MainWindow.xaml replace the ToolBarTray with the following markup:

```
<local:TextEditorToolbar x:Name="toolbar"
                         DockPanel.Dock="Top" />
```

7. Run the application.

8. Try dragging and resizing the toolbars. If a Toolbar is too small to display all its contents, the down arrow on the right will be enabled and you can click it to display the additional icons in a Popup. You can see the effects of this in Figure 8.2.

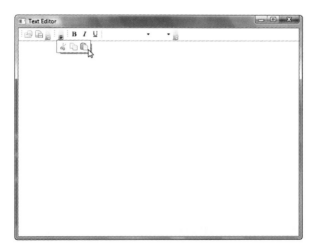

FIGURE 8.2
An application toolbar with overflow.

Recall that Xml Namespace declarations can be placed on elements in XAML to import non-WPF types into the markup. The syntax is: xmlns:*name*="clr-namespace:*clrNamespace*;assembly=*assembly.dll*". If the assembly is the same as the one in which the XAML exists, you do not have to declare it. The name "local" is commonly used in this scenario.

By the Way

LISTING 8.1 Toolbars in a User Control

```
<UserControl x:Class="TextEditor.TextEditorToolbar"
             xmlns="http://schemas.microsoft.com/winfx/2006/xaml/presentation"
             xmlns:x="http://schemas.microsoft.com/winfx/2006/xaml"
             Loaded="UserControl_Loaded">
    <ToolBarTray>
        <ToolBar>
            <Button ToolTip="Open">
                <Image Source="Icons/folder_page.png" />
            </Button>
            <Button ToolTip="Save">
                <Image Source="Icons/page_save.png" />
            </Button>
        </ToolBar>
        <ToolBar>
            <Button ToolTip="Cut">
                <Image Source="Icons/cut.png" />
            </Button>
            <Button ToolTip="Copy">
                <Image Source="Icons/page_copy.png" />
            </Button>
            <Button ToolTip="Paste">
                <Image Source="Icons/page_paste.png" />
            </Button>
        </ToolBar>
        <ToolBar>
            <ToggleButton x:Name="boldButton"
                          ToolTip="Bold">
                <Image Source="Icons/text_bold.png" />
            </ToggleButton>
            <ToggleButton x:Name="italicButton"
                          ToolTip="Italic">
                <Image Source="Icons/text_italic.png" />
            </ToggleButton>
            <ToggleButton x:Name="underlineButton"
                          ToolTip="Underline">
                <Image Source="Icons/text_underline.png" />
            </ToggleButton>
            <Separator />
            <ComboBox x:Name="fonts"
                      MinWidth="100"
                      ItemsSource="{x:Static Fonts.SystemFontFamilies}"
                      ToolTip="Font" />
            <ComboBox x:Name="fontSize"
                      MinWidth="40"
                      ToolTip="Font Size" />
        </ToolBar>
    </ToolBarTray>
</UserControl>
```

We've added quite a few more `Toolbars` to the `ToolBarTray`. The first two are similar in nature, but the third needs some additional explanation.

As you may have guessed by now, a `ToolBar` can host any type of item. We've taken advantage of this rich functionality to add a set of `ToggleButtons` and two

ComboBoxes, visually set apart with a Separator. We've encountered ToggleButton before, and it's obvious what the purpose of Separator is. ComboBox, on the other hand, is a complex control. It is similar to ListBox, with which it shares many properties because of their common ancestor: Selector. For this application we used the same technique to set up a list of fonts as we did in the Font Viewer, but we have used a different technique to set up the list of font sizes. In this case, when the UserControl loads, we are manually adding available font sizes to the Items collection of the ComboBox. We do this by attaching an event handler to the Loaded event of the UserControl and calculating sizes with a simple for loop.

From time to time you may want more control over the layout of toolbars in a ToolBarTray. To prevent a ToolBar from being movable, add the attached property ToolBarTray.IsLocked with a value of true to any ToolBar. If you need to control the positioning of toolbars, you can set their Band and BandIndex properties. These represent the row and column within the tray, respectively.

Did you Know?

Using a Menu

The Menu is one of the most common controls used in applications and provides a simple hierarchy of commands available to the user at any given time. Our next task is to further build up our application's available options by fleshing out its main menu.

1. Add a new UserControl to the project and give it the name **TextEditorMenu.xaml**.

2. Replace the generated XAML with the markup found in Listing 8.2.

3. Add the following code to the TextEditorMenu.xaml.cs file:

```
private void About_Click(object sender, RoutedEventArgs e)
{
    MessageBox.Show(
        "Teach Yourself WPF in 24 Hours - Text Editor",
        "About"
        );
}
```

4. Open the MainWindow.xaml and locate the Menu. Replace it with the following markup:

```
<local:TextEditorMenu x:Name="menu"
                      DockPanel.Dock="Top" />
```

5. Run the application and browse the menu using your mouse or keyboard. See Figure 8.3.

6. Select Help, About to see the MessageBox.

LISTING 8.2   A Menu Contained by a User Control

```
<UserControl x:Class="TextEditor.TextEditorMenu"
             xmlns="http://schemas.microsoft.com/winfx/2006/xaml/presentation"
             xmlns:x="http://schemas.microsoft.com/winfx/2006/xaml">
    <Menu>
        <MenuItem Header="_File">
            <MenuItem Header="_New" />
            <MenuItem Header="_Open" />
            <MenuItem Header="_Save" />
            <MenuItem Header="Save As" />
            <Separator />
            <MenuItem Header="_Print" />
            <Separator />
            <MenuItem Header="Close" />
        </MenuItem>
        <MenuItem Header="_Edit">
            <MenuItem Header="_Undo" />
            <MenuItem Header="_Redo" />
            <Separator />
            <MenuItem Header="Cu_t" />
            <MenuItem Header="_Copy" />
            <MenuItem Header="_Paste" />
            <MenuItem Header="_Delete" />
        </MenuItem>
        <MenuItem Header="_Help">
            <MenuItem Header="_About"
                      Click="About_Click" />
        </MenuItem>
    </Menu>
</UserControl>
```

A Menu has a Click event like a Button and a Header property that works the same as Content on Button. You can see this in the implementation of the About menu option. Right now you may be wondering why we haven't hooked up Click handlers to all the menu items, like we did with About. You may have noticed that we didn't wire handlers to anything in the toolbars as well. Wiring all these handlers and writing their code would be *painful*. This is magnified by the fact that several menu options do the same thing as the toolbars, which could result in duplicate code. We're going to skip wiring most options for now, in favor of using a more elegant solution presented in a later hour.

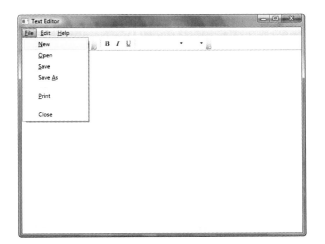

FIGURE 8.3
An application
with menu and
toolbar.

Working with RichTextBox

The RichTextBox shares many features in common with its brother, TextBox. The most obvious difference is that RichTextBox supports formatted text. You won't find a Text property on this control, but you will find a Document property of type FlowDocument. This special type of object is used to represent documents that are optimized for free-flowing text with column and pagination support. You've already been introduced to some of the types of items that a FlowDocument can display when we discussed Inlines and the TextBlock control. Inlines, however, are only a small part of what a FlowDocument is capable of rendering. A full discussion of FlowDocument and its capabilities is beyond the scope of this book, but we will use the RichTextBox to both load and save this type of document for the purposes of the Text Editor.

LISTING 8.3 Implementing the DocumentManager

```
using System.IO;
using System.Windows;
using System.Windows.Controls;
using System.Windows.Documents;
using Microsoft.Win32;

namespace TextEditor
{
    public class DocumentManager
    {
        private string _currentFile;
        private RichTextBox _textBox;

        public DocumentManager(RichTextBox textBox)
```

LISTING 8.3 Continued

```
    {
        _textBox = textBox;
    }

    public bool OpenDocument()
    {
        OpenFileDialog dlg = new OpenFileDialog();

        if (dlg.ShowDialog() == true)
        {
            _currentFile = dlg.FileName;

            using (Stream stream = dlg.OpenFile())
            {
                TextRange range = new TextRange(
                    _textBox.Document.ContentStart,
                    _textBox.Document.ContentEnd
                    );

                range.Load(stream, DataFormats.Rtf);
            }

            return true;
        }

        return false;
    }

    public bool SaveDocument()
    {
        if (string.IsNullOrEmpty(_currentFile)) return SaveDocumentAs();
        else
        {
            using (Stream stream =
                new FileStream(_currentFile, FileMode.Create))
            {
                TextRange range = new TextRange(
                    _textBox.Document.ContentStart,
                    _textBox.Document.ContentEnd
                    );

                range.Save(stream, DataFormats.Rtf);
            }

            return true;
        }
    }

    public bool SaveDocumentAs()
    {
        SaveFileDialog dlg = new SaveFileDialog();

        if (dlg.ShowDialog() == true)
        {
            _currentFile = dlg.FileName;
```

LISTING 8.3 Continued

```
            return SaveDocument();
        }

        return false;
    }
  }
}
```

1. Add a new class to the project and give it the name **DocumentManager.cs**.

2. Use the code in Listing 8.3 to implement the DocumentManager.

3. Change the MainWindow.xaml.cs to look like this:

```
using System.Windows;
using System.Windows.Controls;
using System.Windows.Input;

namespace TextEditor
{
    public partial class MainWindow : Window
    {
        private DocumentManager _documentManager;

        public MainWindow()
        {
            InitializeComponent();

            _documentManager = new DocumentManager(body);

            if (_documentManager.OpenDocument())
                status.Text = "Document loaded.";
        }
    }
}
```

4. Run the application. Select an .rtf file to edit or click Cancel to begin editing a new document.

> **By the Way**
>
> The status object is an instance of TextBox hosted inside the StatusBar. We haven't mentioned StatusBar up to this point because it functions like little more than a simple container for other elements. It is an ItemsControl that lays out its children like a DockPanel by default. We'll discuss ItemsControl in great depth in a later hour. StatusBar is useful for displaying simple controls that notify the user or provide important dynamic information that should always be available.

Building the Document Manager is an application of the principle of Separation of Concerns that we talked about in Hour 3, "Introducing the Font Viewer." We don't want our main window to get too cluttered with code for saving and loading documents, so we invent a new class with this sole responsibility. Our MainWindow will use an instance of the DocumentManager whenever it needs this functionality.

We are not going to wire all the methods of the DocumentManager up to menus and toolbars, because we will be covering that in great depth in the next two hours. However, it is important that you see how the DocumentManager gets .rtf documents in and out of the RichTextBox. The magic of saving and loading happens entirely through the power of the TextRange class. A TextRange represents a concrete selection of content within a document. In the case of both save and load operations, we create the range from the document's start to its end because we want to replace the entire document by loading or save the entire document. You can, however, create a range from any portion of the document. After we have a TextRange, we call either the Save or Load method, passing in a Stream to write/read from and an option from the DataFormats enum. In this case we are interested only in .rtf, but you can save/load other types of documents as well by specifying a different DataFormats value.

Another point of interest about this code is the use of the OpenFileDialog and the SaveFileDialog. These are both standard dialog boxes provided by the framework for these common tasks. We are using them in the most basic way by accessing their FileName for use in creating a FileStream or calling the OpenFile method to get a Stream directly from the dialog. They each have many options and additional features available for more fine-grained control over saving and loading, though.

You can restrict the file types available for saving and loading documents through file dialogs by setting the Filter property. It should be set to a list of alternating display names and file extensions, each separated by a pipe line. For example, if you wanted to allow only .rtf and .txt files you would use something like this: dlg.Filter = "Rich Text Document¦*.rtf¦Text Document¦*.txt".

Summary

At this point we have constructed a solid UI for our Text Editor application. It is based on a layout derived from similar software and has a full application menu and default toolbars. We learned how to configure our toolbars to use icons, creating a more attractive look and feel, and we created a more maintainable application by splitting various parts into `UserControls`. To top it off, we can read `.rtf` and a variety of other formats into a `RichTextBox` using some simple classes and built-in dialog boxes.

Q&A

Q. *Menus are nice with text, but I'd really like to display an icon on the left as well. Is this easily manageable?*

A. Yes. All `MenuItem` elements have an `Icon` property that you can set. It works similar to the `Content` property of a `Button`.

Q. *You mentioned briefly that* `FlowDocument` *is very powerful. What are some of the other features that it supports?*

A. There are quite a few. Some of the major features supported by `FlowDocument` are `Block` elements like `Paragraph`, `Section`, `List`, and `Table`. When these elements are combined with those mentioned earlier in this hour, almost any document layout can be achieved.

Workshop

Quiz

1. What type of elements can be hosted in a `ToolBar`?

2. What class is used to save and load the content of a `RichTextBox`?

3. What is the simplest and most common way to componentize a complex UI?

Answers

1. A `ToolBar` can host any type of .NET class.

2. To save or load the content of a `RichTextBox`, use the `TextRange` class.

3. The easiest way to break up a complex UI is to create separate `UserControls` for related parts and reference them from the original UI.

Activities

1. Expand the Text Editor to be capable of loading `.rtf`, `.txt`, and `.xaml` files. Make sure to include appropriate filtering on the dialog boxes.

2. Research the previously mentioned `FlowDocument` `Blocks`.

3. Spend some time with `ListBox` and `ComboBox`. Compare and contrast the two.

HOUR 9

Getting a Handle on Events

What You'll Learn in This Hour:

▶ Routed events
▶ Bubbling and tunneling
▶ Arguments for routed events
▶ Attached events
▶ Preview events
▶ Generic event handlers

WPF has introduced a rich system for tracking and responding to events. In this hour, we explore how this new event system functions, how it interacts with traditional events, and how you can leverage its power in your applications. Understanding this event model can be a little challenging. We'll be digging deeper into the technology than in the previous hours.

What Are Routed Events?

An application in WPF consists of many elements in a *tree*. This can be seen in all our examples so far. A TextBlock could be nested inside a StackPanel, which could be inside a Grid, which could be in another StackPanel, and so on, until we finally arrive at the root Application. This can be very useful for composing the interface visually, but it presents a complication when we are interpreting user input.

For example, perhaps we want to respond to the MouseLeftButtonDown event on the following Border element:

```
<Border>
    <StackPanel>
        <TextBlock>Click Me!</TextBlock>
        <Image Source="Icons/folder_page.png" />
    </StackPanel>
</Border>
```

Image, TextBlock, and StackPanel also raise the MouseLeftButtonDown event. In fact, MouseLeftButtonDown is implemented on a low-level class, UIElement, which all the elements in WPF inherit from. This means we have four possible sources for the event, depending on which of these elements is actually clicked. In turn, we need to write four handlers.

To avoid this complexity, WPF introduces the concept of *routed events*. Routed events are similar to dependency properties in that they are part of the WPF library and they are built on top of mechanisms that already exist in the common language runtime (CLR).

If a user clicks the Image in our preceding example, WPF would *route* the event along the tree of elements until a handler was found. If no handler is implemented, the event continues beyond the Border all the way to the root element (which can be a Window or a Page).

Routed events can travel in two directions, depending on how the event is defined. The naming might be a little confusing because of the tree metaphor. Events are said to *bubble* up through the tree when they are moving toward the root element. Events are *tunneling* down when they are moving toward the leaves or away from the root element.

Understanding RoutedEventArgs

You are already familiar with standard event handlers. The signature for an event handler looks something like this:

```
void Handle_Event(object sender, EventArgs e)
```

The second parameter might be a derivative of EventArgs, depending on the class raising the event.

Routed events are handled the same way except that the basic signature uses a RoutedEventArgs.

```
void Handle_RoutedEvent(object sender, RoutedEventArgs e)
```

If you dig into it, you will discover that RoutedEventArgs derives from EventArgs as well. In this sense, routed events are really standard events with extra information passed in the argument—extra information that WPF uses to work its magic. Table 9.1 lists the properties specific to RoutedEventArgs.

TABLE 9.1   Properties Specific to RoutedEventArgs

Name	Description
Source	The object that raised the event. This is a property you will generally be interested in. It's useful to note that with routed events this is likely to be different from the sender.
OriginalSource	This returns *original reporting source*. That is the object that *really* raised the event. This property does not change as the event travels along its route.
Handled	A bool that lets you know if the event has already been handled. You should mark this true in your own handlers.
RoutedEvent	This identifies the type of event that was raised. Many events have the same signature, and a single handler might be responsible for several events.

Understanding the differences between Source, OriginalSource, and the sender argument can be confusing.

Let's write a small application that will help us explore these properties and how they are used.

1. Launch Visual Studio and create a new WPF Application named **UnderstandingRoutedEventArgs**.

2. In Window1.xaml, we are going to use a ListBox and a couple of items to demonstrate how events are routed. Add the following markup inside the Grid element:

```
<ListBox Margin="10"
         Background="BurlyWood">
    <ListBoxItem>
        <Border Margin="4"
                Padding="4"
                Background="Khaki"
                CornerRadius="6">
            <TextBlock>Cats</TextBlock>
        </Border>
    </ListBoxItem>
    <ListBoxItem>
        <Border Margin="4"
                Padding="4"
                Background="Khaki"
```

```
                           CornerRadius="6">
                       <TextBlock>Dogs</TextBlock>
                   </Border>
               </ListBoxItem>
           </ListBox>
```

3. Begin adding an attribute on the Grid element MouseLeftButtonDown. IntelliSense should kick in, and you should receive a prompt for creating a new event handler as shown in Figure 9.1.

FIGURE 9.1
Adding an event handler using IntelliSense from XAML.

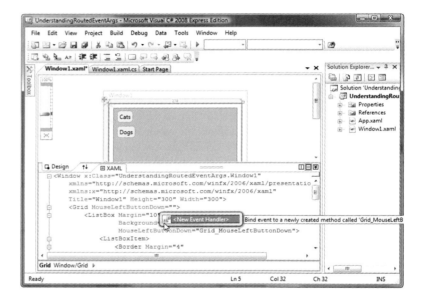

If you prefer to add it manually, place the following attribute on the Grid.

```
MouseLeftButtonDown="Grid_MouseLeftButtonDown"
```

In the code-behind, add the following event handler:

```
private void Grid_MouseLeftButtonDown(object sender,
➥MouseButtonEventArgs e)
{
}
```

4. Inside the handler, we'll add some code to help us see what is going on. Add the following inside the event handler Grid_MouseLeftButtonDown:

```
object source = e.Source;
object originalSource = e.OriginalSource;
```

The parameter `MouseButtonEventArgs` is derived from `RoutedEventArgs`. We're adding these variables to make it easier to see the values in the debugger.

5. Place a breakpoint on the closing bracket of `Grid_MouseLeftButtonDown`. See where the breakpoint is in Figure 9.2. Run the application, and click somewhere on the `ListBox` well below the bottom `ListBoxItem`.

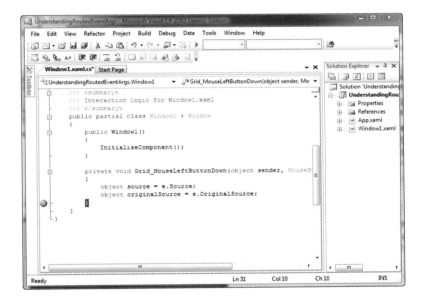

6. When you hit the breakpoint, examine the Locals pane in Visual Studio. If the Locals pane is not visible, select Window, Reset Window Layout from the menu. The Locals pane should look like Figure 9.3.

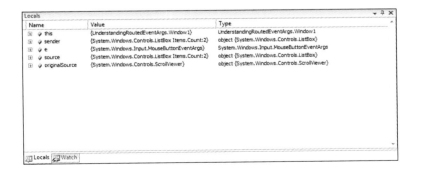

Notice that the values of sender, source, and originalSource are all different.

As mentioned previously, source contains the value we expect. It references the ListBox, and that is the element that we clicked. The ListBox element, however, is a composite of other elements. We can see this by examining the value of originalSource. It is referencing a ScrollViewer. There's no ScrollViewer in our markup, so where did this element come from? The ScrollViewer is one of the elements that make up the ListBox. Many of the more complex controls in WPF are composites of simpler controls and elements such as Border, StackPanel, and ScrollViewer. (This will become clearer when we cover control templates in Hour 21, "Using Control Templates.")

In this case, the ListBox is vertically stretching to fill the Window. The ListBoxItem elements collapse to be as small as possible. The internal ScrollViewer stretches to fill the entire ListBox, and this is the element that we really clicked.

Finally, sender is referencing the Grid element where we attached the event handler. The Grid is the sender because that is where we captured the event. Stop the application now.

7. To further demonstrate how the sender is set, let's bind the ListBox to the same event. Copy the MouseLeftButtonDown attribute from the Grid and add it on the ListBox. Don't remove it from the Grid, though. The ListBox now looks like this:

```
<ListBox Margin="10"
         Background="BurlyWood"
         MouseLeftButtonDown="Grid_MouseLeftButtonDown">
...
</ListBox>
```

8. Run the application again, and click the ListBox as before. When you hit the breakpoint, examine the Locals, and you will see that the sender is now the same as source. That is, the sender is the ListBox because that is where we attached the event handler.

9. Press F5, or select Debug, Continue. We hit the breakpoint a second time! This is because the event continues to travel along its route. This time the sender is the Grid again.

10. Stop the debugger, and add the following line to the event handler:

```
e.Handled = true;
```

This will tell the routed event system that we are finished with the event. We consider it to be "handled," and we are no longer interested.

11. Run the application again, and click the ListBox as before. Press F5 to continue past the breakpoint. We no longer hit the breakpoint twice. Because we set Handled to true, the event never makes it to the handler attached to the Grid.

Using Routed Events

Most of the time you will not be concerned with the specifics of routed events, and you will often handle them as if they were simply standard CLR events. The scenarios where you'll really need to understand and leverage routed events occur when you are building (or compositing) your own custom controls.

You can also leverage them by creating a generic event handler on a parent element. Let's create another simple application that uses a single generic handler to capture a routed event from a couple of different elements.

1. Launch Visual Studio and create a new WPF Application named **GenericEventHandler**.

2. In Window1.xaml, we are going to add a StackPanel containing a few Button elements. Replace the Grid element with the following markup:

```
<StackPanel>
    <Button Content="Red" Foreground="Red"/>
    <Button Content="Green" Foreground="Green" />
    <Button Content="Blue" Foreground="Blue" />
</StackPanel>
```

3. Begin to add an attribute to the StackPanel named ButtonBase.Click. IntelliSense will again intervene, and you can accept its defaults. The final attribute should look like this:

```
ButtonBase.Click="StackPanel_Click"
```

It will also inject the event handler into the code-behind:

```
private void StackPanel_Click(object sender, RoutedEventArgs e)
{
}
```

StackPanel does not have its own Click event. However, we can use an *attached event* to reference the events raised by its child elements. Attached events work very much like attached properties. They take the form of Type.EventName, where Type is the name of the class that owns the event.

You might be surprised to see ButtonBase.Click instead of Button.Click. IntelliSense chooses ButtonBase for us because it is the control that Button derives from, and Button itself does not implement any events. Actually, you can use either of the two interchangeably here, and the application will behave the same.

4. Let's add a place to provide the user with some feedback when we click one of our buttons. Add the following TextBlock under the last Button in the StackPanel:

```
<TextBlock x:Name="Output"
           HorizontalAlignment="Center"
           Text="What color will you choose?" />
```

5. Modify the handler StackPanel_Click to look like this:

```
private void StackPanel_Click(object sender, RoutedEventArgs e)
{
    Button button = (Button) e.Source;
    Output.Text = string.Format(
                    "You chose the color {0}!",
                    button.Content);
    Output.Background = button.Foreground;
}
```

6. Run the application and click the various buttons. We can respond to all the events from the Button elements in a single handler that is attached to their container.

Handling Events in the Text Editor

Let's apply some of what we have learned so far to our Text Editor. When we left off in Hour 8, we had encapsulated the entire markup for the ToolBarTray in a user control. In the ToolBarTray we include two ComboBox elements—one for selecting the font family and another for selecting the font size; however, we have not yet implemented any functionality.

We want to respond to the SelectionChanged event raised by the ComboBox elements and apply the new values to the currently selected text in the RichTextBox. The problem is that the ComboBox elements are now encapsulated deep in the

UserControl, and they are no longer in the same scope as our RichTextBox. We'd like to handle the SelectionChanged event in the same scope as our instance of _documentManager. Using the attached events we just discussed, we are able to do just that!

Let's go ahead and add this to the Text Editor.

1. Open the TextEditor project that we began in Hour 8.

2. Open MainWindow.xaml and locate the UserControl we named toolbar, and then modify the markup so that it matches the following:

```
<local:TextEditorToolbar x:Name="toolbar"
                         DockPanel.Dock="Top"
                         ComboBox.SelectionChanged=
                         ➥"TextEditorToolbar_SelectionChanged" />
```

Notice that IntelliSense did not help us out here. IntelliSense doesn't know anything about the internal composition of the UserControl.

We are attaching an event handler to the UserControl itself that will handle all the SelectionChanged events raised by any ComboBox element that it contains. Currently, we only have two, but it's important to realize that any ComboBox elements added in the future will be picked up by this handler.

3. Open the code-behind for MainWindow.xaml, and let's begin to implement the handler we just referenced:

```
private void TextEditorToolbar_SelectionChanged(object sender,
➥SelectionChangedEventArgs e)
{
    ComboBox source = e.OriginalSource as ComboBox;
    if (source == null) return;

    switch (source.Name)
    {
        case "fonts":
            //change the font face
            break;
        case "fontSize":
            //change the font size
            break;
    }

    body.Focus();
}
```

ComboBox.SelectionChanged is a routed event, and thus SelectionChangedEventArgs is a descendant of RoutedEventArgs. We can use the OriginalSource property to get a reference to the ComboBox that raises the event from inside the UserControl.

Because we are handling events raised by multiple elements, we need to identify which element we are dealing with. We use a `switch` statement based on the `Name` of the `ComboBox`. If you examine the XAML of the `UserControl`, you'll see that we named our `ComboBox` elements `fonts` and `fontSize`.

Changing the font family and the font size involves formatting the contents of the `RichTextBox`, and that should be the responsibility of the `DocumentManager` class, so we've temporarily added some place holder comments in the event handler that we'll fill in after we extend `DocumentManager`.

On the last line of the method, `body.Focus()` returns the focus to the `RichTextBox` from the `ComboBox` we selected.

4. Open `DocumentManager.cs` in the editor. The class encapsulates a `RichTextBox`, which in turn exposes a property called `Selection`. This property represents the currently selected text in the `RichTextBox`. `Selection` is of type `TextSelection`, and it has a method, `ApplyPropertyValue`. This method accepts a dependency property and a value for setting the property. We can use this method to format the currently selected text. Add the following method to `DocumentManager`:

```
public void ApplyToSelection(DependencyProperty property,
➥object value)
{
    if (value != null)
        _textBox.Selection.ApplyPropertyValue(property, value);
}
```

5. Now we can flesh out the implementation of
   `TextEditorToolbar_SelectionChanged`:

```
private void TextEditorToolbar_SelectionChanged(object sender,
➥SelectionChangedEventArgs e)
{
    ComboBox source = e.OriginalSource as ComboBox;
    if (source == null) return;

    switch (source.Name)
    {
        case "fonts":
            _documentManager.ApplyToSelection(TextBlock.
            ➥FontFamilyProperty, source.SelectedItem);
            break;
        case "fontSize":
            _documentManager.ApplyToSelection(TextBlock.
            ➥FontSizeProperty, source.SelectedItem);
            break;
```

```
        }
        body.Focus();
    }
```

All we are really doing is delegating the work to the `DocumentManager` class.

6. Run the application, enter some text, and try to change the font family and size.

Making the Text Editor Work as Expected

The Text Editor is beginning to feel like a useful application, and we haven't written very much code at all! However, users generally have a lot of expectations about the way an application ought to behave, especially if the functionality is as common as a text editor. If you play around with the application at this point, you'll notice that the items on the toolbar do not change their state when you select formatted text in the `RichTextBox`. For example, if you type the following sentence:

The quick brown fox jumps over the lazy dog.

And you increase the font size of "jumps" and then click "dog," the `ComboBox` displaying the font size does not change to reflect the size of the selected text. This isn't the behavior that we have come to expect from similar applications. Let's change the Text Editor to behave as we expect.

> In general, it is a dangerous thing for developers to try to anticipate user needs. If you are developing software for someone else and you need to manage time and cost, avoid adding features the client hasn't asked for. As software developers, we love thinking about the future, and contingencies, and what a user might need. Unfortunately, this often leads to bloated applications, unused features, and a cluttered interface. Not to mention the time lost that could have been used for developing features that are actually needed today. This is especially true in WPF, where adding sophisticated interfaces is easy. If you genuinely believe that a feature is necessary, present the idea to the client and have it become an explicit and acknowledged requirement.
>
> This principle in software development, of building just what is needed now, is often called *YAGNI*—that is, *You Aren't Gonna Need It*.

Watch Out!

1. We know that we want to update the toolbar when the user changes the selected text in the RichTextBox. We can use the SelectionChanged event to do this. In MainWindow.xaml, modify the RichTextBox so that it matches the following markup:

```
<RichTextBox x:Name="body"
             SelectionChanged="body_SelectionChanged"
             SpellCheck.IsEnabled="True"
             AcceptsReturn="True"
             AcceptsTab="True"
             BorderThickness="0 2 0 0"/>
```

2. We're not sure yet what we should do in the event handler. We'll start with the minimal implementation for body_SelectionChanged in the code-behind for MainWindow.xaml.

```
private void body_SelectionChanged(object sender, RoutedEventArgs e)
{
    //update the tool bar
}
```

The completed markup for MainWindow.xaml is shown in Listing 9.1.

LISTING 9.1   The Markup for MainWindow.xaml in the Text Editor

```
<Window x:Class="TextEditor.MainWindow"
        xmlns="http://schemas.microsoft.com/winfx/2006/xaml/presentation"
        xmlns:x="http://schemas.microsoft.com/winfx/2006/xaml"
        xmlns:local="clr-namespace:TextEditor"
        Title="Text Editor"
        Height="600"
        Width="800">
    <DockPanel>
        <local:TextEditorMenu x:Name="menu"
                              DockPanel.Dock="Top" />

        <local:TextEditorToolbar x:Name="toolbar"
                                 DockPanel.Dock="Top"
                                 ComboBox.SelectionChanged=
                                 ➥"TextEditorToolbar_SelectionChanged" />

        <StatusBar DockPanel.Dock="Bottom">
            <TextBlock x:Name="status" />
        </StatusBar>

        <RichTextBox x:Name="body"
                     SelectionChanged="body_SelectionChanged"
                     SpellCheck.IsEnabled="True"
                     AcceptsReturn="True"
                     AcceptsTab="True"
                     BorderThickness="0 2 0 0"/>
    </DockPanel>
</Window>
```

3. Let's think about this for a minute. We'd like to synchronize a lot of items on the toolbar with the selected text. We've already identified font size and font family, but there are also toggles for bold, underline, and italic.

All the controls are embedded in the UserControl we named toolbar. We can't access them directly, so we need to add a method to the UserControl to help us out.

Tackling all five of the formatting options is too much to think about at once, so we'll begin with synchronizing just the font size.

4. Open the code-behind for TextEditorToolbar.xaml, and we'll add a method called SynchronizeWith that we will pass a TextSelection instance into. We'll call this method to synchronize the toolbar with the currently selected text.

```
public void SynchronizeWith(TextSelection selection)
{
    object size =
    ➥selection.GetPropertyValue(TextBlock.FontSizeProperty);
    if (size != DependencyProperty.UnsetValue)
    {
        fontSize.SelectedValue = (double)size;
    }
}
```

First, we get the font size from the TextSelection argument. We need to call the GetPropertyValue method on selection. This is because we're dealing with a dependency property that's owned by TextBlock. After we get the value, we check to make sure that the dependency property has a valid value. Finally, we set the SelectedValue on the ComboBox named fontSize.

DependencyProperty.UnsetValue is a special value used by dependency properties to indicate that the property has not been set. When you work with dependency properties, use this instead of null. See the official documentation for more information.

Did you Know?

---

5. Run the application now, enter some text, and then change the font size using the ComboBox. Try setting a few different sizes on various places in the text. Click around the different sized text and you will notice that the value in the ComboBox is updated to reflect the selected text. Also note that the ComboBox displays nothing for text that has not been explicitly sized.

6. Now let's do the same thing for the bold toggle button. The "boldness" of the font is referred to as the font's weight. We happen to have another dependency property, `FontWeightProperty`, available to us. We can add the following code to the `SynchronizeWith` method:

```
object weight = selection.GetPropertyValue (TextBlock.FontWeightProperty);
if (weight != DependencyProperty.UnsetValue)
{
   boldButton.IsChecked = ((FontWeight)weight == FontWeights.Bold);
}
```

7. The code for the font's weight is very similar to the code for the font's size. If you suspect that the other three properties will be similar, you are correct. This is a good candidate for refactoring, both to simplify our code and to make it more readable. You can use the following abstraction for all the properties. Add this method to `TextEditorToolbar`:

```
private void Synchronize<T>(TextSelection selection,
➥DependencyProperty property, Action<T> methodToCall)
{
    object value = selection.GetPropertyValue(property);
    if (value != DependencyProperty.UnsetValue) methodToCall((T)value);
}
```

This may be a bit confusing, so let's go over it carefully. The `Synchronize` method is generic. When we call it, we need to specify a type that corresponds to the type of the dependency property. We provide the `TextSelection` to examine, the dependency property we are interested in, and a delegate that's responsible for synchronizing the control on the toolbar.

By the Way

You might not have encountered the generic delegate Action<T> before. Action<T> is a simple delegate definition built in to the .NET framework. It's equivalent to declaring

```
delegate void Action<T>(T obj);
```

in your code. It's very handy in situations like this, where we would like a delegate method that doesn't return anything and accepts a single argument of a specific type. If you are unfamiliar with delegates or generics in general, you should take a few moments to read about this feature of the CLR online.

With this new approach, we'll need methods to pass as the delegates.
Following are the two methods we'll use for the font size and font weight.
Go ahead and add them to the code-behind for `TextEditorToolbar.xaml`:

```
private void SetFontSize(double size)
{
    fontSize.SelectedValue = size;
}

private void SetFontWeight(FontWeight weight)
{
    boldButton.IsChecked = weight == FontWeights.Bold;
}
```

8. Now let's bring these new methods together in our refactored event handler:

```
public void SynchronizeWith(TextSelection selection)
{
    Synchronize<double>(selection, TextBlock.FontSizeProperty,
    ➥ SetFontSize);
    Synchronize<FontWeight>(selection, TextBlock.
    ➥FontWeightProperty, SetFontWeight);
}
```

9. Something that is not immediately obvious is that we have introduced a sort
   of feedback loop between the controls on the toolbar and the `RichTextBox`.
   The handler for `SelectionChanged` on `RichTextBox` changes the values of the
   controls on the toolbar; in turn, these controls change the formatting on the
   text box. It's not really a loop, inasmuch as the controls on the toolbar do not
   raise the `SelectionChanged` event. Nevertheless, you'll find the format unexpectedly changing.

   We can compensate for this by adding a Boolean to the `UserControl` indicating whether we are in the process of synchronizing the toolbar. Add the following property using the new automatic property syntax:

```
public bool IsSynchronizing {get; private set;}
```

   Now we can modify the handler to set the value of this property:

```
public void SynchronizeWith(TextSelection selection)
{
    IsSynchronizing = true;

    Synchronize<double>(selection, TextBlock.FontSizeProperty,
    ➥ SetFontSize);
    Synchronize<FontWeight>(selection, TextBlock.
    ➥FontWeightProperty, SetFontWeight);

    IsSynchronizing = false;
}
```

The complete code, including the remaining three properties, is shown in Listing 9.2.

LISTING 9.2   The Code-Behind for `TextEditorToolbar.xaml`

```csharp
using System.Windows;
using System.Windows.Controls;
using System.Windows.Media;
using System.Windows.Documents;
using System;

namespace TextEditor
{
    /// <summary>
    /// Interaction logic for TextEditorToolbar.xaml
    /// </summary>
    public partial class TextEditorToolbar : UserControl
    {
        public TextEditorToolbar()
        {
            InitializeComponent();
        }

        public bool IsSynchronizing { get; private set; }

        private void UserControl_Loaded(object sender, RoutedEventArgs e)
        {
            for (double i = 8; i < 48; i += 2)
            {
                fontSize.Items.Add(i);
            }
        }

        public void SynchronizeWith(TextSelection selection)
        {
            IsSynchronizing = true;

            Synchronize<double>(selection, TextBlock.FontSizeProperty,
            ➥ SetFontSize);
            Synchronize<FontWeight>(selection, TextBlock.FontWeightProperty,
            ➥ SetFontWeight);
            Synchronize<FontStyle>(selection, TextBlock.FontStyleProperty,
            ➥ SetFontStyle);
            Synchronize<TextDecorationCollection>(selection,
            ➥ TextBlock.TextDecorationsProperty, SetTextDecoration);
            Synchronize<FontFamily>(selection, TextBlock.FontFamilyProperty,
            ➥ SetFontFamily);

            IsSynchronizing = false;
        }

        private static void Synchronize<T>(TextSelection selection,
        ➥DependencyProperty property, Action<T> methodToCall)
        {
            object value = selection.GetPropertyValue(property);
            if (value != DependencyProperty.UnsetValue) methodToCall((T)value);
        }
```

LISTING 9.2   Continued

```
    private void SetFontSize(double size)
    {
        fontSize.SelectedValue = size;
    }

    private void SetFontWeight(FontWeight weight)
    {
        boldButton.IsChecked = weight == FontWeights.Bold;
    }

    private void SetFontStyle(FontStyle style)
    {
        italicButton.IsChecked = style == FontStyles.Italic;
    }

    private void SetTextDecoration(TextDecorationCollection decoration)
    {
        underlineButton.IsChecked = decoration == TextDecorations.Underline;
    }

    private void SetFontFamily(FontFamily family)
    {
        fonts.SelectedItem = family;
    }
  }
}
```

10. We need to open the code-behind for the MainWindow.xaml and modify the
    event handler TextEditorToolbar_SelectionChanged to check for the
    IsSynchronizing property. Here's the modified handler:

```
        private void TextEditorToolbar_SelectionChanged(object sender,
        ➥SelectionChangedEventArgs e)
        {
            if (toolbar.IsSynchronizing) return;

            ComboBox source = e.OriginalSource as ComboBox;
            if (source == null) return;

            switch (source.Name)
            {
                case "fonts":
                    _documentManager.ApplyToSelection(TextBlock.
                    ➥ FontFamilyProperty, source.SelectedItem);
                    break;
                case "fontSize":
                    _documentManager.ApplyToSelection(TextBlock.
                    ➥ FontSizeProperty, source.SelectedItem);
                    break;
            }

            body.Focus();
        }
```

The complete code-behind for MainWindow.xaml is shown in Listing 9.3.

11. Run the application. At this point, you need to use Ctrl+B, Ctrl+U, and
Ctrl+I to modify the formatting of the text. These keyboard gestures are built
in to the RichTextBox.

LISTING 9.3   The Code-Behind for MainWindow.xaml

```csharp
using System.Windows;
using System.Windows.Controls;
using System.Windows.Input;

namespace TextEditor
{
    public partial class MainWindow : Window
    {
        private DocumentManager _documentManager;

        public MainWindow()
        {
            InitializeComponent();
            _documentManager = new DocumentManager(body);
        }

        private void TextEditorToolbar_SelectionChanged(object sender,
        ➥SelectionChangedEventArgs e)
        {
            if (toolbar.IsSynchronizing) return;

            ComboBox source = e.OriginalSource as ComboBox;
            if (source == null) return;

            switch (source.Name)
            {
                case "fonts":
                    _documentManager.ApplyToSelection(TextBlock.
                    ➥FontFamilyProperty, source.SelectedItem);
                    break;
                case "fontSize":
                    _documentManager.ApplyToSelection(TextBlock.
                    ➥FontSizeProperty, source.SelectedItem);
                    break;
            }

            body.Focus();
        }

        private void body_SelectionChanged(object sender, RoutedEventArgs e)
        {
            toolbar.SynchronizeWith(body.Selection);
        }
    }
}
```

Preview Events

If you examine the documentation, you'll notice that all the controls in WPF have events beginning with `Preview`. Many of these preview events are owned by the `UIElement` class that all the controls in WPF derive from. For example, `UIElement` defines an event `PreviewKeyDown`. This event is raised when a key is pressed and the element is in focus.

So how does `PreviewKeyDown` differ from the `KeyDown` event, which is also owned by `UIElement`? If you check the documentation for `KeyDown`, it reads the same as `PreviewKeyDown`.

Both of these are routed events, but the difference between the two is that one bubbles and the other tunnels. Remember we mentioned earlier that bubbling means the event is moving up toward the root element, and tunneling means the event is moving down toward its origin. The prefix `Preview` is a convention adopted in WPF to show that an event is a counterpart to another event. Thus `PreviewKeyDown` is the counterpart to `KeyDown`.

When you press a key with an element in focus, first the `PreviewKeyDown` event is raised by the root element and tunnels down the tree to the actual element that was in focus; then the `KeyDown` event is raised and bubbles back up to the root.

Consider the following very simple markup for a `Window`:

```
<Window x:Class="PreviewEvents.Window1"
        xmlns="http://schemas.microsoft.com/winfx/2006/xaml/presentation"
        xmlns:x="http://schemas.microsoft.com/winfx/2006/xaml"
        Title="Example of Preview Events"
        Height="300"
        Width="300">
    <Grid>
        <TextBox />
    </Grid>
</Window>
```

When a user clicks in the `TextBox` and then presses a key, the event travels as shown in Figure 9.4.

In one way, the pair of events behaves as a single event. If you mark the preview event as handled, WPF will not invoke the handler for its counterpart.

FIGURE 9.4
A preview event
tunneling and
the correspon-
ding event
bubbling.

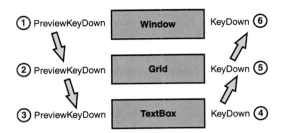

You probably will not be concerned with preview events very often. However, from time to time, you may encounter a scenario where they will come in handy. To help us visualize how these events are routed, let's create a simple project.

1. Create a new project called **PreviewEvents**.

2. Open Window1.xaml and enter the markup from Listing 9.4. Notice that we wire the KeyDown and PreviewKeyDown events for every element to a single handler.

LISTING 9.4   Window1.xaml **Captures All the** KeyDown **Events**

```
<Window x:Class="PreviewEvents.Window1"
        xmlns="http://schemas.microsoft.com/winfx/2006/xaml/presentation"
        xmlns:x="http://schemas.microsoft.com/winfx/2006/xaml"
        KeyDown="Handler"
        PreviewKeyDown="Handler"
        Title="Window1" Height="300" Width="300">
    <DockPanel KeyDown="Handler"
               PreviewKeyDown="Handler">
        <ListBox x:Name="Output"
                 DockPanel.Dock="Left"
                 Margin="0 0 10 0"
                 KeyDown="Handler"
                 PreviewKeyDown="Handler"/>
        <Grid KeyDown="Handler"
              PreviewKeyDown="Handler">
            <StackPanel KeyDown="Handler"
                        PreviewKeyDown="Handler">
                <Button KeyDown="Handler"
                        PreviewKeyDown="Handler"
                        Content="My Button"/>
                <TextBox KeyDown="Handler"
                         PreviewKeyDown="Handler"
                         Text="My TextBox"/>
            </StackPanel>
        </Grid>
    </DockPanel>
</Window>
```

3. Now we implement the handler. The entire code-behind is in Listing 9.5. This handler logs the events by adding items to the ListBox. Preview events are prefixed with "v" to indicate that they are tunneling down; the KeyDown events are prefixed with "^" to indicate that they are bubbling up.

We then check to see if sender is the original source of the event. If so, we are at the bottom. That is the point where the event stops tunneling and begins to bubble. This is actually a hack and it won't work for the ListBox, but it's good enough for this demonstration.

Finally, we check to see if sender is the root element. If it is, we are at the end of the event's route.

LISTING 9.5   Window1.xaml.cs Implements a General Handler

```
using System.Windows.Input;

namespace PreviewEvents
{
    public partial class Window1
    {
        public Window1()
        {
            InitializeComponent();
        }

        private void Handler(object sender, KeyEventArgs e)
        {
            bool isPreview = e.RoutedEvent.Name.StartsWith("Preview");
            string direction = isPreview ? "v" : "^";

            Output.Items.Add(string.Format("{0} {1}",
                                    direction,
                                    sender.GetType().Name));

            if (sender == e.OriginalSource && isPreview)
                Output.Items.Add("-{bounce}-");

            if (sender == this && !isPreview)
                Output.Items.Add(" -end- ");
        }
    }
}
```

4. Run the application. Click various elements and then press a key. This should help you gain an understanding of how the events are routed in WPF.

Summary

WPF adds a lot to the standard events found in the CLR. The principles and techniques surrounding routed events are important to keep in mind because they can help you simplify your code and make your application easier to maintain.

We discussed how routed events can either bubble or tunnel through the element tree in a WPF application, and we examined the properties available on RoutedEventArgs and gained an understanding of how to use them.

Q&A

Q. *List the four properties on* RoutedEventArgs *we discussed.*

A. The four properties are Source, OriginalSource, RoutedEvent, and Handled.

Q. *When a key is pressed, and an element is in focus, which event is raised first,* PreviewKeyDown *or* KeyDown?

A. PreviewKeyDown is raised before the KeyDown event.

Q. *In which direction does an event travel when it is bubbling?*

A. An event is said to be traveling up the element tree, toward the root element when it is bubbling.

Workshop

Quiz

1. Describe the possible differences in the value of the sender argument in a routed event handler, and the value of RoutedEventArgs.Source.

2. Given the following snippet of XAML, what would the markup look like if you attached a single event handler to handle the TextChanged event for all the TextBox elements?

```
<Grid>
    <Grid.ColumnDefinitions>
        <ColumnDefinition />
        <ColumnDefinition />
        <ColumnDefinition />
    </Grid.ColumnDefinitions>
```

```
        <TextBox Grid.Column="0" />
        <TextBox Grid.Column="1" />
        <TextBox Grid.Column="2" />
    </Grid>
```

Answers

1. `RoutedEventArgs.Source` will contain a reference to the object that raised the event as defined by the class that owns the event, whereas the `sender` argument will contain a reference to the object where the event handler was attached. The `sender` argument can be thought of as the last object that touched the event.

2. One possible solution would be the following markup:

```
<Grid TextBoxBase.TextChanged="Grid_TextChanged">
        <Grid.ColumnDefinitions>
            <ColumnDefinition />
            <ColumnDefinition />
            <ColumnDefinition />
        </Grid.ColumnDefinitions>
        <TextBox Grid.Column="0" />
        <TextBox Grid.Column="1" />
        <TextBox Grid.Column="2" />
    </Grid>
```

HOUR 10

Commands

What You'll Learn in This Hour:

- ▶ Binding commands
- ▶ Built-in commands for WPF
- ▶ Creating your own custom commands
- ▶ Input bindings

In modern applications, a user often can execute a command in more than one way. WPF provides a convenient facility for wiring multiple *gestures* to a single command in an application (such as cut or paste).

What Are Commands?

Consider a sophisticated application such as Microsoft Word. You can perform hundreds of functions with the application. A good number of those functions can be executed in more ways than one. If you want to bold some selected text, you could click the Bold icon on the toolbar, or you could press Ctrl+B on the keyboard, or (with Word 2007) you could right-click and select the Bold icon from the context menu. All three methods execute the same action—making the text bold. We call these user actions *gestures*.

Generally, a gesture is some way that a user provides input to an application. Most commonly, and especially in business applications, gestures are nothing more than mouse clicks or keyboard presses. Going back to the Word example, the action itself, making the text bold, could be implemented in the event handler for each of the gestures we listed. That would cause a lot of duplicated code, and if you began to add more gestures to support the same action, the maintainability would really suffer.

The action of making the text bold can be abstracted into a *command*. In WPF, a command is a function or action that can be bound to an input gesture. This declarative binding is similar to the technique of data binding and helps reduce the code that we need to maintain.

Aside from supporting the overall concept of commands, WPF has five built-in libraries of commands. We'll be using a couple of these in our Text Editor. The libraries are listed in Table 10.1.

TABLE 10.1   Built-In Command Libraries in WPF

ApplicationCommands	This library contains commonly used commands such as Cut, Copy, Paste, New, Open, Save, Undo, Close and many others.
ComponentCommands	These are commands for moving around inside an application. These can easily be confused with some of the editing commands as well as navigation commands. The commands in this library are for more general use than the other two. Here you will find commands such as MoveDown, ExtendSelectionLeft, ScrollByLine, SelectToEnd, and many others.
EditingCommands	This library is helpful for dealing with text. It includes commands for alignment, formatting, and the navigation of text. Some examples of command names are ToggleBold, AlignLeft, and DecreaseFontSize.
MediaCommands	These are commands for controlling audio and video in your applications. Some typical commands are Play, Pause, and IncreaseVolume.
NavigationCommands	These commands are most useful for navigating in an application built around a web browser metaphor. Commands include BrowseForward, NextPage, PreviousPage, Refresh, and Search.

Using Commands

The toolbar in our Text Editor application has several buttons for manipulating the text, but they don't do anything yet. Let's leverage the power of the built-in commands to extend our application.

1. Open the `TextEditor` project in Visual Studio.

2. Before we make any changes to the code, run the application, enter some text, and make it bold using Crtl+B.

3. WPF binds the `EditingCommands.ToggleBold` command to the keyboard gesture Ctrl+B by default. You can see the default binding for the built-in commands in the official documentation.

4. We would like our Bold icon on the toolbar to execute the same command. Open `TextEditorToolbar.xaml`, and locate the `ToggleButton` we named `boldButton`. Modify the opening tag to match the following:

```
<ToggleButton x:Name="boldButton"
              Command="EditingCommands.ToggleBold"
              ToolTip="Bold">
```

5. We point the `Command` attribute of the `ToggleButton` to the static property `EditingCommands.ToggleBold`. Run the application again. You can make the text bold with either the keyboard or the toolbar now.

6. Go ahead and add the bindings for `ApplicationCommands.Cut`, `ApplicationCommands.Copy`, `ApplicationCommands.Paste`, `EditingCommands.ToggleItalic`, and `EditingCommands.Underline`. The complete markup for `TextEditorToolbar.xaml` is shown in Listing 10.1.

LISTING 10.1   Markup for TextEditorToolbar.xaml

```
<UserControl x:Class="TextEditor.TextEditorToolbar"
             xmlns="http://schemas.microsoft.com/winfx/2006/xaml/presentation"
             xmlns:x="http://schemas.microsoft.com/winfx/2006/xaml"
             Loaded="UserControl_Loaded">
    <ToolBarTray>
        <ToolBar>
            <Button ToolTip="Open">
                <Image Source="Icons/folder_page.png" />
            </Button>
            <Button ToolTip="Save">
                <Image Source="Icons/page_save.png" />
            </Button>
        </ToolBar>
        <ToolBar>
            <Button Command="ApplicationCommands.Cut"
                    ToolTip="Cut">
                <Image Source="Icons/cut.png" />
            </Button>
            <Button Command="ApplicationCommands.Copy"
                    ToolTip="Copy">
                <Image Source="Icons/page_copy.png" />
            </Button>
            <Button Command="ApplicationCommands.Paste"
```

LISTING 10.1   Continued

```
                ToolTip="Paste">
            <Image Source="Icons/page_paste.png" />
        </Button>
    </ToolBar>
    <ToolBar>
        <ToggleButton x:Name="boldButton"
                    Command="EditingCommands.ToggleBold"
                    ToolTip="Bold">
            <Image Source="Icons/text_bold.png" />
        </ToggleButton>
        <ToggleButton x:Name="italicButton"
                    Command="EditingCommands.ToggleItalic"
                    ToolTip="Italic">
            <Image Source="Icons/text_italic.png" />
        </ToggleButton>
        <ToggleButton x:Name="underlineButton"
                    Command="EditingCommands.ToggleUnderline"
                    ToolTip="Underline">
            <Image Source="Icons/text_underline.png" />
        </ToggleButton>
        <Separator />
        <ComboBox x:Name="fonts"
                MinWidth="100"
                ItemsSource="{x:Static Fonts.SystemFontFamilies}"
                ToolTip="Font"/>
        <ComboBox x:Name="fontSize"
                MinWidth="40"
                ToolTip="Font Size"/>
    </ToolBar>
    </ToolBarTray>
</UserControl>
```

Binding Commands to the Menu

Our toolbar is mostly functioning now, except for the open and save commands. However, our menu bar is pretty useless. We can bind the same commands to the menu bar with very little effort.

1. Open the `UserControl` we named `TextEditorMenu.xaml`.

2. Initially, we defined the menu items along these lines:

```
<MenuItem Header="_Edit">
    <MenuItem Header="_Undo" />
    <MenuItem Header="_Redo" />
    <Separator />
    <MenuItem Header="Cu_t" />
    <MenuItem Header="_Copy" />
    <MenuItem Header="_Paste" />
    <MenuItem Header="_Delete" />
</MenuItem>
```

This is only the Edit portion of the menu. We are going to replace this portion of the menu with the following:

```
<MenuItem Header="_Edit">
    <MenuItem Command="ApplicationCommands.Undo" />
    <MenuItem Command="ApplicationCommands.Redo" />
    <Separator />
    <MenuItem Command="ApplicationCommands.Cut" />
    <MenuItem Command="ApplicationCommands.Copy" />
    <MenuItem Command="ApplicationCommands.Paste" />
    <MenuItem Command="EditingCommands.Delete" />
</MenuItem>
```

3. Run the application, and examine the Edit menu as shown in Figure 10.1. Notice that even though we removed the `Header` attribute from `MenuItem`, the name of the command is displayed. Additionally, we see the corresponding keyboard shortcut displayed on each menu item. Both the name and the keyboard shortcut are provided from the command object to which we are binding. However, if you hold down the Alt key, you will see that we are no longer able to navigate the menu from the keyboard. We could correct this by providing the original `Header` attributes along with the `Command`.

FIGURE 10.1
The Edit menu using command bindings.

Customizing Commands

You might be curious to know why we did not go ahead and add command bindings for the open and save commands on the toolbar or the menu. All the commands we have used so far are generic, whereas a command such as `Open` or `New` is specific to the application. We need to define what `ApplicationCommands.New` means in the context of our application.

Let's define a few of these application specific commands. We'll begin with `New`. We would like the `New` command to replace the document open in our Text Editor with a new instance of `FlowDocument`.

1. We decided earlier that the responsibility of managing the document would reside in the class `DocumentManager`. Open the class in the editor and add the following method:

```
public void NewDocument()
{
    _currentFile = null;
    _textBox.Document = new FlowDocument();
}
```

This is a fairly simple method. Remember that _currentFile is a string representing the path to a currently loaded document. We set it to null because it does not yet exist on the disk. Then we provide a new instance of FlowDocument to the RichTextBox.

2. Now we need a way to bind this new method to the ApplicationCommands. New command. Everything that derives from UIElement has a collection called CommandBindings. CommandBindings is a library of commands available to UIElement and any of its child elements. In our case, we'll add a binding to the Window, which means that the binding will be accessible in our UserControl elements as well.

   Open MainWindow.xaml, and immediately beneath the opening Window element add the following:

   ```
   <Window.CommandBindings>
       <CommandBinding Command="ApplicationCommands.New"
                       Executed="NewDocument" />
   </Window.CommandBindings>
   ```

   The command binding must point to an event handler with an ExecutedRoutedEventArgs parameter. NewDocument will be that event handler, but we have not yet implemented it.

3. Open the code-behind for MainWindow.xaml, and add the following method:

   ```
   private void NewDocument(object sender, ExecutedRoutedEventArgs e)
   {
       _documentManager.NewDocument();
       status.Text = "New Document";
   }
   ```

   Here we call our DocumentManager.NewMethod, as well as setting some text in the status bar to let users know what they did.

4. At this point the command binding is ready for use, but we have not yet bound any gestures to it. If you run the application and place a breakpoint in the event handler we just added, you will discover that the keyboard shortcut Ctrl+N is bound to the ApplicationCommands.New by default.

5. Let's bind `ApplicationCommands.New` to a menu item. Close the application, and open `TextEditorMenu.xaml` in the editor. Find the `MenuItem` whose `Header` attribute is _New and change it to

```
<MenuItem Command="ApplicationCommands.New" />
```

6. You can now select File, New from the menu bar, in addition to using the Ctrl+N shortcut; both gestures execute the same code. Run the application and see.

Adding More Commands to the Text Editor

Now that we have a feel for how commands and command bindings work, it will be very easy to flesh out some of the additional features of the Text Editor. In the following steps, we will not be doing anything new, but we'll utilize both button and menu gestures.

1. Open the code-behind for `MainWindow.xaml` in the editor. We'll begin by adding the additional event handlers we will need for general document management. Here are the handlers to add:

```
private void OpenDocument(object sender, ExecutedRoutedEventArgs e)
{
    if (_documentManager.OpenDocument())
        status.Text = "Document loaded.";
}

private void SaveDocument(object sender, ExecutedRoutedEventArgs e)
{
    if (_documentManager.SaveDocument())
        status.Text = "Document saved.";
}

private void SaveDocumentAs(object sender,
➥ExecutedRoutedEventArgs e)
{
    if (_documentManager.SaveDocumentAs())
        status.Text = "Document saved.";
}

private void ApplicationClose(object sender,
➥ExecutedRoutedEventArgs e)
{
    Close();
}
```

The last handler isn't really for managing documents, but it is convenient for us to take care of it at this time. The other handlers, aside from updating the status, delegate to the corresponding methods on _documentManager. We've already implemented these methods in previous hours, so there is very little work for us to do here.

2. Let's add the markup to MainWindow.xaml to map the command bindings to these event handlers. The Window.CommandBindings element should look like this:

```
<Window.CommandBindings>
    <CommandBinding Command="ApplicationCommands.New"
                    Executed="NewDocument" />
    <CommandBinding Command="ApplicationCommands.Open"
                    Executed="OpenDocument" />
    <CommandBinding Command="ApplicationCommands.Save"
                    Executed="SaveDocument" />
    <CommandBinding Command="ApplicationCommands.SaveAs"
                    Executed="SaveDocumentAs" />
    <CommandBinding Command="ApplicationCommands.Close"
                    Executed="ApplicationClose" />
</Window.CommandBindings>
```

3. Now we need to tie these command bindings to specific gestures. We start by adding them to the toolbar. Open TextEditorToolbar.xaml in the editor. The first child element of the ToolBarTray includes buttons for opening and saving documents. Modify the child ToolBar element as follows:

```
<ToolBar>
    <Button Command="ApplicationCommands.Open"
            ToolTip="Open">
        <Image Source="Icons/folder_page.png" />
    </Button>
    <Button Command="ApplicationCommands.Save"
            ToolTip="Save">
        <Image Source="Icons/page_save.png" />
    </Button>
</ToolBar>
```

4. Open TextEditorMenu.xaml and change the MenuItem elements in the first part of the menu to look like this:

```
<MenuItem Header="_File">
    <MenuItem Command="ApplicationCommands.New" />
    <MenuItem Command="ApplicationCommands.Open" />
    <MenuItem Command="ApplicationCommands.Save" />
    <MenuItem Command="ApplicationCommands.SaveAs" />
    <Separator />
    <MenuItem Command="ApplicationCommands.Close" />
</MenuItem>
```

5. That's all. We've now mapped all our commands to at least one command binding.

Determining If a Command Is Available

It's very common that at times, you won't want a command to be available. For example, it doesn't make sense for the Save command to be available when there is nothing to save. Of course, you will want to give a visual indication to the user that the command is not available. This is normally in the form of a menu or button being disabled.

Command bindings raise an event called CanExecute. We can handle this event and inform the binding if the command is available.

1. Open MainWindow.xaml and modify the CommandBinding for Save to match the following:

```
<CommandBinding Command="ApplicationCommands.Save"
                CanExecute="SaveDocument_CanExecute"
                Executed="SaveDocument" />
```

2. The MainWindow won't know if the document is available for saving, so we'll need to modify DocumentManager to provide this information. Add the following method to DocumentManager:

```
public bool CanSaveDocument()
{
    return !string.IsNullOrEmpty(_currentFile);
}
```

3. In the code-behind for MainWindow.xaml, we'll need to add the following handler:

```
private void SaveDocument_CanExecute(object sender,
➥CanExecuteRoutedEventArgs e)
{
    e.CanExecute = _documentManager.CanSaveDocument();
}
```

4. Run the application. If you examine the File menu, you will see that the Save command is disabled. However, if you first perform a Save As, which sets a value for _currentFile, the command becomes available.

Creating an Input Binding

If you run the Text Editor as we've built it so far, and examine the shortcuts key listed under the File menu, you'll notice that ApplicationCommands.SaveAs did not define a default shortcut. You can define your custom gesture for a command using an *input binding*. Input bindings are similar to the command bindings we discussed earlier in the hour. UIElement defines a collection of input bindings that are automatically available to all of the element's children. Usually, you'll create your input bindings at the Window level of your application.

There are two types of input bindings: KeyBinding and MouseBinding. As you might have guessed, KeyBinding is for activating commands with the keyboard, and MouseBinding is for activating them with the mouse.

It wouldn't really be useful, but let's bind a gesture with the mouse to the SaveAs command, perhaps turning the wheel while holding down control.

1. Open MainWindow.xaml, and just after the command bindings add the following:

```
<Window.InputBindings>
    <MouseBinding Gesture="Control+WheelClick"
                  Command="ApplicationCommands.SaveAs" />
</Window.InputBindings>
```

2. Run the application. Hold down the Control key, roll your mouse wheel, and you'll be presented with the Save As dialog.

The Gesture attribute of the MouseBinding element can be set to any combination of values from the MouseAction enumeration and the ModifierKeys enumeration; both enumerations are in the System.Windows.Input namespace. A value from MouseAction is required, but a ModifierKeys is optional. If both values are used, separate them with a +.

Using a KeyBinding is very similar; if we wanted to define Shift+S to invoke SaveAs, it would look like this:

```
<Window.InputBindings>
    <KeyBinding Key="S"
                Modifiers="Shift"
                Command="ApplicationCommands.SaveAs" />
</Window.InputBindings>
```

The primary difference is that we set these values for two different attributes, instead of just one. In this case, Key is the required attribute, whereas Modifiers is optional. Modifiers expects a value from the same ModifierKeys enumeration we used in the MouseBinding. However, the attribute Key expects a value from the Key enumeration also defined in the System.Windows.Input namespace.

You can also define multiple modifiers for a binding, for example, to include the Alt key along with the previous key binding:

```
<KeyBinding Key="S"
            Modifiers="Shift+Alt"
            Command="ApplicationCommands.SaveAs" />
```

There are a couple of "gotchas" that you might run into when defining gestures for your commands. First, the syntax for combining values in the `ModifierKeys` enumeration uses the plus (+) character. This is not the standard operator for combining flags. Usually, you would use the pipeline (|) character. In fact, everywhere else in WPF, the pipeline is what you use. `ModifierKeys` is the exception.

The second problem you might encounter is specifying an input binding with a gesture that is already in use elsewhere in the application. The gestures are all routed events, and if they are marked as handled before they arrive at the element where your event handler is defined, you'll never see them.

Watch Out!

Summary

Commands and command bindings are a powerful way to simplify your code. The libraries of built-in commands enable you to add rich functionality to your application declaratively. With command bindings you can reduce the complexity of your code while still giving users options for executing commands.

We were able to apply these ideas to our Text Editor, and we've seen how commands and their binding operate in real working software.

Q&A

Q. *Of the five built-in command libraries, which one is likely to be the most commonly used?*

A. The `ApplicationCommands` library has the most general set of commands. It's the library that you will want to familiarize yourself with first. The other four libraries have more domain-specific commands. The second most common is probably the `EditingCommands` library used for manipulating text.

Q. *What's the difference between a command, its source, its target, and its binding?*

A. Even though we didn't explicitly discuss this, there are four central concepts underlying commands. The command itself is the action that's going to be executed. The source is the object that is invoking the command, such as a button or menu. The target is the subject that the command is affecting, such as the currently selected text. Finally, the binding is the object that links the actual implementation of the action to the command.

Workshop

Quiz

1. What are the two types of input bindings that you can create, and how are they different?

2. To use a built-in command that requires an application-specific implementation, such as `ApplicationCommands.New`, you must have certain items defined in both your XAML and your code. What are the items necessary for a minimal functioning use of such a command?

Answers

1. WPF provides `KeyBinding` and `MouseBinding`. `KeyBinding` allows you to define gestures for commands that consist of a keystroke possibly combined with one or more modifiers, whereas `MouseBinding` allows you to define gestures for the mouse that can also be optionally combined with modifiers on the keyboard.

2. The command will need to be wired to an event handler using the `CommandBindings` collection. The event handler will need to be implemented in such a way as to be meaningful in the context of the application. Finally, the command will need a means of being executed by the user, such as an input binding or being set to the `Command` property of a `Button` or `MenuItem`.

Activities

1. Read over the various enumerations we have discussed in the `System.Windows.Input` namespace. A basic knowledge of the values available will come in handy as you are building your own application.

2. Read over the lists of built-in commands as well. Remember that there are five different libraries. The two most important ones are `ApplicationCommands` and `EditingCommands`.

HOUR 11

Output

What You'll Learn in This Hour:

▶ Printing
▶ Visuals
▶ Bitmaps

Up to now, we have focused almost entirely on the capability of WPF to render output to users via a graphical display. WPF has many capabilities, though, and is not limited to this single form of output. Modern software must enable users to consume their data in a variety of formats.

Making the Text Editor Print

At this point, our text editor is almost finished. One major feature is missing: printing. It turns out that printing the contents of a RichTextBox is quite easy. Let's get to it:

1. Open the Text Editor project in Visual Studio and open the MainWindow.xaml file.

2. Add the following to the window's CommandBindings:

   ```
   <CommandBinding Command="ApplicationCommands.Print"
                   Executed="PrintDocument" />
   ```

3. Open the MainWindow.xaml.cs and add the following code:

   ```
   private void PrintDocument(object sender, ExecutedRoutedEventArgs e)
   {
       PrintDialog dlg = new PrintDialog();

       if (dlg.ShowDialog() == true)
       {
           dlg.PrintDocument(
   ```

```
                            (((IDocumentPaginatorSource)body.Document).DocumentPaginator),
                            "Text Editor Printing"
                            );
            }
        }
```

4. Open TextEditorMenu.xaml and add the following to the File menu before the Close option:

```
<Separator />
<MenuItem Command="ApplicationCommands.Print" />
```

5. Run the application and try printing something.

The preceding code gets the job done but is quite naïve and doesn't take proper consideration of paper size or margins. Depending on what you attempted to print, your printer may have spit out a blank page, or it may have positioned or wrapped the text in an odd way. To move toward a more realistic printing mechanism, we'll have to use some more advanced printing APIs.

Implementing a Custom Document Paginator

In our first attempt to print the contents of the RichTextBox, we cast the Document as an IDocumentPaginatorSource. It turns out that we can use this interface to get a DocumentPaginator for the text box. A DocumentPaginator is a special type of class that WPF can use to request individual pages of a document. The printing system uses this to move through the entire document, printing one page at a time. The only problem is that the default paginator doesn't seem to take page size or margins seriously. To fix this, we'll implement our own custom paginator.

1. In the Text Editor solution, add a new class called **PrintingPaginator.cs**.

2. Use Listing 11.1 to implement the body of the class.

LISTING 11.1   A Custom DocumentPaginator

```
using System.Windows;
using System.Windows.Documents;
using System.Windows.Media;

namespace TextEditor
{
    public class PrintingPaginator : DocumentPaginator
    {
        private readonly DocumentPaginator _originalPaginator;
```

LISTING 11.1 Continued

```
private readonly Size _pageSize;
private readonly Size _pageMargin;

public PrintingPaginator(
    DocumentPaginator paginator,
    Size pageSize,
    Size margin)
{
    _originalPaginator = paginator;
    _pageSize = pageSize;
    _pageMargin = margin;

    _originalPaginator.PageSize = new Size(
        _pageSize.Width - _pageMargin.Width*2,
        _pageSize.Height - _pageMargin.Height*2
        );

    _originalPaginator.ComputePageCount();
}

public override bool IsPageCountValid
{
    get { return _originalPaginator.IsPageCountValid; }
}

public override int PageCount
{
    get { return _originalPaginator.PageCount; }
}

public override Size PageSize
{
    get { return _originalPaginator.PageSize; }
    set { _originalPaginator.PageSize = value; }
}

public override IDocumentPaginatorSource Source
{
    get { return _originalPaginator.Source; }
}

public override DocumentPage GetPage(int pageNumber)
{
    DocumentPage originalPage =
        _originalPaginator.GetPage(pageNumber);

    ContainerVisual fixedPage = new ContainerVisual();

    fixedPage.Children.Add(originalPage.Visual);

    fixedPage.Transform = new TranslateTransform(
        _pageMargin.Width,
        _pageMargin.Height
        );

    return new DocumentPage(
```

LISTING 11.1   Continued

```
                fixedPage,
                _pageSize,
                AdjustForMargins(originalPage.BleedBox),
                AdjustForMargins(originalPage.ContentBox)
                );
        }

        private Rect AdjustForMargins(Rect rect)
        {
            if(rect.IsEmpty) return rect;
            else
            {
                return new Rect(
                    rect.Left + _pageMargin.Width,
                    rect.Top + _pageMargin.Height,
                    rect.Width,
                    rect.Height
                    );
            }
        }
    }
}
```

Our custom paginator wraps the original and adds some special functionality. Notice that many of the new properties pass through to the original. The constructor begins by setting the original's page size to a size reflected by the requested size and margins and then asks the underlying paginator to figure out how many pages we have. After the constructor, the most important function is GetPage. WPF calls this method each time it requires a page for display or print. Our override provides a print appropriate page by doing the following things:

1. Obtain the original page from the original paginator.

2. Wrap the page in a ContainerVisual so that it is easier to manipulate. (We'll talk about Visuals in more detail later this hour.)

3. Use a TranslateTransform to move the contents of the ContainerVisual from position (0,0) to (leftMargin, topMargin) so that the page is printed in the correct spot. (More on Transform in a later hour.)

4. Return a new page with its content and bleed adjusted according to the margins.

This paginator will give us exactly what we want, but we now need an easy way to hook this up to our PrintDialog.

Developing a Print Manager

Following the pattern we established with the DocumentManager, we'll create a PrintManager to help keep our printing code isolated. This will promote a clean and maintainable solution should we desire to add additional functionality later or need to fix bugs.

1. Begin by adding two new references to the Text Editor project. Right-click the project and select Add Reference... From the .NET tab select ReachFramework and System.Printing (use Ctrl+click for multiselect) and click OK. These two assemblies contain advanced printing features we'll be using in the PrintManager.

2. Add a new class to the project called **PrintManager.cs**.

3. Use Listing 11.2 to implement the PrintManager.

4. Open MainWindow.xaml.cs and add the following field:

   ```
   private readonly PrintManager _printManager;
   ```

5. Add the following to the MainWindow constructor:

   ```
   _printManager = new PrintManager(body);
   ```

6. Change the PrintDocument method of MainWindow to be as follows:

   ```
   private void PrintDocument(object sender, ExecutedRoutedEventArgs e)
   {
       if(_printManager.Print())
           status.Text = "Document sent to printer.";
   }
   ```

7. Run the program and try printing a document. You should have a correctly sized page with one inch margins.

LISTING 11.2   The PrintManager

```
using System.IO;
using System.Printing;
using System.Windows;
using System.Windows.Controls;
using System.Windows.Documents;

namespace TextEditor
{
    public class PrintManager
    {
        public static readonly int DPI = 96;
        private readonly RichTextBox _textBox;
```

LISTING 11.2   Continued

```
public PrintManager(RichTextBox textBox)
{
    _textBox = textBox;
}

public bool Print()
{
    PrintDialog dlg = new PrintDialog();

    if(dlg.ShowDialog() == true)
    {
        PrintQueue printQueue = dlg.PrintQueue;

        DocumentPaginator paginator = GetPaginator(
            printQueue.UserPrintTicket.PageMediaSize.Width.Value,
            printQueue.UserPrintTicket.PageMediaSize.Height.Value
            );

        dlg.PrintDocument(paginator, "TextEditor Printing");

        return true;
    }

    return false;
}

public DocumentPaginator GetPaginator(
    double pageWidth,
    double pageHeight)
{
    TextRange originalRange = new TextRange(
        _textBox.Document.ContentStart,
        _textBox.Document.ContentEnd
        );

    MemoryStream memoryStream = new MemoryStream();

    originalRange.Save(memoryStream, DataFormats.Xaml);

    FlowDocument copy = new FlowDocument();

    TextRange copyRange = new TextRange(
        copy.ContentStart,
        copy.ContentEnd
        );

    copyRange.Load(memoryStream, DataFormats.Xaml);

    DocumentPaginator paginator =
        ((IDocumentPaginatorSource) copy).DocumentPaginator;

    return new PrintingPaginator(
        paginator,
        new Size(
            pageWidth,
            pageHeight),
```

LISTING 11.2 Continued

```
                new Size(
                    DPI,
                    DPI
                    )
                );
        }
    }
}
```

> PageMediaSize.Width and PageMediaSize.Height are *nullable types*. Therefore
> we must access their real values through the Value property.

Did you Know?

There's a lot happening in this code, so let's break it down beginning with the Print method. Here's what happens:

1. A PrintDialog is created and shown to the user.

2. If the user selects a printer and clicks OK, we use the PrintDialog to obtain a PrintQueue. This is our gateway to extensive printer information and functionality.

3. Using the PrintQueue we obtain a PrintTicket through the UserPrintTicket property. The PrintTicket provides us with the paper size. (ReachFramework and System.Printing are the homes of PrintQueue and PrintTicket.)

4. We call the helper method GetPaginator, passing in the paper dimensions, and we use the result with the PrintDialog's Print method to send the information to the printer.

An explanation of the GetPaginator method is important as well. You might expect this method to be simple, given that we have already implemented a custom paginator; however, there are a few "gotchas." Here is how the GetPaginator method works:

1. Use TextRange to obtain the contents of the document.

2. Make a copy of the document by saving it to a MemoryStream and reloading it into a new FlowDocument. This is the big "gotcha." Because of the use of a custom paginator, the original FlowDocument will no longer be suitable for use within the RichTextBox. Therefore, to preserve the contents of the text box and enable users to continue to interact with the document after printing, we clone it before making any changes.

3. Use the cloned document to obtain the default `DocumentPaginator`.

4. Create an instance of our custom `PrintPaginator`, passing in the default paginator, the page dimensions originally obtained from the `PrintTicket`, and specifying one-inch margins (based on WPF's 96dpi rendering).

5. Return the custom paginator to the calling code.

The code in the previous two sections is a bit more technical than what we have seen in previous hours. However, it is still relatively simple when you consider the wealth of features you are getting. This code fully enables you to print any rich text content and it automatically handles word wrapping and pagination.

Adding Print Preview

Now that we have done the hard work of creating a custom paginator for our text editor, it is relatively easy to create a print preview feature as well. Here's how we do it:

1. Add a new window to the Text Editor project called **PrintPreviewDialog.xaml**.

2. Use Listing 11.3 to implement the markup for the user interface and Listing 11.4 for the code-behind.

3. Open the `MainWindow.xaml` and add the following `CommandBinding` to the `CommandBindings` collection:

```
<CommandBinding Command="ApplicationCommands.PrintPreview"
                Executed="PrintPreview" />
```

4. Add the following code to the `PrintManager.cs`:

```
public void PrintPreview()
{
    PrintPreviewDialog dlg = new PrintPreviewDialog(this);
    dlg.ShowDialog();
}
```

5. Add the following code to the `MainWindow.xaml.cs`:

```
private void PrintPreview(object sender, ExecutedRoutedEventArgs e)
{
    _printManager.PrintPreview();
}
```

6. Add the following markup to the `TextEditorMenu.xaml` just above the definition of the `Print` command:

```
<MenuItem Command="ApplicationCommands.PrintPreview" />
```

7. Run the application, enter some text, and select `Print Preview` from the menu. You can see the results in Figure 11.1.

LISTING 11.3   PrintPreviewDialog.xaml

```
<Window x:Class="TextEditor.PrintPreviewDialog"
        xmlns="http://schemas.microsoft.com/winfx/2006/xaml/presentation"
        xmlns:x="http://schemas.microsoft.com/winfx/2006/xaml"
        Title="Print Preview"
        Height="600"
        Width="450">
    <DockPanel>
        <StackPanel DockPanel.Dock="Bottom"
                    Orientation="Horizontal"
                    HorizontalAlignment="Center">
            <Button Content="&lt;"
                    Click="PreviousClick" />
            <TextBlock Text="{Binding CurrentPage}"
                    Margin="4 2 0 0" />
            <TextBlock Text=" of "
                    Margin="0 2 0 0" />
            <TextBlock Text="{Binding ElementName=pageViewer,
                                ➥ Path=DocumentPaginator.PageCount}"
                    Margin="0 2 4 0" />
            <Button Content="&gt;"
                    Click="NextClick" />
        </StackPanel>
        <Viewbox Margin="10">
            <Grid>
                <Border Background="Gray"
                        Opacity=".5"
                        Margin=".5 .5 0 0"
                        Width="85"
                        Height="110"
                        CornerRadius=".25" />
                <Border BorderBrush="Black"
                        BorderThickness=".1"
                        Background="White"
                        Width="85"
                        Height="110"
                        Margin="-.5 -.5 0 0">
                    <DocumentPageView x:Name="pageViewer" />
                </Border>
            </Grid>
        </Viewbox>
    </DockPanel>
</Window>
```

LISTING 11.4   PrintPreviewDialog.xaml.cs

```
using System.Windows;

namespace TextEditor
{
    public partial class PrintPreviewDialog : Window
    {
        public static readonly DependencyProperty CurrentPageProperty =
            DependencyProperty.Register(
                "CurrentPage",
                typeof(int),
                typeof(PrintPreviewDialog)
                );

        private readonly PrintManager _manager;
        private int _pageIndex;

        public PrintPreviewDialog(PrintManager printManager)
        {
            InitializeComponent();

            _manager = printManager;
            DataContext = this;
            ChangePage(0);
        }

        public int CurrentPage
        {
            get { return (int) GetValue(CurrentPageProperty); }
            set { SetValue(CurrentPageProperty, value); }
        }

        private void PreviousClick(object sender, RoutedEventArgs e)
        {
            ChangePage(_pageIndex - 1);
        }

        private void NextClick(object sender, RoutedEventArgs e)
        {
            ChangePage(_pageIndex + 1);
        }

        private void ChangePage(int requestedPage)
        {
            pageViewer.DocumentPaginator = _manager.GetPaginator(
                8.5*PrintManager.DPI,
                11*PrintManager.DPI
                );

            if(requestedPage < 0)
                _pageIndex = 0;
            else if(requestedPage >= pageViewer.DocumentPaginator.PageCount)
                _pageIndex = pageViewer.DocumentPaginator.PageCount - 1;
            else _pageIndex = requestedPage;
```

LISTING 11.4   Continued

```
        pageViewer.PageNumber = _pageIndex;
        CurrentPage = _pageIndex + 1;
    }
  }
}
```

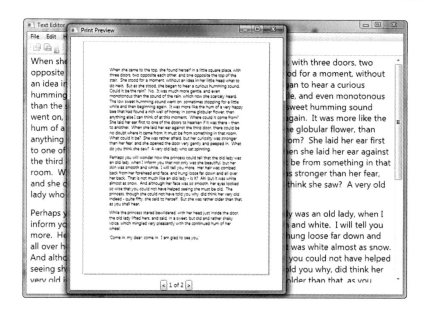

FIGURE 11.1
Print preview
in action.

Custom Dependency Properties

Listing 11.4 demonstrates the creation of a custom dependency property. We
have talked about dependency properties before, but have not detailed how to create them. We typically use this technique only when we need a property on a
`Window`, `UserControl`, or custom control that must support data binding or other
`FrameworkElement`-related features, such as animation or styling. The typical pro-
cedure for creating a dependency property is to declare a public, static field using
`DependencyProperty.Register`. It is advised that you append the word
"Property" onto the field name. There are several overloads of the `Register`
method, but at a minimum you must declare the actual property name, type, and
owning type. You should then create instance getters and setters by using the
static `GetValue` and `SetValue` methods inherited from `DependencyObject`. Use
your dependency property's field as the key to these methods.

You should take notice of several things in both the XAML and the code-behind.
Beginning with the XAML, notice how a `Grid` was used to relatively position two

Border elements. This creates the illusion of a drop shadow because the gray Border is drawn first and the white Border with the content is drawn on top. We mentioned these techniques back in Hour 4, "Handling Application Layout." Also, we made use of a very powerful control called DocumentPageView. This control is capable of using a DocumentPaginator to display one read-only DocumentPage at a time. Because this control is capable of handling only one page, we must manually handle the user's pagination requests. Most of the code in the code-behind is devoted to this. The most interesting part is the use of a custom dependency property to track the currently displayed page. By setting the window's DataContext to itself, we are able to bind to this property from XAML and update the user interface whenever we change pages.

It turns out that DocumentPageView is one of several controls that WPF has for displaying read-only documents. If you intend to work extensively with documents or author applications that involve lots of onscreen reading, you should investigate the controls in Table 11.1.

TABLE 11.1   WPF Document Controls

Name	Usage
DocumentPageView	Displays a single page using a DocumentPaginator.
DocumentViewer	Displays a FixedDocument with a rich set of controls for document navigation, printing, zooming, search, and so on.
FlowDocumentReader	Displays a FlowDocument with the capability to view the document in different modes such as one page, two-page book style, or scrolling view.
FlowDocumentPageViewer	Displays only a paginated view of a FlowDocument.
FlowDocumentScrollViewer	Displays only a scrolling view of a FlowDocument.

Outputting Bitmaps

Printing isn't the only method of output for your user interface, graphics, or documents. Another fully supported option is bitmap output. It is quite easy after you are aware of the important pieces. In this section we are going to enable our Text Editor to automatically save a screenshot of itself anytime an unhandled exception occurs. This provides contextual information for anyone trying to fix bugs, making it easier for them to reproduce the problem.

1. Open the `App.xaml.cs` file and use Listing 11.5 to alter its contents.

2. Open the `TextEditorMenu.xaml` file and add the following `MenuItem` wherever you desire:

```
<MenuItem Header="Throw Exception"
          Click="Exception_Click" />
```

3. Open the `TextEditorMenu.xaml.cs` file and add the following event handler code:

```
private void Exception_Click(object sender, RoutedEventArgs e)
{
    throw new Exception();
}
```

4. Run the application and select the menu item to throw an exception. Exit the application and browse to `bin\Debug\ErrorReports`. You should find a `.png` screenshot of the application when the error occurred. See Figure 11.2.

> When you run the program, the unhandled exception will cause Visual Studio to stop execution of the application. You must stop the debugger manually before you can proceed.

By the Way

> It is a good practice to always handle the UnhandledException event on AppDomain. This event is fired whenever an exception bubbles up far enough to cause an application crash. There is not much that can be done to save the application at this point; however, it is a good opportunity to log important details about the problem.

Did you Know?

LISTING 11.5 App.xaml.cs

```
using System;
using System.IO;
using System.Windows;
using System.Windows.Media;
using System.Windows.Media.Imaging;

namespace TextEditor
{
    public partial class App : Application
    {
        public App()
        {
            AppDomain.CurrentDomain.UnhandledException
                += UnhandledExceptionOccurred;
        }
```

LISTING 11.5   Continued

```
private static void UnhandledExceptionOccurred(
    object sender,
    UnhandledExceptionEventArgs e)
{
    Window win = Current.MainWindow;

    RenderTargetBitmap bmp = new RenderTargetBitmap(
        (int) win.Width,
        (int) win.Height,
        96,
        96,
        PixelFormats.Pbgra32
        );

    bmp.Render(win);

    string errorPath = Path.Combine(
        AppDomain.CurrentDomain.BaseDirectory,
        "ErrorReports"
        );

    if(!Directory.Exists(errorPath))
        Directory.CreateDirectory(errorPath);

    BitmapEncoder encoder = new PngBitmapEncoder();
    encoder.Frames.Add(BitmapFrame.Create(bmp));

    string filePath = Path.Combine(
        errorPath,
        string.Format("{0:MMddyyyyhhmmss}.png", DateTime.Now)
        );

    using(Stream stream = File.Create(filePath))
    {
        encoder.Save(stream);
    }
}
}
}
```

Did you Know?   Use Path.Combine to safely and correctly build up directory and file paths.

The most important parts of the previous code are those dealing with
RenderTargetBitmap and BitmapEncoder. The rest of the code manipulates the file
system. RenderTargetBitmap provides WPF with a destination for its rendering. You
can think of it as a virtual surface that WPF draws on. Before WPF can render to this
target, we have to set its size, dpi, and pixel format. In this case, we are rendering to
a surface that is the same size as the window itself, with WPF's default dpi and a
fairly common sRGB 32-bit pixel format. After we set up the target, we call Render
and pass in a Visual. We have mentioned visuals briefly before. In WPF, a Visual

is a very low-level class that "anything that can be seen" inherits from. This means that almost everything can be rendered to a bitmap in this way.

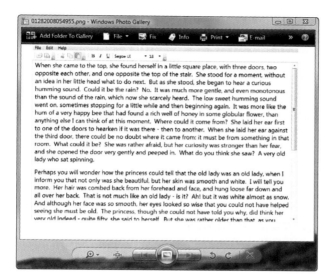

FIGURE 11.2
Viewing a bitmap rendering of the main application window.

Understanding Where Visuals Fit In

So far we've talked about several low-level classes in WPF, but haven't provided a clear picture of how they relate. Figure 11.3 shows the inheritance hierarchies of the important base types we've talked about so far.

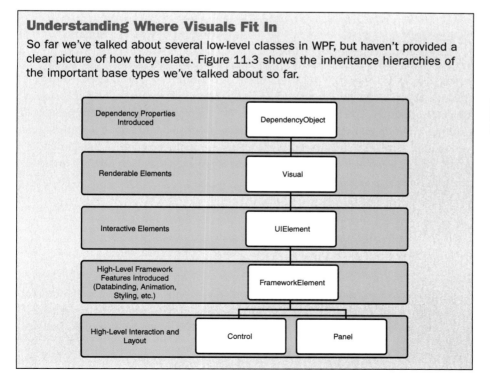

FIGURE 11.3
Basic WPF class hierarchy.

You can see that `Visual` is much lower level than most of the types we have been discussing. You won't work with this element directly, but it is important to know what does and does not inherit from Visual, because it directly affects what WPF can render. In later hours we will revisit visuals and expand on the possibilities that they enable.

After we have rendered the `Visual` to a target, we need to decide on a bitmap encoding. A variety of classes inherit from `BitmapEncoder`. In this case we are using `PngBitmapEncoder`, but you can also use encoders for GIF, JPEG, or BMP. After we have chosen an encoder, we use the render target to add a frame and then call `Save` to push the encoded data to a `FileStream`. That's all. You can even render 3D images to a bitmap using this same technique.

Watch Out!

If you attempt to use `RenderTargetBitmap` with a `Visual` that has never actually been displayed on the screen, you may not receive the results that you want. In this case, you must manually invoke WPF's layout mechanism before rendering. If the visual is a `UIElement`, you can do this by calling its `Measure` and `Arrange` methods.

Summary

We covered a lot of ground in this hour. These last pages on printing and other forms of output have really rounded out the Text Editor. We have gained a strong understanding of the variety of output options and explored a couple of the most common scenarios. You now have the tools you need to tackle some fairly advanced printing and imaging scenarios, and you have completed building a very nice application. The Text Editor is the second of four major applications we will be building, and it should serve as a great demonstration of your technical capabilities and a resource for future development.

Q&A

Q. *Is using a* `DocumentPaginator` *the only way to print in WPF?*

A. No. There are at least two other methods of printing in WPF. The `PrintDialog` has a method called `PrintVisual`, which is capable of printing anything that inherits from `Visual`. Also, you can use static methods on `PrintQueue` to create an `XpsDocumentWriter`, which enables other advanced printing scenarios.

Q. *You mention* FixedDocument. *What is the difference between* FixedDocument *and* FlowDocument?

A. A FlowDocument is one that is not set to any predetermined layout. Thus, its content is free to be reflowed according to various runtime factors. This document was designed primarily for an optimized experience when reading from the screen. FixedDocument represents a series of fixed layout pages. Its content cannot be dynamically laid out by WPF at runtime. It can only be displayed as defined. Comparing FlowDocument to FixedDocument is similar to comparing HTML to PDF.

Workshop

Quiz

1. What is the base class for all renderable types in WPF?

2. In what two assemblies will you find classes related to advanced printing?

3. What type is used to render WPF output to a bitmap?

Answers

1. All elements that are renderable must inherit from Visual.

2. ReachFramework and System.Printing contain types related to advanced printing scenarios.

3. Use RenderTargetBitmap to render WPF visuals to a bitmap.

Activities

1. An extensive and related topic to everything in this hour is XPS documents. XPS stands for XML Paper Specification. Spend some time researching this topic and the WPF libraries that are related.

2. Table 11.1 lists several document viewing controls that WPF has to offer. Experiment with each of these controls.

3. Investigate further the custom dependency and attached properties.

4. The error reporting mechanism in the Text Editor is less than adequate. Try extending it to write the details of the exception to a file in addition to saving the screenshot.

PART III

Visualizing Data

HOUR 12

Building a Contact Manager

What You'll Learn in This Hour:

▶ Model-View-Controller and Model-View-Presenter
▶ Solution organization
▶ Designing the Contact Manager
▶ Data and other application dependencies

Hour 12 represents a milestone in your WPF learning. Previously we have focused solely on the technical aspects of WPF. But now you have sufficient mastery of the basics, and we are free to move into more interesting topics. In the upcoming hours we will begin to use more advanced techniques—techniques that are central to building real applications. We also dig into architectural issues and offer WPF-based, practical solutions that can be used in most of the situations you will encounter.

Design a Contact Manager

We chose the idea of a contact manager because it is an example of a typical business application that a developer might be called on to build. It presents many of the challenges that are common to building business applications and is a great place to explore best practices and demonstrate common design patterns. Although we'll be keeping the list of features small in this application, we still have to deal with the same issues larger projects face, and we will present a consistent architecture that works well for average projects and can be easily evolved to handle more complex scenarios. The Contact Manager will have the following features:

▶ New, Edit, Save, Delete of contacts.

▶ Search contacts by last and first names.

▶ Use a tabbed interface to allow editing of multiple contacts simultaneously.

▶ View contacts as Contact Cards or in a list view.

▶ Allow the tabbed region of the interface to scale for easier reading.

▶ Apply a consistent look and feel throughout.

In addition to these high-level features, there are several architectural practices we would like to adhere to:

▶ Base the application architecture on the *Model-View-Presenter* pattern.

▶ Make healthy use of user controls to break up complex interfaces.

▶ Employ the principle of *Separation of Concerns* to prevent "different types of code" from being intermingled.

▶ Use WPF Resources and Styles to build a more maintainable and flexible solution.

Choosing an Architecture

Dozens of books, articles, blogs, and other resources discuss how to architect an interactive application. Within them you are likely to discover a variety of patterns and practices that people employ to make their software more manageable, but one pattern seems to appear consistently: *Model-View-Controller (MVC)*. MVC, despite its popularity, is commonly misunderstood. This may be because it tends to manifest itself differently in different scenarios—that is, web versus desktop applications. Regardless, the spirit of the pattern is the same. In MVC there are three types of objects in communication:

▶ Model objects represent the business concerns that are specific to the application being built. In our contact manager, a Contact would be an example of a model object.

▶ Views are the actual visible components of an application. They are most likely represented by WPF controls.

▶ Controllers traditionally functioned as mediators between the human and the application by handling user input from the mouse or keyboard.

One major problem exists with the preceding descriptions. Controller doesn't seem to fit exactly with modern UI toolkits like WPF. Very rarely would one need to write code to manually handle user input. These tasks are now handled by the various controls themselves. What is really needed is an application-centric component that can mediate between the View and the Model. This component would be capable of responding to View interactions and translating those into application commands. In the context of a contact manager, these commands would be actions like *SaveContact*, *DeleteContact*, *Search*, and the like.

The mismatch between the MVC pattern and modern UI frameworks has been recognized by many people. Over time a new pattern called *Model-View-Presenter* has evolved from MVC. The MVP pattern addresses the preceding issues and functions in a way that is more harmonious with WPF's advanced controls and data binding. For this reason, we will be using MVP to develop the Contact Manager.

Creating the Solution and Application Shell

As projects increase in complexity, more care should be taken to keep things organized. Let's begin by putting together the basic structure of our Contact Manager solution.

1. Open Visual Studio and create a new WPF Application called **ContactManager**.

2. Add the following folders to the solution: Model, Presenters, Resources, UserControls and Views. This will help us keep the different types of classes organized.

3. Add two user controls to the UserControls folder. Call them SideBar.xaml and SearchBar.xaml.

4. Remove the hardcoded height and width from the XAML files of each of the user controls.

5. Rename Window1 to **Shell**. Don't forget to update the App.xaml file with the changes.

6. Use the code in Listing 12.1 to implement the XAML for Shell.xaml.

7. Run the application to see the beginning of the Contact Manager shell. You can see the results in Figure 12.1.

LISTING 12.1   Shell.xaml

```xaml
<Window x:Class="ContactManager.Shell"
        xmlns="http://schemas.microsoft.com/winfx/2006/xaml/presentation"
        xmlns:x="http://schemas.microsoft.com/winfx/2006/xaml"
        xmlns:uc="clr-namespace:ContactManager.UserControls"
        Title="Contact Manager"
        Height="600"
        Width="800">
    <DockPanel>

        <uc:SearchBar DockPanel.Dock="Top" />

        <StatusBar DockPanel.Dock="Bottom">
            <StatusBarItem DockPanel.Dock="Right">
                <Slider x:Name="zoomSlider"
                        Width="125"
                        Value="1"
                        Minimum=".5"
                        Maximum="2" />
            </StatusBarItem>

            <StatusBarItem DockPanel.Dock="Right">
                <TextBlock>Zoom:</TextBlock>
            </StatusBarItem>

            <StatusBarItem>
                <TextBlock Text="{Binding StatusText}" />
            </StatusBarItem>
        </StatusBar>

        <Expander DockPanel.Dock="Left"
                  ExpandDirection="Right"
                  IsExpanded="True"
                  BorderThickness="0 1 1 1"
                  BorderBrush="Gray"
                  Margin="0 2 0 0"
                  Padding="2">
            <Expander.Header>
                <TextBlock Text="Contacts"
                           FontSize="14"
                           FontWeight="Bold">
                    <TextBlock.LayoutTransform>
                      <RotateTransform Angle="90" />
                    </TextBlock.LayoutTransform>
                </TextBlock>
            </Expander.Header>

            <uc:SideBar />

        </Expander>

        <TabControl x:Name="tabs"
                    Grid.Column="2"
                    Margin="5 0">
            <TabControl.LayoutTransform>
                <ScaleTransform ScaleX="{Binding ElementName=zoomSlider,
                                        ➥ Path=Value}"
```

LISTING 12.1 Continued

```
                                    ScaleY="{Binding ElementName=zoomSlider,
                                    ➥ Path=Value}" />
                </TabControl.LayoutTransform>
            </TabControl>

        </DockPanel>
</Window>
```

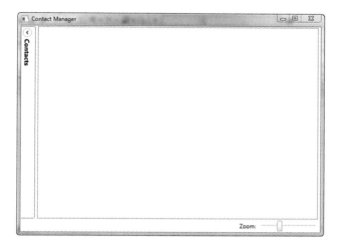

The application looks empty because we haven't created our Model or any Views to display it. We'll get to that shortly. In the meantime, there are some important things to study in the shell. First, we started with the canonical DockPanel as our root layout decision. We docked our two user controls to the top and left sides, added a status bar to the bottom, and left the remaining space to be filled with our tabbed views. We will build out the user controls later. For now, let's take a look at the new controls that have been introduced in the shell.

Expander

The Expander is a simple control whose primary purpose is to allow the user to collapse or expand a named region of the interface. A developer can use the Header property to label the region. This property is of type object, so it can be filled with a simple string or with any type of UI. (Notice how we used a RotateTransform to ensure that the header text looks natural. We'll discuss this more later.) The IsExpanded property can be used to get or set the current state of the Expander, and the ExpandDirection property determines to which side the control expands when the toggle button is clicked.

Slider

A `Slider` allows the selection of a double value by dragging a "handle" between a `Minimum` and `Maximum` value. Besides setting the range of the control, you can use properties like `Interval`, `SmallChange`, and `LargeChange` to affect how dramatically dragging the slider updates the `Value` property.

TabControl

A tabbed interface is common in many applications, and WPF's `TabControl` enables the Contact Manager to achieve this same functionality without too much hassle. `TabControl` inherits from `ItemsControl`, so it has many of the properties and events of previously mentioned controls, such as `ListBox` and `ComboBox`. We'll discuss this family of controls in detail in Hour 16, "Visualizing Lists." The most common use for a `TabControl` is to display a collection of `TabItem` controls. The Contact Manager will do just this, by adding tabs dynamically based on what the user needs to do. Additionally, the `TabControl` can be scaled to the user's preference via the data binding between the `ScaleTransform` and the `Slider`.

Defining the Model

Because the basics of a contact manager are fairly well known, we can dive directly into building the model. The model is made up of several classes. We'll begin by building the *entities* and *value objects*:

1. Add a new class to the solution called **Notifier.cs**. Make sure to add this directly under the solution because it will be used by several aspects of the application.

2. Use the following code to implement the `Notifier`:

```
using System;
using System.ComponentModel;

namespace ContactManager
{
    [Serializable]
    public abstract class Notifier : INotifyPropertyChanged
    {
        [field: NonSerialized]
        public event PropertyChangedEventHandler PropertyChanged;

        protected virtual void OnPropertyChanged(string propertyName)
        {
            if (PropertyChanged != null)
            {
                PropertyChanged(
                    this,
```

```
                            new PropertyChangedEventArgs(propertyName)
                        );
                    }
                }
            }
        }
```

3. Under the Model folder, create a new class named **Address.cs**. Use the code in Listing 12.2 to implement the class.

4. Also under the Model folder, create a class named **Contact.cs**. Implement this class with the code found in Listing 12.3.

LISTING 12.2   Address.cs

```
using System;

namespace ContactManager.Model
{
    [Serializable]
    public class Address : Notifier
    {
        private string _city;
        private string _country;
        private string _line1;
        private string _line2;
        private string _state;
        private string _zip;

        public string City
        {
            get { return _city; }
            set
            {
                _city = value;
                OnPropertyChanged("City");
            }
        }

        public string Country
        {
            get { return _country; }
            set
            {
                _country = value;
                OnPropertyChanged("Country");
            }
        }

        public string Line1
        {
            get { return _line1; }
            set
            {
                _line1 = value;
```

LISTING 12.2   Continued

```
                OnPropertyChanged("Line1");
            }
        }

        public string Line2
        {
            get { return _line2; }
            set
            {
                _line2 = value;
                OnPropertyChanged("Line2");
            }
        }

        public string State
        {
            get { return _state; }
            set
            {
                _state = value;
                OnPropertyChanged("State");
            }
        }

        public string Zip
        {
            get { return _zip; }
            set
            {
                _zip = value;
                OnPropertyChanged("Zip");
            }
        }
    }
}
```

LISTING 12.3   Contact.cs

```
using System;

namespace ContactManager.Model
{
    [Serializable]
    public class Contact : Notifier
    {
        private Address _address = new Address();
        private string _cellPhone;
        private string _firstName;
        private string _homePhone;
        private Guid _id = Guid.Empty;
        private string _imagePath;
        private string _jobTitle;
        private string _lastName;
        private string _officePhone;
```

LISTING 12.3   Continued

```
private string _organization;
private string _primaryEmail;
private string _secondaryEmail;

public Guid Id
{
    get { return _id; }
    set
    {
        _id = value;
        OnPropertyChanged("Id");
    }
}

public string ImagePath
{
    get { return _imagePath; }
    set
    {
        _imagePath = value;
        OnPropertyChanged("ImagePath");
    }
}

public string FirstName
{
    get { return _firstName; }
    set
    {
        _firstName = value;
        OnPropertyChanged("FirstName");
        OnPropertyChanged("LookupName");
    }
}

public string LastName
{
    get { return _lastName; }
    set
    {
        _lastName = value;
        OnPropertyChanged("LastName");
        OnPropertyChanged("LookupName");
    }
}

public string Organization
{
    get { return _organization; }
    set
    {
        _organization = value;
        OnPropertyChanged("Organization");
    }
}
```

LISTING 12.3   Continued

```
public string JobTitle
{
    get { return _jobTitle; }
    set
    {
        _jobTitle = value;
        OnPropertyChanged("JobTitle");
    }
}

public string OfficePhone
{
    get { return _officePhone; }
    set
    {
        _officePhone = value;
        OnPropertyChanged("OfficePhone");
    }
}

public string CellPhone
{
    get { return _cellPhone; }
    set
    {
        _cellPhone = value;
        OnPropertyChanged("CellPhone");
    }
}

public string HomePhone
{
    get { return _homePhone; }
    set
    {
        _homePhone = value;
        OnPropertyChanged("HomePhone");
    }
}

public string PrimaryEmail
{
    get { return _primaryEmail; }
    set
    {
        _primaryEmail = value;
        OnPropertyChanged("PrimaryEmail");
    }
}

public string SecondaryEmail
{
    get { return _secondaryEmail; }
    set
```

LISTING 12.3   Continued

```
        {
            _secondaryEmail = value;
            OnPropertyChanged("SecondaryEmail");
        }
    }

    public Address Address
    {
        get { return _address; }
        set
        {
            _address = value;
            OnPropertyChanged("Address");
        }
    }

    public string LookupName
    {
        get { return string.Format("{0}, {1}", _lastName, _firstName); }
    }

    public override string ToString()
    {
        return LookupName;
    }

    public override bool Equals(object obj)
    {
        Contact other = obj as Contact;
        return other != null && other.Id == Id;
    }
    }
}
```

So far the model code is pretty straightforward. It is composed of two classes that collectively make up a contact *aggregate*. These classes are the home of the basic properties we want to track. Each class, as well as the base Notifier class, is decorated with the [Serializable] attribute. A production quality application would probably save its contacts in some sort of database. Because we are striving to keep this example free of unnecessary complexity, we will be serializing them to disk. .NET requires the [Serializable] attribute in order to do this.

An important supporting class that is also part of the model is found in Listing 12.4.

1. Add a new class to the Model folder called **States.cs**.

2. Use the code in Listing 12.4 to implement this class.

LISTING 12.4   States.cs

```
using System.Collections.Generic;

namespace ContactManager.Model
{
    public static class States
    {
        private static readonly List<string> _names;

        static States()
        {
            _names = new List<string>(50);

            _names.Add("Alabama");
            _names.Add("Alaska");
            _names.Add("Arizona");
            _names.Add("Arkansas");
            _names.Add("California");
            ... Continue with state names ...
        }

        public static IList<string> GetNames()
        {
            return _names;
        }
    }
}
```

Abstract the Data Store

Almost every business application has some sort of data store that it uses to persist important information across application restarts. In most cases a database is used, but sometimes XML or flat files are used instead. For simplicity's sake, the Contact Manager will use a binary encoded flat file to persist contact data. Regardless of what the underlying data store is, every well-architected solution hides this technicality from the rest of the application. A common pattern is to execute all data-related activity through a *repository* class:

1. Add a new class to the Model folder called **ContactRepository.cs**.

2. Use the code in Listing 12.5 to implement this class.

LISTING 12.5   ContactRepository.cs

```
using System;
using System.Collections.Generic;
using System.IO;
using System.Linq;
using System.Runtime.Serialization.Formatters.Binary;
```

LISTING 12.5   Continued

```
namespace ContactManager.Model
{
    public class ContactRepository
    {
        private List<Contact> _contactStore;
        private readonly string _stateFile;

        public ContactRepository()
        {
            _stateFile = Path.Combine(
                AppDomain.CurrentDomain.BaseDirectory,
                "ContactManager.state"
                );

            Deserialize();
        }

        public void Save(Contact contact)
        {
            if (contact.Id == Guid.Empty)
                contact.Id = Guid.NewGuid();

            if (!_contactStore.Contains(contact))
                _contactStore.Add(contact);

            Serialize();
        }

        public void Delete(Contact contact)
        {
            _contactStore.Remove(contact);
            Serialize();
        }

        public List<Contact> FindByLookup(string lookupName)
        {
            IEnumerable<Contact> found =
                from c in _contactStore
                where c.LookupName.StartsWith(
                    lookupName,
                    StringComparison.OrdinalIgnoreCase
                    )
                select c;

            return found.ToList();
        }

        public List<Contact> FindAll()
        {
            return new List<Contact>(_contactStore);
        }

        private void Serialize()
        {
            using (FileStream stream =
                File.Open(_stateFile, FileMode.OpenOrCreate))
```

LISTING 12.5   Continued

```
        {
            BinaryFormatter formatter = new BinaryFormatter();
            formatter.Serialize(stream, _contactStore);
        }
    }

    private void Deserialize()
    {
        if (File.Exists(_stateFile))
        {
            using (FileStream stream =
                File.Open(_stateFile, FileMode.Open))
            {
                BinaryFormatter formatter = new BinaryFormatter();

                _contactStore =
                    (List<Contact>)formatter.Deserialize(stream);
            }
        }
        else _contactStore = new List<Contact>();
    }
}
}
```

The important part of a repository is that it abstracts away the actual data store so that other parts of the application are able to work with a high-level API and not concern themselves with *how* the data is stored. They care only *that* the data is stored. If the underlying infrastructure needs to be changed or optimized at some point in the future, a developer needs to change only the internals of the repository; no other code need be affected. You may want to run the application, but you will see no extra behavior as a result of our model definition, even though it contains all the code necessary to meet the "business need." For our application to become useful, we still need to create the other two parts of the MVP triad: Views and Presenters.

Summary

In this hour we took a deep dive into the subject of WPF application architecture. It is an important topic for those who want to use their WPF skills in building any but the most trivial of applications. We've examined the MVC pattern and discussed how an evolution of this pattern, MVP, works well with WPF. We built out the complete Model (the M in MVP) and cleanly organized it within an overall solution structure. The pieces put into place here will lay a strong foundation for everything that will be built on top in the next few hours.

Q&A

Q. *You mentioned the MVC and MVP patterns, but are there any other patterns that are common in interactive application architecture?*

A. Yes. There are dozens of patterns. Two more patterns that are related to MVP and are likely to aid in WPF development are *Supervising-Controller* and *Passive-View*.

Q. *Where do the model-related terms like entity, value object, aggregate, and repository come from?*

A. In 2003, Eric Evans wrote a fantastic book called *Domain-Driven Design: Tackling Complexity in the Heart of Software* (Addison-Wesley, 2003, ISBN: 978-0-321-12521-7). This book is focused on exploring how to build rich software models and is the source of many model-related terms that have come into common use.

Workshop

Quiz

1. Which part of the MVC pattern doesn't fit WPF exactly and why?

2. In an MVP pattern, what is the role of the 'M'?

3. What is a repository and how does it apply the principle of Separation of Concerns (SoC)?

Answers

1. The Controller in the original MVC triad does not fit well with WPF's design. This is because many of the responsibilities that the Controller had in the original pattern have been taken over by WPF's rich control set.

2. The M in MVP stands for Model. The primary purpose of this part of the application is to represent business-specific constructs in software.

3. A repository is a type of class that hides the actual data storage mechanism from the rest of the application. It embodies SoC by separating any data-related code from other classes and encapsulating it in a way that hides the internal complexity from unconcerned parties.

Activities

1. Spend some time on the Internet researching MVC and MVP.

2. Rewrite the `ContactRepository` to store contacts in a database. Do not change the public interface of the class.

3. Research "Domain Driven Design," a topic deeply concerned with the building of rich business models.

HOUR 13

Presenters and Views

What You'll Learn in This Hour:

▶ Application level presenters
▶ Screen-level presenters
▶ Presenter/View communication
▶ Dependency injection

With the Model we built in Hour 12 and an understanding of the MVP pattern, it's time to complete the triad by building the first presenters and views of our application. Presenters are the home of application logic, and they often mediate between the View and the Model. Therefore, presenters are a core piece of the Contact Manager. They receive special attention this hour along with the patterns that enable them to communicate with views.

Creating a Custom Base Class for Presenters

In the process of developing this application, we will build several presenters for managing various aspects of the Contact Manager. There are a couple of things that all these presenters will have in common. These features make View/Presenter collaboration easier and will enable various aspects of the shell infrastructure that we are going to build. Let's create a base class to implement the common presenter features:

1. In the Contact Manager solution, create a new class in the `Presenters` folder called **PresenterBase.cs**.

2. Use the code in Listing 13.1 to implement the class.

3. Build the application to confirm that you have entered the code correctly.

LISTING 13.1   PresenterBase.cs

```
namespace ContactManager.Presenters
{
    public class PresenterBase<T> : Notifier
    {
        private readonly string _tabHeaderPath;
        private readonly T _view;

        public PresenterBase(T view)
        {
            _view = view;
        }

        public PresenterBase(T view, string tabHeaderPath)
        {
            _view = view;
            _tabHeaderPath = tabHeaderPath;
        }

        public T View
        {
            get { return _view; }
        }

        public string TabHeaderPath
        {
            get { return _tabHeaderPath; }
        }
    }
}
```

We have chosen to inherit our base class from Notifier. Recall from Hour 12, "Building a Contact Manager," that this class gives us a basic implementation of INotifyPropertyChanged, which enables more powerful data binding in WPF. Besides data binding, presenters often need additional mechanisms to request information from the view or tell it to display something. The generic property T allows each presenter to talk to its associated view as necessary. Finally, the TabHeaderPath exists to support the tabbed UI infrastructure we are building. This property provides the data binding *property path* to bind to the Tab's header.

Completing the Tab UI Infrastructure

We began developing the tabbed UI in Hour 12 by implementing the basic XAML in the Shell.xaml file. Before we can fully use it, we need to add a bit of "intelligence" to it. Let's do that now.

1. Open `Shell.xaml.cs` in the code editor.

2. Add the following method to enable adding presenter-based views to the shell:

```
public void AddTab<T>(PresenterBase<T> presenter)
{
    TabItem newTab = null;

    for(int i = 0; i < tabs.Items.Count; i++)
    {
        TabItem existingTab = (TabItem) tabs.Items[i];

        if(existingTab.DataContext.Equals(presenter))
        {
            tabs.Items.Remove(existingTab);
            newTab = existingTab;
            break;
        }
    }

    if(newTab == null)
    {
        newTab = new TabItem();

        Binding headerBinding = new Binding(presenter.TabHeaderPath);
        BindingOperations.SetBinding(
            newTab,
            TabItem.HeaderProperty,
            headerBinding
            );

        newTab.DataContext = presenter;
        newTab.Content = presenter.View;
    }

    tabs.Items.Insert(0, newTab);
    newTab.Focus();
}
```

3. Add the following method to enable removing presenter-based views from the shell:

```
public void RemoveTab<T>(PresenterBase<T> presenter)
{
    for (int i = 0; i < tabs.Items.Count; i++)
    {
        TabItem item = (TabItem)tabs.Items[i];

        if (item.DataContext.Equals(presenter))
        {
            tabs.Items.Remove(item);
            break;
        }
    }
}
```

4. Make sure you include the following using statement at the top of the Shell.cs:

```
using ContactManager.Presenters;
```

5. Compile the application.

The AddTab method loops through the existing tabs to make sure that one is not already present for the given presenter. If no existing tab is found, one is created and a binding is set on the tab's header using the TabHeaderPath. The new tab's DataContext is set to the presenter and its Content is set to the associated view. Finally, the new or existing tab is inserted into the beginning of the list and given focus.

RemoveTab is quite simple. To remove a presenter's tab, it searched through the list of tab items, comparing each DataContext (previously set in AddTab) to the presenter. When a match is found, the tab is removed.

Implementing the Application Presenter

In a typical application, there is a need for an *Application Controller* or *Application Presenter*. This special type of presenter provides common application-level functionality to other presenters and manages various other cross-presenter issues. We'll build this now so that its capabilities will be available for future use:

1. Add a new class to the Presenters folder called **ApplicationPresenter.cs**.

2. Use the code in Listing 13.2 to implement this class.

3. Open Shell.xaml.cs and change the constructor to the match the following:

```
public Shell()
{
    InitializeComponent();
    DataContext = new ApplicationPresenter(this, new ContactRepository());
}
```

4. Make sure to include the following using statement at the top of Shell.cs:

```
using ContactManager.Model;
```

5. Compile the application.

LISTING 13.2   ApplicationPresenter.cs

```
using System;
using System.Collections.ObjectModel;
using ContactManager.Model;

namespace ContactManager.Presenters
{
    public class ApplicationPresenter : PresenterBase<Shell>
    {
        private readonly ContactRepository _contactRepository;
        private ObservableCollection<Contact> _currentContacts;
        private string _statusText;

        public ApplicationPresenter(
            Shell view,
            ContactRepository contactRepository)
            : base(view)
        {
            _contactRepository = contactRepository;

            _currentContacts = new ObservableCollection<Contact>(
                _contactRepository.FindAll()
                );
        }

        public ObservableCollection<Contact> CurrentContacts
        {
            get { return _currentContacts; }
            set
            {
                _currentContacts = value;
                OnPropertyChanged("CurrentContacts");
            }
        }

        public string StatusText
        {
            get { return _statusText; }
            set
            {
                _statusText = value;
                OnPropertyChanged("StatusText");
            }
        }

        public void Search(string criteria)
        {
            if (!string.IsNullOrEmpty(criteria) && criteria.Length > 2)
            {
                CurrentContacts = new ObservableCollection<Contact>(
                    _contactRepository.FindByLookup(criteria)
                    );

                StatusText = string.Format(
                    "{0} contacts found.",
                    CurrentContacts.Count
                    );
            }
```

LISTING 13.2   Continued

```
            else
            {
                CurrentContacts = new ObservableCollection<Contact>(
                    _contactRepository.FindAll()
                    );

                StatusText = "Displaying all contacts.";
            }
        }

        public void NewContact()
        {
            OpenContact(new Contact());
        }

        public void SaveContact(Contact contact)
        {
            if (!CurrentContacts.Contains(contact))
                CurrentContacts.Add(contact);

            _contactRepository.Save(contact);

            StatusText = string.Format(
                "Contact '{0}' was saved.",
                contact.LookupName
                );
        }

        public void DeleteContact(Contact contact)
        {
            if (CurrentContacts.Contains(contact))
                CurrentContacts.Remove(contact);

            _contactRepository.Delete(contact);

            StatusText = string.Format(
                "Contact '{0}' was deleted.",
                contact.LookupName
                );
        }

        public void CloseTab<T>(PresenterBase<T> presenter)
        {
            View.RemoveTab(presenter);
        }

        public void OpenContact(Contact contact)
        {
            throw new NotImplementedException();
        }

        public void DisplayAllContacts()
        {
            throw new NotImplementedException();
        }
    }
}
```

The ApplicationPresenter exposes the necessary functionality that several components (views and other presenters) will need to get their work done. Notice that the method names on the presenter mostly reflect the features we said we would support at the beginning of Hour 12. These features include things such as searching contacts and creating, saving, and deleting contacts. The CloseTab method will be used by other presenters as well as the OpenContact method.

Some important architectural decisions were made in the implementation of this class and how it works into the overall application design. Let's mention a few:

▶ Notice that the constructor is dependent on two other classes: an instance of Shell and an instance of ContactRepository. This technique is known as *constructor injection* and is a specific type of *dependency injection*. DI is a technique that is commonly used to help enforce the principle of Separation of Concerns (SoC), which we have mentioned on several occasions. Dependency injection allows the presenter to worry about application-level functionality and to easily interact with other classes to accomplish complex tasks.

▶ Examine the Search method. This is a great example of how the ApplicationPresenter adds application-level logic to the low-level search capabilities of the repository. The presenter should not know the details of how search is accomplished, but it is responsible for determining under what conditions it should occur.

▶ The new, save, and delete methods follow the same pattern as Search. They are concerned only with the application-level issues surrounding the given command. For all other issues, they delegate to the repository.

▶ The CloseTab method on this presenter allows other child presenters to close themselves by user request. Notice how the ApplicationPresenter forwards this request on to the View. The presenter, essentially, does not care how the view removes the tab; this is a view's responsibility. It simply asks for it to be done.

▶ Finally, we instantiate the presenter and set it to the DataContext property on the Shell. This enables data binding for the CurrentContacts collection and the StatusText property. Additionally, this presenter will be available to the user controls SideBar and SearchBar because they will automatically inherit the DataContext value from their parent.

Enhancing the Shell

Now that we have some application functionality brewing, we need a way to access it through the user interface. In Hour 12 we created two stub user controls that we plugged into the `Shell`. Let's build out one of them a little more now:

1. Open `SideBar.xaml` and alter the markup to match the following:

```
<UserControl x:Class="ContactManager.UserControls.SideBar"
             xmlns="http://schemas.microsoft.com/winfx/2006/xaml/
             ➥presentation"
             xmlns:x="http://schemas.microsoft.com/winfx/2006/xaml">
    <DockPanel>
        <StackPanel DockPanel.Dock="Bottom"
                    Margin="4">
            <Button Content="New Contact"
                    Click="New_Click" />
            <Button Content="View All"
                    Click="ViewAll_Click" />
        </StackPanel>
        <ScrollViewer VerticalScrollBarVisibility="Auto">
            <ItemsControl Width="250"
                          VerticalAlignment="Stretch"
                          BorderThickness="0"
                          ItemsSource="{Binding CurrentContacts}">
            </ItemsControl>
        </ScrollViewer>
    </DockPanel>
</UserControl>
```

2. Open `SideBar.xaml.cs` and alter its code according to the listing that follows:

```csharp
using System.Windows;
using System.Windows.Controls;
using ContactManager.Presenters;

namespace ContactManager.UserControls
{
    public partial class SideBar : UserControl
    {
        public SideBar()
        {
            InitializeComponent();
        }

        public ApplicationPresenter Presenter
        {
            get { return DataContext as ApplicationPresenter; }
        }

        private void New_Click(object sender, RoutedEventArgs e)
        {
            Presenter.NewContact();
        }
```

```
        private void ViewAll_Click(object sender, RoutedEventArgs e)
        {
            Presenter.DisplayAllContacts();
        }
    }
}
```

3. Run the application to see the results of the changes.

We mentioned in the previous section that the `ApplicationPresenter` would be inherited through the `DataContext` property. We are taking advantage of that here. Because of our application architecture, the view's button clicks can delegate to the presenter for appropriate action.

ScrollViewer

The `SideBar` uses a `ScrollViewer` control to create a scrollable region inside the view. `ScrollViewer` is a `ContentControl`. It is capable of providing a scrollable interface for anything set to its `Content` property. This control provides several special properties. Two that are most commonly used are `VerticalScrollBarVisibility` and `HorizontalScrollBarVisibility`. These properties allow you to define when the scrollbars will become visible. Setting the value to `Auto` keeps the scrollbars hidden until the `Content` is too large for the display area and requires scrolling.

ItemsControl

The `ItemsControl` used in the preceding markup has been mentioned at several points in previous hours. It is the base class for more complex list controls such as `ListBox`, `ComboBox`, and `TabControl`. An `ItemsControl` implements the minimum code necessary to display a list of items. We'll discuss this control and its inheritors in great detail in Hour 16, "Visualizing Lists."

Building an Edit Contact Screen

Running the Contact Manager and clicking New Contact will result in an exception being thrown because we haven't implemented the edit contact screen. Implementing this piece requires creating a presenter, view, and making some minor additions to the `ApplicationPresenter`. Let's get to work:

1. Create a new `UserControl` called **EditContactView.xaml** in the Views folder.

2. Use the markup in Listing 13.3 to implement this view.

3. Add a new class to the Presenters folder called **EditContactPresenter.cs**.

4. Use the code in Listing 13.4 to implement this class.

5. Open the EditContactView.xaml.cs and make it match the code in Listing 13.5.

6. Open the ApplicationPresenter and change the OpenContact method to the following:

```
public void OpenContact(Contact contact)
{
    if (contact == null) return;

    View.AddTab(
        new EditContactPresenter(
            this,
            new EditContactView(),
            contact
            )
        );
}
```

7. Run the application. Click New Contact. Enter some contact details and save. Try using the zoom slider. You should be able to see the effects more clearly than before.

LISTING 13.3   EditContactView.xaml

```xml
<UserControl x:Class="ContactManager.Views.EditContactView"
        xmlns="http://schemas.microsoft.com/winfx/2006/xaml/presentation"
        xmlns:x="http://schemas.microsoft.com/winfx/2006/xaml">
    <DockPanel Margin="5">
        <Border DockPanel.Dock="Top">
            <DockPanel LastChildFill="False">
                <TextBlock DockPanel.Dock="Left"
                        Text="{Binding Contact.LastName}" />
                <TextBlock DockPanel.Dock="Left"
                        Text=", " />
                <TextBlock DockPanel.Dock="Left"
                        Text="{Binding Contact.FirstName}" />
                <TextBlock DockPanel.Dock="Right"
                        Text="{Binding Contact.Organization}" />
            </DockPanel>
        </Border>

        <StackPanel DockPanel.Dock="Bottom">
            <Button Content="Save"
                    Click="Save_Click" />
            <Button Content="Delete"
                    Click="Delete_Click" />
            <Button Content="Close"
                    Click="Close_Click" />
        </StackPanel>
```

LISTING 13.3   Continued

```xml
<WrapPanel>
    <GroupBox>
        <GroupBox.Header>
            <Border>
                <TextBlock Text="General" />
            </Border>
        </GroupBox.Header>

        <Grid>
            <Grid.ColumnDefinitions>
                <ColumnDefinition Width="100" />
                <ColumnDefinition Width="Auto" />
                <ColumnDefinition Width="175" />
            </Grid.ColumnDefinitions>
            <Grid.RowDefinitions>
                <RowDefinition Height="Auto" />
                <RowDefinition Height="Auto" />
                <RowDefinition Height="Auto" />
                <RowDefinition Height="Auto" />
            </Grid.RowDefinitions>

            <Grid Grid.RowSpan="4">
                <Border Background="Gray"
                        CornerRadius="6"
                        Margin="2 2 0 0"
                        Opacity=".5" />
                <Border Margin="2 2 4 4"
                        Background="White" />
                <Viewbox Margin="2 2 4 4">
                    <Image Source="{Binding Contact.ImagePath}" />
                </Viewbox>
                <Border BorderThickness="2"
                        Background="Transparent"
                        CornerRadius="6"
                        Margin="0 0 2 2" />
                <Button Background="White"
                        Click="SelectImage_Click" />
            </Grid>

            <Label Grid.Column="1"
                   Content="_First Name:"
                   Target="{Binding ElementName=firstName}" />
            <TextBox x:Name="firstName"
                     Grid.Column="2"
                     Text="{Binding Contact.FirstName}" />

            <Label Grid.Row="1"
                   Grid.Column="1"
                   Content="_Last Name:"
                   Target="{Binding ElementName=lastName}" />
            <TextBox x:Name="lastName"
                     Grid.Row="1"
                     Grid.Column="2"
                     Text="{Binding Contact.LastName}" />
```

LISTING 13.3   Continued

```xml
                        <Label Grid.Row="2"
                               Grid.Column="1"
                               Content="Or_ganization:"
                               Target="{Binding ElementName=organization}" />
                        <TextBox x:Name="organization"
                                 Grid.Row="2"
                                 Grid.Column="2"
                                 Text="{Binding Contact.Organization}" />

                        <Label Grid.Row="3"
                               Grid.Column="1"
                               Content="_Job Title:"
                               Target="{Binding ElementName=jobTitle}" />
                        <TextBox x:Name="jobTitle"
                                 Grid.Row="3"
                                 Grid.Column="2"
                                 Text="{Binding Contact.JobTitle}" />
                    </Grid>
                </GroupBox>
            </WrapPanel>
        </DockPanel>
</UserControl>
```

LISTING 13.4   EditContactPresenter.cs

```csharp
using ContactManager.Model;
using ContactManager.Views;

namespace ContactManager.Presenters
{
    public class EditContactPresenter : PresenterBase<EditContactView>
    {
        private readonly ApplicationPresenter _applicationPresenter;
        private readonly Contact _contact;

        public EditContactPresenter(
            ApplicationPresenter applicationPresenter,
            EditContactView view,
            Contact contact)
            : base(view, "Contact.LookupName")
        {
            _applicationPresenter = applicationPresenter;
            _contact = contact;
        }

        public Contact Contact
        {
            get { return _contact; }
        }

        public void SelectImage()
        {
            string imagePath = View.AskUserForImagePath();
```

LISTING 13.4 Continued

```
                if (!string.IsNullOrEmpty(imagePath))
                    Contact.ImagePath = imagePath;
        }

        public void Save()
        {
            _applicationPresenter.SaveContact(Contact);
        }

        public void Delete()
        {
            _applicationPresenter.CloseTab(this);
            _applicationPresenter.DeleteContact(Contact);
        }

        public void Close()
        {
            _applicationPresenter.CloseTab(this);
        }

        public override bool Equals(object obj)
        {
            EditContactPresenter presenter = obj as EditContactPresenter;
            return presenter != null && presenter.Contact.Equals(Contact);
        }
    }
}
```

LISTING 13.5 EditContactView.xaml.cs

```
using System.Windows;
using System.Windows.Controls;
using ContactManager.Presenters;
using Microsoft.Win32;

namespace ContactManager.Views
{
    public partial class EditContactView : UserControl
    {
        public EditContactView()
        {
            InitializeComponent();
        }

        public EditContactPresenter Presenter
        {
            get { return DataContext as EditContactPresenter; }
        }

        private void Save_Click(object sender, RoutedEventArgs e)
        {
            Presenter.Save();
        }
```

LISTING 13.5   Continued

```
    private void Delete_Click(object sender, RoutedEventArgs e)
    {
        Presenter.Delete();
    }

    private void Close_Click(object sender, RoutedEventArgs e)
    {
        Presenter.Close();
    }

    private void SelectImage_Click(object sender, RoutedEventArgs e)
    {
        Presenter.SelectImage();
    }

    public string AskUserForImagePath()
    {
        OpenFileDialog dlg = new OpenFileDialog();
        dlg.ShowDialog();
        return dlg.FileName;
    }
  }
}
```

Although the Contact Manager doesn't *look* very attractive (see Figure 13.1), it is now functioning and supported by a solid architecture.

FIGURE 13.1
A functioning Contact Manager.

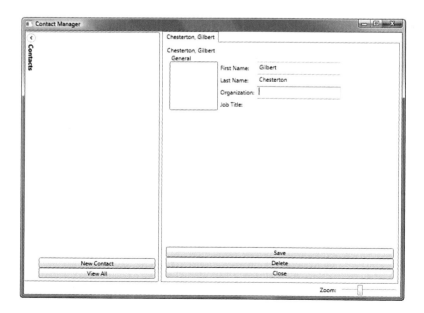

We've introduced a lot of code and markup in the previous section, but most of it is pretty straightforward. Looking at the EditContactView.xaml, you will find pretty typical markup compared to what we've been working with in previous chapters. In the next hour, we are going to make some changes to this markup that greatly beautify it. For now, it works.

EditContactPresenter follows similar patterns as ApplicationPresenter does. Notice how it takes an instance of the application presenter in its constructor. This is essential to this particular implementation of the MVP pattern. Much of what the presenter does is delegated to the application presenter; the rest, such as determining a filename, is delegated to the view. Pay special attention to the override of Equals. Our tab infrastructure requires this to prevent multiple copies of the same contact being open at the same time.

When you compile this application, you may get several compiler warnings, depending on your Visual Studio settings. These warnings are related to the overriding of the Equals method on several classes. In a real-world application, you would want to override GetHashCode, the == operator, and the != operator anytime you override Equals. Because it is not necessary for our example, we have left these implementations out for the purpose of simplification.

Did you Know?

When it comes to the EditContactView.xaml.cs code-behind, we have followed the same pattern as in previous examples. The one interesting thing to take note of is the AskUserForImagePath method. This allows the presenter to ask the view for this information without needing to be concerned with how it is done. In this case, the view uses an OpenFileDialog to locate an image, but it could have used any number of means.

Summary

This hour has introduced the final important pieces into our solution; presenters and views. We've looked at a lot of code and markup, but we've seen how a well-thought-out architecture can keep code simple and isolated. Separation of Concerns has played a key role in our design, enabling repository logic to be separated from application-wide logic, which in turn is separated from screen-specific logic.

Q&A

Q. *MVC and MVP are interesting and useful patterns. Where can I go to find more examples of this being used in the context of WPF?*

A. Sadly, there isn't much literature available on implementing these patterns in WPF yet. More and more developers are seeing the benefits of designing applications in this fashion, so there is likely to be more guidance soon. In the meantime, investigate how other platforms have tackled these issues.

Q. *Why doesn't WPF have more built-in support for the MVP pattern?*

A. The creators of WPF, in trying to cater to a very wide range of customers, have left these issues out of the core design of WPF. In doing this, they have given developers the flexibility to solve complex UI problems in a variety of ways. The method presented in this book is one of several variations.

Workshop

Quiz

1. Describe the role of an application controller/presenter.

2. Describe the role of a subordinate or screen-related presenter.

Answers

1. An application presenter is responsible for managing items that have application-wide scope. This could be state that is accessed or manipulated by various parts of the application, or it could be UI infrastructure methods that other presenters require to function properly. Examples of what such methods might enable are adding tabs to a central view and allowing a presenter to add custom menu options or toolbar buttons.

2. All other presenters besides the application presenter tend to function in a subordinating role. They exist to help the application presenter do its job. Some may function by separating out additional application-wide responsibilities, whereas others may exist to manage the presentation of a specific screen within the application.

Activities

1. Research "Martin Fowler," if you have not already. Browse his website and read up on some common UI related patterns.

2. Extract interfaces for the existing views and presenters. Alter the constructors of the presenters to depend on interfaces rather than concrete classes. In a real-world application, all code would work against interfaces rather than concrete classes. This enables further decoupling and ease of testing throughout the application.

3. Spend some time on the Internet researching "dependency injection" and the related term "inversion of control." Several open source frameworks ease the use of these techniques: StructureMap, Windsor, and Spring.net. You may find it valuable to investigate these tools because they are likely to be of great use on any medium or large projects you may develop.

HOUR 14

Resources and Styles

What You'll Learn in This Hour:

- ▶ Defining resources
- ▶ Defining styles
- ▶ Using static versus dynamic resources
- ▶ Stylizing the Contact Manager

In Hours 12 and 13 we worked hard to build a solid application architecture. We decided to use an MVP pattern and we organized the solution structure appropriately. Using MVP or MVC is a good approach to building almost any UI, but there are other important issues that must be dealt with as well. As applications grow, they depend more and more on resources such as graphics and colors. Over the development of a solution, a common "look and feel" may be designed, or it may emerge on its own. In previous Windows technologies, these styles would likely be strewn across various classes, creating a maintenance nightmare. The designers of WPF were well aware of these problems and created a rich and dynamic solution, as discussed in this hour.

Defining Resources

WPF uses a special type called a `ResourceDictionary` to store reusable "pieces" of an application. Some of the most common reusable pieces are colors and brushes used to create an application's color theme. The `Application` type has a `Resources` property of type `ResourceDictionary` that a developer can use to store application-scoped resources. Resources are often marked with a `Key` for easy access by other parts of the UI. It turns out that this is a great way to define a color theme for your application. Let's go ahead and do this for the Contact Manager:

1. Open the Contact Manager solution in Visual Studio.

2. Open the App.xaml file for editing.

3. Use the XAML in Listing 14.1 as the markup for this file.

LISTING 14.1   App.xaml

```
<Application x:Class="ContactManager.App"
             xmlns="http://schemas.microsoft.com/winfx/2006/xaml/presentation"
             xmlns:x="http://schemas.microsoft.com/winfx/2006/xaml"
             StartupUri="Shell.xaml">
    <Application.Resources>
        <Color x:Key="lightBlueColor">#FF145E9D</Color>
        <Color x:Key="darkBlueColor">#FF022D51</Color>
        <Color x:Key="redColor">#FFAA2C27</Color>
        <Color x:Key="greenColor">#FF656A03</Color>
        <Color x:Key="brownColor">#FF513100</Color>
    </Application.Resources>
</Application>
```

Everything that inherits from FrameworkElement has a Resources property. This creates a hierarchical set of resources for the application. Items declared in App.Resources are visible to the entire application. Resources defined for a particular UserControl would be visible only to that control. If that UserControl had a Grid that defined resources, those items would be visible only to the children of the Grid, and so on. Additionally, resources in a more fine-grained scope can override items in a larger scope. For example, some styles defined in a particular UserControl could override styles declared at the application level. As you can see, WPF provides for some very complex resource scoping needs.

Declaring resources is simple. All you have to do is add the XAML definition of the object you want to store to a ResourceDictionary (usually through the Resources property at the desired scope). Typically, you add a Key to the resource so that it can be referenced elsewhere. Looking back at Listing 14.1, you can see how simple this is to do.

Color

WPF colors can be declared in a variety of ways. It is most common to use hexadecimal notation as we have. This notation always begins with a # and uses two digits each for the alpha, red, green, and blue values. We'll discuss colors in greater detail in Hour 19, "Colors and Brushes."

Combining Resources

One powerful aspect of resources is that they can be combined to create new resources. This composability enables developers to factor their XAML so that they can reduce duplication and enable easier maintenance. Let's use our colors to create a set of *brushes* for the Contact Manager now:

1. Open App.xaml for editing.

2. Just below the previously defined Color resources, add the following XAML:

```
<SolidColorBrush x:Key="lightBlueBrush"
                 Color="{StaticResource lightBlueColor}" />
<SolidColorBrush x:Key="darkBlueBrush"
                 Color="{StaticResource darkBlueColor}" />
<SolidColorBrush x:Key="redBrush"
                 Color="{StaticResource redColor}" />
<SolidColorBrush x:Key="greenBrush"
                 Color="{StaticResource greenColor}" />
<SolidColorBrush x:Key="brownBrush"
                 Color="{StaticResource brownColor}" />
```

Colors cannot be applied to most WPF element properties like Background or Foreground. These properties require the use of a Brush. In the preceding XAML we have used our previously defined colors to create several instances of SolidColorBrush. We have done this using the StaticResource markup extension. You will recall from earlier hours that Binding is a markup extension. Binding, along with StaticResource, make up the two most common extensions that you will use in WPF. Using the StaticResource extension allows you to reference a previously defined resource by its Key value. When you reference a resource in this fashion, WPF will start at the local scope and search broader and broader scopes until it finds a resource with the specified key.

Brushes

Interestingly, we have been using brushes for quite some time now. Every time we declared something like Background="Blue" we have been using some built-in default brushes. WPF has all sorts of brushes that you can paint with. The simple SolidColorBrush is only one example of how you can declare your own brushes. We'll discuss this and other options in more detail in Hour 19.

Using Resources in the UI

Now that we have some brushes, we should apply them to our currently plain user interface. Let's start by filling in one of the missing pieces introduced in Hour 12:

1. Open `SearchBar.xaml` located under the `UserControls` folder in the solution.

2. Use the markup in Listing 14.2 for the contents of this file.

3. Open the `SearchBar.xaml.cs` file and use the code in Listing 14.3 to finish off the user control's implementation.

4. Run the application. You should see something similar to Figure 14.1.

LISTING 14.2   SearchBar.xaml

```
<UserControl x:Class="ContactManager.UserControls.SearchBar"
        xmlns="http://schemas.microsoft.com/winfx/2006/xaml/presentation"
        xmlns:x="http://schemas.microsoft.com/winfx/2006/xaml">
    <Border Background="{StaticResource lightBlueBrush}"
        CornerRadius="6"
        Margin="4"
        Padding="4">
        <DockPanel LastChildFill="False">
            <TextBlock DockPanel.Dock="Left"
                    Text="Contact Manager"
                    FontWeight="Bold"
                    Foreground="White"
                    VerticalAlignment="Center"
                    FontSize="22"
                    FontFamily="Trebuchet" />
                <TextBox x:Name="searchText"
                    DockPanel.Dock="Right"
                    Width="150"
                    Background="White"
                    TextChanged="SearchText_Changed" />
                <Label DockPanel.Dock="Right"
                    Content="Search:"
                    FontWeight="Bold"
                    Foreground="White" />
            </DockPanel>
    </Border>
</UserControl>
```

LISTING 14.3   SearchBar.xaml.cs

```
using System.Windows.Controls;
using ContactManager.Presenters;

namespace ContactManager.UserControls
{
    public partial class SearchBar : UserControl
    {
```

LISTING 14.3 Continued

```
public SearchBar()
{
    InitializeComponent();
}

public ApplicationPresenter Presenter
{
    get { return DataContext as ApplicationPresenter; }
}

private void SearchText_Changed(object sender, TextChangedEventArgs e)
{
    Presenter.Search(searchText.Text);
}
    }
}
```

FIGURE 14.1
A Contact Manager with a colorful search bar.

Looking back over the previous two listings, you'll see that nothing is terribly new. The SearchBar.xaml creates the interface, and the SearchBar.xaml.cs wires up the presenter in the fashion discussed in Hour 13. The one interesting point is in the Border's use of the StaticResource lightBlueBrush. Because this Brush is defined at the application's resources, it is available for use here.

Factoring Resource Files

In complex applications, you may have a large amount of application scoped resources. Piling all these resources into the `App.xaml` file can turn into a maintenance issue very quickly. WPF provides a way to split resources into separate files. Let's go ahead and do this with our application:

1. On the `Resources` folder, right-click and select Add, New Item.

2. In the dialog that appears, select Resource Dictionary (WPF) and name the new file **ColorsAndBrushes.xaml**.

3. Remove the defined colors and brushes from `App.xaml` and add them to the new `ColorsAndBrushes.xaml` `ResourceDictionary`.

4. Add the following markup to the `Application.Resources` in `App.xaml`:

```
<ResourceDictionary>
    <ResourceDictionary.MergedDictionaries>
        <ResourceDictionary Source="Resources\ColorsAndBrushes.xaml" />
    </ResourceDictionary.MergedDictionaries>
</ResourceDictionary>
```

5. Run the application and observe that the appearance is the same as previously seen in Figure 14.1.

One very useful feature of resource dictionaries is the capability to merge them to create new dictionaries. In this example, we create a resource for storing only our colors, and we merged this resource into the main application dictionary.

StaticResource Versus DynamicResource

So far, we have referenced all our resources using the `StaticResource` markup extension. You can also use resources with the `DynamicResource` extension. But what is the difference? Simply put, `DynamicResource` allows the resource to change after the point of reference, whereas `StaticResource` does not. This most often applies when you're using system resources. For example, if you wanted to use a color from `SystemColors`, you would use a `DynamicResource`. This allows for the scenario where the user changed the system color theme *while* your application was running. If a `DynamicResource` was used, your application would update its colors on-the-fly whereas they would remain the same with a `StaticResource`. Because of the dynamic nature of the so-named resource, it is more resource intensive and less performant than `StaticResource`. You should prefer to use `StaticResource` and fall back to `DynamicResource` only when you need the special capabilities it offers.

Defining Styles

Almost anything can be added to a resource dictionary, but perhaps the most common items to define there are *styles*. Styles allow a way to declare common property values on any FrameworkElement. If you have a web background, then you will find WPF styles are similar to CSS. The best way to understand their purpose is to see them in action. Let's add some basic styles to our application:

1. Add a new ResourceDictionary to the Resources folder called **DefaultStyles.xaml**.

2. Use the markup in Listing 14.4 to implement the resource dictionary.

3. Open App.xaml and add the following to ResourceDictionary.MergedDictionaries:

   ```
   <ResourceDictionary Source="Resources\DefaultStyles.xaml" />
   ```

4. Run the application and click New Contact. There are some subtle changes in the appearance of various elements as pictured in Figure 14.2.

LISTING 14.4   DefaultStyles.xaml

```
<ResourceDictionary
    xmlns="http://schemas.microsoft.com/winfx/2006/xaml/presentation"
    xmlns:x="http://schemas.microsoft.com/winfx/2006/xaml">
    <Style TargetType="{x:Type Button}">
        <Setter Property="Margin"
                Value="4" />
    </Style>
    <Style TargetType="{x:Type GroupBox}">
        <Setter Property="Margin"
                Value="5" />
        <Setter Property="Padding"
                Value="5" />
        <Setter Property="BorderThickness"
                Value="2" />
    </Style>
    <Style TargetType="{x:Type Label}">
        <Setter Property="FontWeight"
                Value="Bold" />
        <Setter Property="FontSize"
                Value="12" />
        <Setter Property="HorizontalAlignment"
                Value="Right" />
    </Style>
    <Style TargetType="{x:Type TextBox}">
        <Setter Property="FontWeight"
                Value="Normal" />
        <Setter Property="FontSize"
                Value="12" />
        <Setter Property="Margin"
```

LISTING 14.4   Continued

```
                Value="2" />
        </Style>
        <Style TargetType="{x:Type ComboBox}">
            <Setter Property="FontWeight"
                    Value="Normal" />
            <Setter Property="FontSize"
                    Value="12" />
            <Setter Property="Margin"
                    Value="2" />
        </Style>
    </ResourceDictionary>
```

FIGURE 14.2
A meagerly
styled user
interface.

Every `Style` must have a `TargetType` to declare to what it should be applied. Styles are straightforward resources because they are mostly composed of *setters*. By using a `Setter` a developer can declare a reusable property/value pair that can be applied to the `TargetType`. This is done by setting the `Property` attribute to the name of a property on the `TargetType` and the `Value` attribute to the desired value. `Setter` values can be simple or complex objects. In light of what we have already discussed, at least one thing about styles should jump out at you. They have no `Key` defined. A `Style` resource is a special case because its key can be implicitly based on its `TargetType` value. This allows WPF to automatically apply styles to elements whose type matches the `TargetType` property within the given scope. For example, because these styles are defined at the application level, every `Button` in the entire application will have its `Margin` property set to 4.

Although Styles can be implicitly keyed from their `TargetType`, they can also be explicitly keyed like a standard resource. Let's add some explicit styles to our application:

1. Open `DefaultStyles.xaml`.

2. Add the following markup to the resource dictionary below the previously defined styles:

```xml
<Style x:Key="openButton"
       TargetType="{x:Type Button}">
    <Setter Property="Content"
            Value="+" />
    <Setter Property="Background"
            Value="Transparent" />
    <Setter Property="BorderBrush"
            Value="Transparent" />
    <Setter Property="VerticalAlignment"
            Value="Top" />
    <Setter Property="HorizontalAlignment"
            Value="Right" />
    <Setter Property="Margin"
            Value="0 5 10 0" />
    <Setter Property="Padding"
            Value="0" />
    <Setter Property="FontWeight"
            Value="Bold" />
</Style>
<Style x:Key="buttonPanel"
       TargetType="{x:Type StackPanel}">
    <Setter Property="Orientation"
            Value="Horizontal" />
    <Setter Property="HorizontalAlignment"
            Value="Right" />
    <Setter Property="VerticalAlignment"
            Value="Bottom" />
</Style>
<Style x:Key="header"
       TargetType="{x:Type Border}">
    <Setter Property="Background"
            Value="{StaticResource darkBlueBrush}" />
    <Setter Property="CornerRadius"
            Value="6" />
    <Setter Property="Padding"
            Value="10 5 10 5" />
    <Setter Property="TextBlock.Foreground"
            Value="White" />
```

```
    <Setter Property="TextBlock.FontSize"
           Value="20" />
    <Setter Property="TextBlock.FontWeight"
           Value="Bold" />
</Style>
<Style x:Key="groupBoxHeader"
       TargetType="{x:Type Border}">
    <Setter Property="CornerRadius"
           Value="4" />
    <Setter Property="Padding"
           Value="5 1 5 1" />
    <Setter Property="TextBlock.Foreground"
           Value="White" />
    <Setter Property="TextBlock.FontSize"
           Value="14" />
    <Setter Property="TextBlock.FontWeight"
           Value="Bold" />
</Style>
```

If you run the application, you will notice that nothing changes. Styles defined with a Key, even though they have a `TargetType`, must be assigned on an element before they take effect. In this case, `TargetType` must still be declared so that the XAML parser can ensure that the wrong style is not applied to an incompatible type.

Using Keyed Styles

Keyed styles are used like any other resource. Every `FrameworkElement` has a `Style` property that you can set using the `StaticResource` extension. Let's make a dramatic change to our user interface by extending it and applying our new styles throughout:

1. Open `EditContactView.xaml`.

2. Replace the markup with the extended and stylized XAML found in Listing 14.5.

3. Run the application and click New Contact.

4. Click the Change Picture button to add a photo of the contact. You should see the dramatically altered interface depicted in Figure 14.3.

FIGURE 14.3
A fully realized and styled contact UI.

LISTING 14.5   EditContactView.xaml

```xaml
<UserControl x:Class="ContactManager.Views.EditContactView"
        xmlns="http://schemas.microsoft.com/winfx/2006/xaml/presentation"
        xmlns:x="http://schemas.microsoft.com/winfx/2006/xaml">
    <DockPanel Margin="5">
        <Border DockPanel.Dock="Top"
                Style="{StaticResource header}">
            <DockPanel LastChildFill="False">
                <TextBlock DockPanel.Dock="Left"
                        Text="{Binding Contact.LastName}" />
                <TextBlock DockPanel.Dock="Left"
                        Text=", " />
                <TextBlock DockPanel.Dock="Left"
                        Text="{Binding Contact.FirstName}" />
                <TextBlock DockPanel.Dock="Right"
                        Text="{Binding Contact.Organization}" />
            </DockPanel>
        </Border>

        <StackPanel DockPanel.Dock="Bottom"
                Style="{StaticResource buttonPanel}">
            <Button Content="Save"
                Click="Save_Click" />
            <Button Content="Delete"
                Click="Delete_Click" />
            <Button Content="Close"
                Click="Close_Click" />
        </StackPanel>
```

LISTING 14.5   Continued

```xml
<WrapPanel>
    <GroupBox BorderBrush="{StaticResource lightBlueBrush}">
        <GroupBox.Header>
            <Border Background="{StaticResource lightBlueBrush}"
                    Style="{StaticResource groupBoxHeader}">
                <TextBlock Text="General" />
            </Border>
        </GroupBox.Header>

        <Grid>
            <Grid.ColumnDefinitions>
                <ColumnDefinition Width="100" />
                <ColumnDefinition Width="Auto" />
                <ColumnDefinition Width="175" />
            </Grid.ColumnDefinitions>
            <Grid.RowDefinitions>
                <RowDefinition Height="Auto" />
                <RowDefinition Height="Auto" />
                <RowDefinition Height="Auto" />
                <RowDefinition Height="Auto" />
            </Grid.RowDefinitions>

            <Grid Grid.RowSpan="4">
                <Border Background="Gray"
                        CornerRadius="6"
                        Margin="2 2 0 0"
                        Opacity=".5" />
                <Border Margin="2 2 4 4"
                        Background="White" />
                <Viewbox Margin="2 2 4 4">
                    <Image Source="{Binding Contact.ImagePath}" />
                </Viewbox>
                <Border BorderBrush="{StaticResource lightBlueBrush}"
                        BorderThickness="2"
                        Background="Transparent"
                        CornerRadius="6"
                        Margin="0 0 2 2" />
                <Button Style="{StaticResource openButton}"
                        Background="White"
                        Foreground="{StaticResource lightBlueBrush}"
                        BorderBrush="{StaticResource lightBlueBrush}"
                        ToolTip="Change Picture"
                        Click="SelectImage_Click" />
            </Grid>

            <Label Grid.Column="1"
                    Content="_First Name:"
                    Target="{Binding ElementName=firstName}" />
            <TextBox x:Name="firstName"
                    Grid.Column="2"
                    Text="{Binding Contact.FirstName}" />

            <Label Grid.Row="1"
                    Grid.Column="1"
                    Content="_Last Name:"
                    Target="{Binding ElementName=lastName}" />
```

LISTING 14.5 Continued

```xml
        <TextBox x:Name="lastName"
                Grid.Row="1"
                Grid.Column="2"
                Text="{Binding Contact.LastName}" />

        <Label Grid.Row="2"
                Grid.Column="1"
                Content="Or_ganization:"
                Target="{Binding ElementName=organization}" />
        <TextBox x:Name="organization"
                Grid.Row="2"
                Grid.Column="2"
                Text="{Binding Contact.Organization}" />

        <Label Grid.Row="3"
                Grid.Column="1"
                Content="_Job Title:"
                Target="{Binding ElementName=jobTitle}" />
        <TextBox x:Name="jobTitle"
                Grid.Row="3"
                Grid.Column="2"
                Text="{Binding Contact.JobTitle}" />
    </Grid>
</GroupBox>

<GroupBox BorderBrush="{StaticResource greenBrush}">
    <GroupBox.Header>
        <Border Background="{StaticResource greenBrush}"
                Style="{StaticResource groupBoxHeader}">
            <TextBlock Text="Address" />
        </Border>
    </GroupBox.Header>

    <Grid>
        <Grid.ColumnDefinitions>
            <ColumnDefinition Width="Auto" />
            <ColumnDefinition Width="150" />
            <ColumnDefinition Width="Auto" />
            <ColumnDefinition Width="150" />
        </Grid.ColumnDefinitions>
        <Grid.RowDefinitions>
            <RowDefinition Height="Auto" />
            <RowDefinition Height="Auto" />
            <RowDefinition Height="Auto" />
            <RowDefinition Height="Auto" />
        </Grid.RowDefinitions>

        <Label Content="Line _1:"
                Target="{Binding ElementName=line1}" />
        <TextBox x:Name="line1"
                Grid.Column="1"
                Grid.ColumnSpan="3"
                Text="{Binding Contact.Address.Line1}" />

        <Label Grid.Row="1"
                Content="Line _2:"
```

LISTING 14.5   Continued

```
                    Target="{Binding ElementName=line2}" />
            <TextBox x:Name="line2"
                    Grid.Row="1"
                    Grid.Column="1"
                    Grid.ColumnSpan="3"
                    Text="{Binding Contact.Address.Line2}" />

            <Label Grid.Row="2"
                    Content="Ci_ty:"
                    Target="{Binding ElementName=city}" />
            <TextBox x:Name="city"
                    Grid.Row="2"
                    Grid.Column="1"
                    Text="{Binding Contact.Address.City}" />

            <Label Grid.Row="2"
                    Grid.Column="2"
                    Content="_State:"
                    Target="{Binding ElementName=state}" />
            <ComboBox x:Name="state"
                    Grid.Row="2"
                    Grid.Column="3"
                    SelectedItem="{Binding Contact.Address.State}" />

            <Label Grid.Row="3"
                    Content="_Zip:"
                    Target="{Binding ElementName=zip}" />
            <TextBox x:Name="zip"
                    Grid.Row="3"
                    Grid.Column="1"
                    Text="{Binding Contact.Address.Zip}" />

            <Label Grid.Row="3"
                    Grid.Column="2"
                    Content="Countr_y:"
                    Target="{Binding ElementName=country}" />
            <TextBox x:Name="country"
                    Grid.Row="3"
                    Grid.Column="3"
                    Text="{Binding Contact.Address.Country}" />
        </Grid>
    </GroupBox>

    <GroupBox BorderBrush="{StaticResource redBrush}">
        <GroupBox.Header>
            <Border Background="{StaticResource redBrush}"
                    Style="{StaticResource groupBoxHeader}">
                <TextBlock Text="Phone" />
            </Border>
        </GroupBox.Header>

        <Grid>
            <Grid.ColumnDefinitions>
                <ColumnDefinition Width="Auto" />
                <ColumnDefinition Width="150" />
            </Grid.ColumnDefinitions>
```

LISTING 14.5   Continued

```xml
        <Grid.RowDefinitions>
            <RowDefinition Height="Auto" />
            <RowDefinition Height="Auto" />
            <RowDefinition Height="Auto" />
        </Grid.RowDefinitions>

        <Label Content="_Office:"
               Target="{Binding ElementName=office}" />
        <TextBox x:Name="office"
                 Grid.Column="1"
                 Text="{Binding Contact.OfficePhone}" />

        <Label Grid.Row="1"
               Content="_Cell:"
               Target="{Binding ElementName=cell}" />
        <TextBox  x:Name="cell"
                 Grid.Row="1"
                 Grid.Column="1"
                 Text="{Binding Contact.CellPhone}" />

        <Label Grid.Row="2"
               Content="_Home:"
               Target="{Binding ElementName=home}" />
        <TextBox  x:Name="home"
                 Grid.Row="2"
                 Grid.Column="1"
                 Text="{Binding Contact.HomePhone}" />

    </Grid>
</GroupBox>

<GroupBox BorderBrush="{StaticResource brownBrush}">
    <GroupBox.Header>
        <Border Background="{StaticResource brownBrush}"
                Style="{StaticResource groupBoxHeader}">
            <TextBlock Text="Email" />
        </Border>
    </GroupBox.Header>

    <Grid>
        <Grid.ColumnDefinitions>
            <ColumnDefinition Width="Auto" />
            <ColumnDefinition Width="200" />
        </Grid.ColumnDefinitions>
        <Grid.RowDefinitions>
            <RowDefinition Height="Auto" />
            <RowDefinition Height="Auto" />
        </Grid.RowDefinitions>

        <Label Content="_Primary:"
               Target="{Binding ElementName=primaryEmail}" />
        <TextBox x:Name="primaryEmail"
                 Grid.Column="1"
                 Text="{Binding Contact.PrimaryEmail}" />
```

LISTING 14.5   Continued

```
                      <Label Grid.Row="1"
                             Content="S_econdary:"
                             Target="{Binding ElementName=secondaryEmail}" />
                      <TextBox  x:Name="secondaryEmail"
                                Grid.Row="1"
                                Grid.Column="1"
                                Text="{Binding Contact.SecondaryEmail}" />
                  </Grid>
               </GroupBox>
            </WrapPanel>
         </DockPanel>
      </UserControl>
```

In the previous markup, we have added several additional GroupBox controls to display the rest of the information that our Contact class is tracking. The layouts, controls, and data bindings are all very similar to what we have seen in previous hours. If you take a close look at the markup, you will find many instances where we have set the Style property of an element using a StaticResource. We have referenced our application-wide styles by name, and we could have referenced any number of locally scoped styles just as easily. Applying styles to a UI is that simple.

Did you Know?

> In real applications, user interface markup can get very large due to its complexity. Therefore, it is important to begin recognizing commonalities in appearance as early as possible so that they can be extracted into a Style and located elsewhere. If you notice that you are declaring the same colors, fonts, margins, etc. on elements repeatedly, it's time to implement some styles.

Factoring Styles

Sometimes different styles can have a lot in common. For example, you might want to use the same font appearance on all your buttons *and* labels, but you don't want to declare this over and over. WPF has a simple facility for letting you inherit styles one from another. Take a look at the following markup:

```
<Style x:Key="baseControlStyle"
       TargetType="{x:Type Control}">
   <Setter Property="FontFamily"
           Value="Arial" />
   <Setter Property="FontSize"
           Value="12" />
</Style>
<Style TargetType="{x:Type Button}"
       BasedOn="{StaticResource baseControlStyle}">
   <Setter Property="Margin"
           Value="4" />
```

```
    </Style>
    <Style TargetType="{x:Type Label}"
            BasedOn="{StaticResource baseControlStyle}">
        <Setter Property="HorizontalAlignment"
                Value="Right" />
        <Setter Property="FontWeight"
                Value="Bold" />
    </Style>
```

By using the `BasedOn` property you can reference other styles and effectively enable style inheritance. The basic constraint is that you must determine a compatible base class for all the styles involved. In this case, both `Button` and `Label` inherit from `Control`.

Summary

This hour introduced one of the most powerful WPF features: Styles. With styles there is a new set of possibilities available and a greater ease of development and maintenance of application UIs. Resources are the typical home of styles but they are not limited to storing them alone. Any CLR object with a parameterless constructor can be stored inside a resource dictionary and easily accessed later by key. As you work more with WPF, you will find that combining these features deeply enables rich, dynamic application development.

Q&A

Q. *How do I work with resources in code?*

A. Every `FrameworkElement` has a `Resources` property. This property works like a standard dictionary object, so you can both add and retrieve values from it normally. After you retrieve a resource, you are free to do with it as you please.

Q. *Can styles be manipulated in code?*

A. Yes. Like resources, every `FrameworkElement` has a `Style` property that you can get or set to an instance of a `Style`. `Style` has a collection called `Setters` to which you can add instances of `Setter`. The `Setter` lets you easily define properties and values. Both `Style` and `Setter` have several constructors that make instantiation more convenient.

Workshop

Quiz

1. Briefly describe how resources are located.

2. How are styles applied?

Answers

1. When WPF needs to find a resource, it first examines the Resources of the current element. If the resource with the requested Key is not found, WPF will look at that element's parent's Resources. WPF will follow this pattern until it reaches the root element in the UI. If the resource has not yet been found, it will look at the Application.Resources.

2. Styles can be applied by TargetType or Key. If an element has a specific style declared with a key, that style will override all other styles applied to that element. If no style is explicitly set, WPF will search for a style defined with a matching TargetType and apply it if found within the visible scopes; otherwise, the WPF default style will be used. A developer can always override individual aspects of a style by explicitly setting the properties on an element.

Activities

1. Research "Resources" on MSDN. Investigate some of the deeper implications of using dynamic versus static resources.

2. Review the styles presented in this hour. Determine if there is a way to extract some base styles and make the appropriate changes.

3. Experiment with the application's color theme. Create a new color theme for the application by changing only resource values.

HOUR 15

Digging Deeper into Data Binding

What You'll Learn in This Hour:

- ▶ Sources for data binding
- ▶ Sorting, filter, and converting values
- ▶ Using data templates, and how they differ from styles
- ▶ Understanding collection views

We began our discussion of data binding in Hour 6, "Introducing Data Binding," and even then we saw a lot of what data binding is capable of. In this hour, we further explore this star feature of WPF and see how we can apply it to our Contact Manager application.

Handling Advanced Data Binding Scenarios

You can do a lot with the techniques for data binding that we discussed in Hour 6. However, you will find that you frequently need to format, or convert, the data that you are binding. For example, if you are binding a `DateTime` value to a `TextBlock`, you'll want to control how the date is rendered. Should it render as 5/22/1998 or as May 22nd, 1998?

The situation is even more complicated when you are binding to collections. Suppose that you want to filter a collection that you have bound to a `ListBox`. You don't want to filter the actual underlying collection, just what is rendering in the control. A problem also occurs when you add or remove items from a collection. Most enumerables don't provide any notification to the data bindings when items are added or removed.

Adding the Contact List

Let's extend our Contact Manager to demonstrate how we can handle these problems. We're going to add another view to the application that will present all the contacts in a more traditional grid view. We'll include columns for names, telephone numbers, and email addresses. More important, we're going to format the telephone numbers that are rendered in this view. We'll also examine the code we introduced in Hour 13, "Presenters and Views," for binding the text on tab headers.

1. Open the Contact Manager project in Visual Studio.

2. Right-click the Views folder and select Add, User Control.

   Name this new view **ContactListView.xaml**.

3. Now we can create the associated presenter for this view. Right-click the Presenters folder and select Add, Class.

   Name the presenter **ContactListPresenter.cs**.

4. We'll begin with a basic implementation of the presenter that will support opening and closing the view, but not much else. Modify ContactListPresenter.cs so that it matches the following:

```
public class ContactListPresenter : PresenterBase<ContactListView>
{
    private readonly ApplicationPresenter _applicationPresenter;

    public ContactListPresenter(
        ApplicationPresenter applicationPresenter,
        ContactListView view)
        : base(view, "TabHeader")
    {
        _applicationPresenter = applicationPresenter;
    }

    public string TabHeader
    {
        get { return "All Contacts"; }
    }

    public void Close()
    {
        _applicationPresenter.CloseTab(this);
    }

    public override bool Equals(object obj)
    {
        return obj != null && GetType() == obj.GetType();
    }
}
```

5. All the code we just added is either to satisfy the requirements of the base class or to support the tabbed interface that will host the associated view. Remember that the `ApplicationPresenter` is the coordinator for the entire application, and we use an instance of it to handle closing the tab. The view will need a button to call `Close()` on the presenter. We'll also make the layout of this view similar to `EditContactView.xaml` by docking the Close button at the bottom. Replace the `Grid` element in `ContactListView.xaml` with the following markup:

```
<DockPanel Margin="5">
    <StackPanel DockPanel.Dock="Bottom"
                Style="{StaticResource buttonPanel}">
        <Button Content="Close"
                Click="Close_Click" />
    </StackPanel>
</DockPanel>
```

We also want to remove the `Height` and `Width` attributes from the UserControl so that it will stretch to fill the entire tab.

6. Now add the following handler to the code-behind:

```
public ContactListPresenter Presenter
{
    get { return DataContext as ContactListPresenter; }
}

private void Close_Click(object sender, RoutedEventArgs e)
{
    Presenter.Close();
}
```

You'll also need to add the following using statement at the top of the file:

```
using ContactManager.Presenters;
```

7. Finally, we need a way to access this new view. Open `ApplicationPresenter.cs` and locate the `DisplayAllContacts` method we added in Hour 13, "Presenters and Views." Replace the method with the following code:

```
public void DisplayAllContacts()
{
    View.AddTab(
        new ContactListPresenter(
            this,
            new ContactListView()
            )
        );
}
```

8. Run the application and you'll see that clicking the View All button in the sidebar opens a new view, albeit useless at the moment, and the Close button on the view closes the tab.

Binding Data in Code

In Hour 13, we wrote the following method on the code-behind for `Shell.xaml` that was responsible for adding tabs to the interface.

```
public void AddTab<T>(PresenterBase<T> presenter)
{
    TabItem newTab = null;

    for (int i = 0; i < tabs.Items.Count; i++)
    {
        TabItem existingTab = (TabItem)tabs.Items[i];

        if (existingTab.DataContext.Equals(presenter))
        {
            tabs.Items.Remove(existingTab);
            newTab = existingTab;
            break;
        }
    }

    if (newTab == null)
    {
        newTab = new TabItem();

        Binding headerBinding = new Binding(presenter.TabHeaderPath);
        BindingOperations.SetBinding(
            newTab,
            TabItem.HeaderProperty,
            headerBinding
            );

        newTab.DataContext = presenter;
        newTab.Content = presenter.View;
    }

    tabs.Items.Insert(0, newTab);
    newTab.Focus();
}
```

This method programmatically binds some data to the header on the tab. Let's outline the logic inside this method.

1. We loop through all the currently open tabs.

2. If we discover that the presenter we are trying to add is already open, we remove the tab. We store a reference to it, and we reinsert it again at the end of the method.

3. If we didn't find an existing tab for the presenter (`newTab == null`), we create a new tab for the presenter.

4. When creating a new tab, we create a binder for the header, we set the data context of the tab to the presenter, and then we inject the presenter's view into the tab.

5. We insert the tab at the head of the collection and give it the focus.

The code for binding the tab header is a bit tricky, so let's dig into it further. The `Binding` class is analogous to the `Binding` markup extension. It's an entity in and of itself that represents the relationship between the source and the target of the data binding. The constructor for `Binding` accepts a path to the target. The path tells the binding how to get the target data, starting from the data context of the source. In this code, the path is provided from the presenter.

If we examine the constructor of `ContactListPresenter`, we'll see that we set the value of `TabHeaderPath` to `TabHeader`. In this context, the code

```
Binding headerBinding = new Binding(presenter.TabHeaderPath);
```

is equivalent to the markup extension `{Binding Path=TabHeader}`. All the parameters you find on the markup extension are properties on the `Binding` class.

Keep in mind that we are setting the data context of `newTab` to the presenter. This means that it will look on the instance of `ContactListPresenter` for a property named `TabHeader`. We wrote this property to return the string `All Contacts`.

`BindingOperations` is a utility class used for manipulating bindings. We use the `SetBinding` method to establish the relationship between the tab and the presenter. `SetBinding` takes three parameters. The first is the target of the data binding. The second is the dependency property on the target that we are binding to. (Recall that dependency properties are available as static members on their parent class.) The third parameter is the binding we just created.

In summary, there are three steps to create a functioning data binding:

1. Create an instance of `Binding`.

2. Establish the relationship between the target and the binding with `BindingOperations.SetBinding()`.

3. Set the data context on the target to the source of the data.

Before we move on, let's consider how the tab binding works with `EditContactPresenter`. When we examine its constructor we see that it is setting

TabHeaderPath to Contact.LookupName. Because EditContactPresenter has a property Contact of type Contact, this binds the tab's header to the LookupName property on the presenter's Contact property. Furthermore, Contact implements INotifyPropertyChanged. This means that any updates to the Contact.LookupName are immediately reflected in the tab header.

In practice, you rarely need to manipulate bindings programmatically. However, from time to time you will encounter situations such as this that do require it.

Observing Change in Collections

As we mentioned in Hour 6, for data binding to work, the source of the data must communicate any changes to the binding. The three methods of communication we discussed in Hour 6 are shown in Table 15.1.

TABLE 15.1   Communicating Change with Data Bindings

Name	Description
Dependency properties	WPF controls all make use of the dependency property system. You can use dependency properties in your own classes, but often it will be overkill to do so.
INotifyPropertyChanged	Classes that implement this interface raise an event when one of their properties changes. This is fairly lightweight compared to implementing dependency properties. It is also the notification mechanism we are using for the model classes with the Contact Manager.
Event naming convention	If neither of the preceding methods are used, WPF automatically looks for events that follow a naming convention. The convention is the name of the property with the suffix Changed.

These three approaches are primarily concerned with properties changing on single instances of an object. How do we handle the situation when we are adding or removing items from a collection?

In general we are talking about classes that implement IList or IList<T>. These classes have Add and Remove methods for changing the contents of the collection. The classes that ship with .NET that implement these interfaces don't include a mechanism for change notification. On the whole that's what we want, because change notification is expensive.

WPF includes the INotifyCollectionChanged interface to help us solve the problem. It is the sibling of INotifyPropertyChanged. Even better, WPF includes a default implementation of this interface, a generic class, ObservableCollection<T>.

You probably will never use INotifyCollectionChanged. With the advent of generics, it's pretty rare that we ever need to implement our own collections. ObservableCollection<T> provides all the functionality that you'll generally need.

In Hour 13, we added a field to ApplicationPresenter:

```
private ObservableCollection<Contact> _currentContacts;
```

Then in the constructor, we initialized _currentContacts, like this:

```
_currentContacts = new ObservableCollection<Contact>(
    _contactRepository.FindAll()
    );
```

You can pass in an instance of List<T> into the constructor of ObservableCollection<T>. This is very handy because most of the time we care to use only an ObservableCollection<T> in the presentation layer.

Demonstrating an Observable Collection

Let's get back to the Contact Manager now. First, we'll expose our set of contacts in the ContactListPresenter, and then we'll demonstrate how changes to the collection are reflected in the UI.

1. Open ContactListPresenter.cs.

2. Add the following using statements to the top of the file:

   ```
   using System.Collections.ObjectModel;
   using ContactManager.Model;
   ```

3. Now add the following property:

   ```
   public ObservableCollection<Contact> AllContacts
   {
       get { return _applicationPresenter.CurrentContacts; }
   }
   ```

   All we are doing with this property is exposing the collection so that it is accessible in the view.

4. Open ContactListView.xaml. We're going to display the number of contacts at the top of the view. Add the following markup as the first element inside the DockPanel.

```xml
<Border DockPanel.Dock="Top"
        Style="{StaticResource header}">
    <StackPanel Orientation="Horizontal">
        <TextBlock Text="All Contacts (" />
        <TextBlock Text="{Binding AllContacts.Count}" />
        <TextBlock Text=")" />
    </StackPanel>
</Border>
```

Notice how we are reusing the style header that we defined in Hour 14.

5. Run the application and click the View All button. Our new view will be displayed. Notice the current count, but don't close the tab. Now add and save a new contact. When you switch back to the All Contact tab, you will find that the count has been updated.

Displaying the List View

Now that we have an observable collection of contacts on our presenter, let's modify the view to display them in grid form. We're going to use the ListView control to display them. The ListView is derived from ListBox, but it allows you to provide a "view" for rendering the items. WPF ships with only one view, the GridView. It allows us to display our collection items in a tabular format. We'll discuss ListView further in the next hour.

1. Open ContactListView.xaml.

2. After the StackPanel, add the following markup. It will be the last element in the DockPanel.

```xml
<ListView Margin="5"
          ItemsSource="{Binding AllContacts}">
    <ListView.View>
        <GridView>
            <GridViewColumn Header="Last Name"
                    DisplayMemberBinding="{Binding LastName}" />
            <GridViewColumn Header="First Name"
                    DisplayMemberBinding="{Binding FirstName}" />
            <GridViewColumn Header="Work Phone"
                    DisplayMemberBinding="{Binding OfficePhone}" />
            <GridViewColumn Header="Cell Phone"
                    DisplayMemberBinding="{Binding CellPhone}" />
            <GridViewColumn Header="Email Address"
                    DisplayMemberBinding="{Binding PrimaryEmail}" />
        </GridView>
    </ListView.View>
</ListView>
```

3. Run the application. Make sure you have some contacts, and click the View All button. The application should resemble Figure 15.1.

FIGURE 15.1
Contacts in a
list view.

Data Templates

Data templates are one of the two types of templates used in WPF. They provide a way to describe how data should be visualized in terms of UI elements. This is different from deciding how to render a `DateTime` value, or formatting a telephone number. We'll cover that scenario later this hour.

Data templates are a composition of UI elements. Many controls have properties of type `DataTemplate`. For example, `ItemsControl.ItemTemplate` and `GridView.CellTemplate`.

Data templates are best explained with an example. In our new list view, we would like to include a button on each row for displaying an individual contact.

1. Open `ContactListView.xaml` again, and locate the `GridView` element nested inside the `ListView`.

2. We're going to add a new column to the `GridView`. Add the following as the first element in the `GridView`:

```
<GridViewColumn>
    <GridViewColumn.CellTemplate>
        <DataTemplate>
            <Button Style="{StaticResource openButton}" />
        </DataTemplate>
    </GridViewColumn.CellTemplate>
</GridViewColumn>
```

The new column contains a button, and we are applying a style we defined in Hour 14.

3. If you run the application, you'll see that the first column has a button on each row. However, we haven't wired the buttons to do anything yet. We need to go back to the presenter and implement the behavior we want.

4. Open `ContactListPresenter.cs` and add the following method:

```
public void OpenContact(Contact contact)
{
    _applicationPresenter.OpenContact(contact);
}
```

Again, we are just passing through to the method on the `ApplicationPresenter`.

5. Now we can return to `ContactListView.xaml`. On the `ListView`, add the following attribute:

```
Button.Click="OpenContact_Click"
```

In the code-behind, implement the handler with:

```
private void OpenContact_Click(object sender, RoutedEventArgs e)
{
    Button button = e.OriginalSource as Button;

    if(button != null)
        Presenter.OpenContact(button.DataContext as Contact);
}
```

You'll also need to add a using statement at the top of the file:

```
using ContactManager.Model;
```

6. You can now run the application and open contacts from the list view. It should resemble Figure 15.2.

Notice in step 5 that we cast the `DataContext` of the button to a `Contact` before we pass it to the presenter. The data context for the data template is set for each contact in the collection.

Also, notice how we used the attached property `Button.Click` to wire the handler for all the buttons in the `ListView`. We first discussed this technique in Hour 9, "Getting a Handle on Events."

In the next hour, we'll show you how data templates can be used with much more impressive results.

FIGURE 15.2
The list view using a data template.

By the Way

Sometimes it can get confusing to know which feature of WPF is appropriate in a given scenario. There's some overlap in the things that styles, data templates, and control templates are able to do. To add to the confusion, you can embed styles in your data templates, control templates in your styles, and so on. Here are a few thoughts to help you decide what to use:

Styles are the simplest of the three, so if you are able to achieve what you want using styles, that is the best choice. Keep in mind that styles allow you to set nonvisual properties as well.

Control templates define the UI elements that compose a given control. That's a lot more complicated than merely setting some properties. You should use control templates only when you really need to.

Data templates resemble control templates in that they allow you to compose UI elements. They are often used with list controls to define how items in a list should be rendered.

It's good practice to store all three in your application's resources. This helps reduce noise and makes your markup more readable. Additionally, it is a common practice to set control templates using styles.

Formatting Bound Data

We've mentioned more than once the need to format or convert data when binding it to the UI. When working with data bindings in WPF, you can use a *converter* to transform the data. Converters are used to format data being displayed in the UI, but they can also be used to translate user input into the desired format.

We'll demonstrate this with the telephone numbers we use in the Contact Manager. For example, we would like to consistently display telephone numbers in one of the following formats, depending on the number of digits provided:

▶ ###-####

▶ (###) ###-####

▶ +# (###) ###-####

We'd also like to store the phone numbers in a consistent format. We'll keep it simple and store just the digits.

Converters are classes that implement IValueConverter. The interface has two methods, Convert and ConvertBack. Convert is used when data flows from the source to the target. ConvertBack is used when data flows back to the source (in a two-way binding).

Both methods take four parameters. The first is value, and it is the actual data to be manipulated. The second is the type of the target data. The third is for general use and can be used to parameterize your converter. We'll discuss it later. The fourth is the cultural information about the executing context.

Let's implement a class for handling telephone numbers in the Contact Manager:

1. Right-click the Presenters folder, and add a new class named **PhoneConverter.cs**.

2. Add the using statements:
```
using System.Windows.Data;
using System.Globalization;
```

3. Modify the class declaration:
```
public class PhoneConverter: IValueConverter
```

4. We'll handle the ConvertBack method later; in the meantime we'll just stub it out:
```
public object ConvertBack(object value, Type targetType,
➥object parameter, CultureInfo culture)
{
    return null;
}
```

5. Next, we'll implement the Convert method as follows:

```
public object Convert(object value, Type targetType,
➥object parameter, CultureInfo culture)
{
    string result = value as string;

    if(!string.IsNullOrEmpty(result))
    {
        string filteredResult = string.Empty;

        foreach(char c in result)
        {
            if(Char.IsDigit(c))
                filteredResult += c;
        }

        long theNumber = System.Convert.ToInt64(filteredResult);

        switch (filteredResult.Length)
        {
            case 11:
                result = string.Format("{0:+# (###) ###-####}", theNumber);
                break;
            case 10:
                result = string.Format("{0:(###) ###-####}", theNumber);
                break;
            case 7:
                result = string.Format("{0:###-####}", theNumber);
                break;
        }
    }

    return result;
}
```

Let's review the logic in the Convert method:

- First, we take the incoming data and cast it as a string.

- We filter out all the non-numeric characters and store the result.

- We convert the filtered result into an Int64. This makes it easier to format the number.

- We choose a format based on the number of digits (that is the length of the Int64).

- Finally, we use the powerful String.Format to apply the correct format for the number.

> ## Using Linq
>
> We have not been making use of the new language enhancements included with .NET 3.5. WPF is a lot to learn by itself, although this is a good example of where Linq would fit it.
>
> We filter out the non-numeric characters from the phone number using a `foreach` loop to build up a new string. Here's the exact snippet:
>
> ```
> string filteredResult = string.Empty;
>
> foreach (char c in result)
> {
>     if (Char.IsDigit(c))
>         filteredResult += c;
> }
> ```
>
> We could have accomplished the same thing using Linq:
>
> ```
> var filterQuery = from c in result
>         where Char.IsDigit(c)
>         select c;
>
> string filteredResult = new string(filterQuery.ToArray());
> ```
>
> In both cases, `result` is the incoming, unfiltered phone number, and c is a char. Admittedly, using Linq in this example does not reduce the amount of code. Neither would a newcomer to Linq find this statement more readable. However, when the logic becomes more complex, Linq begins to shine. Additionally, after you are acquainted with the syntax, you will find the Linq version more readable as well.

Hooking Up a Converter

Now we need to wire this converter to the necessary bindings. You may have already noticed that the `Binding` class has a property called `Converter` that accepts `IValueConverter`. We need to assign an instance of `PhoneConverter` to that property.

1. Open `App.xaml`. We're going to create an instance of `PhoneConverter` in the resource dictionary for the application.

2. Because `PhoneConverter` is part of our code, and not part of WPF, we need to create a namespace alias to reference the class. Add the following attribute to the `Application` element:

   ```
   xmlns:Presenters="clr-namespace:ContactManager.Presenters"
   ```

3. Inside the ResourceDictionary element, add the following:

```
<Presenters:PhoneConverter x:Key="phoneConverter" />
```

The complete markup for `App.xaml` is shown in Listing 15.1.

LISTING 15.1   Converter in Application Resources

```
<Application x:Class="ContactManager.App"
             xmlns="http://schemas.microsoft.com/winfx/2006/xaml/presentation"
             xmlns:x="http://schemas.microsoft.com/winfx/2006/xaml"
             xmlns:Presenters="clr-namespace:ContactManager.Presenters"
             StartupUri="Shell.xaml">
    <Application.Resources>

        <ResourceDictionary>
            <ResourceDictionary.MergedDictionaries>
                <ResourceDictionary Source="Resources\ColorsAndBrushes.xaml" />
                <ResourceDictionary Source="Resources\DefaultStyles.xaml" />
            </ResourceDictionary.MergedDictionaries>

            <Presenters:PhoneConverter x:Key="phoneConverter" />

        </ResourceDictionary>

    </Application.Resources>
</Application>
```

4. Open `ContactListView.xaml` and locate the `GridViewColumn` bound to `OfficePhone`. Change the binding to the following:

```
{Binding Path=OfficePhone, Converter={StaticResource phoneConverter}}
```

We had to explicitly provide `Path` because we now have more than one parameter. Additionally, the value for `Converter` is another markup extension, one that pulls the instance of `PhoneConverter` out of the resources. You can embed markup extensions inside other markup extensions.

5. Change the binding for the cell phone column as well:

```
{Binding Path=CellPhone, Converter={StaticResource phoneConverter}}
```

6. Run the application, and make sure that you have some contacts with phone numbers. Open All Contacts and see how the converter works.

Converting Back

Now we need to handle the second half of the converter. Here we are going to convert the user input into the format we really want. The logic we want to use is already present in the `Convert` method. We'll extract it for reuse, and then use it in `ConvertBack`.

1. Open PhoneConverter.cs.

2. Add the following method to the class:

```
private static string FilterNonNumeric(string stringToFilter)
{
    if (string.IsNullOrEmpty(stringToFilter)) return string.Empty;

    string filteredResult = string.Empty;

    foreach (char c in stringToFilter)
    {
        if (Char.IsDigit(c))
            filteredResult += c;
    }

    return filteredResult;
}
```

3. Now we can modify `Convert` to use this new function. The result is this:

```
public object Convert(object value, Type targetType,
➥object parameter, CultureInfo culture)
{
    string result = value as string;

    if (!string.IsNullOrEmpty(result))
    {
        string filteredResult = FilterNonNumeric(result);

        long theNumber = System.Convert.ToInt64(filteredResult);

        switch (filteredResult.Length)
        {
            case 11:
                result = string.Format("{0:+# (###) ###-####}", theNumber);
                break;
            case 10:
```

```
                    result = string.Format("{0:(###) ###-####}", theNumber);
                    break;
                case 7:
                    result = string.Format("{0:###-####}", theNumber);
                    break;
            }
        }

        return result;
    }
```

4. Now, implementing `ConvertBack` is very simple:

```
public object ConvertBack(object value, Type targetType,
↪object parameter, CultureInfo culture)
{
    return FilterNonNumeric(value as string);
}
```

The complete code for `PhoneConverter` is shown in Listing 15.2.

5. To see `ConvertBack` in action, we need to apply the converter someplace where data binding is two-way. Open the `EditContactView.xaml`.

6. Locate the three `TextBox` elements that are bound to the telephone numbers. They are named `office`, `cell`, and `home`. Modify the binding on each to match the following pattern:

```
{Binding Path=Contact.OfficePhone,
↪Converter={StaticResource phoneConverter}}
```

7. Run the application and create a new contact. Enter some telephone numbers without formatting. Notice that the numbers are formatted as soon as the field loses focus.

LISTING 15.2   The PhoneConverter Class

```
using System;
using System.Globalization;
using System.Windows.Data;

namespace ContactManager.Presenters
{
    public class PhoneConverter : IValueConverter
    {
        public object Convert(object value, Type targetType,
        ↪object parameter, CultureInfo culture)
        {
            string result = value as string;

            if (!string.IsNullOrEmpty(result))
            {
```

LISTING 15.2   Continued

```
            string filteredResult = FilterNonNumeric(result);

            long theNumber = System.Convert.ToInt64(filteredResult);

            switch (filteredResult.Length)
            {
                case 11:
                    result = string.Format("{0:+# (###) ###-####}",
                    ➥theNumber);
                    break;
                case 10:
                    result = string.Format("{0:(###) ###-####}", theNumber);
                    break;
                case 7:
                    result = string.Format("{0:###-####}", theNumber);
                    break;
            }
        }

        return result;
    }

    private static string FilterNonNumeric(string stringToFilter)
    {
        if (string.IsNullOrEmpty(stringToFilter)) return string.Empty;

        string filteredResult = string.Empty;

        foreach (char c in stringToFilter)
        {
            if (Char.IsDigit(c))
                filteredResult += c;
        }

        return filteredResult;
    }

    public object ConvertBack(object value, Type targetType,
    ➥ object parameter, CultureInfo culture)
    {
        return FilterNonNumeric(value as string);
    }
  }
}
```

Parameterizing Converters

You can provide additional information to a converter through the
ConverterParameter. Even though we don't need it for the Contact Manager, I'll
provide a brief example. You might have a converter with the following method:

```
public object Convert(object value, Type targetType,
➥object parameter, CultureInfo culture)
{
    string formattedText = parameter as string;
    if (string.IsNullOrEmpty(formattedText)) return value;
    return string.Format(formattedText, value);
}
```

Then in our markup, we could create a binding like

```
{Binding Path=OfficePhone, Converter={StaticResource phoneConverter},
      ➥ConverterParameter='TEL:{0}'}
```

The resulting output would be equivalent to

```
string.Format("TEL:{0}", OfficePhone);
```

That's something of a contrived example, but it should give you the general idea. This is an easy way to make your converters more generic.

Understanding Collection Views

This is a topic that really confused me when I first encountered it. I think it's best to start by considering the problem we need to solve. In our Contact Manager, we have a collection of contacts. Specifically, we are working with an ObservableCollection<Contact> on the ApplicationPresenter. Both the sidebar and the list view bind directly to this collection. Additionally, when we add a contact we are inserting it into this collection. So far, this is what we want because changes produced in one part of the application are immediately reflected in other parts.

Now imagine that we want to filter the contacts on the sidebar, or perhaps sort the contacts in the list view. If we change the collection, it changes everywhere, and that's not what we want. We don't want sorting in the list view to affect the sidebar.

The solution is to use an intermediary object, or a *collection view*. The CollectionView class is part of WPF and acts as a wrapper around the collection we are interested in manipulating. The collection view tracks additional information about the collection, such as sorting, filtering, and grouping currently selected items.

Fortunately, WPF automatically uses a collection view whenever we bind to a collection. This is what enables a ListBox, or any item control, to track what is currently selected. That means we don't have to solve the problem ourselves. The solution is built in to the framework!

WPF uses three types of collection views depending on the underlying collection. Table 15.2 lists the three types.

TABLE 15.2   Types of Collection Views in WPF

Name	Description
CollectionView	The default view for collections that only implement IEnumberable.
ListCollectionView	Used for collections that implement IList.
BindingListCollectionView	For collections implementing IBindingList.

It's important to understand that a collection view does not change the underlying collection. This means that you can have multiple views of the same collection and they don't interfere with one another. Two ListBox controls bound to the same collection track their currently selected items independently.

Collection Views and XAML

To work with collection views in XAML, we have to introduce another class, CollectionViewSource. As the official documentation is careful to point out, a collection view source is not the same thing as a collection view. It's a proxy that allows us to declare a collection view in markup.

CollectionViewSource has a property View that allows you to access the collection view. Also, it has a Source property that you explicitly assign to the collection you are interested in.

Let's use CollectionViewSource in the Contact Manager to keep the contacts sorted by their lookup name in the list view.

1. Open ContactListView.xaml.

2. Add a namespace alias to the UserControl element:

   ```
   xmlns:ComponentModel=
   ➥"clr-namespace:System.ComponentModel;assembly=WindowsBase"
   ```

3. We'll create a resources element for the user control and add the collection view source. Immediately after the opening UserControl tag add the following:

   ```
   <UserControl.Resources>
       <CollectionViewSource x:Key="contactSource"
                         Source="{Binding AllContacts}">
           <CollectionViewSource.SortDescriptions>
               <ComponentModel:SortDescription PropertyName="LookupName" />
   ```

```
        </CollectionViewSource.SortDescriptions>
      </CollectionViewSource>
  </UserControl.Resources>
```

4. Now we need to modify the binding on the ListView to use the new CollectionViewSource, instead of the AllContacts property directly. The new binding on ListView will look like this:

```
{Binding Source={StaticResource contactSource}}
```

5. If you run the application now (assuming you have an adequate number of contacts), you will see that contacts on the list view are sorted.

There is a great deal more that can be said regarding binding lists and how to use collection views—much more than we have room for in this book. An excellent online resource is the blog of Beatriz Costa. Beatriz was part of the data binding test team for WPF, and she has a lot of insight. Her blog can be found at www.beacosta.com/blog/.

By the Way

Summary

We covered a lot of ground in this hour. You should now have a basic understanding of how to create and manipulate bindings in code. We used converters to help us format our telephone numbers; we used data templates to link buttons to contacts; and we demonstrated how we can apply sorting through the use of collection views.

Even so, there's still a lot more that you can do with data binding.

Q&A

Q. *Do the column headers in a* ListView *provide any default functionality—for example, sorting?*

A. No, the ListView, or rather the underlying GridView, does not provide any of the sorting or grouping functionality that you might expect. However, you can easily write code to provide the functionality.

Q. *Why is the data binding for the tab header written in code, instead of being declared in XAML?*

A. The reason that the data binding is handled in code for the tabs is that we don't know at design time which tabs will be open in the interface. To declare a data binding in XAML, we need to be able to make certain assumptions about the interface. Typically, that's not an issue, but it is in this scenario.

Q. *Why did we place the* PhoneConverter *into the application resources? Is there any benefit aside from reducing the amount of markup?*

A. When we declare a PhoneConverter in the resources, it creates a single instance that is used for the entire application. If we were to declare the converter inline, we would be creating a new instance for each binding.

Workshop

Quiz

1. If you are data binding to a DateTime value, and you'd like to display the date as a short date—that is, mm/dd/yyyy—what's the best choice for accomplishing this?

2. If your application requires you to create a custom collection, what would you need to do for that collection to participate in data binding?

Answers

1. You could create a class that implements IValueConverter and formats the date as a short date. Additionally, you could create the class to accept a date format string in the ConverterParameter, and in your binding you could provide the appropriate values for a short date.

2. Your custom collection would need to implement INotifyCollectionChanged and call the corresponding methods when its internal state was modified.

HOUR 16

Visualizing Lists

In many of the previous hours, we have made use of various controls for displaying lists. We have touched them only on a surface level, frequently mentioning that we would cover them in detail at a later time. In this hour we finally dig into this powerful portion of the WPF control hierarchy and explore many of the great possibilities that it enables.

The Control Hierarchy

Take a few minutes to study Figures 16.1 and 16.2. If you look closely, you'll see almost every control we have discussed thus far in the book represented somewhere in one of these two charts. There are a few notable exceptions, but almost every control we have used either inherits from ItemsControl or ContentControl. We know that ContentControl has a Content property that allows it to render almost anything, and we've seen references to ItemsControl throughout the book as it relates to lists. We could state that the primary difference between these two base classes is that ContentControl supports the rendering of a single item, whereas ItemsControl supports the rendering of multiple items.

FIGURE 16.1
The most com-
mon list-related
classes.

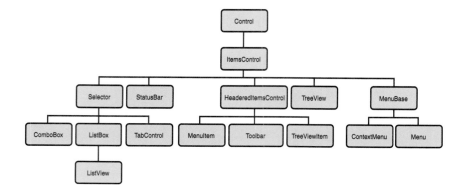

FIGURE 16.2
The most com-
mon content-
related classes.

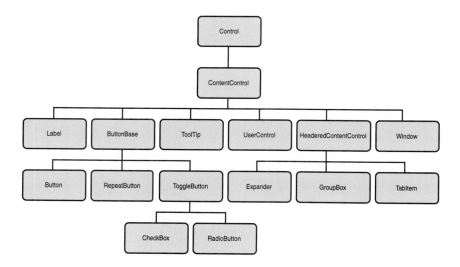

For the remainder of this hour, we look at several important features of all
ItemsControl derivatives. We'll also pay special attention to classes that inherit
from Selector. As we uncover important aspects of these base classes, we'll extend
the Contact Manager with some new features.

Dissecting ItemsControl

Looking back over Figure 16.1 we can see just how many controls there are that are
related to ItemsControl. The good part about this is that everything we discuss here
regarding the base class can be applied to the usage of every derivative.

Items

The first order of business with an ItemsControl is being able to tell it what items should be displayed. This can be accomplished in two ways. The simplest and most intuitive way is to add items to its Items collection by calling the Add method and passing in the item. This can also be done in XAML by declaring multiple child elements. To see an example of where we have used this technique, open Shell.xaml in the Contact Manager. Near the top of the markup you see the definition of a StatusBar. We know from Figure 16.1 that StatusBar is an ItemsControl. In this case, its Items collection is being explicitly populated by three instances of StatusBarItem. In many cases you will want your lists to be data driven. For this second scenario, ItemsControl exposes an ItemsSource property. You can set any IEnumerable collection as the value and the ItemsControl will use this to generate the Items collection. If you open the SideBar.xaml, you will see an example of where we have used data binding to set the ItemsSource collection.

The performance of ItemsControl and some advanced data binding scenarios are influenced by what type of collection you use for the ItemsSource. In general, ObservableCollection is the best in terms of performance and features, followed by List, and ending with plain old IEnumerable.

By the Way

Rendering

Setting up the items for an ItemsControl is pretty straightforward, but understanding how those items get rendered can be a little confusing. In the case of the above-mentioned StatusBar, it's fairly obvious that it renders the StatusBarItem instances. But what about the ItemsControl in SideBar.xaml? It's bound to a list of Contact instances. How does WPF determine how to render these? Following is a list of the steps that ItemsControl goes through to render the instances in its Items collection:

1. If the item inherits from Visual, WPF already knows how to render this type and will treat it normally.

2. If the item does not inherit from Visual (like Contact), the ItemsControl will look for special instructions as detailed in the following:

   ▶ If the DisplayMemberPath property is set, the ItemsControl creates a TextBlock and binds its Text property to the property of the item indicated by DisplayMemberPath.

   ▶ If the ItemTemplate is set to a DataTemplate, the ItemsControl uses
      the template to render each item.

   ▶ If the ItemTemplateSelector is set, WPF executes your custom code
      (a special class inheriting from DataTemplateSelector), expecting you
      to provide it with a DataTemplate based on the particular item in the
      collection.

   ▶ If none of the preceding properties is set, the ItemsControl searches the
      Resources hierarchy looking for a DataTemplate that matches the item
      type. If none is found, the ToString method on the item is called and a
      TextBlock is used to display this value.

3. After the visuals are created for the display of the item, the ItemsControl uses
its ItemContainerGenerator to wrap that visual in an appropriate container.
For example, if you were using a ComboBox, it would wrap the visual in a
ComboBoxItem.

4. The generated container would then be styled according to the following rules:

   ▶ If the ItemContainerStyle is set, the ItemsControl will use it to style
      each container.

   ▶ If the ItemContainerStyleSelector was set, it would execute your cus-
      tom code (a special class inheriting from StyleSelector), expecting
      you to provide it with a Style based on the particular item in the
      collection.

   ▶ If none of the preceding properties is set, the ItemsControl searches the
      Resources hierarchy looking for a Style that matches the container
      type. If one is not found, the default style will be applied.

ItemContainerGenerator

As alluded to previously, every ItemsControl has an ItemContainerGenerator.
This class is responsible for generating appropriate containers for the data-bound
UI. In the case of a ListBox, its generator would create instances of ListBoxItem,
but in the case of ComboBox, the generator would produce instances of
ComboBoxItem. Normally, a developer doesn't need to interact with this directly.
However, occasionally there is a need to determine what container instance is host-
ing a particular piece of data or vice versa. To do this, ItemContainerGenerator
has several methods. We have found the most useful methods to be
ItemFromContainer and ContainerFromItem.

DataTemplateSelector

Sometimes a user interface's portrayal of data needs to be based on complex logic
and can only be determined at runtime. In these cases, rather than setting the
`ItemTemplate` for an `ItemsControl`, you want to use a `DataTemplateSelector`.
To implement your special display logic, you must inherit from this class and override its `SelectTemplate` method. The code should look something like this:

```
public class MyTemplateSelector : DataTemplateSelector
{
    public override DataTemplate SelectTemplate(object item, DependencyObject
    ➥container)
    {
        DataTemplate dataTemplate;

        //custom logic for determining the template

        return dataTemplate;
    }
}
```

The custom selector is generally instantiated in a `Resources` collection so that it can
be referenced elsewhere and so that it can reference other templates stored in the
resources also. At runtime, the `item` parameter of the `SelectTemplate` method
refers to the data that is being displayed by the template, and the `container`
parameter refers to the UI container that is hosting the data (such as a
`ListBoxItem`). Typically, your custom selector implementation exposes properties
for the different templates it needs so that they could be bound to other resources.
The `SelectTemplate` method then programmatically determines which of these
templates to use based on properties of the data item. By tackling the problem this
way, you can still define your templates in XAML (bound using `StaticResource`),
but have your custom selection logic in code.

> There is another way to alter the appearance of templates at runtime without
> resorting to custom code: *Triggers*. Triggers are discussed in Hour 22.

StyleSelector

`StyleSelector` follows the same pattern as `DataTemplateSelector`, except that it
has a `SelectStyle` method. The parameters are the same as `SelectTemplate` in
the previous example, and the techniques used are the same as well.

As you can see, the `ItemsControl` is very flexible and can receive its item rendering
instructions in a variety of ways. The most common scenarios are to either set
`DisplayMemberPath` or to use a `DataTemplate`. In the case of `SideBar.xaml`, the
default `ToString` is used. We'll change this shortly.

Layout

The flexibility of `ItemsControl` is not limited to the rendering of its individual items, but also allows for the customization of their layout. To customize the layout, you set the `ItemsPanel` property to an instance of `ItemsPanelTemplate`. This template describes what type of `Panel` should be used to lay out the items. By default a `VirtualizingStackPanel` is used by most descendants of `ItemsControl`. This is a special type of `StackPanel` that is smart enough to not attempt the rendering of nonvisible elements. You could tell the `ItemsControl` to use a `Grid`, a `Canvas`, or any other `Panel`, though.

Another way in which the layout of an `ItemsControl` can be customized is by setting the `GroupStyle` (or the `GroupStyleSelector`) property. Using a `CollectionViewSource`, you can specify how items should be grouped. The `ItemsControl` understands these groups and will attempt to render them according to the `GroupStyle`.

An immense number of features are packed into this one control. Remember that everything that inherits from `ItemsControl` (everything in Figure 16.1) has these capabilities. Let's apply some of these features specifically in our Contact Manager.

Customizing the SideBar

We are now going to work with the `SideBar.xaml`. Currently it displays a very simple, barely usable list of contacts. We'll spice it up using some of our newfound knowledge. Let's get started working on that now:

1. Open the Contact Manager project in Visual Studio if it is not already open.

2. Open the `SideBar.xaml` file.

3. Replace the current `ItemsControl` markup with what is found in Listing 16.1.

4. Run the application. Create a few contacts and observe the appearance of the sidebar. You should see something similar to Figure 16.3.

LISTING 16.1   An ItemsControl with ItemTemplate

```
<ItemsControl Width="250"
              VerticalAlignment="Stretch"
              BorderThickness="0"
              ItemsSource="{Binding CurrentContacts}">
    <ItemsControl.ItemTemplate>
```

LISTING 16.1   Continued

```xml
<DataTemplate>
    <Grid Margin="2">
        <Border Margin="2 2 0 0"
                CornerRadius="4"
                Background="Gray"
                Opacity=".5" />
        <Border BorderBrush="{StaticResource redBrush}"
                BorderThickness="2"
                CornerRadius="4"
                Background="White"
                Margin="0 0 2 2"
                Padding="3">
            <Grid>
                <Grid.ColumnDefinitions>
                    <ColumnDefinition Width="Auto" />
                    <ColumnDefinition />
                </Grid.ColumnDefinitions>
                <Grid.RowDefinitions>
                    <RowDefinition />
                    <RowDefinition />
                    <RowDefinition />
                </Grid.RowDefinitions>

                <TextBlock Grid.ColumnSpan="2"
                           FontWeight="Bold"
                           Text="{Binding LookupName}" />

                <TextBlock Grid.Row="1"
                           Text="   Office: " />
                <TextBlock Grid.Row="1"
                           Grid.Column="1"
                           Text="{Binding Path=OfficePhone,
                           ➥ Converter={StaticResource
                           ➥ phoneConverter}}"/>

                <TextBlock Grid.Row="2"
                           Text="   Email: " />
                <TextBlock Grid.Row="2"
                           Grid.Column="1"
                           Text="{Binding PrimaryEmail}" />
            </Grid>
        </Border>
        <Button Style="{StaticResource openButton}" />
    </Grid>
</DataTemplate>
    </ItemsControl.ItemTemplate>
</ItemsControl>
```

FIGURE 16.3
A templated
contact list.

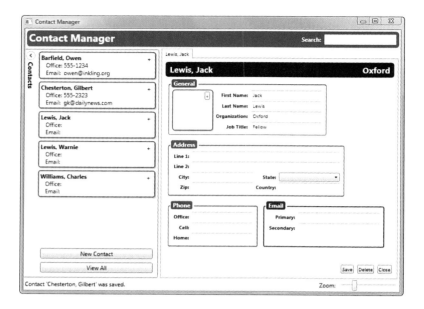

It may not have occurred to you when we first introduced data templates in Hour 15, "Digging Deeper into Data Binding," but you can use any type of element to create your template. In this case we've simulated a "contact card" style. Notice that from within a `DataTemplate` you can make full use of styles and converters (and even other templates). You can even catch events:

1. Add the following attached event declaration to the `ItemsControl`:

   ```
   ButtonBase.Click="OpenContact_Click"
   ```

2. In the `SideBar.xml.cs` add the following event handler:

   ```
   private void OpenContact_Click(object sender, RoutedEventArgs e)
   {
       Button button = e.OriginalSource as Button;

       if (button != null)
           Presenter.OpenContact(button.DataContext as Contact);
   }
   ```

3. Don't forget to add the using statement to the top of the file:

   ```
   using ContactManager.Model;
   ```

4. Run the application. You should now be able to use the plus (+) buttons on each of the contact cards to open the contact.

As you can see, `DataTemplates` used as an `ItemTemplate` behave naturally, bubbling and tunneling events the same as anything else. We're almost finished with the sidebar now. Let's add some sorting to finish things off:

1. At the top of the `UserControl` add the following resources definition:

```
<UserControl.Resources>
    <CollectionViewSource x:Key="contactSource"
                          Source="{Binding CurrentContacts}">
        <CollectionViewSource.SortDescriptions>
            <cm:SortDescription PropertyName="LookupName" />
        </CollectionViewSource.SortDescriptions>
    </CollectionViewSource>
</UserControl.Resources>
```

2. For the `SortDescription` to work, you need to add this Xml Namespace Declaration:

```
xmlns:cm="clr-namespace:System.ComponentModel;assembly=WindowsBase"
```

3. Change the `ItemsControl.ItemsSource` to use our new `CollectionViewSource` with this binding:

```
ItemsSource="{Binding Source={StaticResource contactSource}}"
```

4. Run the application, and you should have a fully interactive and sorted contact list.

As you can see, `ItemsControl` is quite powerful. We could not demonstrate every feature in this example, but we wanted to make you aware of the possibilities. We'll use additional features such as `ItemsPanel` and `GroupStyle` in Hour 17, "Building a Media Viewer," so you'll be ready for it when you see it.

Applying Data Templates

A `DataTemplate` is similar to a `Style` in the way that it can be set. For example, we could have stored the preceding template in `Resources` somewhere and given it an `x:Key`. We could then have set the `ItemTemplate` property using `StaticResource`. Another way in which `DataTemplate` is similar to `Style` is that it has a `DataType` property that functions the same as a style's `TargetType`. So, we could have declared our template with this property `DataType="{x:Type ns:Contact}"` (where ns is a declared namespace) and it would have worked as well. Another important thing to know is that data templates work with `ContentControl` and its inheritors. So you could set the `Content` property to a `Contact`, for example, and the `ContentControl` would search the `Resources` for an appropriate template, too.

Studying Selector

If we look again at Figure 16.1 we see that there is another important base class descended directly from ItemsControl. The Selector class is probably the next most important to understand because its functionality is shared by several very commonly used controls: ComboBox, ListBox, ListView, and TabControl. Selector takes all the functionality of ItemsControl and adds to it the capability to select one or more items. Several important properties come into play at this level. We would like to discuss those properties which we have found the most useful.

To begin with, you can determine which item is selected (or set the selected item) using the SelectedItem property. You can achieve the same effect by working with the SelectedIndex property. This second property represents which element index in the Items collection is selected. Anytime the selection changes, the SelectionChanged event is fired. You can handle this directly or using attached events, as we did with the ComboBox in the Text Editor toolbar from Hour 9. One final property to note is IsSynchronizedWithCurrentItem, which allows you to synchronize the selection across multiple selectors. For example, you might have two ComboBox instances bound to the same collection, and they need to keep their SelectedItem synchronized.

Using Selector

We've been using controls that inherit from Selector since the very beginning. But let's take one more opportunity to examine some XAML and consider it based on our new understanding:

1. Open the EditContactView.xaml file and locate the ComboBox element. You may want to use the Visual Studio shortcut, Ctrl+F, to more quickly find it.

2. Notice that the SelectedItem property, which it inherits from Selector, is data bound to our model.

3. ComboBox also has an ItemsSource property it inherits from ItemsControl that is not yet set, preventing the control from actually displaying any states. To fix this, open App.xaml.

4. We are going to declare a global data source for our state list. Add the following markup to the application Resources collection, inside the ResourceDictionary:

```
<ObjectDataProvider  x:Key="stateNames"
                     MethodName="GetNames"
                     ObjectType="{x:Type Model:States}" />
```

5. You will need to add the following namespace declaration to the XAML
    as well:

    ```
    xmlns:Model="clr-namespace:ContactManager.Model"
    ```

6. Return to the `EditContactView.xaml` and go to the `ComboBox`. Add the
    following attribute to the `ComboBox`:

    ```
    ItemsSource="{Binding Source={StaticResource stateNames}}"
    ```

7. Run the application. You should now be able to select states in the `ComboBox`.

8. Exit the application and return to Visual Studio.

9. Add the following attribute to the `ComboBox`:

    ```
    IsSynchronizedWithCurrentItem="True"
    ```

10. Run the application again. Open several tabs with contacts in them. Change
    the selected `State` in one of the combo boxes.

11. Go to another tab. Notice that the `State` change in one tab has affected
    the other.

12. Exit the application and return to Visual Studio.

13. Remove the `IsSynchronizedWithCurrentItem` attribute because this is not
    the behavior that we want in this situation.

Hopefully this last task helped you to see how each of the base classes contributed
functionality to `ComboBox`. Also, it is important to understand just how the
`IsSynchronizedWithCurrentItem` property works, because using this in some
scenarios can cause surprising and undesirable behavior.

To make the `States` available to our `ComboBox`, we've used a new technique. The
`ObjectDataProvider` is a simple class that lets us point to an `ObjectType` and a
`Method`. At runtime, the provider locates the `ObjectType` and calls the method to
obtain a set of data. By placing this in the application resources, we have made
available a single state list that the entire application can use.

Summary

In this hour we have taken a deep dive into the world of ItemsControl. As one of the most important base classes in WPF, this control provides a great deal of functionality that will affect much of what you build with this technology. This control allows for the rendering of multiple items, allowing for custom templating and stylization of each item in the list. Additionally, ItemsControl can arrange its items using any type of Panel and can perform grouping of items as well. For selectable lists, WPF offers Selector and its descendents, each one meeting a specific UI need and providing a wealth of UI possibilities.

Q&A

Q. *What are some of the other important base classes besides* ContentControl *and* ItemsControl?

A. A couple of other base classes that you should be familiar with are RangeBase and TextBoxBase.

Q. *I can control the layout of items using the* ItemsPanel *property, but if I am using grouping, can I control how the groups are arranged?*

A. Yes. GroupStyle has a number of useful properties. Among them is a Panel property.

Workshop

Quiz

1. Name four ways that a DataTemplate can be applied to the items of an ItemsControl.

2. If you want to have the SelectedItem property kept in sync across multiple selectors, what property must you set?

Answers

1. The DataTemplate could be declared inline using the ItemTemplate property. It could also be declared in a Resources collection and applied either by key or type. Finally, a DataTemplateSelector can be used to apply the template based on advanced runtime conditions.

2. You must set the IsSynchronizedWithCurrentItem to True.

Activities

1. Besides ObjectDataProvider, WPF provides an XmlDataProvider. Spend some time researching this other data source provider.

2. Move the DataTemplate declared in this chapter into a resources collection. Hint: You may have to reorganize some other resources as well.

PART IV

Creating Rich Experiences

HOUR 17

Building a Media Viewer

What You'll Learn in This Hour:

▶ Building a functioning media viewer application
▶ Learning how to play audio and video
▶ Implementing another version of the MVP pattern

With the first three parts of this book behind us, we've uncovered most of what the typical developer needs to be successful with WPF. However, we are not going to stop here, because we have yet to take advantage of several of the most innovative and powerful features in WPF. To really let WPF shine, we are going to build a media-based application. This will send us on a deep dive into the fantastic UI customization that WPF enables through graphics, animations, and control templating, among other things.

Defining the Requirements

For the book's final application, we wanted to do something with a little more pizzazz. We decided that one of best ways to demonstrate the full capabilities of WPF is to bring together several types of media in an attractive and useful presentation. Thus the Media Viewer concept was born. The requirements for this application are simple:

1. Provide users with an attractive menu screen through which they can choose to experience a variety of media types.

2. Allow users to view pictures, listen to music, and watch video.

3. Provide a highly stylized and customized user experience.

4. Leverage all the best practices and techniques that reasonably apply from previous hours.

Setting Up the Solution

We'll begin this hour by setting up a general solution structure like we have on several previous occasions. We'd like to note that the following code is the product of a lot of thought, trial, error, and refactoring. It's less likely that you would start out with the following structure, but more common that this design would emerge over time, as it did in our case. However, the first few steps should be fairly familiar to you by now:

1. Open Visual Studio and create a new WPF Application called **MediaViewer**.

2. Add the following folders to the solution: Model, Presenters, Resources, UserControls, and Views.

3. Change Window1.xaml to **MainWindow.xaml** and make the appropriate changes in the code-behind and in the App.xaml file.

4. Use the following XAML to implement the markup for MainWindow.xaml:

```
<Window x:Class="MediaViewer.MainWindow"
        xmlns="http://schemas.microsoft.com/winfx/2006/xaml/presentation"
        xmlns:x="http://schemas.microsoft.com/winfx/2006/xaml"
        Title="Media Viewer"
        Height="600"
        Width="800"
        Loaded="MainWindow_Loaded">
    <DockPanel>
        <Button DockPanel.Dock="Top"
                Content="Media Player"
                Click="Header_Click"/>
        <ContentControl x:Name="currentView" />
    </DockPanel>
</Window>
```

5. Ensure that the MainWindow.xaml.cs file contains the handlers for the events MainWindow_Loaded and Header_Click as defined in the XAML. One way to do this is to right-click the name of the handler in the XAML and select the Navigate to Event Handler option from the context menu.

6. Add the following code to the MainWindow class in the MainWindow.xaml.cs:

```
public void TransitionTo(object view)
{
    currentView.Content = view;
}
```

7. Add a new class to the Presenters folder called ApplicationController.cs and use the code in Listing 17.1 as the implementation.

8. Now update the code in MainWindow.xaml.cs to match that found in Listing 17.2.

LISTING 17.1 ApplicationController.cs

```
using System;
using System.IO;
using Microsoft.Win32;

namespace MediaViewer.Presenters
{
    public class ApplicationController
    {
        private readonly MainWindow _shell;

        public ApplicationController(MainWindow shell)
        {
            _shell = shell;
        }

        public void ShowMenu()
        {
        }

        public void DisplayInShell(object view)
        {
            GC.Collect();
            GC.WaitForPendingFinalizers();

            _shell.TransitionTo(view);
        }

        public string RequestDirectoryFromUser()
        {
            OpenFileDialog dialog = new OpenFileDialog();

            dialog.InitialDirectory = Environment.GetFolderPath(
                Environment.SpecialFolder.MyDocuments
                );

            dialog.Title = "Please choose a folder.";
            dialog.CheckFileExists = false;
            dialog.FileName = "[Get Folder]";
            dialog.Filter = "Folders|no.files";

            if ((bool)dialog.ShowDialog())
            {
                string path = Path.GetDirectoryName(dialog.FileName);
                if (!string.IsNullOrEmpty(path)) return path;
            }

            return string.Empty;
        }
    }
}
```

LISTING 17.2   MainWindow.xaml.cs

```
using System.Windows;
using MediaViewer.Presenters;

namespace MediaViewer
{
    public partial class MainWindow : Window
    {
        public MainWindow()
        {
            InitializeComponent();
            DataContext = new ApplicationController(this);
        }

        public ApplicationController Controller
        {
            get { return (ApplicationController)DataContext; }
        }

        public void TransitionTo(object view)
        {
            currentView.Content = view;
        }

        private void MainWindow_Loaded(object sender, RoutedEventArgs e)
        {
            Controller.ShowMenu();
        }

        private void Header_Click(object sender, RoutedEventArgs e)
        {
            Controller.ShowMenu();
        }
    }
}
```

The design we have chosen for the main window is quite simple: a Button and a ContentControl. Recall from earlier chapters that ContentControl is the base class for many other WPF controls. It defines a simple, yet handy, property called Content. In our MainWindow layout, we are using the ContentControl as a place-holder for views that will be switched in and out by our application. You can see how this works by looking at the code for the TransitionTo method in the code-behind. Note that both event handlers in the code-behind delegate responsibility to the ShowMenu method on the ApplicationController, which itself is instantiated in the MainWindow constructor. This allows the menu screen to be shown at startup as well as anytime the user clicks our button header.

The ApplicationController is one of the most important classes in the application because it enables almost everything else to work. The single instance of this class will be passed around to various presenters (don't forget that we are using an MVP pattern), giving them access to its core functionality. Look at the `DisplayInShell` method. This method enables other presenters to display their view in the main shell. Notice how it does some memory management before asking the view to handle the transition. Because we are going to be dealing with media files, we want to make sure that we clean up after ourselves frequently. The `ApplicationController` will ensure that this happens before a new view is displayed. Also, take a look at the `RequestDirectoryFromUser` method. Sometimes a presenter will need to ask the user for a directory to search for media. We have chosen to expose this functionality through the `ApplicationPresenter` as well. WPF, at present, doesn't offer a standard dialog box for folder selection, so we have demonstrated a simple workaround using the `OpenFileDialog`. The only other unexplained code is the `ShowMenu` method, which is the subject of the next section.

Implementing the Menu Screen

The menu screen is what the users see when they first load the application and what they return to when they choose to experience different types of media. We'll build a simple and intuitive screen for this purpose and prepare the way for the real meat of the application.

1. Begin by adding a new user control to the `Views` folder called `MenuView.xaml`.

2. Use the markup from Listing 17.3 to implement the view. Make sure that the declared event handlers are created in the code-behind.

3. Add a new class to the `Presenters` folder called `MenuPresenter.cs`. Use the code in Listing 17.4 to fill out the implementation.

4. Change the code-behind file `MenuView.xaml.cs` to match Listing 17.5.

5. Change the `ShowMenu` method in the `ApplicationController` to the following:

```
public void ShowMenu()
{
    new MenuPresenter(this);
}
```

6. Run the application. You should see something similar to Figure 17.1.

LISTING 17.3   MenuView.xaml

```xaml
<UserControl x:Class="MediaViewer.Views.MenuView"
             xmlns="http://schemas.microsoft.com/winfx/2006/xaml/presentation"
             xmlns:x="http://schemas.microsoft.com/winfx/2006/xaml">
    <Grid TextBlock.FontSize="72">
        <Grid.ColumnDefinitions>
            <ColumnDefinition />
            <ColumnDefinition />
        </Grid.ColumnDefinitions>
        <Grid.RowDefinitions>
            <RowDefinition />
            <RowDefinition />
        </Grid.RowDefinitions>

        <Button Content="Video"
                Grid.ColumnSpan="2"
                Click="Video_Click" />
        <Button Content="Music"
                Grid.Row="1"
                Click="Music_Click" />
        <Button Content="Pictures"
                Grid.Row="1"
                Grid.Column="1"
                Click="Pictures_Click" />
    </Grid>
</UserControl>
```

LISTING 17.4   MenuPresenter.cs

```csharp
using MediaViewer.Views;

namespace MediaViewer.Presenters
{
    public class MenuPresenter
    {
        private readonly ApplicationController _controller;

        public MenuPresenter(ApplicationController controller)
        {
            _controller = controller;
            _controller.DisplayInShell(new MenuView(this));
        }

        public void DisplayPictures()
        {
        }

        public void ListenToMusic()
        {
        }

        public void WatchVideo()
        {
        }
    }
}
```

LISTING 17.5   MenuView.xaml.cs

```
using System.Windows;
using System.Windows.Controls;
using MediaViewer.Presenters;

namespace MediaViewer.Views
{
    public partial class MenuView : UserControl
    {
        public MenuView(MenuPresenter presenter)
        {
            InitializeComponent();
            DataContext = presenter;
        }

        public MenuPresenter Presenter
        {
            get { return (MenuPresenter) DataContext; }
        }

        private void Video_Click(object sender, RoutedEventArgs e)
        {
            Presenter.WatchVideo();
        }

        private void Music_Click(object sender, RoutedEventArgs e)
        {
            Presenter.ListenToMusic();
        }

        private void Pictures_Click(object sender, RoutedEventArgs e)
        {
            Presenter.DisplayPictures();
        }
    }
}
```

If you were comfortable with the architecture presented when we built the Contact Manager, the previously introduced code should seem quite natural. Again, we are using an MVP pattern to separate our view logic from our presenter logic. Because of this, when events on the MenuView fire, the results of the action are handled by the MenuPresenter. This keeps our classes concise and easy to maintain. The MenuView is a simple interface with three big buttons, allowing users to easily choose the path they are most interested in. The presenter actions for each of these buttons will be filled in later this hour after we have built our model.

FIGURE 17.1
The Media
Viewer menu
screen.

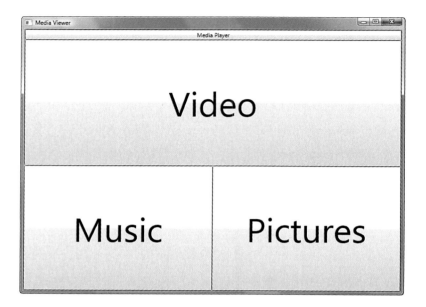

Building the Model

The basic functionality of our application is geared around loading files and rendering them, either to the screen or to the computer audio device. All we need for a model in this case is a thin wrapper around the `FileInfo` class that .NET provides. Displaying images turns out to be a little more complicated in our scenario, however, so we'll derive a special model class for them.

1. Add a new class to the `Model` folder called `Media.cs`. Use the code in Listing 17.6 for the implementation.

2. Add a second class to the `Model` folder with the name `Picture.cs`. Use the code in Listing 17.7 for this class.

LISTING 17.6   Media.cs

```
using System;
using System.ComponentModel;
using System.IO;

namespace MediaViewer.Model
{
    public class Media : INotifyPropertyChanged
    {
        protected FileInfo _fileInfo;
        protected Uri _uri;
```

LISTING 17.6 Continued

```csharp
    public string Name
    {
        get { return Path.GetFileNameWithoutExtension(_fileInfo.Name); }
    }

    public string Directory
    {
        get { return _fileInfo.Directory.Name; }
    }

    public Uri Uri
    {
        get { return _uri; }
    }

    public void SetFile(FileInfo fileInfo)
    {
        _fileInfo = fileInfo;
        _uri = new Uri(_fileInfo.FullName);

        OnPropertyChanged("Name");
        OnPropertyChanged("Directory");
        OnPropertyChanged("Uri");
    }

    public event PropertyChangedEventHandler PropertyChanged;

    protected virtual void OnPropertyChanged(string propertyName)
    {
        if (PropertyChanged != null)
        {
            PropertyChanged(
                this,
                new PropertyChangedEventArgs(propertyName)
                );
        }
    }
  }
}
```

LISTING 17.7 Picture.cs

```csharp
using System;
using System.IO;
using System.Threading;
using System.Windows;
using System.Windows.Media;
using System.Windows.Media.Imaging;
using System.Windows.Threading;

namespace MediaViewer.Model
{
    public class Picture : Media
    {
```

LISTING 17.7   Continued

```
    private ImageSource _thumbnail;

    public ImageSource Thumbnail
    {
        get
        {
            if(_thumbnail == null)
            {
                ThreadPool.QueueUserWorkItem(
                    LoadImage
                    );
            }

            return _thumbnail;
        }
    }

    private void LoadImage(object state)
    {
        byte[] buffer = File.ReadAllBytes(_fileInfo.FullName);
        MemoryStream mem = new MemoryStream(buffer);

        BitmapDecoder decoder = BitmapDecoder.Create(
            mem,
            BitmapCreateOptions.None,
            BitmapCacheOption.None
            );

        _thumbnail = decoder.Frames[0];

        Application.Current.Dispatcher.Invoke(
            DispatcherPriority.Normal,
            (Action)delegate { OnPropertyChanged("Thumbnail"); }
            );
    }
  }
}
```

The Media class is pretty straightforward. It provides change notification and easily data-bindable properties around the values of a FileInfo class, which can be set using the SetFile method. The Picture class is where the interesting code is. As you'll see shortly, loading a large number of pictures into a UI can be a time-consuming operation. We would like our picture view to be able to display thumbnails of the images as each one is loaded, rather than waiting until all images are loaded. To accomplish this, we've built a bit of simple multithreaded code into our model. When the thumbnail is requested, if it is not already loaded, we use ThreadPool. QueueUserWorkItem to load the image on one of the .NET background threads. This is done in the LoadImage method. The process goes like this:

1. Use the `FileInfo` to read in all the bytes of the image.

2. Create a `MemoryStream` from the image bytes.

3. Use the stream to create a `BitmapDecoder` by calling the static `Create` method. This method takes several options that allow a developer to customize how the bitmap is decoded. We have specified not to use any particular options.

4. Set the `_thumbnail` field to the first frame of the decoder.

5. Fire the `PropertyChanged` event on the UI thread.

Most of this code is typical file loading and decoding (very similar to what was presented in Hour 11, "Output.") The important part is the call to `Application.Current.Dispatcher.Invoke`. This method executes the delegate on the UI thread according to the specified `DispatcherPriority`. This is important because WPF is not guaranteed to work properly with events firing on threads other than the UI thread.

The Dispatcher

The `Dispatcher` in WPF is an object with which you can queue work for execution. It prioritizes the work and then executes each item from beginning to end on the UI thread. Multithreading is often used to create a more responsive application by allowing long-running or intense activities to execute on a background thread. If these activities need to update the UI, they should use the `Dispatcher` to do so, as we have in the preceding code. Only the minimum necessary code should be queued with the `Dispatcher` to keep the application from becoming unresponsive. This is an advanced topic, and you will not likely encounter the `Dispatcher` unless you begin writing more multithreaded applications, but be aware of its existence. If you would like to learn more, you should begin with these MSDN resources: http://msdn2.microsoft.com/en-us/library/ms750441.aspx and http://msdn2.microsoft.com/en-us/magazine/cc163328.aspx.

Creating the Picture Screen

With our model built, we can actually proceed to displaying some real media files. Let's begin by creating the screen and associated code for viewing pictures on your computer:

1. To the `Views` folder, add a new user control called `PictureView.xaml`. Use the markup in Listing 17.8 to create the view.

2. Add a new class to the `Presenters` folder named `MediaPresenter.cs`. The code in Listing 17.9 should be used to implement this class.

3. Add the following using statements to `MenuPresenter.cs`:

```
using System;
using System.Windows.Controls;
using MediaViewer.Model;
```

4. Add the following helper method to the `MenuPresenter` class:

```
private void Display<View, MediaType>(
    string mediaPath,
    params string[] extensions
    )
    where View : UserControl, new()
    where MediaType : Media, new()
{
    MediaPresenter<MediaType> presenter =
        new MediaPresenter<MediaType>(mediaPath, extensions);

    View view = new View();
    view.DataContext = presenter;

    _controller.DisplayInShell(view);
}
```

5. Change the `DisplayPictures` method to be as follows:

```
public void DisplayPictures()
{
    string myPicturesPath = Environment.GetFolderPath(
        Environment.SpecialFolder.MyPictures
        );

    Display<PictureView, Picture>(
        myPicturesPath,
        "*.jpg", "*.gif", "*.png", "*.bmp"
        );
}
```

6. Make sure that you have some picture files in your `MyPictures` folder.

7. Run the application. Click the Pictures button on the main menu. You should see something like Figure 17.2.

We've put a cap of 50 on the number of files loaded. This allows us to greatly simplify this sample application by easily preventing issues that could be caused by loading too many pictures into memory. In a real application you would remove this limit and restructure the code to carefully load only visible images and remove them from memory after they go out of view. This technique is called *UI Virtualization* and is beyond the scope of this book.

LISTING 17.8 PictureView.xaml

```xml
<UserControl x:Class="MediaViewer.Views.PictureView"
             xmlns="http://schemas.microsoft.com/winfx/2006/xaml/presentation"
             xmlns:x="http://schemas.microsoft.com/winfx/2006/xaml"
             xmlns:cm="clr-
    ➥namespace:System.ComponentModel;assembly=WindowsBase">
    <UserControl.Resources>
        <CollectionViewSource x:Key="pictureSource"
                              Source="{Binding Media}">
            <CollectionViewSource.SortDescriptions>
                <cm:SortDescription PropertyName="Name" />
            </CollectionViewSource.SortDescriptions>
            <CollectionViewSource.GroupDescriptions>
                <PropertyGroupDescription PropertyName="Directory" />
            </CollectionViewSource.GroupDescriptions>
        </CollectionViewSource>
    </UserControl.Resources>

    <ScrollViewer HorizontalScrollBarVisibility="Disabled"
                  VerticalScrollBarVisibility="Auto">
        <ItemsControl ItemsSource="{Binding
                                    ➥Source={StaticResource pictureSource}}">
            <ItemsControl.ItemsPanel>
                <ItemsPanelTemplate>
                    <WrapPanel />
                </ItemsPanelTemplate>
            </ItemsControl.ItemsPanel>
            <ItemsControl.ItemTemplate>
                <DataTemplate>
                    <Image Source="{Binding Thumbnail}"
                           Width="75"
                           Height="75"
                           Margin="4">
                        <Image.ToolTip>
                            <StackPanel>
                                <Image Source="{Binding Thumbnail}"
                                       Width="400"
                                       Height="400" />
                                <TextBlock Text="{Binding Name}" />
                            </StackPanel>
                        </Image.ToolTip>
                    </Image>
                </DataTemplate>
            </ItemsControl.ItemTemplate>
            <ItemsControl.GroupStyle>
                <GroupStyle>
                    <GroupStyle.ContainerStyle>
                        <Style TargetType="{x:Type GroupItem}">
                            <Setter Property="Margin"
                                    Value="5" />
                        </Style>
                    </GroupStyle.ContainerStyle>
                </GroupStyle>
            </ItemsControl.GroupStyle>
        </ItemsControl>
    </ScrollViewer>
</UserControl>
```

LISTING 17.9   MediaPresenter.cs

```csharp
using System.Collections.ObjectModel;
using System.IO;
using MediaViewer.Model;

namespace MediaViewer.Presenters
{
    public class MediaPresenter<T>
        where T : Media, new()
    {
        private readonly string[] _fileExtensions;
        private readonly string _mediaPath;
        private ObservableCollection<Media> _media;

        public MediaPresenter(string mediaPath, params string[] extensions)
        {
            _mediaPath = mediaPath;
            _fileExtensions = extensions;
        }

        public ObservableCollection<Media> Media
        {
            get
            {
                if(_media == null) LoadMedia();
                return _media;
            }
        }

        private void LoadMedia()
        {
            if(string.IsNullOrEmpty(_mediaPath)) return;

            _media = new ObservableCollection<Media>();
            DirectoryInfo directoryInfo = new DirectoryInfo(_mediaPath);

            foreach(string extension in _fileExtensions)
            {
                FileInfo[] pictureFiles = directoryInfo.GetFiles(
                    extension,
                    SearchOption.AllDirectories
                    );

                foreach(FileInfo fileInfo in pictureFiles)
                {
                    if(_media.Count == 50) break;

                    T media = new T();
                    media.SetFile(fileInfo);
                    _media.Add(media);
                }
            }
        }
    }
}
```

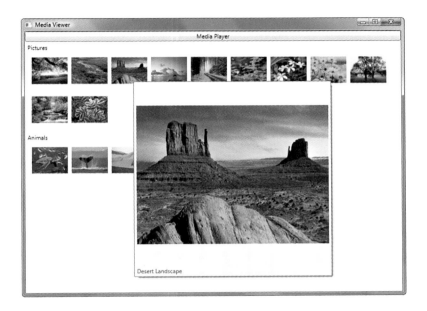

FIGURE 17.2
The Media
Viewer display-
ing pictures.

Looking over the `PictureView.xaml`, we don't see anything we haven't seen in a previous hour. We are simply taking full advantage of `ItemsControl` to provide a custom `ItemsPanel`, `ItemTemplate`, and `GroupStyle` for display of our picture objects. Notice that we are binding to our custom `Thumbnail` property.

The `MediaPresenter` is the interesting part of this section. Its sole job is to use a folder path and set of file extensions to populate an easily bindable `Media` collection with objects. This version of the class came about with much experimentation on our part. We specifically constructed it so that we could generically use it as the presenter for not only `PictureView` but the yet to be discussed `MusicView` and `VideoView`. The generic constraints enable the presenter to create `Media` instances or `Song` instances depending on the need. This is more clearly seen in the changes made to `MenuPresenter`. Out of a desire to reuse as much code as possible, we have created a generic method called `Display`. This method's generic parameters allow us to easily specify what view and media type should be created, and it takes care of instantiating them and hooking up all the necessary pieces. You'll see us take advantage of this when we add code for other media types. But, before we do that, we need to learn more about media playback.

Understanding Media

WPF has powerful media playback capabilities. Most simple tasks can be accomplished through the use of the MediaElement. This single FrameworkElement derivative allows for the full playback and control of the most common types of audio and video today. The MediaElement does not expose a UI for media control, so we will have to build one ourselves. Because we will need this for both audio and video playback, we'll build a user control that we can plug into any view that we need.

1. In the UserControls folder, create a new user control called **MediaPlayer. xaml**.

2. Use the markup in Listing 17.10 and the code in Listing 17.11 to implement the control.

LISTING 17.10   MediaPlayer.xaml

```xaml
<UserControl x:Class="MediaViewer.UserControls.MediaPlayer"
        xmlns="http://schemas.microsoft.com/winfx/2006/xaml/presentation"
        xmlns:x="http://schemas.microsoft.com/winfx/2006/xaml">
    <DockPanel>
        <Grid DockPanel.Dock="Bottom">
            <Grid.ColumnDefinitions>
                <ColumnDefinition Width="*" />
                <ColumnDefinition Width="*" />
                <ColumnDefinition Width="*" />
                <ColumnDefinition Width="*" />
                <ColumnDefinition Width="*" />
                <ColumnDefinition Width="*" />
                <ColumnDefinition Width="*" />
            </Grid.ColumnDefinitions>
            <Button Grid.Column="2"
                    Content="Stop"
                    Click="Stop_Click" />
            <Button Grid.Column="3"
                    Content="Play"
                    Click="Play_Click" />
            <ToggleButton Grid.Column="4"
                        Content="Mute"
                        IsChecked="{Binding ElementName=mediaElement,
                        ➥Path=IsMuted}" />
            <Slider Grid.Column="5"
                    Minimum="0"
                    Maximum="1"
                    Value="{Binding ElementName=mediaElement, Path=Volume}"/>
        </Grid>
        <Slider x:Name="progressSlider"
                DockPanel.Dock="Bottom"
                Minimum="0"
                LargeChange="1000"
                PreviewMouseLeftButtonDown="progressSlider_MouseDown"
                PreviewMouseLeftButtonUp="progressSlider_MouseUp"/>
```

LISTING 17.10   Continued

```xml
        <MediaElement x:Name="mediaElement"
                      DockPanel.Dock="Top"
                      LoadedBehavior="Manual"
                      MediaOpened="mediaElement_MediaOpened"
                      MediaEnded="mediaElement_MediaEnded"/>
    </DockPanel>
</UserControl>
```

LISTING 17.11   MediaPlayer.xaml.cs

```csharp
using System;
using System.Windows;
using System.Windows.Controls;
using System.Windows.Input;
using System.Windows.Media;
using System.Windows.Media.Animation;
using MediaViewer.Model;

namespace MediaViewer.UserControls
{
    public partial class MediaPlayer : UserControl
    {
        public static readonly DependencyProperty MediaProperty =
            DependencyProperty.Register(
                "Media",
                typeof(Media),
                typeof(MediaPlayer));

        private bool _userMovingSlider;

        public MediaPlayer()
        {
            InitializeComponent();
        }

        public Media Media
        {
            get { return GetValue(MediaProperty) as Media; }
            set { SetValue(MediaProperty, value); }
        }

        private void mediaElement_MediaOpened(object sender, RoutedEventArgs e)
        {
            progressSlider.Maximum =
        ➥mediaElement.NaturalDuration.TimeSpan.TotalMilliseconds;
        }

        private void Play_Click(object sender, RoutedEventArgs e)
        {
            MediaClock clock = mediaElement.Clock;

            if(clock != null)
            {
                if(clock.IsPaused) clock.Controller.Resume();
                else clock.Controller.Pause();
            }
```

LISTING 17.11   Continued

```
        else
        {
            if(Media == null) return;

            MediaTimeline timeline = new MediaTimeline(Media.Uri);
            clock = timeline.CreateClock();
            clock.CurrentTimeInvalidated += Clock_CurrentTimeInvalidated;
            mediaElement.Clock = clock;
        }
    }

    private void Stop_Click(object sender, RoutedEventArgs e)
    {
        mediaElement.Clock = null;
    }

    private void mediaElement_MediaEnded(object sender, RoutedEventArgs e)
    {
        mediaElement.Clock = null;
    }

    private void Clock_CurrentTimeInvalidated(object sender, EventArgs e)
    {
        if(mediaElement.Clock == null || _userMovingSlider) return;

        progressSlider.Value =
            mediaElement.Clock.CurrentTime.Value.TotalMilliseconds;
    }

    private void progressSlider_MouseDown(
        object sender,
        MouseButtonEventArgs e)
    {
        _userMovingSlider = true;
    }

    private void progressSlider_MouseUp(object sender,
➥MouseButtonEventArgs e)
    {
        MediaClock clock = mediaElement.Clock;

        if(clock != null)
        {
            TimeSpan offest = TimeSpan.FromMilliseconds(
                progressSlider.Value
                );

            clock.Controller.Seek(
                offest,
                TimeSeekOrigin.BeginTime
                );
        }

        _userMovingSlider = false;
    }
  }
}
```

The `MediaPlayer.xaml` markup contains a typical layout of controls that could control media. We set up element bindings for muting and controlling the volume and added buttons for the standard functions. To more effectively control the `MediaElement`, we wired a number of events that are handled in the code-behind.

The `MediaPlayer.xaml.cs` is where the real magic happens. We begin by creating a custom dependency property so that we will be able to bind to the media, and after that, the events take over. Here is how things work:

▶ When a user clicks play, the event handler checks to see if a media file is already playing. If not, it uses the `Media` to create a `MediaTimeline`. This timeline exposes a clock that can be used to monitor and control the playback of the media. The clock is assigned to the so-named property on the `MediaElement`.

▶ When the `Clock` property changes, the `MediaElement` attempts to load the file. When this is complete, the `MediaOpened` event fires. Our handler for this event makes sure to set the `progressSlider.Maximum` to the length of the media.

▶ As the media begins playing, the `CurrentTimeInvalidated` event on the clock begins firing. The handler for this event updates the position of the `progressSlider` as long as there is a clock (the media is loaded) and the user is not manually dragging the slider.

▶ If the user is dragging the slider, we use its value to `Seek` to the appropriate position in the media. This is done by using the `Controller` property on the clock, which exposes a variety of methods for fine-grained control of media playback.

▶ If the media ends or the stop button is pressed, we remove the `Clock` by setting the property to `null` on the `MediaElement`.

▶ The user can also pause/resume media playback by using the Play button. This works only if there is a valid clock.

Now that we have a reusable media player control, all we have to do is create the video and music views that use it.

Finalizing the Media Player Functionality

All we have left to do is create our final two views and hook them into the overall application navigation:

1. Add a new user control to the Views folder called MusicView.xaml. Use the markup from Listing 17.12 to implement this view.

2. Add another user control to the Views folder and name it VideoView.xaml. Use the markup from Listing 17.13 for it.

3. Open the MenuPresenter.cs and change the ListenToMusic and WatchVideo methods to match the following:

```
public void ListenToMusic()
{
    Display<MusicView, Media>(
        Environment.GetFolderPath(Environment.SpecialFolder.MyMusic),
        "*.wma", "*.mp3"
        );
}

public void WatchVideo()
{
    Display<VideoView, Media>(
        _controller.RequestDirectoryFromUser(),
        "*.wmv"
        );
}
```

4. Run the application. You now have a fully functional media viewer. See Figure 17.3.

Due to some quirks in Visual Studio, adding these user controls and their accompanying code may cause some problems for the design-time view. Don't worry, just compile the code, and the problem should fix itself.

LISTING 17.12   MusicView.xaml

```
<UserControl x:Class="MediaViewer.Views.MusicView"
            xmlns="http://schemas.microsoft.com/winfx/2006/xaml/presentation"
            xmlns:x="http://schemas.microsoft.com/winfx/2006/xaml"
            xmlns:cm="clr-namespace:System.ComponentModel;assembly=WindowsBase"
            xmlns:uc="clr-namespace:MediaViewer.UserControls">
    <UserControl.Resources>
        <CollectionViewSource x:Key="songSource"
                            Source="{Binding Media}">
```

LISTING 17.12   Continued

```
            <CollectionViewSource.SortDescriptions>
                <cm:SortDescription PropertyName="Name" />
            </CollectionViewSource.SortDescriptions>
            <CollectionViewSource.GroupDescriptions>
                <PropertyGroupDescription PropertyName="Directory" />
            </CollectionViewSource.GroupDescriptions>
        </CollectionViewSource>
    </UserControl.Resources>

    <DockPanel>
        <uc:MediaPlayer DockPanel.Dock="Top"
                        Margin="4"
                        Media="{Binding ElementName=songList,
                          ➥Path=SelectedItem}"/>
        <ListBox x:Name="songList"
                 ItemsSource="{Binding Source={StaticResource songSource}}"
                 DisplayMemberPath="Name">
            <ListBox.GroupStyle>
                <GroupStyle>
                    <GroupStyle.ContainerStyle>
                        <Style TargetType="{x:Type GroupItem}">
                            <Setter Property="Margin"
                                    Value="5" />
                        </Style>
                    </GroupStyle.ContainerStyle>
                </GroupStyle>
            </ListBox.GroupStyle>
        </ListBox>
    </DockPanel>
</UserControl>
```

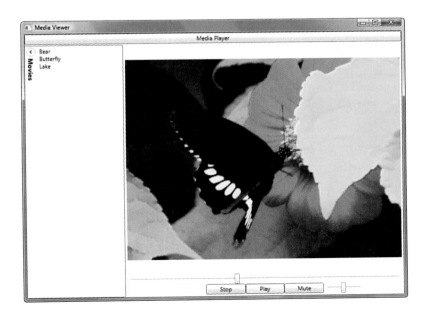

FIGURE 17.3
The Media
Viewer playing a
movie.

LISTING 17.13   VideoView.xaml

```xml
<UserControl x:Class="MediaViewer.Views.VideoView"
             xmlns="http://schemas.microsoft.com/winfx/2006/xaml/presentation"
             xmlns:x="http://schemas.microsoft.com/winfx/2006/xaml"
             xmlns:uc="clr-namespace:MediaViewer.UserControls"
             xmlns:cm="clr-
                 ➥namespace:System.ComponentModel;assembly=WindowsBase">
    <UserControl.Resources>
        <CollectionViewSource x:Key="movieSource"
                              Source="{Binding Media}">
            <CollectionViewSource.SortDescriptions>
                <cm:SortDescription PropertyName="Name" />
            </CollectionViewSource.SortDescriptions>
        </CollectionViewSource>
    </UserControl.Resources>

    <DockPanel>
        <Expander DockPanel.Dock="Left"
                  ExpandDirection="Right"
                  IsExpanded="True"
                  BorderThickness="0 1 1 1"
                  BorderBrush="Gray"
                  Margin="0 2 0 0"
                  Padding="2">
            <Expander.Header>
                <TextBlock Text="Movies"
                           FontSize="14"
                           FontWeight="Bold">
                    <TextBlock.LayoutTransform>
                      <RotateTransform Angle="90" />
                    </TextBlock.LayoutTransform>
                </TextBlock>
            </Expander.Header>
            <ListBox x:Name="movieList"
                     Width="175"
                     BorderThickness="0"
                     ItemsSource="{Binding Source={StaticResource movieSource}}"
                     DisplayMemberPath="Name" />
        </Expander>
        <uc:MediaPlayer Media="{Binding ElementName=movieList,
                            ➥Path=SelectedItem}"
                        Margin="4"/>
    </DockPanel>
</UserControl>
```

There's not much to be said about this XAML. Now that we have our MediaPlayer control built, all we do is plug it into the two views. Each of these views binds to the Media collection on its presenter and displays a list of available media with the SelectedItem bound to the player.

Summary

We've built an entire application this hour. It's designed using an MVP pattern that keeps the classes small and organized so that it will be easy to maintain and extend. Hopefully you are beginning to see the benefits of this approach by now. The views and associated presenters allow for intuitive browsing of photos and playback of common audio and video files. We've even built a reusable media player to simplify the views and help provide a standard user interface for the application. In future hours we'll focus on improving the look and feel of this application with many of WPF's most powerful features.

Q&A

Q. You briefly demonstrated `MediaTimeline` **and** `MediaClock` **for manually controlling media playback. Is there anything else these classes are used for?**

A. Yes. These classes are central to the synchronization of Media and WPF animations.

Q. Where does the `Dispatcher` **come from?**

A. The `Dispatcher` is created by WPF when you start an application. It is strongly tied to the Windows "message pump." You can access the `Dispatcher` from any object that derives from `DispatcherObject`. This is the lowest level class (directly above `object` and below `DependencyObject`) in the WPF class hierarchy.

Workshop

Quiz

1. What is the name of the `FrameworkElement` most commonly used to work with media in WPF?

2. List the common file dialogs that WPF supports.

Answers

1. MediaElement is used to play back a variety of audio and video formats.

2. The common file dialogs that WPF supports include SaveFileDialog, OpenFileDialog, and PrintDialog. WPF does not presently have a common dialog for folder selection, font selection, or print preview.

Activities

1. Use your WPF knowledge and experience up to this point to create a custom folder selection dialog. Change the Media Viewer to use your custom dialog.

2. Research "UI Virtualization." As a parallel to that, you may want to investigate the IScrollInfo interface.

HOUR 18

Drawing with Shapes

What You'll Learn in This Hour:

▶ Using Shapes

▶ Drawing with the Path element

▶ Understanding stroke and fill

▶ Working with complex shapes

Just like the rest of WPF, the API for 2D drawing is both extensive and powerful. Our goal in this hour is to equip you with the basics you need to start working with WPF quickly, as well as providing a foundation for learning if your projects have a need to go deeper.

Drawing Basic Shapes

The WPF has a number of basic shapes built in. The shapes are

▶ Line

▶ Polyline

▶ Polygon

▶ Rectangle

▶ Ellipse

▶ Path

All these classes live in the namespace System.Windows.Shapes.

Lines and Strokes

The best way to understand how these shapes work is to see them in action. Let's create a simple project for the purpose of understanding these classes.

1. Create a new project in Visual Studio called **LearningShapes**.

2. Open Window1.xaml and add the following markup inside the Grid.

   ```
   <Line X1="0" Y1="0" X2="100" Y2="100" Stroke="Red" />
   ```

3. Make sure that you are using the Split Pane view to view Window1.xaml. Visual Studio's live preview will display the XAML without your having to run the application. This makes it very easy for us to play with the various shapes. Figure 18.1 shows what Window1.xaml looks like at this point.

FIGURE 18.1
Previewing a simple line in the IDE.

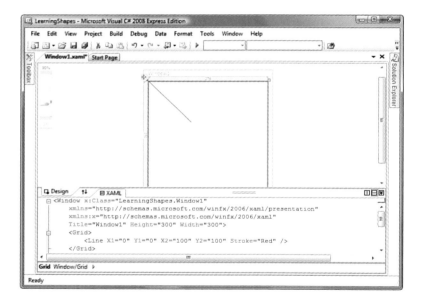

As you can see, Line draws a line between two points. For Line to render something visible, you need to provide at least one of the coordinate pairs and the stroke. The X and Y properties default to zero, so technically we could have omitted X1 and Y1 in the preceding example.

The coordinates are specified with respect to the upper-left corner of the element that contains the line. So when Y1 is 25, it means that the point is 25 pixels from the top. Increasing Y1 would move the point downward. Likewise, increasing X1 would move the point toward the right.

You can provide values for the coordinates that go beyond the bounds of the container. You can even provide negative values if you need to.

The Stroke property tells WPF what color the line should be. (Actually, it's a not a color, but a *brush*. Brushes are a lot more interesting than simple colors. We'll go into that in the next hour.) The Stroke property is common to all the shapes classes.

Let's explore some of the other properties related to the stroke. We'll draw two lines on top of each other for comparison.

1. In Window1.xaml, replace the line with the following markup:

```
<Line X1="20" Y1="20"
      X2="200" Y2="100"
      Stroke="Black"
      StrokeThickness="30" />
```

2. This draws a very thick black line. The StrokeThickness tells WPF how thick the line should be in pixels. Now, we'll draw a brightly colored line on top of it. Add this markup immediately after the previous Line:

```
<Line X1="20" Y1="20"
      X2="200" Y2="100"
      Stroke="Fuchsia"
      StrokeThickness="20"
      StrokeStartLineCap="Round"
      StrokeEndLineCap="Square"
      StrokeDashCap="Triangle"
      StrokeDashArray="1.6 1.3" />
```

3. The resulting lines are shown in Figure 18.2.

We have specified *line caps* for the fuchsia line using the StrokeStartLineCap and StrokeEndLineCap. A line cap tells WPF how to draw the ends of the line. Notice that the upper-left point of the black line is flat, and that the corresponding point on the fuchsia line is rounded. The StrokeStartLineCap defines the cap for the point of the line designated by X1 and Y1. StrokeEndLineCap handles the point designated by X2 and Y2.

The preceding example actually demonstrates all the possible values for line caps and how they are rendered. The default value for a line cap is Flat. Note that all line caps except for Flat extend beyond the endpoint of the line. That's why the ends of the fuchsia line overlap the ends of the black line, even though they are the same length.

FIGURE 18.2
Demonstrating
the stroke-
related
properties.

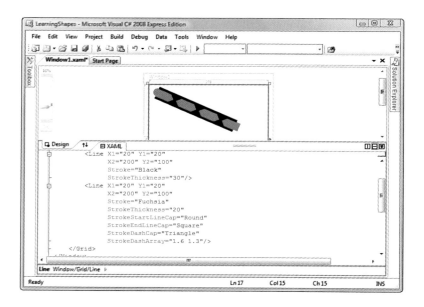

`StrokeDashArray` is a property that allows us to define the dashes and gaps in a line. The values in the array alternate between the length of the dash and the length of the gap. The values are also relative to the thickness of the stroke. So a value of 1.0 means that the length of the corresponding dash or gap is equal to the width of the stroke.

In our example, we are telling WPF to draw a dash that is 1.6 times the width of the stroke followed by a gap 1.3 times the width of the stroke. The array is not limited to two values; you can make something much more complicated if you like.

Listing 18.1 contains markup demonstrating some possible lines. Notice that the common properties of the lines have been moved into the resources.

LISTING 18.1   Several Lines in Window1.xaml

```
<Window x:Class="LearningShapes.Window1"
        xmlns="http://schemas.microsoft.com/winfx/2006/xaml/presentation"
        xmlns:x="http://schemas.microsoft.com/winfx/2006/xaml"
        Title="Window1" Height="300" Width="300">
    <StackPanel>
        <StackPanel.Resources>
            <Style TargetType="{x:Type Line}">
                <Setter Property="Stroke" Value="Black" />
                <Setter Property="StrokeThickness" Value="10" />
                <Setter Property="X2" Value="260" />
                <Setter Property="Margin" Value="10" />
            </Style>
```

LISTING 18.1   Continued

```
      </StackPanel.Resources>

      <Line />
      <Line StrokeDashArray="1 1" />
      <Line StrokeDashArray="0.5 1.5"/>
      <Line StrokeDashArray="1 2 0.1 0.2 0.3 0.4"/>

      <!-- a dotted line-->
      <Line StrokeDashArray="0 1.5"
            StrokeDashCap="Round"/>

      <Line StrokeDashArray="0 1.5"
            StrokeDashCap="Triangle"/>

   </StackPanel>
</Window>
```

Sometimes the preview isn't accurate when displaying the results of your XAML.
Figure 18.3 shows what Listing 18.1 looks like when executed.

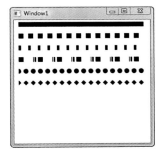

FIGURE 18.3
Examples of
lines with
dashes.

Simple Shapes and Fills

Polyline allows you to draw a line with multiple segments. It has a property,
Points, that is similar to the StrokeDashArray. It takes a series of values that alternate between x and y coordinates. The following XAML snippets are equivalent:

```
<Polyline Points="10 10 200 10" Stroke="Red"/>
<Line X1="10" Y1="10" X2="200" Y2="10" Stroke="Red" />
```

They both draw a red line from 10,10 to 200,10. With Polyline you can continue to
add segments. We could draw a square with the following snippet:

```
<Polyline Points="10,10 200,10 200,210 10,210 10,10" Stroke="Red"/>
```

Notice that in this snippet I have included commas to help group the x and y pairs. The commas are ignored by WPF; occasionally, you will see them used to delimit the pairs themselves, such as in this snippet:

```
<Polyline Points="10 10,200 10,200 210,10 210,10 10" Stroke="Red"/>
```

A Polyline can handle thousands of points. However, it's difficult to manage that many points in XAML. In those cases, you will very likely be adding the points in code.

The Polygon shape is nearly identical to the Polyline. The primary difference is that a Polyline is open and a Polygon is closed. For example, we could create a square with the following snippet:

```
<Polygon Points="10 10 50 10 50 60 10 60" Stroke="Green"/>
```

Notice that our polygon has one less set of x,y values. This is because a Polygon automatically connects the end point with the start point.

In addition to Stroke, all the shapes also have a Fill property. Fill is analogous to the Background property that you have already seen on controls. Let's try drawing a few shapes and adding some fills.

1. Create a new window in your LearningShapes project named Poly.xaml. Replace the Grid with a WrapPanel. Set the Background of the Window to Pink to add some contrast.

2. First, we'll draw a Polyline. Add the following inside the WrapPanel:

```
<Polyline Points="10 10 50 10 50 60 10 60"
          Stroke="Red"
          StrokeThickness="4"
          Fill="Orange"/>
```

Notice that the left side of the square does not contain a stroke.

3. Add a Polygon to the WrapPanel with this markup:

```
<Polygon Points="10 10 50 10 50 60 10 60"
         Fill="Yellow"
         Stroke="Green"
         StrokeThickness="6"
         StrokeLineJoin="Round"/>
```

This Polygon has the same points as the preceding Polyline, but there is a stroke on the left side. We've also added the StrokeLineJoin property. It tells the stroke how to render at the *vertices* or corners of the Polygon. In this case we are rounding the corners. It's hard to notice the effect unless the stroke has some thickness.

4. Our next Polygon demonstrates mitered corners. We need some angles that aren't perpendicular to see this effect.

```
<Polygon Points="10 10, 30 20, 50 10, 50 60, 30 50, 10 60"
         Stroke="Green"
         StrokeThickness="6"
         StrokeLineJoin="Miter"
         StrokeMiterLimit="1"
         Fill="Yellow" />
```

The StrokeMiterLimit determines how much of the corners are cut off. Values less than 1 are meaningless. You can experiment here by changing the property to something like 1.2. StrokeThickness also affects how visible the miter is.

5. A Polygon can intersect itself as well. This next one crosses itself twice:

```
<Polygon Points="10 10, 30 60, 50 10, 50 60, 30 10, 10 60"
         Fill="Yellow" />
```

6. Here's the markup for a star:

```
<Polygon Margin="10 10 0 0"
         Points="25 0, 33 17, 50 19, 38 32, 40 50,
         25 42, 10 50, 12 32, 0 19, 17 17"
     Fill="Yellow" />
```

We included the margin on the star to add some spaces; all our previous shapes are already offset by 10,10. It's also useful to note that our collection of points can span multiple lines. The extra whitespace is ignored.

7. Finally, put the entire WrapPanel element inside of a ViewBox. The complete markup for Poly.xaml is shown in Listing 18.2. Set Poly.xaml to be the StartupUri in App.xaml and run the application. Resize the window and you can get a better look at the behavior of the strokes. Figure 18.4 shows the application.

LISTING 18.2   Polyline, Polygons, and Fills

```
<Window x:Class="LearningShapes.Poly"
        xmlns="http://schemas.microsoft.com/winfx/2006/xaml/presentation"
        xmlns:x="http://schemas.microsoft.com/winfx/2006/xaml"
        Title="Poly" Height="300" Width="300"
        Background="Pink">
    <Viewbox>
        <WrapPanel>
            <Polyline Points="10 10 50 10 50 60 10 60"
                      Stroke="Red"
                      StrokeThickness="4"
                      Fill="Orange"/>
            <Polygon Points="10 10 50 10 50 60 10 60"
```

LISTING 18.2   Continued

```
                        Fill="Yellow"
                        Stroke="Green"
                        StrokeThickness="6"
                        StrokeLineJoin="Round"/>
            <Polygon Points="10 10, 30 20, 50 10, 50 60, 30 50, 10 60"
                        Stroke="Green"
                        StrokeThickness="6"
                        StrokeLineJoin="Miter"
                        StrokeMiterLimit="1"
                        Fill="Yellow" />
            <Polygon Points="10 10, 30 60, 50 10, 50 60, 30 10, 10 60"
                        Fill="Yellow" />
            <Polygon Margin="10 10 0 0"
                        Points="25 0, 33 17, 50 19, 38 32, 40 50,
                        25 42, 10 50, 12 32, 0 19, 17 17"
                        Fill="Yellow" />
        </WrapPanel>
    </Viewbox>
</Window>
```

FIGURE 18.4
The polyline and
polygons.

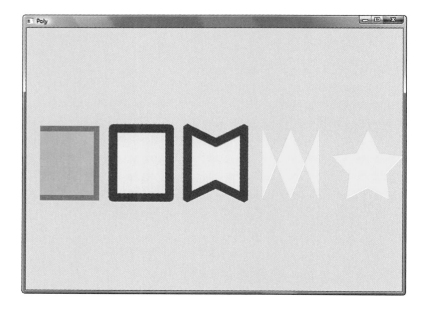

Both Polygon and Polyline have a property called FillRule. FillRule controls which portions of a Polygon or Polyline are filled in. FillRule is meaningful only under certain conditions when you have a complicated shape that intersects with itself multiple times. If the fill of a shape is not what you expect, looking up this property in the documentation is a good place to start.

By the Way

Ellipses and Rectangles

Often you will find that `Line`, `Polyline`, and `Polygon` are overkill. The two classes that you are likely to use frequently are `Ellipse` and `Rectangle`.

They are similar to the shapes we've already encountered. `Fill` and all the stroke properties we discussed are still applicable. However, with both `Ellipse` and `Rectangle` you do not need to specify any points. Instead, you provide the desired `Width` and `Height`. For circles and squares, set `Width` and `Height` to the same value.

By default, `Ellipse` and `Rectangle` are positioned at 0,0 with respect to their parent element. To relocate them you have to use `Margin`. The exception is when they are placed in a `Canvas`. In that case, you use the attached properties `Canvas.Left` and `Canvas.Top`. As it turns out, `Canvas` is the container you'll most commonly place shapes in.

A Header for the Media Viewer

Let's use a few `Ellipse` elements to create a logo for Media Viewer.

1. Open the `MediaViewer` project in Visual Studio.

2. We'll begin by defining a palette that we'll use to theme the application. Add a new resource dictionary under the `Resources` folder named `ColorsAndBrushes.xaml`.

3. Add the following brushes to our new resource dictionary:

```
<SolidColorBrush x:Key="yellowBrush" Color="#FFFFB03B"/>
<SolidColorBrush x:Key="orangeBrush" Color="#FFB64926"/>
<SolidColorBrush x:Key="redBrush" Color="#FF8E2800"/>
```

4. Let's also go ahead and create a resource dictionary for all styles that we will use. Add it under `Resources` and name it `DefaultStyles.xaml`. We'll use both the styles and the brushes applicationwide, so let's merge these dictionaries into the main dictionary for the application. Open `App.xaml`.

5. Inside `Application.Resources` add the following:

```
<ResourceDictionary>
    <ResourceDictionary.MergedDictionaries>
        <ResourceDictionary Source="Resources\ColorsAndBrushes.xaml" />
        <ResourceDictionary Source="Resources\DefaultStyles.xaml" />
    </ResourceDictionary.MergedDictionaries>
</ResourceDictionary>
```

6. Now we are ready to start the real work. Open `MainWindow.xaml`. We're going to add a header to our application. It will contain the Home button that returns to the main menu, the logo and title of the application, and it will be accessible from each of the views in the application.

7. Replace the existing `Button` element with the following:

```
<StackPanel DockPanel.Dock="Top"
            Orientation="Horizontal"
            Margin="0 0 0 8">

    <Button Content="Return to Main Menu"
            Click="Header_Click"/>

    <TextBlock Text="Media Viewer"
               VerticalAlignment="Center" />
</StackPanel>
```

8. Our logo for the application is very simple. It's three overlapping circles of different colors. In between the `Button` and the `TextBlock`, add the following:

```
<Canvas>
    <Ellipse Fill="{StaticResource redBrush}"
             Width="20" Height="20"
             Canvas.Top="5"/>
    <Ellipse Fill="{StaticResource orangeBrush}"
             Width="20" Height="20"
             Canvas.Top="5" Canvas.Left="6"/>
    <Ellipse Fill="{StaticResource yellowBrush}"
             Width="20" Height="20"
             Canvas.Top="5" Canvas.Left="12"/>
</Canvas>
```

Look at the live preview in the design pane and notice that the `TextBlock` is on top of the `Canvas` and that our ellipses extend beyond the bounds of the `StackPanel`. This isn't how we want the header to look. We'd like to have the logo completely inside the `StackPanel`, and we'd like to have the `TextBlock` to the right of the logo. You can see this illustrated in Figure 18.5.

The problem is that the `Canvas` element has no `Width` or `Height`. Unlike other panels, it does not expand to contain its children. They spill outside of its bounds. If we provide a `Width` of 35 and a `Height` of 25, the elements align as we expect.

9. Instead of plain text, let's use a `Polygon` to draw the silhouette of a house inside our home button. We'll remove the `Content` property and add a `Polygon` element. The result will be this:

```
<Button Background="{StaticResource redBrush}"
        Click="Header_Click">
```

```
        <Polygon Fill="{StaticResource yellowBrush}"
                Points="0,10 11,0 22,10 18,10 18,20 4,20 4,10" />
</Button>
```

If you are trying to follow the points, the `Polygon` begins at the left-most edge of the roof.

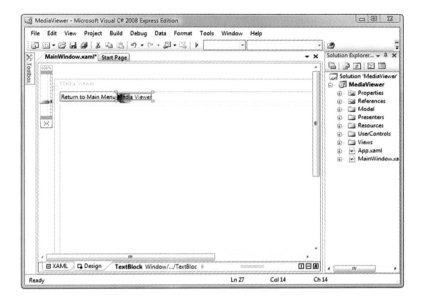

FIGURE 18.5
The logo isn't
quite right.

10. While we are working on the header, let's style the title a bit. First, we'll add a brush for coloring text. We'll add it to `ColorsAndBrushes.xaml`:

```
<SolidColorBrush x:Key="textBrush" Color="#FF000000"/>
```

11. Inside `DefaultStyles.xaml`, we need to add a reference to `ColorAndBrushes.xaml`.

```
<ResourceDictionary.MergedDictionaries>
    <ResourceDictionary Source="ColorsAndBrushes.xaml" />
</ResourceDictionary.MergedDictionaries>
```

12. We'll name the style `title`. Place this in `DefaultStyles.xaml`:

```
<Style x:Key="title" TargetType="{x:Type TextBlock}">
    <Setter Property="FontSize" Value="20" />
    <Setter Property="FontWeight" Value="Bold" />
    <Setter Property="Foreground" Value="{StaticResource textBrush}" />
</Style>
```

13. Return to `MainWindow.xaml`. Locate the `TextBlock` and point the style to `title`.

```
<TextBlock Style="{StaticResource title}"
           Text="Media Viewer"
       VerticalAlignment="Center"/>
```

The application now looks like Figure 18.6.

FIGURE 18.6
The header with a logo and a fancy Home button.

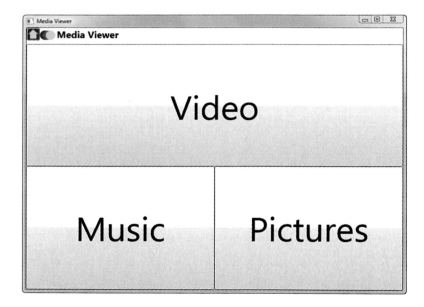

The complete markup for `MainWindow.xaml` is shown in Listing 18.3.

LISTING 18.3   MainWindow.xaml with Some Styling

```
<Window x:Class="MediaViewer.MainWindow"
        xmlns="http://schemas.microsoft.com/winfx/2006/xaml/presentation"
        xmlns:x="http://schemas.microsoft.com/winfx/2006/xaml"
        Title="Media Viewer"
        Height="600"
        Width="800"
        Loaded="MainWindow_Loaded">
    <DockPanel>
        <StackPanel DockPanel.Dock="Top"
                    Orientation="Horizontal"
                    Margin="0 0 0 8">
            <Button Background="{StaticResource redBrush}"
                    Click="Header_Click">
                <Polygon Fill="{StaticResource yellowBrush}"
                         Points="0,10 11,0 22,10 18,10 18,20 4,20 4,10" />
            </Button>
```

LISTING 18.3 Continued

```xml
        <Canvas Width="35" Height="25">
            <Ellipse Fill="{StaticResource redBrush}"
                    Width="20" Height="20"
                    Canvas.Top="5"/>
            <Ellipse Fill="{StaticResource orangeBrush}"
                    Width="20" Height="20"
                    Canvas.Top="5" Canvas.Left="6"/>
            <Ellipse Fill="{StaticResource yellowBrush}"
                    Width="20" Height="20"
                    Canvas.Top="5" Canvas.Left="12"/>
        </Canvas>
        <TextBlock Style="{StaticResource title}"
                Text="Media Viewer"
                VerticalAlignment="Center"/>
    </StackPanel>
    <ContentControl x:Name="currentView" />
    </DockPanel>
</Window>
```

Styling the Media Controls

Let's turn our attention to `MediaPlayer.xaml`. This user control contains the stop, play/pause, and mute buttons used in our application. Ultimately, we want the user control to look like Figure 18.7.

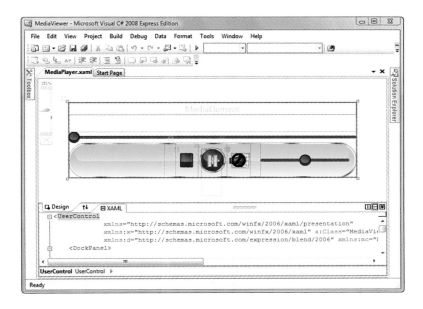

FIGURE 18.7
`MediaPlayer.xaml` after it is completely styled.

To do this, we're going to need to modify the layout somewhat. This brings up an important aspect of WPF applications. We can significantly modify the layout of elements in the application without breaking the application.

1. Open `MediaPlayer.xaml`.

2. Locate the `Grid` element that is just inside the `DockPanel`. Modify the opening tag so that it looks like this:

```
<Grid DockPanel.Dock="Bottom"
      HorizontalAlignment="Center"
      Width="400" Height="50"
      Background="{StaticResource yellowBrush}">
```

3. If you look back at Figure 18.7, you will notice that the control is divided into thirds. The first third is empty, the middle third contains the three buttons, and the final third contains the slider for adjusting the volume. To achieve this, we need to group the three buttons together, as well as reduce the number of columns in our outermost `Grid` to three. After making these changes, our `Grid` now looks like this:

```
<Grid DockPanel.Dock="Bottom"
      HorizontalAlignment="Center"
      Width="400" Height="50"
      Background="{StaticResource yellowBrush}">
    <Grid.ColumnDefinitions>
        <ColumnDefinition Width="*" />
        <ColumnDefinition Width="*" />
        <ColumnDefinition Width="*" />
    </Grid.ColumnDefinitions>
    <Grid Grid.Column="1"
          HorizontalAlignment="Center">
        <Grid.ColumnDefinitions>
            <ColumnDefinition Width="Auto" />
            <ColumnDefinition Width="Auto" />
            <ColumnDefinition Width="Auto" />
        </Grid.ColumnDefinitions>
        <Button Content="Stop"
                Click="Stop_Click" />
        <Button Grid.Column="1"
                Content="Play"
                Click="Play_Click" />
        <ToggleButton Grid.Column="2"
                      Content="Mute"
                      IsChecked="{Binding ElementName=mediaElement,
                                          Path=IsMuted}" />
    </Grid>
    <Slider Grid.Column="2"
            Minimum="0"
            Maximum="1"
            Value="{Binding ElementName=mediaElement, Path=Volume}"/>
</Grid>
```

On both `Grid` elements, we set the `HorizontalAlignment` to `Center` both to center the element in its parent and to make it collapse to the size of its content. To see the difference, remove the alignment on the innermost `Grid`. You'll see in the live preview that it expands to fill all the space in the center column of its parent `Grid`.

We set the `Width` of the column in the outer `Grid` to * because we want them to all be the same size, whereas we set the column in the inner grid to `Auto` so that they will collapse to the size of their content.

4. Now, we'll use a `Rectangle` to make the Stop button look like the traditional Stop buttons on media players. Replace the Stop button with this:

```
<Button Click="Stop_Click">
    <Rectangle Width="18" Height="20"
               Fill="{StaticResource redBrush}"
               RadiusX="1" RadiusY="1"
               Stroke="{StaticResource orangeBrush}"
               StrokeThickness="1"/>
</Button>
```

The `Rectangle` element behaves just like the `Ellipse`. The `Rectangle` includes `RadiusX` and `RadiusY` properties. These allow you to round the corners on a `Rectangle`. They are similar to `CornerRadius` on `Border`, but provide finer-grained control. Try changing their values and observing the change in the preview before we move on. The current value is very subtle.

5. The Play button is a little more complicated. We want the content of the button to change depending on the state of the player. We'll actually implement this when we discuss triggers in Hour 22. In the meantime, we add the content for both play and pause, and we'll just hide the pause content.

The icon for play is a simple triangle that we'll draw with a `Polygon`. For the Pause button, we want two parallel bars. There's actually several ways to achieve this. We'll use two `Rectangle` elements inside a `Canvas` for the time being.

Also, a `Button` can have only one child, so we'll place both of these inside a `Grid`. The new markup for the play button is the following:

```
<Button Grid.Column="1"
        Click="Play_Click">
    <Grid>
        <Polygon Fill="{StaticResource yellowBrush}"
                 Stroke="Gray"
                 Points="0,0 18,10 0,18" />
        <Canvas Visibility="Hidden">
            <Rectangle Height="18"
                       Fill="{StaticResource yellowBrush}"
```

```
                            Stroke="{StaticResource orangeBrush}"
                            Width="6"/>
                <Rectangle Height="18"
                            Fill="{StaticResource yellowBrush}"
                            Stroke="{StaticResource orangeBrush}"
                            Width="6"
                            Canvas.Left="8"/>
            </Canvas>
        </Grid>
    </Button>
```

6. Go ahead and run the application to see how the styling looks.

Paths and Complex Drawings

Even with all the classes we've discussed so far, limitations still exist. For example, we said earlier that we would like the mute button to look like Figure 18.8.

FIGURE 18.8
The mute button after styling.

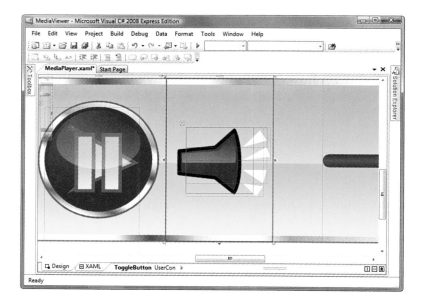

However, we haven't yet discussed a way of drawing a shape that consists of straight lines and curves. In fact, the curves we've seen so far are ellipses.

WPF has a shape class called Path that allows you to define any sort of shape you can imagine. It is a powerful tool, and has many features. We are only going to scratch the surface of what you can do with it.

Path is not as intuitive as the other shapes. It may be easier to think of a Path element as a series of commands telling WPF what to draw. (Yes, that's more imperative than declarative.) You can think of the commands as moving a virtual pen around the display. For example, you might have a set of commands like this:

▶ Move the pen to point A.

▶ Draw a line to point B.

▶ Draw another line to point C.

▶ Draw a curved line to point D.

▶ Close the shape with a line back to point A.

Figure 18.9 helps illustrate this idea. Realize that you are not telling WPF to draw a line from A to B; rather, the pen is already at A, and you are drawing a line to B. That automatically makes B the beginning of the next segment.

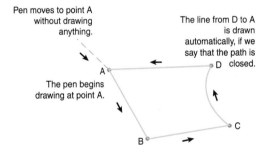

FIGURE 18.9
Moving and drawing with the pen.

Path has Fill and the same stroke properties as the previous shapes. However, it has a property called Data. You can set Data using a PathGeometry element or using a special syntax we'll discuss later in the hour. I'll show you some examples of each, but a thorough coverage of the subject is beyond the scope of this book.

Let's use the PathGeometry element to begin drawing the mute button.

1. Open MediaPlayer.xaml.

2. Locate the ToggleButton that we bound to mediaElement. We're going to remove the Content attribute and place a Canvas inside the ToggleButton. The Canvas will contain a Path drawing the silhouette of a speaker, a second Path that will be the glossy highlight on the speaker, and a series of Polygon elements that will be the sound coming out of the speaker. The resulting markup looks like this:

```
<ToggleButton Grid.Column="2"
              IsChecked="{Binding ElementName=mediaElement,
                                    Path=IsMuted}">
    <Canvas Width="20" Height="20">
        <!-- the speaker -->
        <Path Fill="{StaticResource yellowBrush}"
              Stroke="{StaticResource redBrush}"
              StrokeLineJoin="Round">
            <Path.Data>
                <PathGeometry>
                    <PathFigure StartPoint="12,5"
                                IsClosed="True">
                        <LineSegment Point="0,6" />
                        <PolyLineSegment Points="0,14 12,15 17,20" />
                        <ArcSegment Point="17,0"
                                    Size="30,30"/>
                    </PathFigure>
                </PathGeometry>
            </Path.Data>
        </Path>
        <!-- highlight -->
        <Path Fill="White">
            <Path.Data>
                <PathGeometry>
                    <PathFigure StartPoint="13,6"
                                IsClosed="True">
                        <PolyLineSegment Points="1,7 1,11 17.5,11" />
                        <ArcSegment Point="16.5,2"
                                    Size="30,30"/>
                    </PathFigure>
                </PathGeometry>
            </Path.Data>
        </Path>
        <!-- sound waves -->
        <Polygon Points="20,5 25,0 27,3"
                 Fill="{StaticResource redBrush}" />
        <Polygon Points="20,10 28,9 27,6"
                 Fill="{StaticResource redBrush}" />
        <Polygon Points="20,13 26,17 27,13"
                 Fill="{StaticResource redBrush}" />
        <Polygon Points="20,17 24,21 26,18"
                 Fill="{StaticResource redBrush}" />
    </Canvas>
</ToggleButton>
```

3. The user control should now look like Figure 18.10. Run the application and
take a look at the new mute button.

Let's take a closer look at the Path, in particular the PathGeometry element.

```
<PathGeometry>
    <PathFigure StartPoint="12,5"
                IsClosed="True">
        <LineSegment Point="0,6" />
        <PolyLineSegment Points="0,14 12,15 17,20" />
```

```
        <ArcSegment Point="17,0"
                    Size="30,30"/>

    </PathFigure>
</PathGeometry>
```

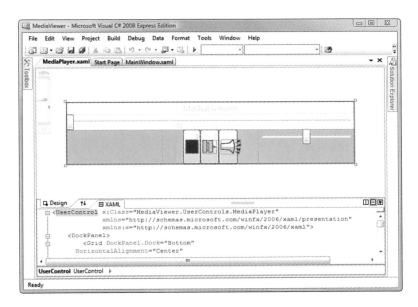

FIGURE 18.10
The
MediaPlayer
user control
so far.

The first child element is PathFigure. A path figure is a single shape within the
path. You are allowed to have multiple figures in the path. For example, if you
wanted two circles in your path that were not touching, you could use two figures
to accomplish this. On the figure we set IsClosed to True; this automatically draws
a line from the last point to the first point. It's the same difference that we found
between a PolyLine and a Polygon. The StartPoint property is the point where we
will begin drawing our figure. This is equivalent to point A in Figure 18.9.

Inside PathFigure, we have a series of segments. The first element, LineSegment,
draws a single straight line from 12,5 to 0,6. That's the top-left line of the speaker.
The second element, PolyLineSegment, draws three lines. The first of the three lines
goes from 0,6 to 0,14. It's the right-most line on the speaker. The remaining two lines
are the bottom of the speaker. We could easily have incorporated the first
LineSegment into the PolyLineSegment, but we left it in for demonstration purposes.

The final segment draws the curved front of the speaker. The Size property indicates
the radii of the ellipse that we are taking the arc from. Because we need a gentle
curve for the face of the speaker, we used a large ellipse.

There are seven types of segments in all.

▶ ArcSegment

▶ BezierSegment

▶ LineSegment

▶ PolyBezierSegment

▶ PolyLineSegment

▶ PolyQuadraticBezierSegment

▶ QuadraticBezierSegment

Covering all these segments is beyond the scope of the book. However, if you are interested in knowing more about computer graphics in general, you should take some time to research these classes as well as the principles underlying them.

ArcSegment has many more features than what we've mentioned here. Take a look at the official documentation if you would like to know more about the class.

One important thing to note about PathFigure and the segment classes is that they are available for data binding and animation. However, that they support these features means that they come with extra overhead. There's a lightweight alternative if you don't need those features.

Stream Geometry

Stream geometry is an alternative to path geometry. It uses a special syntax or mini-language for defining geometries.

If you use a tool such as Expression Blend or Expression Design to draw shapes in XAML, you will discover that most of the output is Path elements. However, these paths do not use figures. Instead, they employ the special mini-language in the Data attribute. For example, the XAML to produce the speaker that we just examined could also be expressed as the following:

```
<Path Fill="{StaticResource yellowBrush}"
      Stroke="{StaticResource redBrush}"
      Data="M12,5 L0,6 0,14 12,15 17,20 A30,30,0,0,0,17,0 z" />
```

This notation is much more concise than the original:

```
<Path Fill="{StaticResource yellowBrush}"
      Stroke="{StaticResource redBrush}"
      StrokeLineJoin="Round">
```

```
    <Path.Data>
        <PathGeometry>
            <PathFigure StartPoint="12,5"
                        IsClosed="True">
                <LineSegment Point="0,6" />
                <PolyLineSegment Points="0,14 12,15 17,20" />
                <ArcSegment Point="17,0"
                            Size="30,30"/>
            </PathFigure>
        </PathGeometry>
    </Path.Data>
</Path>
```

If you look carefully at the Data attribute, you'll notice that it is a combination of letters and points. Just like in other places where we have encountered sets of points, the commas are optional. The points themselves are the same points used in the figure segments.

> M is a command to move to a given point.
>
> L indicates that the following points are line segments.
>
> A uses the following seven points to draw an arc segment.
>
> Z is the command to close the figure.

There are many more commands. Additionally, commands are case sensitive. Uppercase letters work with absolute coordinates, and lowercase letters with relative coordinates. (Relative coordinates are often easier to understand.)

You can use this language to define path geometry as well. It is set to the Figures property on PathGeometry. However, most of the time you encounter it, it will be in the context of stream geometry.

If you are interested in learning more, check the official documentation under the topic of "Path Markup Syntax."

Summary

This hour has been only an introduction to the topic of drawing in WPF. Nevertheless, a lot can be done just with the material we covered in this hour. Additionally, you are now better equipped to dig deeper into the graphics capabilities of WPF.

Q&A

Q. *Why do we have two separate resource dictionaries in this project?*

A. There is not a technical reason for splitting up the resource dictionaries. In fact, we could store all the resources for styling directly in App.xaml. However, it makes it easier to located resources when they are partitioned into separate files. If we used a single dictionary for all the resources, it would be very large by the time we were finished.

Q. *Are there any drawbacks to having multiple resources dictionaries?*

A. Yes, in fact there are. The primary drawback is that WPF has to load the resources in a particular order. This will become more evident as we progress. However, your resources dictionaries usually end up with a chain of dependencies. For example, DefaultStyles.xaml depends on ColorsAndBrushes.xaml.

Q. *How does the topic of shapes and 2D drawing relate to 3D in WPF?*

A. There is not much of a correlation between what we discussed in this hour and using 3D in WPF. However, there is another means of drawing in 2D. Frequently, it uses Geometry classes, whereas the techniques we studied here use the Shape classes. It has a lot of similarities to the way WPF handles 3D. For more information, look up System.Windows.Media.Geometry on MSDN.

Workshop

Quiz

1. What's the difference between a closed path or shape and an open one?

2. What are two common properties on all the Shape classes?

Answers

1. Paths that are closed automatically include a line segment connecting their final point to the start point. Open shapes do not connect the start and end points.

2. There are more than a dozen properties on the base class `System.Windows.`
`Shapes.Shape`. The properties we mentioned in this hour are

▶ `Fill`

▶ `Stroke`

▶ `StrokeDashArray`

▶ `StrokeDashCap`

▶ `StrokeEndLineCap`

▶ `StrokeLineJoin`

▶ `StrokeMiterLimit`

▶ `StrokeStartLineCap`

▶ `StrokeThickness`

Activities

1. Look up "Stream Geometry" on MSDN. Gain a better understanding of when
it is appropriate to use path geometry over stream geometry.

2. Research the topic of Bézier curves. You might also find useful information
under the topic of "splines." Build a WPF application that allows you to
manipulate the points of a Bézier curve.

HOUR 19

Colors and Brushes

What You'll Learn in This Hour:

▶ Defining colors
▶ Defining brushes
▶ Different types of brushes
▶ Using colors and brushes

Colors and brushes are at the core of WPF. You can find them in almost every part of the API. Thus far, we have been glossing over them, allowing you to understand them on a mostly intuitive level. However, we now examine them more fully to take further advantage of WPF's powerful features.

Using Colors

We've been using colors from the very beginning of this book, but we first drew attention to them in Hour 14, "Resources and Styles," when we introduced resources. Here's what we showed:

```
<Color x:Key="lightBlueColor">#FF145E9D</Color>
<Color x:Key="darkBlueColor">#FF022D51</Color>
<Color x:Key="redColor">#FFAA2C27</Color>
<Color x:Key="greenColor">#FF656A03</Color>
<Color x:Key="brownColor">#FF513100</Color>
```

You probably determined from this markup that WPF has an important class called Color. This class is the sole mechanism by which WPF understands what colors to paint your UI. However, WPF gives you a great amount of flexibility as to how you define your colors. The most common method is by using hexadecimal notation:

```
<Color x:Key="someColor">#FF0000FF</Color>
```

If you have a web programming background, this should be very familiar. The first two digits of hexadecimal represent the alpha channel (transparency), the next represent red, then green, and finally blue. This gives us eight bits (a maximum value of 255) for each channel, resulting in a total of thirty-two bits. Hexadecimal colors are always preceded by #. With this information, can you determine what color the preceding notation represents?

▶ The first two digits, FF, represent maximum (255) opacity.

▶ The second two digits, 00, represent zero red.

▶ The third two digits, 00, represent zero green.

▶ The last two digits, FF, represent maximum (255) blue.

This tells us that the color defined is a 100% opaque, pure blue. Most design tools represent color in this fashion, and it is the preferred method for the web, so it is little wonder that this is the way you will define most of your colors in WPF. However, several other methods are available to you. Another popular method is to use ARGB values:

```
<Color A="255" R="0" G="0" B="255" />
```

Here we have defined the exact same color as the previous one, in a slightly more verbose fashion, by explicitly setting the alpha (A), red (R), green (G), and blue (B) values. Here's one final (rarely used) mechanism:

```
<Color ScA="1" ScR="0" ScG="0" ScB="1" />
```

This method uses ScRGB to define colors, which represents each of the channels as a `float` value between 0 and 1.

> Should you find yourself needing to create colors manually in code, the Color class has a number of static factory methods for instantiating Color objects with the different schemes. Additionally, the Colors class defines a set of predefined colors based on the Unix X11 named colors. This is what enables XAML to understand the meaning of the word Blue in this markup: <Color>Blue</Color>.

Choosing Colors

With the technical details of color definition out of the way, developers or designers must now turn their attention to the selection of colors. Choosing a nice color scheme is very important. Making a poor choice can result in a hideous application.

In both the Contact Manager and the Media Viewer, we used Adobe's Kuler utility to help us make our choices. You can find it online at http://kuler.adobe.com/. It features many community designed color themes as well as the capability to modify or create new themes based on established principles of color theory.

It's hard to discuss color without talking a little bit about color theory. Whether you decide to use Kuler or just "wing it," having a basic understanding of these principles can help you to succeed where others have failed. The obvious starting point is *primary colors*. Figure 19.1 shows the most basic of color wheels representing the primary colors yellow, red, and blue. These colors are called *primary* because they cannot be formed from mixing any other colors. In fact, all other colors can be formed by mixing them in varying degrees.

FIGURE 19.1
The primary colors.

If you mix each of the primary colors with one other primary color in equal amounts, you will create the *secondary colors* shown in Figure 19.2. This adds the colors orange, purple, and green to our palette.

FIGURE 19.2
The secondary colors.

Finally, if you mix each of the secondary colors with a primary color, you create the *tertiary colors*, shown in Figure 19.3. These colors are named by combining the primary and secondary color name. This gives us the colors yellow-orange, red-orange, red-purple, blue-purple, blue-green and yellow-green.

FIGURE 19.3
The tertiary colors.

After you understand the basic concepts of the color wheel, you need to know how to select colors for your application. You may have heard the term *complementary colors*, which refers to colors that are directly across from each other on the color wheel, or *analogous colors*, which are right next to each other. In general, complementary colors create a strong contrast, whereas analogous colors tend to be more visually bland or mellow. You'll want to experiment with colors that are similar or different in varying degrees until you can find a harmonious palette. Kuler is an application that we have found makes it easy to do this, by easily applying various color "rules" and adjusting until you have a satisfying product.

Introducing Brushes

WPF rarely makes use of colors outright. Most of the time a Brush is used for drawing. Brushes are far more flexible than simple colors because they allow you to combine various colors and other visual effects in a variety of ways. Like colors, we've been using them from the beginning of the book—albeit in a very simplistic way. Let's dive into our media application and learn how to make more use of this core drawing element:

1. Open the Media Viewer in Visual Studio.

2. Open the ColorsAndBrushes.xaml file for editing.

3. Replace the existing resources with the following:

```
<Color x:Key="yellowColor" A="255" R="255" G="176" B="59" />
<Color x:Key="orangeColor" A="255" R="182" G="73" B="38" />
<Color x:Key="redColor" A="255" R="142" G="40" B="0" />
<Color x:Key="textColor" A="255" R="255" G="255" B="255" />
<Color x:Key="bgColor" A="255" R="0" G="0" B="0" />
<Color x:Key="paleColor" A="255" R="255" G="240" B="165" />

<SolidColorBrush x:Key="yellowBrush" Color="{StaticResource yellowColor}"/>
<SolidColorBrush x:Key="orangeBrush" Color="{StaticResource orangeColor}"/>
<SolidColorBrush x:Key="redBrush" Color="{StaticResource redColor}" />
<SolidColorBrush x:Key="textBrush" Color="{StaticResource textColor}"/>
<SolidColorBrush x:Key="bgBrush" Color="{StaticResource bgColor}" />
<SolidColorBrush x:Key="paleBrush" Color="{StaticResource paleColor}"/>
<SolidColorBrush x:Key="glossOutline" Color="#99FFFFFF" />
<SolidColorBrush x:Key="chromeOutline" Color="#FF808080"/>
<SolidColorBrush x:Key="controlOutline" Color="#FF333333" />
```

4. Open the MainWindow.xaml and change the Background property of the Window element to be as follows:

```
Background="{StaticResource bgBrush}"
```

5. Run the application.

What we've accomplished here is pretty simple. Previously we had a series of SolidColorBrushes, all hard-coded with the color details. Using our new knowledge of colors, we have more efficiently factored out several of the colors so that it will be easier for us to reuse them later. We've also gone ahead and defined a few additional colors and brushes that we will use later.

SolidColorBrush

As previously stated, most WPF APIs make use of brushes. The Brush base class has several inheritors, the simplest of which is SolidColorBrush. A SolidColorBrush paints its designated area with a single color, defined by its Color property. That's all there is to it.

> There is a Brushes class that has static SolidColorBrushes for each of the Unix X11 named colors in Colors. This is what we have been using through most of the book. When you see markup like <Button Background="Blue"/> WPF is using the statically defined, named brush on the Brushes class.

By the Way

Leveraging LinearGradientBrush

Using solid colors everywhere can make an application look boring and sometimes unprofessional. In many cases, just the slightest color gradient can make a world of difference. The most common brush used for this purpose is LinearGradientBrush. Let's see how to use it:

1. Open ColorsAndBrushes.xaml and add the following brush definition to the bottom of the resources:

```
<LinearGradientBrush x:Key="yellowGradient"
                     StartPoint="0.5,0"
                     EndPoint="0.5,1">
    <GradientStop Color="{StaticResource yellowColor}"
                  Offset="0.4"/>
    <GradientStop Color="#FFFFF0A5"
                  Offset="1"/>
</LinearGradientBrush>
```

2. Open MediaPlayer.xaml and locate the Play button.

3. Replace the content of the Play button with this markup:

```
<Grid Margin="4 0 0">
    <Polygon Fill="{StaticResource yellowGradient}"
             Stroke="{StaticResource chromeOutline}"
             Points="0,0 18,10 0,18">
    </Polygon>
    <Canvas Visibility="Hidden">
        <Rectangle Height="18"
                   Fill="{StaticResource yellowGradient}"
                   Stroke="{StaticResource chromeOutline}"
```

```
                        Width="6"/>
        <Rectangle Height="18"
                        Fill="{StaticResource yellowGradient}"
                        Stroke="{StaticResource chromeOutline}"
                        Width="6" Canvas.Left="8"/>
        </Canvas>
    </Grid>
```

4. Run the application and navigate to the music view. Take notice of the subtle gradient effect that is now present on the Play button.

Linear gradients are significantly more complex than solid color brushes. The easiest way to understand their features is to look at Figure 19.4, which shows the same gradient, but with some annotations.

FIGURE 19.4
An annotated
LinearGradient-
Brush example.

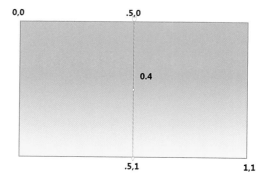

Every linear gradient is defined by a *gradient axis*. In the diagram, this is represented by the arrow-tipped line pointing straight down the middle. The axis is defined in terms of a coordinate space with 0,0 at the top-left corner and 1,1 at the lower right. By using the `StartPoint` and `EndPoint` properties of the `LinearGradientBrush` you can define this axis. By default they are set to 0,0 and 1,1, creating a diagonal gradient from the top-left corner to the bottom right. Because we want a vertical gradient, we have defined the start and end points as 0.5,0 and 0.5,1, respectively. After you have defined the axis, you should declare several instances of `GradientStop`. Each `GradientStop` has a `Color` and an `Offset`. The function of `Color` should be obvious. `Offset` is a decimal value from 0 to 1 that indicates where on the gradient axis the color should begin. If the first offset doesn't begin at 0, a solid color will be rendered up to the point of the first offset. Likewise, if the last offset is less than 1, a solid color will be rendered after the offset. The color between two gradient stop offsets is a linear interpolation of the two. Looking back at Figure 19.4, you can see the offset at 0.4 and the resulting interpolation.

Working with RadialGradientBrush

Besides linear gradients, WPF also offers radial gradient functionality through the RadialGradientBrush. Let's spice up our media player's Stop button:

1. Open ColorsAndBrushes.xaml and add the following markup to the bottom of the resources:

```
<LinearGradientBrush x:Key="glossBrush"
                     StartPoint="0.5,0"
                     EndPoint="0.5,1">
    <GradientStop Color="#00FFFFFF"
                  Offset="0" />
    <GradientStop Color="#66FFFFFF"
                  Offset="1" />
</LinearGradientBrush>

<RadialGradientBrush x:Key="redRadial"
                     GradientOrigin="0.45,0.30">
    <GradientStop Color="{StaticResource orangeColor}"
                  Offset="0" />
    <GradientStop Color="{StaticResource redColor}"
                  Offset="1" />
</RadialGradientBrush>
```

2. Open the MediaPlayer.xaml and replace the contents of the Stop button with the following:

```
<Border Width="18"
        Height="20"
        Background="{StaticResource redRadial}"
        CornerRadius="1"
        BorderBrush="{StaticResource controlOutline}"
        BorderThickness="1">
    <Rectangle HorizontalAlignment="Center"
               VerticalAlignment="Top"
               Margin="0,1,0,0"
               Width="15"
               Height="10"
               Fill="{StaticResource glossBrush}"
               RadiusX="1"
               RadiusY="1" />
</Border>
```

3. Replace the contents of the ToggleButton with the following:

```
<Canvas Width="20"
        Height="20">
    <!-- the speaker -->
    <Path Fill="{StaticResource redRadial}"
          Stroke="{StaticResource controlOutline}"
          StrokeLineJoin="Round">
        <Path.Data>
            <PathGeometry>
                <PathFigure StartPoint="12,5"
```

```
                        IsClosed="True">
                <LineSegment Point="0,6" />
                <PolyLineSegment Points="0,14 12,15 17,20" />
                <ArcSegment Point="17,0"
                            Size="30,30" />
            </PathFigure>
        </PathGeometry>
    </Path.Data>
</Path>
<!-- highlight -->
<Path Fill="{StaticResource glossBrush}">
    <Path.Data>
        <PathGeometry>
            <PathFigure StartPoint="13,6"
                        IsClosed="True">
                <PolyLineSegment Points="1,7 1,11 17.5,11" />
                <ArcSegment Point="16.5,2"
                            Size="30,30" />
            </PathFigure>
        </PathGeometry>
    </Path.Data>
</Path>
<!-- sound waves -->
<Polygon Points="20,5 25,0 27,3"
        Fill="{StaticResource textBrush}" />
<Polygon Points="20,10 28,9 27,6"
        Fill="{StaticResource textBrush}" />
<Polygon Points="20,13 26,17 27,13"
        Fill="{StaticResource textBrush}" />
<Polygon Points="20,17 24,21 26,18"
        Fill="{StaticResource textBrush}" />
</Canvas>
```

4. Run the application and navigate to the music view. Observe the new look of the Stop and Mute buttons.

Like linear gradients, radial gradients are a little difficult to understand without a picture. Take a look at Figure 19.5 to see how the RadialGradientBrush works.

FIGURE 19.5
An annotated RadialGradient-Brush example.

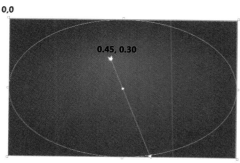

Similar to the LinearGradientBrush, all coordinates for the RadialGradientBrush are between 0,0 and 1,1. With a radial gradient, the gradient axis is defined by a line from the GradientOrigin to the perimeter of the ellipse. The gradient stops are relative to this axis and function the same as in a linear gradient. You can see from Figure 19.5 that the position of the gradient origin has been shifted from the exact center of the circle to produce the effect of a light source coming from the upper left. You can further customize the rendering of the gradient by setting the Center, RadiusX, and RadiusY properties. These properties allow you to move and resize the ellipse that governs how the gradient is drawn. Remember, all these properties must be set in terms of the 0,0 to 1,1 coordinate space.

> Declaring simple linear and radial gradients directly in XAML can be cumbersome. Although it is certainly possible to create brushes like this by hand, you will likely get the desired effects more quickly by using a tool such as Expression Blend or Adobe Illustrator to create them.

Did you Know?

> Both LinearGradientBrush and RadialGradientBrush inherit from GradientBrush. This base class provides a number of properties that are common to both—GradientStops is the most obvious. However, several other lesser-used properties can be helpful in advanced scenarios. These include ColorInterpolationMode, MappingMode, and SpreadMethod.

By the Way

Understanding DrawingBrush

WPF provides quite a few built-in brushes. One very powerful brush is DrawingBrush. It's commonly used to paint backgrounds with complex images. Let's take a look at how this is done.

1. Open ColorsAndBrushes.xaml and add the following brush definitions to the bottom of the resources:

```
<LinearGradientBrush x:Key="chromeBrush"
                     StartPoint="0.73,-0.053"
                     EndPoint="0.341,0.967"
                     SpreadMethod="Repeat">
    <GradientStop Color="#FF727272"
                  Offset="0.54" />
    <GradientStop Color="#FFFFFFFF"
                  Offset="1" />
    <GradientStop Color="#FFFFFFFF"
                  Offset="0" />
    <GradientStop Color="#FFDADADA"
                  Offset="0.46" />
```

```xml
          <GradientStop Color="#FFFFFFFF"
                        Offset="0.37" />
          <GradientStop Color="#FFB7B7B7"
                        Offset="0.30" />
          <GradientStop Color="#FFEEEEEE"
                        Offset="0.82" />
          <GradientStop Color="#FF858585"
                        Offset="0.90" />
          <GradientStop Color="#FFFFFFF2"
                        Offset="0.61" />
      </LinearGradientBrush>

      <DrawingBrush x:Key="MediaControlPanelBackground"
                    Stretch="UniformToFill">
          <DrawingBrush.Drawing>
              <DrawingGroup>
                  <GeometryDrawing Brush="{StaticResource chromeBrush}">
                      <GeometryDrawing.Pen>
                          <Pen Brush="{StaticResource chromeOutline}"
                               Thickness="0.5" />
                      </GeometryDrawing.Pen>
                      <GeometryDrawing.Geometry>
                          <RectangleGeometry RadiusX="25"
                                             RadiusY="25"
                                             Rect="0 0 400 50" />
                      </GeometryDrawing.Geometry>
                  </GeometryDrawing>
                  <GeometryDrawing Brush="{StaticResource yellowGradient}">
                      <GeometryDrawing.Geometry>
                          <RectangleGeometry RadiusX="23"
                                             RadiusY="23"
                                             Rect="2 2 396 46" />
                      </GeometryDrawing.Geometry>
                  </GeometryDrawing>
                  <GeometryDrawing Brush="{StaticResource glossBrush}">
                      <GeometryDrawing.Geometry>
                          <RectangleGeometry RadiusX="10"
                                             RadiusY="10"
                                             Rect="10 6 380 20" />
                      </GeometryDrawing.Geometry>
                  </GeometryDrawing>
              </DrawingGroup>
          </DrawingBrush.Drawing>
      </DrawingBrush>
```

2. Open the `MediaPlayer.xaml`. Locate the root `Grid` and change its `Background` property as follows:

```
Background="{StaticResource MediaControlPanelBackground}"
```

3. Let's make one more cosmetic change. Locate the volume slider and change its markup to match this:

```xml
<Slider Grid.Column="2"
        VerticalAlignment="Center"
        Margin="0,0,10,0"
```

```
                Minimum="0"
                Maximum="1"
                Value="{Binding Path=Volume, ElementName=mediaElement}" />
```

4. Run the application and navigate to the music view to see the changes. You should see something similar to Figure 19.6.

Notice how the use of the SpreadMethod property affects the rendering of the LinearGradientBrush when it is used for the Pen in the outline of the drawing.

By the Way

FIGURE 19.6
Media Player controls with custom brushes.

The DrawingBrush enables a wealth of complex scenarios that cannot be handled by simple gradient brushes. It allows you to specify an entire drawing that can then be used to paint anything that accepts a Brush. Notice the use of the Stretch property. Setting this to UniformToFill allows the drawing to scale to fit its target surface while preserving the aspect ratio. (This is analogous to the Stretch property on Viewbox.) DrawingBrush uses WPF geometries rather than shapes. The geometry classes are lower level and perform better, thus they are better suited to being contained by a brush. They have all the capabilities of shapes plus more.

Applying a VisualBrush

The last brush we are going to discuss is the VisualBrush. It is by far the most powerful brush that WPF has to offer. Let's see why:

1. Open MediaPlayer.xaml and replace the MediaElement with the following markup:

```
<Grid DockPanel.Dock="Top">
    <Grid.RowDefinitions>
        <RowDefinition Height="3*" />
        <RowDefinition Height="1*" />
    </Grid.RowDefinitions>
    <MediaElement x:Name="mediaElement"
                  VerticalAlignment="Bottom"
                  LoadedBehavior="Manual"
                  MediaOpened="mediaElement_MediaOpened"
                  MediaEnded="mediaElement_MediaEnded" />
    <Rectangle x:Name="reflection"
               Grid.Row="1"
               Width="{Binding Path=ActualWidth, ElementName=mediaElement}"
               MinHeight="24">
        <Rectangle.Fill>
            <VisualBrush Visual="{Binding ElementName=mediaElement}" />
        </Rectangle.Fill>
        <Rectangle.OpacityMask>
            <LinearGradientBrush EndPoint="0.5,0.5"
                                 StartPoint="0.5,0">
                <GradientStop Color="#72000000"
                              Offset="0" />
                <GradientStop Color="#00FFFFFF"
                              Offset="1" />
            </LinearGradientBrush>
        </Rectangle.OpacityMask>
    </Rectangle>
</Grid>
```

2. Run the application and navigate to the video view. Select a folder with videos and play a video. You should see something similar to Figure 19.7.

Everything that inherits from UIElement has an OpacityMask property of type Brush. This means that you can apply arbitrary brushes to any element, which will affect its opacity. The LinearGradientBrush that has been applied to the Rectangle causes our reflection to fade out and appear more realistic.

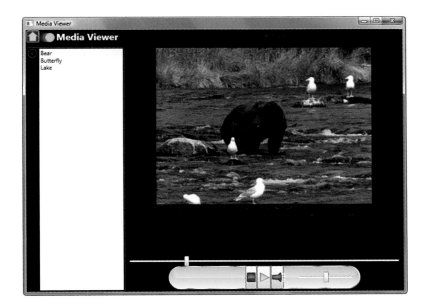

FIGURE 19.7
A video playing with reflection.

The VisualBrush is WPF's most powerful brush because it can paint its target with anything that inherits from Visual. Recall from earlier hours that Visual is one of the lowest-level base classes in WPF. Everything that can be visualized inherits from it. Thus, a VisualBrush can paint a surface with shapes, video, controls, and even 3D content, enabling many seemingly impossible scenarios. You can either create a visual specifically for the brush or use data binding as we have to bind the brush's visual to another element in the UI. The effect of our VisualBrush binding is that we have a reflection of our playing video. One thing is wrong with our reflection, though. It doesn't look quite right because it isn't flipped like it would be in reality. We'll fix this in the next hour.

A VisualBrush is very powerful, but it is also the most resource-intensive option. Use it sparingly.

Watch Out!

Both DrawingBrush and VisualBrush inherit from TileBrush. This base class has a slew of additional properties for controlling alignment, tiling, and scaling of the brush when it is mapped onto a surface. TileBrush also has one other descendent, ImageBrush, which works similarly to the other brushes, but paints with an image.

By the Way

Summary

In this hour we have finally given fair attention to WPF's color and brush capabilities. Now that we have uncovered some of WPF's hidden power, think back over earlier parts of the book when we used simple SolidColorBrushes. Every time we set a Background, Foreground, Fill, or Pen property, we were using WPF's brush mechanism but only in the most simplistic way. With the knowledge you now have, you can customize any UI in seemingly endless ways just by changing the properties or type of a brush.

Q&A

Q. *You mentioned that* Geometry *can be used to create a* DrawingBrush. *Does it have any other interesting uses?*

A. Yes. Besides using Geometry in drawings and brushes, it can be used to define animation paths and clipping regions.

Q. *Are there any other unique uses for brushes besides the ones shown in this hour?*

A. There are dozens of interesting ways to use brushes. A couple of neat ideas are using brushes as the Foreground for text or to texture a 3D image. (Though outside of the scope of this book, all brushes can be applied to 3D models.)

Workshop

Quiz

1. What are the different types of brushes that WPF offers?

2. What are the four channels of a WPF Color object?

Answers

1. SolidColorBrush, LinearGradientBrush, RadialGradientBrush, DrawingBrush, VisualBrush and ImageBrush.

2. Alpha, Red, Green, Blue.

Activities

1. Look back over the Contact Manager. Change some of the SolidColorBrushes used to style the application into other types of brushes.

2. Research ImageBrush and its base class TileBrush.

3. Create a VisualBrush that paints a background with a visual composed of controls.

HOUR 20

Transforms and Effects

What You'll Learn in This Hour:

▶ Render versus Layout transforms

▶ Built-in transforms

▶ Brush transforms

▶ Bitmap effects

With WPF's rich support for shapes, geometry, colors, and brushes, it would seem that you can create almost anything. However, some visuals would be difficult or impossible to achieve without the use of geometric transforms or special bitmap effects. It's these two technology pieces that we'll use to complete our graphics arsenal.

Understanding Transforms

In WPF, a group of classes exist that inherit from Transform. These classes include TranslateTransform, SkewTransform, RotateTransform, ScaleTransform, MatrixTransform, and TransformGroup. We'll cover all of these except MatrixTransform, because it is only necessary in rare cases. Let's build an application to see how they work:

1. Open Visual Studio and create a new WPF Application. Name the project **TransformDemo**.

2. Use the code from Listing 20.1 to implement the markup for Window1.xaml.

3. Run the application and observe the different pieces of text. You should see something like Figure 20.1.

LISTING 20.1   Window1.xaml

```xml
<Window x:Class="TransformDemo.Window1"
        xmlns="http://schemas.microsoft.com/winfx/2006/xaml/presentation"
        xmlns:x="http://schemas.microsoft.com/winfx/2006/xaml"
        Title="Transforms"
        TextBlock.FontSize="20"
        SizeToContent="WidthAndHeight">
    <Canvas Height="600"
            Width="800">
        <TextBlock Text="No Transform" />
        <TextBlock Text="Translate Transform">
            <TextBlock.RenderTransform>
                <TranslateTransform X="50"
                                    Y="25" />
            </TextBlock.RenderTransform>
        </TextBlock>
        <TextBlock Canvas.Left="200"
                   Canvas.Top="100"
                   Text="Skew Transform">
            <TextBlock.RenderTransform>
                <SkewTransform AngleX="45" />
            </TextBlock.RenderTransform>
        </TextBlock>

        <TextBlock Canvas.Left="200"
                   Canvas.Top="200"
                   Text="Rotate Transform">
            <TextBlock.RenderTransform>
                <RotateTransform Angle="45" />
            </TextBlock.RenderTransform>
        </TextBlock>

        <TextBlock Canvas.Left="200"
                   Canvas.Top="300"
                   Text="Scale Transform">
            <TextBlock.RenderTransform>
                <ScaleTransform ScaleX="2"
                                ScaleY="11" />
            </TextBlock.RenderTransform>
        </TextBlock>

        <TextBlock Text="Transform Group">
            <TextBlock.RenderTransform>
                <TransformGroup>
                    <TranslateTransform X="400" />
                    <RotateTransform Angle="45" />
                    <SkewTransform AngleX="45" />
                </TransformGroup>
            </TextBlock.RenderTransform>
        </TextBlock>

    </Canvas>
</Window>
```

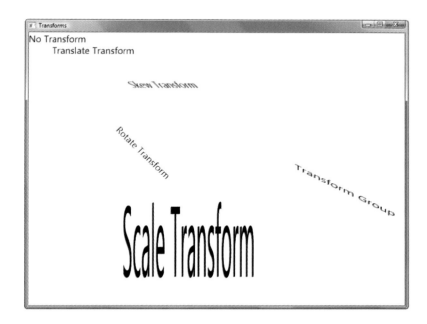

FIGURE 20.1
A set of trans-
formed text
blocks.

As you can see, transforms alter the rendering of the elements they are applied to in various ways. It's easy to use a transform. Every UIElement has a RenderTransform property. Just set this property to a valid transform.

TranslateTransform

The TranslateTransform does nothing more than shift an element away from its current location. The most important properties on TranslateTransform are X and Y. Setting these properties controls how the element will be translated along the x or y axis. Figure 20.1 demonstrates a TextBlock being shifted by 50 pixels on the x axis and 25 on the y.

SkewTransform

SkewTransform distorts the original element by shearing or shifting it along the x or y axis. To control this, you use the AngleX and AngleY properties with values from –90 to 90. You can see from the sample how the skewed TextBlock has been distorted horizontally along the x axis.

RotateTransform

The RotateTransform alters an element by rotating it based on a specified angle. It should be no surprise that this is accomplished by setting the Angle property. Figure 20.1 shows a TextBlock rotated by 45 degrees.

ScaleTransform

If you need to alter an element's size, use ScaleTransform. It has ScaleX and ScaleY properties, which enable this functionality. Setting these properties to different values will cause the element to be stretched along either the x or y axis. A value of 1 represents normal size, whereas using a 2 would double the size. You can see the ScaleTransform demonstrated in Figure 20.1.

TransformGroup

Many times you cannot get the desired transformation by using a single Transform. In this case, you should use the TransformGroup. It has a Children property which can be set to an arbitrary number of Transform instances. Figure 20.1 shows a TransformGroup that combines a TranslateTransform, RotateTransform, and SkewTransform.

When applying multiple transforms by using a TransformGroup, remember that the *order* of the transforms can have a strong impact on the result.

RenderTargetOrigin

RotateTransform, ScaleTransform, and SkewTransform all have CenterX and CenterY properties that control the point around which the element is transformed. By default the center is set at 0,0—the upper-left corner of the element. You can move the center using these properties to change the transform behavior, but this works only if you know the exact size of the element. In many cases you won't know the size. For this scenario UIElement has the property RenderTargetOrigin. You can use this property to specify a point similar to the way the origin for a radial gradient is done. The coordinate must be between 0,0 and 1,1.

Differentiating Render and Layout Transforms

In Listing 20.1 we set the RenderTransform on each TextBlock. If you look closely at the available properties on TextBlock, however, you will discover another Transform property called LayoutTransform. In fact, everything that inherits from FrameworkElement has this property. So, what's the difference between these two properties? Why does FrameworkElement need to add a second way to set the transform? The answer is quite simple. Using a LayoutTransform allows an element to be transformed while still playing by the layout rules of the Panel in which it lives. WPF has such rich layout capabilities that it would be unfortunate if all transforms broke the layout rules. Essentially, a LayoutTransform occurs before a Panel performs layout; thus, any transforms that occur are taken into account when the Panel arranges its children. A RenderTransform happens independently of the layout mechanism. Let's write a program that will show us a clear example of this:

1. Open Visual Studio and create a new WPF Application. Give it the name **LayoutTransformDemo**.

2. Use the markup in Listing 20.2 to implement Window1.xaml.

3. Run the application. You should see something similar to Figure 20.2.

4. Stop the application and return to Window1.xaml.

5. Change all occurrences of LayoutTransform to RenderTransform.

6. Run the application again. You should see several differences, pictured in Figure 20.3.

LISTING 20.2   Window1.xaml with LayoutTransform

```
<Window x:Class="LayoutTransformDemo.Window1"
        xmlns="http://schemas.microsoft.com/winfx/2006/xaml/presentation"
        xmlns:x="http://schemas.microsoft.com/winfx/2006/xaml"
        Title="Layout Transform"
        Height="600"
        Width="800">
    <Grid ShowGridLines="True">
        <Grid.RowDefinitions>
            <RowDefinition />
            <RowDefinition />
        </Grid.RowDefinitions>
```

LISTING 20.2 Continued

```
        <Grid.ColumnDefinitions>
            <ColumnDefinition />
            <ColumnDefinition />
        </Grid.ColumnDefinitions>

        <Button>
            <Button.LayoutTransform>
                <SkewTransform AngleX="45" />
            </Button.LayoutTransform>
        </Button>
        <Button Grid.Row="1"
                Grid.Column="1">
            <Button.LayoutTransform>
                <RotateTransform Angle="45" />
            </Button.LayoutTransform>
        </Button>
    </Grid>
</Window>
```

FIGURE 20.2
The effects of a
LayoutTransform.

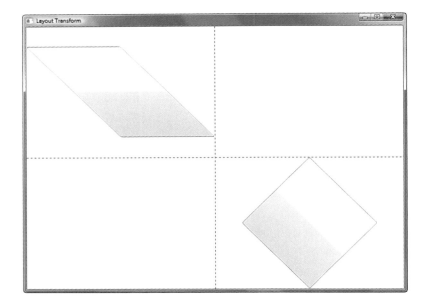

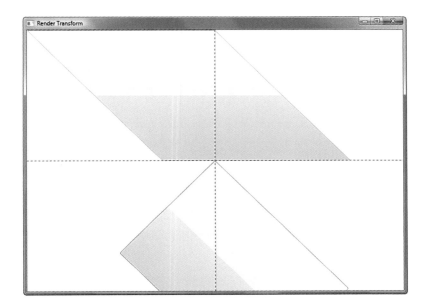

FIGURE 20.3
The effects of a
RenderTransform.

As you can see from Figures 20.2 and 20.3, quite dramatic differences exist in the renderings produced by these two transforms. Because LayoutTransform is designed to work within the confines of a panel's instructions, it cannot affect the final position of the element, and its size will also be restricted. RenderTransform, however, does not have to play by the rules of WPF's layout mechanism. Hopefully this clarifies the ways in which a LayoutTransform differs from a RenderTransform. Experience might lead you to using LayoutTransform more with UI and RenderTransform more with graphics. However, this does not always hold true, so you will need to think through each scenario carefully.

Adding Transforms to the Media Viewer

Now that we've learned about transforms, let's use them to get a few interesting effects in our Media Viewer.

1. Open the Media Viewer in Visual Studio.

2. Open MediaPlayer.xaml and navigate to the Rectangle named "reflection."

3. Replace the rectangle's Fill with this markup:

```
<Rectangle.Fill>
    <VisualBrush Visual="{Binding ElementName=mediaElement}">
        <VisualBrush.Transform>
            <TransformGroup>
```

```
                    <ScaleTransform ScaleY="-1" />
                    <TranslateTransform Y="{Binding Path=ActualHeight,
                              ➥ElementName=reflection}" />
                </TransformGroup>
            </VisualBrush.Transform>
        </VisualBrush>
    </Rectangle.Fill>
```

4. Run the application and navigate to the video view. Play a video and notice the appearance of the reflection. It should look something like Figure 20.4.

5. Stop the application and open `ColorsAndBrushes.xaml`.

6. Replace the `redRadial` brush with the following definition:

```
<RadialGradientBrush x:Key="redRadial"
                     GradientOrigin="0.45,0.30">
    <RadialGradientBrush.RelativeTransform>
        <TranslateTransform X="-0.2"
                            Y="-0.2" />
    </RadialGradientBrush.RelativeTransform>
    <GradientStop Color="{StaticResource orangeColor}"
                  Offset="0" />
    <GradientStop Color="{StaticResource redColor}"
                  Offset="1" />
</RadialGradientBrush>
```

7. Run the application and go to the music view. Look carefully at the stop button and notice that the red gradient has been shifted slightly.

Well, we've finally fixed our video reflection from Hour 19 and made a slight adjustment to one of our gradients. It turns out that you can set a transform on `Brush` as well as `UIElement` and `FrameworkElement`. It is quite common to use transforms in this way. In fact, the three most common uses of transforms are in drawings, brushes, and animations. For another example of using a transform, look at `VideoView.xaml`. For a slightly more interesting example, look back at the Contact Manager. You may recall a data bound transform that we used in the `Shell.xaml`.

You may have noticed that one of the brushes we showed sets the `Transform` and the other sets the `RelativeTransform`. Every `Brush` has these two different transform properties. `RelativeTransform` uses relative coordinates (0,0–1,1) and is applied to the brush before it is mapped onto the target. `Transform` uses exact coordinates and is applied after the brush is mapped onto its target. Depending on the scenario, these two different uses of transforms can have drastically different outcomes. Using a tool such as Expression Blend can help you to get this right and make it easier to experiment with new ideas.

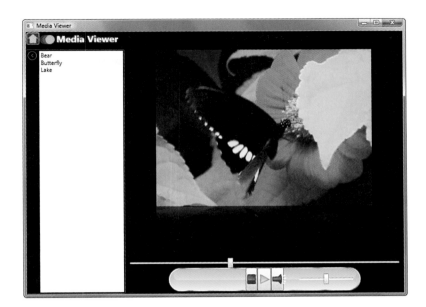

FIGURE 20.4
A video with
a properly
transformed
reflection.

Introducing BitmapEffect

The final piece of WPF's visual puzzle is *bitmap effects*. Every UIElement has a
BitmapEffect property that can be used to add various special shader-like effects to
the element. Several built-in effects represent things that designers use frequently.
All these effects classes derive from the base
System.Windows.Media.Effects.BitmapEffect. Let's jump right in and build an
application to familiarize ourselves with these effects:

1. Open Visual Studio and create a new WPF Application. Name the project
   BitmapEffectDemo.

2. Use the code from Listing 20.3 to implement the markup for Window1.xaml.

3. Run the application and observe the different effects. You should see something like Figure 20.5.

LISTING 20.3 Window1.xaml with BitmapEffect

```
<Window x:Class="BitmapEffectDemo.Window1"
        xmlns="http://schemas.microsoft.com/winfx/2006/xaml/presentation"
        xmlns:x="http://schemas.microsoft.com/winfx/2006/xaml"
        Title="Bitmap Effects"
        Height="600"
        Width="800">
    <Window.Resources>
```

LISTING 20.3   Continued

```xml
        <Style TargetType="{x:Type Button}">
            <Setter Property="FontSize"
                    Value="32" />
            <Setter Property="Margin"
                    Value="10" />
            <Setter Property="FontWeight"
                    Value="Bold" />
        </Style>
    </Window.Resources>

    <UniformGrid Columns="3">
        <Button Content="Drop Shadow">
            <Button.BitmapEffect>
                <DropShadowBitmapEffect />
            </Button.BitmapEffect>
        </Button>

        <Button Content="Outer Glow">
            <Button.BitmapEffect>
                <OuterGlowBitmapEffect GlowColor="Red"
                                       GlowSize="10" />
            </Button.BitmapEffect>
        </Button>

        <Button Content="Blur">
            <Button.BitmapEffect>
                <BlurBitmapEffect Radius="4" />
            </Button.BitmapEffect>
        </Button>

        <Button Content="Emboss">
            <Button.BitmapEffect>
                <EmbossBitmapEffect LightAngle="90"
                                    Relief="2" />
            </Button.BitmapEffect>
        </Button>

        <Button Content="Bevel">
            <Button.BitmapEffect>
                <BevelBitmapEffect LightAngle="90"
                                   Relief=".75" />
            </Button.BitmapEffect>
        </Button>

        <Button Content="Group">
            <Button.BitmapEffect>
                <BitmapEffectGroup>
                    <DropShadowBitmapEffect />
                    <BlurBitmapEffect Radius="4" />
                    <OuterGlowBitmapEffect GlowColor="Red"
                                           GlowSize="2" />
                </BitmapEffectGroup>
            </Button.BitmapEffect>
        </Button>
    </UniformGrid>
</Window>
```

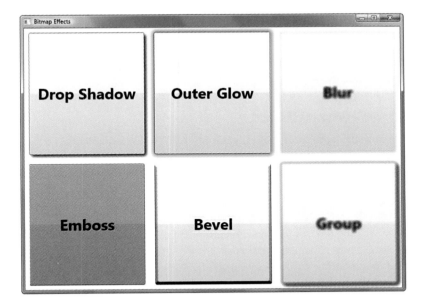

FIGURE 20.5
WPF Bitmap
Effects.

Did you notice the use of the UniformGrid to lay out our Button elements? We haven't used that panel before in the book. UniformGrid is similar to Grid, but automatically lays out its children based on their order. All you have to do is specify the number of rows you want *or* the number of columns. It does the rest.

By the Way

DropShadowBitmapEffect

DropShadowBitmapEffect is one of the most common effects you'll want to apply to an element. It adds a shadow behind the element, cast by a configurable light source. Normally the default effect works for most needs, but you can customize it by using several properties. The most common properties you will use are ShadowDepth, Color, and Direction.

OuterGlowBitmapEffect

The OuterGlowBitmapEffect adds a halo to the element it is applied to. This can add a very nice, subtle effect to text and is great for providing user feedback for MouseOver events. GlowColor and GlowSize are handy properties for controlling the main aspects of the halo.

BlurBitmapEffect

If you want to make an element appear unfocused or blurry, use the `BlurBitmapEffect`. You will likely want to adjust its `Radius` property to set the degree of blurriness.

EmbossBitmapEffect

To add texture or depth to an object, you may want to use an `EmbossBitmapEffect`. To affect the degree of depth and shading, use the `LightAngle` and `Relief` properties.

BevelBitmapEffect

If you want to give the element an appearance of being raised, you can add a `BevelBitmapEffect`. Like `EmbossBitmapEffect`, it has `LightAngle` and `Relief` properties, but it can be further customized by setting its `BevelWidth`, `EdgeProfile`, and `Smoothness`.

BitmapEffectGroup

Should you desire to apply multiple effects to a single element, you would use the `BitmapEffectGroup`. This works in much the same way as the `TransformGroup` we discussed earlier. It has a `Children` collection that you can set to any number of effects.

In the present version of WPF, all bitmap effects are software rendered. This means that they will incur a significant performance hit. Use them sparingly.

For an extra added effect, you can animate the different properties of a BitmapEffect. We look at how to use WPF's animation system in Hour 23, "Animation."

Adding a BitmapEffect to the Media Viewer

You can use bitmap effects to add a nice, subtle touch to the user interface. It's important not to overuse these types of effects because they can hinder the usability of your application. Let's see how we used one in the Media Viewer:

1. Open the Media Viewer in Visual Studio if you have not already.

2. Open the `DefaultStyles.xaml` file and locate the title style.

3. Add the following `Setter` to the title style:

```
<Setter Property="BitmapEffect">
    <Setter.Value>
        <OuterGlowBitmapEffect GlowColor="{StaticResource textColor}"
                               Opacity="0.5" />
    </Setter.Value>
</Setter>
```

4. Run the application and observe the subtle glow on the header's text. It should look something like Figure 20.6.

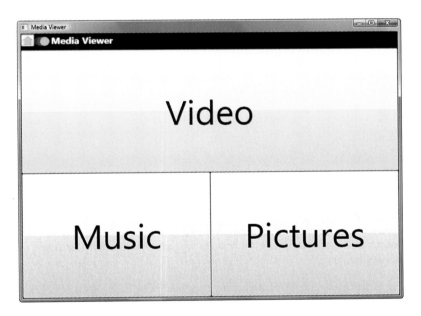

FIGURE 20.6
Text with an
`OuterGlowBitmap-`
`Effect`.

We've chosen to apply the `BitmapEffect` by way of a `Style`. The effect is small, but noticeable. Using these effects wisely can give your application a very professional and elegant appeal.

Future Versions of WPF

At the time of the writing of this book, Microsoft is working on a service update to the .NET 3.5 Framework. This update will fix many issues with the current version of WPF; chief among them is performance. As part of the performance enhancements, WPF's bitmap effects will be overhauled. The present effects are being reworked for hardware acceleration. This will lift many of the current limits that are "practically" imposed on their use, opening up a lot of new possibilities. In addition to fixing the existing effects, Microsoft is adding a new *shader API* which will allow developers to create custom effects using a *shader language*. Shaders are the technology that enables many of the impressive effects seen in today's cutting edge 3D video games.

Summary

Completing Hour 20 is a great accomplishment. You are now equipped to tackle almost any graphical task. When you combine shapes, brushes, transforms, and effects, you can almost let your mind run wild with possibilities. In the next few hours we are going to show you how to make these new visual experience more dynamic with templates, triggers, and animations.

Q&A

Q. *WPF doesn't have the bitmap effect I need. Is there any way to create my own?*

A. At present, the only way to create your own effect is through an unmanaged C++ API. We wouldn't recommend it. However, Microsoft has announced that it will be releasing a hardware accelerated, managed shader API for WPF soon.

Q. *What other uses are there for transforms other than basic visual manipulation?*

A. Transforms are one of the key components in WPF animation. You'll learn more about this in Hour 23.

Workshop

Quiz

1. What are the two types of transforms present on `FrameworkElement`?

2. List the built-in bitmap effects.

Answers

1. The two transforms that are present on `FrameworkElement` are `RenderTransform` and `LayoutTransform`.

2. The built-in bitmap effects are `DropShadowBitmapEffect`, `OuterGlowBitmapEffect`, `BlurBitmapEffect`, `EmbossBitmapEffect`, and `BevelBitmapEffect`.

Activities

1. Revisit the Contact Manager. Apply some bitmap effects to appropriate places.

HOUR 21

Using Control Templates

What You'll Learn in This Hour:

▶ The basics of making control templates

▶ Why you would want to use control templates

▶ Examples of making control templates

▶ Solutions for problems that you'll encounter when authoring your own templates

Control templates are used to define the actual look of a control. With control templates we can make a list box filled with the names of countries look like a map of the world, without affecting the behavior of the list box programmatically. After we cover the basic concepts, you'll find that control templates are easy to understand. The difficulty in working with them is in the details of the individual controls. We go through a few examples in this hour so that you'll be well equipped to write your own control templates.

Understanding Control Templates

You've probably heard people using the phrase "look and feel" when discussing software. People sometimes hear it for years and never stop to consider what it actually means. In the case of control templates, the "look" is what is rendered on the screen, and the "feel" is the actual behavior of a control. For example, a list box of any sort will always present users with a set of items, allowing them to make a selection. That describes the feel, or behavior, of a list box. Visually, it might be a 10×10 grid of little colored squares, one square for each item in the set, or it might be a traditional box with a scrollbar and vertically stacked items. Either option is a different look.

Control templates are a way for you to define the look of a control without affecting its feel. An example is worth a thousand words here. Suppose that we would like to create a button that looks like a smiley face.

1. Create a new project called **ControlTemplates**.

2. In Window1.xaml, create a button with the following:

```
<Button HorizontalAlignment="Center"
        VerticalAlignment="Center">
    <Canvas Width="48" Height="48">
        <Ellipse Width="48" Height="48"
                 Fill="Yellow" />
        <Ellipse Width="8" Height="8"
                 Canvas.Top="12" Canvas.Left="12"
                 Fill="Black"/>
        <Ellipse Width="8" Height="8"
                 Canvas.Top="12" Canvas.Right="12"
                 Fill="Black" />
        <Path Data="M10,30 C18,38 30,38 38,30"
              Stroke="Black" />
    </Canvas>
</Button>
```

3. Run the application, and the result will look like Figure 21.1.

FIGURE 21.1
A button with a smiley face.

We've created a button and placed a canvas inside with a drawing of a smiley face. The problem with this is that our canvas is inside the button. The *chrome* of the button is still present. We want to completely replace the visual representation of our button.

1. We are going to add a control template. But first, to save us some typing, copy and paste our smiley face into the window's resource dictionary:

```
<Window.Resources>
    <Canvas x:Key="Smiley" Width="48" Height="48">
        <Ellipse Width="48" Height="48"
                 Fill="Yellow" />
        <Ellipse Width="8" Height="8"
```

```
                               Canvas.Top="12" Canvas.Left="12"
                               Fill="Black"/>
            <Ellipse Width="8" Height="8"
                               Canvas.Top="12" Canvas.Right="12"
                               Fill="Black" />
            <Path Data="M10,30 C18,38 30,38 38,30"
                               Stroke="Black" />
        </Canvas>
    </Window.Resources>
```

2. We'll modify our button to this:

```
<Button HorizontalAlignment="Center"
        VerticalAlignment="Center">
    <Button.Template>
        <ControlTemplate>
            <Border Background="Black"
                    Padding="4"
                    CornerRadius="4"
                    Child="{StaticResource Smiley}" />
        </ControlTemplate>
    </Button.Template>
</Button>
```

3. The WPF designer isn't able to render a preview. However, run the application and you'll see that our button is now just the black border and smiley face. Be sure to mouse over and click the button. The result is shown in Figure 21.2.

FIGURE 21.2
A button with simple template.

Why isn't the WPF designer able to render the button after we placed the canvas in the resources? The exact reason is somewhat technical; however, the problem illustrates an important point. Items in a resource dictionary are single instances. Essentially, we are creating an instance of a Canvas, and all references in our XAML are pointing to that one instance. A given element can have only one parent. If we attempt to reuse our stored canvas in another location, we'll run into the same error at runtime. You can easily demonstrate the problem by simply duplicating the button we just created.

In practice, it is not very useful to store instances of UIElement in a resource dictionary.

Did you notice that our button no longer has any visual cues for mouseover and click? Those effects are actually part of the built-in control templates. Anytime you implement a control template, you'll have to handle these effects yourself. We'll show you how to handle this when we cover the topic of triggers.

Placing Content Inside the Template

Our smiley face started off in the `Content` property of the button, and after moving it to the template we no longer have any content for the button. It's just the template. In the majority of cases, however, your template isn't meant to provide the actual content; rather, it's a template that your content will be injected into.

1. Add the `Content` attribute back to the `Button` with the value `Smile!`.

```
<Button HorizontalAlignment="Center"
        VerticalAlignment="Center"
        Content="Smile!">
```

2. Run the application and take a look at the button. Where's the content? We haven't told the template what to do with the content, so WPF just ignores it.

3. We need to take two steps for WPF to render the content. First, we need to tell the template what type of control it is a template for. Modify the opening tag of the template to match this:

```
<ControlTemplate TargetType="{x:Type Button}">
```

4. Then the template needs to know where to place the content. There are few special elements called *presenters* that communicate to a template where to place the content. We can modify the template to look like this:

```
<ControlTemplate TargetType="{x:Type Button}">
    <Grid>
        <Border Background="Green"
                Padding="4"
                CornerRadius="4"
                Child="{StaticResource Smiley}" />
        <ContentPresenter HorizontalAlignment="Center" />
    </Grid>
</ControlTemplate>
```

I changed the background of the border to contrast better with the content. Run the application to see the button with its content.

Now you should have a basic feel for control templates. Here are few points to summarize things so far:

▶ Templates are composed out of UI elements.

▶ Templates need to be explicitly told what type of control they are targeting. Use the `TargetType` attribute to do this.

▶ Templates need to know what to do with the control content. We used the `ContentPresenter` element to handle this for a button.

Telling the Template What to Do

We just mentioned the `ContentPresenter`, but two other presenter controls exist as well: `ScrollContentPresenter` and `ItemsPresenter`.

Use `ContentPresenter` when templating any control that has a `Content` property. Examples of these controls are `Label`, `ToolTip`, and `Button`; that is, anything that derives from `ContentControl`.

Use `ItemsPresenter` for any control that has an `Items` property. Some controls using this presenter in their templates are `TreeView`, `Menu`, and `ListBox`. Use this with any control that derives from `ItemsControl`.

`ScrollContentPresenter` is a special case that is used only with the `ScrollViewer` control. It derives from `ContentPresenter`, but implements the `IScrollInfo` interface.

Choosing Panels in Items Controls

A few things about `ItemsControl` warrant more explanation. You may recall from Hour 16, "Visualizing Lists," that `ItemsControl` has a property `ItemsPanel` that allows you to choose a panel for the layout of the actual items. An example might be:

```
<ListBox>
    <ListBox.ItemsPanel>
        <ItemsPanelTemplate>
            <WrapPanel />
        </ItemsPanelTemplate>
    </ListBox.ItemsPanel>
    <ListBox.Items>
        <ListBoxItem Content="Red" />
        <ListBoxItem Content="Green" />
        <ListBoxItem Content="Blue" />
    </ListBox.Items>
</ListBox>
```

We've told this `ListBox` to use a `WrapPanel` instead of its default `StackPanel`. The three items that we've explicitly added to the `ListBox` will be injected into the `WrapPanel`. Now we'll add a control template:

```
<ListBox>
    <ListBox.ItemsPanel>
        <ItemsPanelTemplate>
            <WrapPanel />
        </ItemsPanelTemplate>
    </ListBox.ItemsPanel>
    <ListBox.Items>
        <ListBoxItem Content="Red" />
        <ListBoxItem Content="Green" />
        <ListBoxItem Content="Blue" />
    </ListBox.Items>
    <ListBox.Template>
        <ControlTemplate TargetType="{x:Type ListBox}">
            <Border Background="Pink"
                    Padding="8">
                <ItemsPresenter />
            </Border>
        </ControlTemplate>
    </ListBox.Template>
</ListBox>
```

When the template is rendered, the `WrapPanel` and its children are injected at the location of `ItemsPresenter`.

As you can see, the XAML is growing quickly. There is a shortcut, however.

```
<ListBox>
    <ListBox.Items>
        <ListBoxItem Content="Red" />
        <ListBoxItem Content="Green" />
        <ListBoxItem Content="Blue" />
    </ListBox.Items>
    <ListBox.Template>
        <ControlTemplate TargetType="{x:Type ListBox}">
            <Border Background="Pink"
                    Padding="8">
                <WrapPanel IsItemsHost="True" />
            </Border>
        </ControlTemplate>
    </ListBox.Template>
</ListBox>
```

In this snippet, we no longer set the `ItemsPanel` on the `ListBox`. In addition, no `ItemsPresenter` is in the template. Instead, we specify the panel inline and set the `IsItemsHost` to `True`.

Although this is convenient shorthand, a drawback exists. You are no longer able to set the `ItemsPanel`. The property is ignored when you use `IsItemsHost`. This means that another developer using this control template cannot swap out the panel without modifying the template.

Adding Templates to Our Application

Let's apply some of our knowledge of templates to the Media Viewer. We'll begin with the Home button in the upper-left corner of the application.

1. Open the Media Viewer project.

2. In `MainWindow.xaml`, located the `Button` wired to `Header_Click`. First, we'll remove the `Background` attribute, and then we'll add the template. Modify the button to look like this:

```xml
<Button Background="{StaticResource redBrush}"
        Click="Header_Click">
    <Button.Template>
        <ControlTemplate TargetType="{x:Type Button}">
            <Grid HorizontalAlignment="Center"
                  VerticalAlignment="Center">
                <Ellipse x:Name="chromeEdge"
                         Margin="-2"
                         Width="36" Height="36"
                         Fill="{StaticResource chromeBrush}"
                         Stroke="{StaticResource chromeOutline}"
                         StrokeThickness="0.5">
                </Ellipse>
                <Ellipse x:Name="bg"
                         Width="32" Height="32"
                         Stroke="{StaticResource redBrush}"
                         Fill="{StaticResource redRadial}"/>
                <ContentPresenter HorizontalAlignment="Center"
                                  VerticalAlignment="Center" />
                <Rectangle x:Name="gloss"
                           Margin="3.5"
                           Width="25" Height="16"
                           RadiusX="20" RadiusY="10"
                           Fill="{StaticResource glossBrush}"
                           VerticalAlignment="Top"/>
            </Grid>
        </ControlTemplate>
    </Button.Template>
    <Polygon Fill="{StaticResource yellowGradient}"
             Points="0,10 11,0 22,10 18,10 18,20 4,20 4,10" />
</Button>
```

Let's take a moment to examine what we just did. We have two ellipses, a content presenter, and a rectangle. Because we don't have any columns or rows in the containing grid, these four elements are stacked on top of one another. We set the horizontal and vertical alignment to center to make the Grid collapse to the size of its content.

At the bottom of the stack is the `Ellipse` element we named `chromeEdge`. It's not imperative that we name these elements, but it makes it easier to talk about them.

chromeEdge extends outside the containing grid because of its negative margin. Because it's on the bottom, it's also almost entirely covered by the other elements. The combination of the chromeBrush fill and the chromeOutline stroke provide the illusion of a metallic ring around the button.

The next element, bg, is the primary background of the button. I added the redBrush stroke to further enhance the metallic ring.

Next we have the actual content. Note that we've centered the ContentPresenter in the Grid.

Finally, we use a highly rounded rectangle to give the impression of depth and glossiness. The brush is translucent and actually on top of the content.

When viewed in the designer, MainWindow.xaml will look like Figure 21.3.

FIGURE 21.3
A control template applied to the Home button.

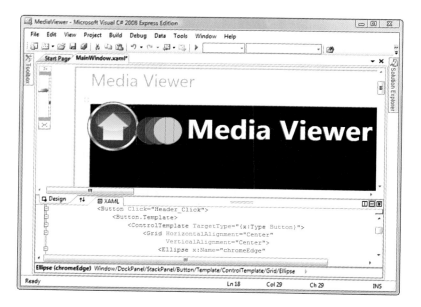

This same control template would look great when used with the Play button in the MediaPlayer user control. We'll need to move the template into a resource dictionary to accomplish this.

It's a good idea to place your control templates in a resource dictionary. Templates are usually lengthy, and they can easily obscure the intent of your markup. You can even apply templates through styles, which reduces the inline markup even more. Finally, it's necessary if you plan to reuse a template.

1. Open `DefaultStyles.xaml`. We're going create a style that we'll apply to both the Home button and the Play button. Add the following:

```
<Style x:Key="fancyButtonStyle" TargetType="{x:Type Button}">
    <Setter Property="Margin" Value="4" />
    <Setter Property="Template">
        <Setter.Value>
            <!-- We'll cut and paste the template here! -->
        </Setter.Value>
    </Setter>
</Style>
```

I also added some margin to the style as well.

2. Now cut the `ControlTemplate` from `MainWindow.xaml` and paste in the spot we left in `DefaultStyles.xaml`.

3. Modify the Home button in `MainWindow.xaml` so that it references the style and no longer has a `Button.Template` child. It should look like this when you are done:

```
<Button Style="{StaticResource fancyButtonStyle}"
        Click="Header_Click">
    <Polygon Fill="{StaticResource yellowGradient}"
            Points="0,10 11,0 22,10 18,10 18,20 4,20 4,10" />
</Button>
```

4. Open `MediaPlayer.xaml` in the `UserControls` directory and locate the `Button` wired to `Play_Click`. Add the following attribute:

```
Style="{StaticResource fancyButtonStyle}"
```

5. I also modified the contents of the Play button slightly to match the new template. The markup for the entire button is:

```
<Button Grid.Column="1"
        Click="Play_Click"
        Style="{StaticResource fancyButtonStyle}">
    <Grid Margin="4 0 0 0">
        <Polygon Fill="{StaticResource yellowGradient}"
                Stroke="{StaticResource chromeOutline}"
                Points="0,0 18,10 0,18">
        </Polygon>
        <Canvas Visibility="Hidden">
            <Rectangle Height="18"
                        Fill="{StaticResource yellowGradient}"
                        Stroke="{StaticResource chromeOutline}"
                        Width="6" />
                <Rectangle Height="18"
                        Fill="{StaticResource yellowGradient}"
                        Stroke="{StaticResource chromeOutline}"
                        Width="6" Canvas.Left="8" />
        </Canvas>
    </Grid>
</Button>
```

6. Run the application and switch to the music view. The Home button and the Play button now use the same template.

7. Creating a template for the Stop and Mute buttons uses the same principles. Here is the style for them:

```
<Style x:Key="mediaButtonStyle" TargetType="{x:Type ButtonBase}">
    <Setter Property="Template">
        <Setter.Value>
            <ControlTemplate TargetType="{x:Type ButtonBase}">
                <Grid Width="32" Height="32"
                      Background="Transparent" >
                    <ContentPresenter VerticalAlignment="Center"
                                      HorizontalAlignment="Center"/>
                    <Border x:Name="highlight"
                            CornerRadius="3"
                            Background="{StaticResource mediaButtonHover}"
                            BorderBrush="{StaticResource glossOutline}"
                            BorderThickness="1">
                    </Border>
                </Grid>
            </ControlTemplate>
        </Setter.Value>
    </Setter>
</Style>
```

Note that both the style and the template target `ButtonBase` instead of `Button`. The style is going to be applied to a `ToggleButton` as well, so we target the base class for both `Button` and `ToggleButton`.

In a later hour, we'll modify this template so that `highlight` is visible only when a mouse is over the button.

8. Our template depends upon the brush `mediaButtonHover`. Let's go ahead and add that to `ColorsAndBrushes.xaml`:

```
<LinearGradientBrush x:Key="mediaButtonHover"
                     StartPoint="0.5,0"
                     EndPoint="0.5,1" >
    <GradientStop Color="#C0FFFFFF" Offset="0"/>
    <GradientStop Color="#00FFFFFF" Offset="0.33"/>
    <GradientStop Color="#00FFFFFF" Offset="0.66"/>
    <GradientStop Color="#C0FFFFFF" Offset="1"/>
</LinearGradientBrush>
```

9. The Stop button now looks like this:

```
<Button Style="{StaticResource mediaButtonStyle}"
        Click="Stop_Click">
    <Border Width="18" Height="20"
            Background="{StaticResource redRadial}"
            CornerRadius="1"
```

```
               BorderBrush="{StaticResource controlOutline}"
               BorderThickness="1"
               SnapsToDevicePixels="False">
        <Rectangle HorizontalAlignment="Center"
                   VerticalAlignment="Top"
                   Margin="0,1,0,0"
                   Width="15" Height="10"
                   Fill="{StaticResource glossBrush}"
                   RadiusX="1" RadiusY="1"/>
    </Border>
</Button>
```

10. The Mute button now looks like this:

```
<ToggleButton Grid.Column="2"
              Style="{StaticResource mediaButtonStyle}"
              IsChecked="{Binding Path=IsMuted,
              ➥ElementName=mediaElement}" >
    <Grid>
        <Canvas Width="20" Height="20">
            <!-- the speaker -->
            <Path Fill="{StaticResource redRadial}"
                Stroke="{StaticResource controlOutline}"
                StrokeLineJoin="Round">
                <Path.Data>
                    <PathGeometry>
                        <PathFigure StartPoint="12,5"
                                    IsClosed="True">
                            <LineSegment Point="0,6" />
                            <PolyLineSegment Points="0,14 12,15 17,20" />
                            <ArcSegment Point="17,0"
                                        Size="30,30"/>
                        </PathFigure>
                    </PathGeometry>
                </Path.Data>
            </Path>
            <!-- highlight -->
            <Path Fill="{StaticResource glossBrush}">
                <Path.Data>
                    <PathGeometry>
                        <PathFigure StartPoint="13,6"
                                    IsClosed="True">
                            <PolyLineSegment Points="1,7 1,11 17.5,11" />
                            <ArcSegment Point="16.5,2"
                                        Size="30,30"/>
                        </PathFigure>
                    </PathGeometry>
                </Path.Data>
            </Path>
            <!-- sound waves -->
            <Polygon Points="20,5 25,0 27,3"
                     Fill="{StaticResource textBrush}" />
            <Polygon Points="20,10 28,9 27,6"
                     Fill="{StaticResource textBrush}" />
            <Polygon Points="20,13 26,17 27,13"
                     Fill="{StaticResource textBrush}" />
```

```
            <Polygon Points="20,17 24,21 26,18"
                        Fill="{StaticResource textBrush}" />
        </Canvas>
      </Grid>
    </ToggleButton>
```

At this point, the music view of the application is really beginning to take shape.

Identifying Special Parts in Templates

ContentPresenter and ItemsPresenter provide support only for a limited number of controls. For example, if you wanted to create a template for a TextBox, how would you communicate to the template which element displays the input? Or if you are creating a ScrollBar, which has many moving parts, how does the template know which elements are which?

Many controls have special *named parts* that must be included in the template for the control to be completely functional. The named parts are simply elements with well-known names that the control expects to be there. The convention established for these well-known names is that they begin with "PART_". The control also expects these elements to be specific types. Table 21.1 lists all controls included with WPF that use named parts, as well as the expected type for each part. (Note that although most of the types are in System.Windows.Controls, some are in System.Windows.Controls.Primitives.)

Controls won't complain if you forget to include a named part—a portion (or all) of the control just won't work.
This is part of Microsoft's "Guidelines for Designing Stylable Controls." The guidelines explicitly state that a control should not throw an exception if the template fails to fulfill the contract.

TABLE 21.1   Named Parts in the Standard WPF Controls

Name	Named Parts
ComboBox	PART_EditableTextBox (TextBox)
	PART_Popup (Popup)
DocumentViewer	PART_ContentHost (ScrollViewer)
	PART_FindToolBarHost (ContentControl)
FlowDocumentPageViewer	PART_FindToolBarHost (Decorator)
FlowDocumentReader	PART_ContentHost (Decorator)
	PART_FindToolBarHost (Decorator)

TABLE 21.1   Continued

Name	Named Parts
FlowDocumentScrollViewer	PART_ContentHost (ScrollViewer) PART_FindToolBarHost (Decorator) PART_ToolBarHost (Decorator)
Frame	PART_FrameCP (ContentPresenter)
GridViewColumnHeader	PART_FloatingHeaderCanvas (Canvas) PART_HeaderGripper (Thumb)
MenuItem	PART_Popup (Popup)
NavigationWindow	PART_NavWinCP (ContentPresenter)
PasswordBox	PART_ContentHost (FrameworkElement)
ProgressBar	PART_Indicator (FrameworkElement) PART_Track (FrameworkElement)
ScrollBar	PART_Track (Track)
ScrollViewer	PART_HorizontalScrollBar (ScrollBar) PART_ScrollContentPresenter (ScrollContentPresenter) PART_VerticalScrollBar (ScrollBar)
Slider	PART_SelectionRange (FrameworkElement) PART_Track (Track)
StickyNoteControl	PART_CloseButton (Button) PART_ContentControl (ContentControl) PART_CopyMenuItem (MenuItem) PART_EraseMenuItem (MenuItem) PART_IconButton (Button) PART_InkMenuItem (MenuItem) PART_PasteMenuItem (MenuItem) PART_ResizeBottomRightThumb (Thumb) PART_SelectMenuItem (MenuItem) PART_TitleThumb (Thumb)
TabControl	PART_SelectedContentHost (ContentPresenter)
TextBoxBase	PART_ContentHost (FrameworkElement)
ToolBar	PART_ToolBarOverflowPanel (ToolBarOverflowPanel) PART_ToolBarPanel (ToolBarPanel)
TreeViewItem	PART_Header (FrameworkElement)

Microsoft's convention is that any control using parts in its template should be decorated with the TemplatePartAttribute for each of the parts. The purpose is to provide design-time support for templating, but it is also helpful for identifying the named parts in the official documentation.

Creating a Template for a Slider

We're going to create a control template for all the slider controls in the Media Viewer. Slider has two named parts, although we will be concerned with only one of them at the moment.

It will be helpful to think about the various parts of the control before we get started. Figure 21.4 shows the anatomy of the Slider.

FIGURE 21.4
The functional
elements of a
Slider.

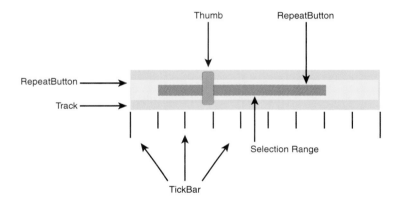

There are 6 functional parts to a Slider:

▶ **Thumb**—This is the element you click and drag to adjust the value of the Slider.

▶ **Track**—This element is responsible for the layout of the RepeatButton elements and the Thumb. This is a named part.

▶ **RepeatButton**—There are two of these elements, one on the left of the Thumb and another on the right. They allow a user to adjust the value when clicking either side of the Thumb.

▶ **TickBar**—This element displays a set of ticks. The Thumb can optionally snap to the ticks marks.

▶ **Selection Range**—This is another named part. Its purpose is to visually indicate a specific range on the slider, although it does not actually restrict the value.

For the Media Viewer, we are going only to the `Track` and `Thumb`. These two are the bare minimum we need to have a functioning `Slider`.

1. Open `DefaultStyles.xaml`.

2. Create a new style using the following:

```
<Style TargetType="{x:Type Slider}">
    <Setter Property="Template">
        <Setter.Value>
            <ControlTemplate TargetType="{x:Type Slider}">
                <Grid x:Name="root">
                    <Border Height="4"
                            CornerRadius="2"
                            Background="{StaticResource sliderBg}">
                    </Border>
                    <Track x:Name="PART_Track">
                        <Track.Thumb>
                            <Thumb />
                        </Track.Thumb>
                    </Track>
                </Grid>
            </ControlTemplate>
        </Setter.Value>
    </Setter>
</Style>
```

Notice that we didn't provide an `x:Key` attribute. This means that the styles will be applied to all the sliders in the application.

3. We need to add the `sliderBg` brush to `ColorsAndBrushes.xaml`. Open this file and add the following:

```
<LinearGradientBrush x:Key="sliderBg"
                     StartPoint="0.5,0" EndPoint="0.5,1">
    <GradientStop Color="{StaticResource redColor}" Offset="0"/>
    <GradientStop Color="{StaticResource orangeColor}" Offset="0.5"/>
    <GradientStop Color="{StaticResource redColor}" Offset="1"/>
</LinearGradientBrush>
```

4. If you run the application now and switch to the music view, you will notice that the sliders look very odd. The `Thumb` is unstyled, and it stretches vertically to the container of the slider. Add the following to `DefaultStyles.xaml`:

```
<Style TargetType="{x:Type Thumb}" >
    <Setter Property="Template">
        <Setter.Value>
```

```
<ControlTemplate TargetType="{x:Type Thumb}">
    <Grid Width="16" Height="16">
        <Ellipse Fill="{StaticResource redRadial}"
                 Stroke="{StaticResource controlOutline}"/>
        <Ellipse Fill="{StaticResource glossBrush}"
                 Margin="2,2,2,4"/>
    </Grid>
</ControlTemplate>
        </Setter.Value>
    </Setter>
</Style>
```

Again, this style applies to all thumbs in the application. A few other controls also use thumbs, so there is potential for conflict. If you discover that your style is showing up in unwanted spots, provide a key and then explicitly reference the style in your slider template. Figure 21.5 shows the results of these new templates.

FIGURE 21.5
The slider with new control templates.

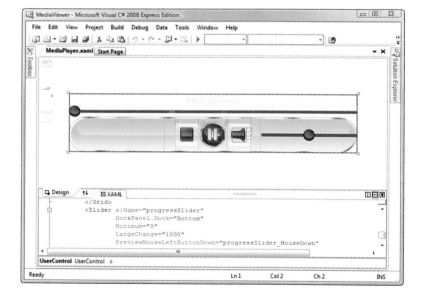

Creating a Flexible Template

Suppose that you would like to provide a single control template for all the buttons in an application. Perhaps all the buttons need to be circles, but you want to be able to set a different background brush for the circle on each button. You can accomplish this using data binding. We can bind elements in a template to the actual control.

Suppose that we have a template, named `CircleButton`, that looks like this:

```
<ControlTemplate x:Key="CircleButton" TargetType="{x:Type Button}">
    <Grid HorizontalAlignment="Center"
          VerticalAlignment="Center"
          MinHeight="36" MinWidth="36">
        <Ellipse Fill="{TemplateBinding Background}" />
        <ContentPresenter />
    </Grid>
</ControlTemplate>
```

In this example, the `Fill` property on the `Ellipse` will be set to the `Background` property of the button that the template is applied to.

Let's see how template binding works by returning the `ControlTemplates` project that we created at the beginning of this hour:

1. Open the project `ControlTemplates`.

2. Modify Windows1.xaml to match Listing 21.1. This creates three buttons in a `StackPanel` that all use the same template. However, the brush for the Fill is different for each button. Figure 21.6 shows how WPF renders this XAML.

LISTING 21.1   Window1.xaml

```
<Window x:Class="ControlTemplates.Window1"
        xmlns="http://schemas.microsoft.com/winfx/2006/xaml/presentation"
        xmlns:x="http://schemas.microsoft.com/winfx/2006/xaml"
        Title="Window1" Height="300" Width="300">
    <StackPanel>
        <StackPanel.Resources>
            <ControlTemplate x:Key="CircleButton"
                             TargetType="{x:Type Button}">
                <Grid HorizontalAlignment="Center"
                      VerticalAlignment="Center"
                      MinHeight="36" MinWidth="36">
                    <Ellipse Fill="{TemplateBinding Background}" />
                    <ContentPresenter TextBlock.FontSize="24"
                                      TextBlock.Foreground="White"
                                      HorizontalAlignment="Center"
                                      VerticalAlignment="Center" />
                </Grid>
            </ControlTemplate>
        </StackPanel.Resources>
        <Button Background="Red"
                Content="1"
                Template="{StaticResource CircleButton}" />
        <Button Background="Green"
                Content="2"
                Template="{StaticResource CircleButton}" />
        <Button Background="Blue"
                Content="3"
                Template="{StaticResource CircleButton}" />
    </StackPanel>
</Window>
```

FIGURE 21.6
A control tem-
plate using tem-
plate binding.

By the Way

Note that we are using attached properties on the ContentPresenter in Listing 21.1. The properties tell WPF to set the FontSize and Foreground for any TextBlock elements that end up in the ContentPresenter. Even though we aren't explicitly using a TextBlock in each of the buttons, we can take advantage of the fact that WPF needs to use a TextBlock to render the string we put in Content.

Template binding is very powerful. Any property on the target type of the template can be bound, including the DataContext and Tag properties.

It is a common practice to keep a control template flexible through the use of template binding. The idea is that you create a default style for your controls that sets the control template. However, you use template binding and set as many of the properties as possible in the style. That way, you can inherit from the default style, overriding specifics as needed, while retaining your control template. When you use this approach, you can think of the control template as the structural portion of your control. I've applied this pattern to the XAML we just looked at, and the result is Listing 21.2.

LISTING 21.2   Window1.xaml Refactored

```
<Window x:Class="ControlTemplates.Window1"
        xmlns="http://schemas.microsoft.com/winfx/2006/xaml/presentation"
        xmlns:x="http://schemas.microsoft.com/winfx/2006/xaml"
        Title="Window1" Height="300" Width="300">
    <StackPanel>
        <StackPanel.Resources>
            <ControlTemplate x:Key="CircleButtonTemplate"
                             TargetType="{x:Type Button}">
                <Grid HorizontalAlignment="Center"
                      VerticalAlignment="Center"
                      MinHeight="{TemplateBinding MinHeight}"
                      MinWidth="{TemplateBinding MinWidth}">
                    <Ellipse Fill="{TemplateBinding Background}" />
```

LISTING 21.2 Continued

```
                    <ContentPresenter TextBlock.FontSize=
                              ➡ "{TemplateBinding FontSize}"
                              TextBlock.Foreground=
                              ➡ "{TemplateBinding Foreground}"
                              HorizontalAlignment="Center"
                              VerticalAlignment="Center" />
            </Grid>
        </ControlTemplate>
        <!--the basic style-->
        <Style x:Key="DefaultCircleButtonStyle"
              TargetType="{x:Type Button}">
            <Setter Property="Template"
                   Value="{StaticResource CircleButtonTemplate}" />
            <Setter Property="Background"
                   Value="Red" />
            <Setter Property="Foreground"
                   Value="White" />
            <Setter Property="FontSize"
                   Value="24" />
            <Setter Property="MinHeight"
                   Value="36" />
            <Setter Property="MinWidth"
                   Value="36" />
        </Style>
        <!--a derived style-->
        <Style x:Key="NewCircleButtonStyle"
              TargetType="{x:Type Button}"
              BasedOn="{StaticResource DefaultCircleButtonStyle}">
            <Setter Property="Background"
                   Value="Green"/>
        </Style>

    </StackPanel.Resources>
    <Button Content="1"
           Style="{StaticResource DefaultCircleButtonStyle}" />
    <Button Content="2"
           Style="{StaticResource NewCircleButtonStyle}" />
    <Button Background="Blue"
           Content="3"
           Style="{StaticResource DefaultCircleButtonStyle}" />
  </StackPanel>
</Window>
```

Listing 21.2 will render the same as the previous listing. Notice that with each button we set the background brush using a different method.

The result of a template binding could also be accomplished using a regular data binding. For example, this data binding:

```
{Binding RelativeSource={RelativeSource TemplatedParent}, Path=Background}
```

is the equivalent of this template binding:

```
{TemplateBinding Background}
```

> Template bindings are preferred because they are both easier to read and more performant. However, they do have some limitations; for example, they can pass data in only one direction: from the control to the template. If you find yourself running into such a limitation, you may need to resort to a data binding.

Additional control templates for the Media Viewer are provided in the appendixes.

The Benefit of Control Templates

As we alluded to at the beginning of this hour, control templates are useful because they allow you to change the visualization and structure of a control without having to modify the behavior of the control. They provide a way to cleanly separate the look from the feel. (We discuss the principle of separating concerns further in Hour 24, "Best Practices.")

This means that you can always treat a `ListBox` as a `ListBox` in code, even though it might have a radically different appearance to the user. Because a `ListBox` can take so many different visual forms, we are able to "develop" new controls simply by creating new templates. Furthermore, control templates make it easier for developers to collaborate with designers to determine what a control should look like.

Summary

The core principles underlying control templates are easy to master. We can readily apply our knowledge of composing a UI to the process of constructing templates. Control templates provide us with the real power to completely theme an application.

The difficulty is with the details, however, as every control has unique needs when defining templates. There are lots of "gotchas," and you will find a frequent need to consult the documentation or examine reference templates.

Q&A

Q. *I need to create templates for a control we didn't cover. Where can I go to find examples?*

A. Expression Blend allows you to "decompose" controls into basic templates. Right-click a control in the Objects and Timeline panel in Blend, and then select Edit Control Parts (Template), Edit a Copy.

Additionally, Blend ships with a set of themed controls called Simple Styles. Adding one of these controls to your application adds a resource dictionary named `SimpleStyles.xaml` to your project. It is full of example templates.

Q. ***Where do the default themes come from? I've noticed that a WPF application without any styles or templates looks different on different computers.***

A. WPF ships with a set of six themes designed to match the default themes and colors on XP and Vista. The themes are stored in various assemblies that follow a naming pattern of `PresentationFramework.[ThemeName].dll`.

Workshop

Quiz

1. What are the two commonly used controls for presenting content and items in a template?

2. What's the purpose of the `TargetType` attribute on a `ControlTemplate`?

Answers

1. The `ContentPresenter` is used for `ContentControl`, and `ItemsPresenter` is used for `ItemsControl`.

2. The `TargetType` attribute tells WPF what the intended type of control is for a given template. This allows WPF to verify that things like template bindings are valid. You can specify a super class for the target type and apply it to any controls that inherit from the class.

Activities

1. Additional control templates and resources for the Media Viewer are available on the web site for this book (see Appendix C, "Project Source (downloadable)" for more information). Download these resources and add them.

2. Extend the control template for the `Slider` to use a `TickBar` and selection range.

HOUR 22

Triggers

What You'll Learn in This Hour:

▶ The rationale for triggers

▶ Trigger types

▶ Applying triggers to the Media Viewer

Triggers are the gateway to a wealth of WPF functionality. Up to now, our graphics and control templates have been fairly static and unresponsive to user input or changes in data. Triggers give us the power to change all that in a simple and intuitive way.

Leveraging Triggers

Triggers are a special feature of `Style`, `ControlTemplate`, `DataTemplate`, and `FrameworkElement`. Through the careful use of triggers, you can declaratively enable your UI and graphics to respond to mouse events, changes in dependency properties, and even changes in your application's data model. Let's look at one of the most common uses of a `Trigger` by adding some responsiveness to our media player buttons:

1. Open Visual Studio and load the Media Viewer project.

2. Open the `DefaultStyles.xaml` and navigate to the `mediaButtonStyle`.

3. Replace the existing `Style` with the following markup:

```
<Style x:Key="mediaButtonStyle"
       TargetType="{x:Type ButtonBase}">
    <Setter Property="Template">
        <Setter.Value>
            <ControlTemplate TargetType="{x:Type ButtonBase}">
                <Grid Width="32"
                      Height="32"
                      Background="Transparent">
                    <ContentPresenter VerticalAlignment="Center"
```

```
                                       HorizontalAlignment="Center" />
                    <Border x:Name="highlight"
                            Visibility="Hidden"
                            CornerRadius="3"
                            Background="{StaticResource mediaButtonHover}"
                            BorderBrush="{StaticResource glossOutline}"
                            BorderThickness="1">
                    </Border>
                </Grid>
                <ControlTemplate.Triggers>
                    <Trigger Property="IsMouseOver"
                             Value="True">
                        <Setter TargetName="highlight"
                                Property="Visibility"
                                Value="Visible" />
                    </Trigger>
                    <Trigger Property="IsPressed"
                             Value="True">
                        <Setter TargetName="highlight"
                                Property="Opacity"
                                Value="0.5" />
                    </Trigger>
                </ControlTemplate.Triggers>
            </ControlTemplate>
        </Setter.Value>
    </Setter>
</Style>
```

4. Run the application and navigate to the music view. Try mousing over the Stop and Mute buttons, as well as clicking them. The highlight effect should respond to your interactions. See Figure 22.1.

FIGURE 22.1
A trigger-based mouseover effect.

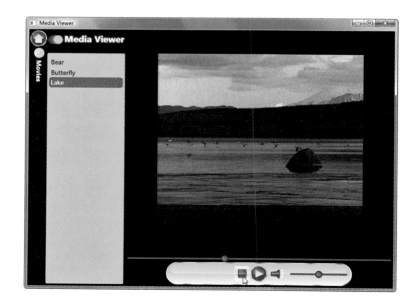

What we've done here is add a `Triggers` section to the `ControlTemplate` for our `mediaButtonStyle`. Here's how it works:

1. When the `Button` is created, WPF applies the `mediaButtonStyle`.

2. By default, the `highlight Border` is not visible.

3. When the user mouses over the `Button`, the `IsMouseOver` property becomes `True`.

4. The first `Trigger` is fired. Its `Setter` locates the element with the name `highlight` and changes its `Visibility` property to `Visible`, causing the `Button` to appear highlighted.

5. When the user presses the `Button`, the `IsPressed` property becomes `True` in addition to the `IsMouseOver`.

6. The second `Trigger` is fired. Its `Setter` changes the `Opacity` of the `highlight` to 0.5.

7. When the user releases the mouse `Button`, the `IsPressed` property becomes `False`.

8. The second `Trigger` has its `Setter` effect removed, causing the `Opacity` to return to 1.

9. When the user moves their mouse off the `Button`, the `IsMouseOver` property becomes `False`.

10. The first `Trigger` has its `Setter` effect removed, causing the `highlight` to revert to a `Visibility` of `Hidden`.

Each `Trigger` in the collection is connected to a specific `Property` and `Value` of the control. When the specified `Property` matches the `Value` declared in the `Trigger`, it uses its `Setters` collection to alter the UI. When the trigger's value ceases to match the property, the effects of the `Setters` are removed. If multiple triggers alter the same UI properties, the last one wins. The `Setter` elements used in a `Trigger` are the same as those used in a `Style`; however, most of the time you will need to specify a `TargetName`. This enables the `Setter` to reach into the `ControlTemplate` and alter the specific part of the template as needed. There's no limit to the number of setters and triggers you can define. The only stipulation is that you must trigger and alter dependency properties only.

*Did you
    Know?*

> If your triggers need to be activated by properties on elements within the
> ControlTemplate, use the SourceName property.

Let's look at another, slightly different, application of triggers within our Media
Viewer by fixing up the Play button:

1. Open the MediaPlayer.xaml file.

2. Replace the contents of the Play button with the following:

```
<Grid Margin="4 0 0 0">
    <Polygon Fill="{StaticResource yellowGradient}"
             Stroke="{StaticResource chromeOutline}"
             Points="0,0 18,10 0,18">
        <Polygon.Style>
            <Style TargetType="{x:Type Polygon}">
                <Style.Triggers>
                    <Trigger Property="DataContext" Value="Playing">
                        <Setter Property="Visibility" Value="Hidden" />
                    </Trigger>
                </Style.Triggers>
            </Style>
        </Polygon.Style>
    </Polygon>
    <Canvas>
        <Rectangle Height="18"
                   Fill="{StaticResource yellowGradient}"
                   Stroke="{StaticResource chromeOutline}"
                   Width="6"/>
        <Rectangle Height="18"
                   Fill="{StaticResource yellowGradient}"
                   Stroke="{StaticResource chromeOutline}"
                   Width="6" Canvas.Left="8"/>
        <Canvas.Style>
            <Style TargetType="{x:Type Canvas}">
                <Setter Property="Visibility" Value="Hidden" />
                <Style.Triggers>
                    <Trigger Property="DataContext" Value="Playing">
                        <Setter Property="Visibility" Value="Visible" />
                    </Trigger>
                </Style.Triggers>
            </Style>
        </Canvas.Style>
    </Canvas>
</Grid>
```

3. Run the application and navigate to the music view. Click the Play button.
   Click again to pause. You should see the graphics change as shown in
   Figure 22.2.

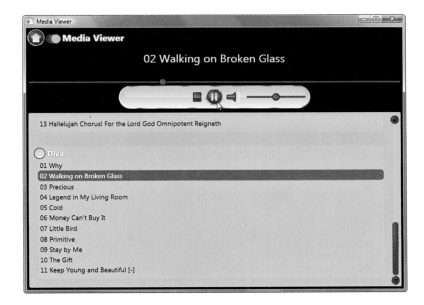

FIGURE 22.2
The media
player uses trig-
gers to switch
between play
and pause.

`Style` has a `Triggers` collection in addition to the one found on `ControlTemplate`. You may want to use this instead if your triggers are only responding to and altering properties on the control, rather than properties on elements *within* the `ControlTemplate`. This is the main difference in the uses of these two similar collections of triggers and the reason we have used it in this second example. In this case we want to change the `Visibility` of the two button graphics based on the state of the player. The `Trigger` is based on the `DataContext` of the `Canvas/Polygon`, which is inherited from the `UserControl`, where we set the different states. This makes the triggering simple.

Using a DataTrigger

As you've seen, basic triggers open up a lot of possibilities. However, sometimes triggering from simple dependency properties is not enough. The `DataTrigger` solves this problem by letting us use any data binding expression as the source of a trigger. Let's fix our Mute button to see how this works:

1. Open `MediaPlayer.xaml` and locate the `ToggleButton` used for muting the sound.

2. Replace the contents of the button with the following XAML:

```xaml
<Grid>
    <Canvas Width="20"
            Height="20">
        <!-- the speaker -->
        <Path Fill="{StaticResource redRadial}"
              Stroke="{StaticResource controlOutline}"
              StrokeLineJoin="Round">
            <Path.Data>
                <PathGeometry>
                    <PathFigure StartPoint="12,5"
                                IsClosed="True">
                        <LineSegment Point="0,6" />
                        <PolyLineSegment Points="0,14 12,15 17,20" />
                        <ArcSegment Point="17,0"
                                    Size="30,30" />
                    </PathFigure>
                </PathGeometry>
            </Path.Data>
        </Path>
        <!-- highlight -->
        <Path Fill="{StaticResource glossBrush}">
            <Path.Data>
                <PathGeometry>
                    <PathFigure StartPoint="13,6"
                                IsClosed="True">
                        <PolyLineSegment Points="1,7 1,11 17.5,11" />
                        <ArcSegment Point="16.5,2"
                                    Size="30,30" />
                    </PathFigure>
                </PathGeometry>
            </Path.Data>
        </Path>
        <!-- sound waves -->
        <Polygon Points="20,5 25,0 27,3"
                 Fill="{StaticResource textBrush}" />
        <Polygon Points="20,10 28,9 27,6"
                 Fill="{StaticResource textBrush}" />
        <Polygon Points="20,13 26,17 27,13"
                 Fill="{StaticResource textBrush}" />
        <Polygon Points="20,17 24,21 26,18"
                 Fill="{StaticResource textBrush}" />
    </Canvas>
    <!--Off symbol-->
    <Canvas>
        <Canvas.Style>
            <Style TargetType="{x:Type Canvas}">
                <Setter Property="Visibility"
                        Value="Hidden" />
                <Style.Triggers>
                    <DataTrigger Binding="{Binding Path=IsMuted,
                        ➥ ElementName=mediaElement}"
                                 Value="True">
                        <Setter Property="Visibility"
                                Value="Visible" />
```

```
                </DataTrigger>
            </Style.Triggers>
        </Style>
    </Canvas.Style>
    <Ellipse Width="20"
             Height="20"
             Stroke="{DynamicResource bgBrush}"
             Canvas.Left="0"
             Canvas.Top="0"
             StrokeThickness="3" />
    <Path Width="13.498"
          Height="16.446"
          Fill="{x:Null}"
          Stretch="Fill"
          Stroke="{DynamicResource bgBrush}"
          StrokeThickness="3"
          Canvas.Left="3.442"
          Canvas.Top="1.319"
          Data="M4.9424596,16.265143 L15.440304,2.8191997" />
    </Canvas>
</Grid>
```

3. Run the application. Navigate to the audio or video view and try muting the sound. You should see something like Figure 22.3.

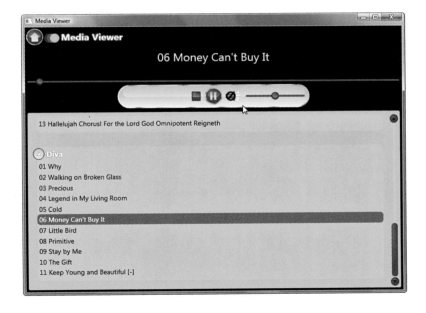

FIGURE 22.3
The media player using a `DataTrigger` to control the mute appearance.

Notice how the "off symbol" Canvas has a Style with a DataTrigger. The two important properties of DataTrigger are Binding and Value. The Binding property allows you to use any valid data binding expression to declare what will be the source of the Trigger. When the bound property is equal to the Value, the Setters are applied. DataTrigger opens up the full power of data binding to be used in styles.

> Because the Binding property of a DataTrigger supports the full breadth of data binding features, you can use an IValueConverter to pump additional logic into your trigger bindings.

Besides their use in styles, data triggers are the main type of trigger used in the Triggers collection of a DataTemplate. The presence of these triggers allows you to change the appearance of rendered data based on property values of the data itself. To see how this works, we'll revisit the Contact Manager.

1. Open the Contact Manager solution in Visual Studio.

2. Open the SideBar.xaml file and locate the DataTemplate.

3. Within the DataTemplate, find the second Border and add this attribute:

   ```
   x:Name="border"
   ```

4. Scroll down to the end of the DataTemplate and add this markup:

   ```
   <DataTemplate.Triggers>
       <DataTrigger Binding="{Binding Address.State}"
                    Value="Florida">
           <Setter TargetName="border"
                   Property="BorderBrush"
                   Value="Orange" />
       </DataTrigger>
   </DataTemplate.Triggers>
   ```

5. Run the application. Create a contact with a Florida address and save. You should see something similar to Figure 22.4.

FIGURE 22.4
A contact list with data triggered coloration.

Adding Animation with EventTrigger

EventTrigger is the final type of trigger that WPF currently offers. Essentially, its purpose is to enable declarative control over animations that are triggered by routed events. Let's see how this works:

1. Return to the Media Viewer and open DefaultStyles.xaml and locate the fancyButtonStyle.

2. Replace this style with the markup found in Listing 22.1.

3. Run the application and navigate to the music or video view. Mouse over the Play button and observe the animation. You should also see the same effect applied to the Home button in the application's header.

LISTING 22.1   fancyButtonStyle

```
<Style x:Key="fancyButtonStyle"
      TargetType="{x:Type Button}">
   <Setter Property="Margin"
          Value="4" />
   <Setter Property="Template">
      <Setter.Value>
         <ControlTemplate TargetType="{x:Type ButtonBase}">
            <Grid HorizontalAlignment="Center"
                  VerticalAlignment="Center">
```

LISTING 22.1   Continued

```
<Ellipse x:Name="chromeEdge"
         Margin="-2"
         Width="36"
         Height="36"
         Fill="{StaticResource chromeBrush}"
         Stroke="{StaticResource chromeOutline}"
         StrokeThickness="0.5"
         RenderTransformOrigin="0.5,0.5">
    <Ellipse.RenderTransform>
        <RotateTransform />
    </Ellipse.RenderTransform>
</Ellipse>
<Ellipse x:Name="bg"
         Width="32"
         Height="32"
         Stroke="{StaticResource redBrush}"
         Fill="{StaticResource redRadial}" />
<ContentPresenter HorizontalAlignment="Center"
                  VerticalAlignment="Center" />
<Rectangle x:Name="gloss"
           Margin="3.5"
           Width="25"
           Height="16"
           Stroke="{StaticResource bgBrush}"
           StrokeThickness="0"
           RadiusX="20"
           RadiusY="10"
           Fill="{StaticResource glossBrush}"
           VerticalAlignment="Top" />
</Grid>
<ControlTemplate.Triggers>
    <EventTrigger RoutedEvent="UIElement.MouseEnter">
        <BeginStoryboard>
            <Storyboard Storyboard.TargetName="chromeEdge"
                        Storyboard.TargetProperty=
                        ➥"RenderTransform.Angle">
                <DoubleAnimation To="90"
                                 Duration="0:0:0.10" />
            </Storyboard>
        </BeginStoryboard>
    </EventTrigger>
    <EventTrigger RoutedEvent="UIElement.MouseLeave">
        <BeginStoryboard>
            <Storyboard Storyboard.TargetName="chromeEdge"
                        Storyboard.TargetProperty=
                        ➥"RenderTransform.Angle">
                <DoubleAnimation To="0"
                                 Duration="0:0:0.10" />
            </Storyboard>
        </BeginStoryboard>
    </EventTrigger>
    <Trigger Property="IsPressed"
             Value="True">
```

LISTING 22.1   Continued

```
                <Setter Property="RenderTransform"
                        TargetName="chromeEdge">
                    <Setter.Value>
                        <TransformGroup>
                            <RotateTransform Angle="90" />
                        </TransformGroup>
                    </Setter.Value>
                </Setter>
            </Trigger>
        </ControlTemplate.Triggers>
    </ControlTemplate>
</Setter.Value>
</Setter>
</Style>
```

Animation is a complex topic and is discussed in depth in Hour 23, so we won't focus on that right now. The important part of this code is the EventTrigger. Notice the important RoutedEvent property, which is used to declare which event will trigger the action. Rather than having a collection of Setter elements, EventTrigger has a collection of TriggerActions. There are several inheritors of TriggerAction. We've used the BeginStoryboard TriggerAction to start an animation. Table 22.1 lists the other types of actions and their purposes.

TABLE 22.1   TriggerAction Inheritors

Name	Description
BeginStoryboard	Begins an animation
SoundPlayerAction	Plays a sound file
PauseStoryboard	Pauses an animation
RemoveStoryboard	Removes an animation
ResumeStoryboard	Resumes a paused animation
SeekStoryboard	Skips the animation ahead to a specified time
SetStoryboardSpeedRatio	Changes the speed of an animation
SkipStoryboardToFill	Skips the animation ahead to the end of its fill
StopStoryboard	Stops an animation

As you can see, many things can be triggered with an EventTrigger. Because WPF defines a wealth of routed events (pretty much every important event), it is easy to wire up animation-related actions to almost anything.

Understanding Trigger Restrictions

If you look back at Listing 22.1, you'll notice that we used two types of triggers in our ControlTemplate: EventTrigger and Trigger. In many cases, WPF allows the use of different types of triggers together. However, WPF places some restrictions on *where* you can use different types of triggers. Table 22.2 lists the different trigger collection locations and pairs them with the appropriate type of triggers to use.

TABLE 22.2   Trigger Usage

Trigger Collection	Allowed Trigger Types
FrameworkElement.Triggers	EventTrigger only.
Style.Triggers	All trigger types allowed.
ControlTemplate.Triggers	All trigger types allowed.
DataTemplate.Triggers	All trigger types allowed, but it is generally a good practice to limit to DataTrigger.

From Table 22.2 it is obvious that the most limiting collection is FrameworkElement.Triggers. Otherwise, WPF is very flexible.

At the time of the writing of this book, the MSDN documentation has some incorrect information regarding the FrameworkElement.Triggers collection. It states that it can be set only on the root visual. However, it can be set at any level within the element hierarchy.

Advanced Trigger Scenarios

Sometimes a situation arises in which a simple Trigger can't express the conditions under which a collection of setters should be applied. For these scenarios, WPF provides the MultiTrigger and the MultiDataTrigger. These represent more advanced versions of Trigger and DataTrigger, respectively. Instead of having a simple Property or Binding and a Value, they each have a collection called Conditions. To leverage this functionality, you add multiple Condition instances to this collection. When all the conditions are met, the setters will be applied. Here's an example of what some XAML might look like for the Contact Manager:

```
<DataTemplate DataType="{x:Type local:Contact}">
    <Border x:Name="border"
            Background="Green">
        <TextBox Foreground="White"
                 Text="{Binding LookupName}" />
    </Border>
    <DataTemplate.Triggers>
        <MultiDataTrigger>
            <MultiDataTrigger.Conditions>
                <Condition Binding="{Binding Organization}"
                           Value="Blue Spire Consulting, Inc." />
                <Condition Binding="{Binding Address.City}"
                           Value="Tallahassee" />
            </MultiDataTrigger.Conditions>
            <MultiDataTrigger.Setters>
                <Setter TargetName="border"
                        Property="Background"
                        Value="Blue" />
            </MultiDataTrigger.Setters>
        </MultiDataTrigger>
    </DataTemplate.Triggers>
</DataTemplate>
```

In this scenario, the border's background would be changed from green to blue only if the Contact.Organization property was equal to "Blue Spire Consulting, Inc." *and* the Contact.Address.City was equal to "Tallahassee." If either of these two conditions is not met, the background remains green.

A Setter can be used to change out an entire Style or ControlTemplate. Often times a complex Style will use triggers to switch out different control templates depending on the values of the control. Just be aware that if the setter is part of a Style, it cannot switch itself out. The same applies to templates.

Did you Know?

Summary

Triggers are a very powerful feature of WPF. They greatly expand the capabilities of Styles, ControlTemplates, and DataTemplates, allowing them to be dynamic and responsive. FrameworkElement is also extended with trigger capabilities for very specific animation-related scenarios. By combining triggers with animations, you can truly harness the power of WPF.

Q&A

Q. *Is it possible to start animations based on a* `Trigger` *or* `DataTrigger`?

A. Yes. Both `Trigger` and `DataTrigger` (as well as `MultiTrigger` and `MultiDataTrigger`) have an `EnterActions` and `ExitActions` collection. The `EnterActions` collection allows you to list instances of `TriggerAction` that should be executed when the trigger is matched. `ExitActions` is a set of `TriggerActions` that will execute when the `Trigger` goes from a matched state to an unmatched state.

Workshop

Quiz

1. What trigger collection supports only `EventTrigger`?

2. What are the four locations where triggers can be set?

Answers

1. `FrameworkElement.Triggers` does not work with `Trigger` or `DataTrigger`. It supports only `EventTrigger`.

2. Triggers can be set on `FrameworkElement`, `Style`, `ControlTemplate`, and `DataTemplate`.

Activities

1. At this point, we have covered every aspect of styles except one rarely used feature. Research `EventSetter` on MSDN to complete your knowledge.

HOUR 23

Animation

What You'll Learn in This Hour:

▶ Some underlying concepts for animation in general
▶ The mechanics of animation in WPF
▶ Creating animations in XAML
▶ How to apply animations to styles and control templates

Animation is one of the more complicated topics to discuss in WPF—not because it is technically more difficult, but because it has many prerequisites. To fully discuss animation, you need to have knowledge of routed events, dependency properties, triggers, and many other aspects of WPF. Hopefully, you have a sense of satisfaction that you are now ready to tackle the subject.

Understanding Animation in General

Before we dig into the tools that WPF provides for creating animations, we should take a moment to understand the fundamentals of animation in general. At its root, an animation is a series of images shown in rapid succession to give the illusion of motion. "Motion" has a broad meaning here, and you could substitute the phrase "continuous change." The practical difficulty of producing animation is that it takes a large number of images to create even a few seconds of motion.

The individual images in an animation are referred to as *frames*. The number of frames per second (fps) is called the *frame rate*. Most television and film is somewhere between 20 and 30fps. The higher the frame rate, the smoother the animation will seem. Computer graphics generally target a frame rate around 60fps.

In traditional hand-drawn animation, each frame is drawn by hand. As you can imagine, this is a somewhat tedious process. Teams of animators are employed to create all the necessary frames. However, a lead animator draws the *key frames*. Key frames are the frames that represent significant points in the motion, such as the start and end points. All the remaining frames, those in between the key frames, are called *tweens*. (That's a contraction of "in between frames.")

The animation system of WPF, as well as that of Adobe Flash, allows you to define the key frames, and then it will handle the tweens for you. For example, say that you have a circle that you want to move along a linear path from the right side of the screen to the left. You can specify the starting position and the ending position of the circle, and then allow WPF to interpolate all the necessary positions in between.

Understanding Animation in WPF

One of the central concepts behind animation in WPF is *timelines*. (In fact, timelines are central to most computer animation frameworks.) A timeline is a segment of time; it has a beginning point and duration. In other words, it is "when does the animation start" and "how long does it last." In some cases, you will designate key frames at certain points along the timelines, but in many cases the key frames will be implied from the beginning and end of the timeline.

In WPF, timelines are represented by classes inheriting from `System.Windows. Media.Animation.Timeline`. There are lots of classes that derive from `Timeline`. Many of them contain `Animation` in their names. For example, `ColorAnimation`, `StringAnimationUsingKeyFrames`, and `PointAnimationUsingPath` are all derived from `Timeline`. These classes are responsible for defining how a value changes over their duration. Take a look at this snippet of XAML:

```
<ColorAnimation From="Yellow" To="Red" Duration="0:0:5"
                Storyboard.TargetProperty="Fill.Color" />
```

This is a timeline responsible for changing a `Color` from yellow to red over the course of 5 seconds. We can provide a string in the format of "hours:minutes: seconds" for the `Duration` property. This timeline has two implicit keyframes. The first is right at the beginning, that is at "0:0:0". The second is at "0:0:5". `ColorAnimation` knows how to interpolate between two `Color` values.

The attached property, `Storyboard.TargetProperty`, is a reference to the property we are animating.

An important concept to grasp here is that these timeline classes are tied to specifc types. `ColorAnimation` knows only how to interpolate between two `Color` values. If you need to animate a property of type `double`, you must use a class like `DoubleAnimation`.

The Storyboard class is a special timeline. You will use it for all the animations that you build in XAML. It's a container timeline that allows you to group other timelines. It can also tell its children which object and property to target for the animation. We'll come back to Storyboard and other timelines in a moment.

To animate something, we need to answer a few questions for WPF:

▶ What object are we targeting for the animation?

▶ Which property on the target object are we going to animate?

▶ When does the animation start? Or what triggers the animation?

▶ How long does the animation last?

▶ How does the property change over the course of the animation?

Let's create a simple project with a simple animation and examine how we can answer these questions in XAML. We'll animate a small red ball moving across the window over the course of 7.5 seconds:

1. Create a new project called **LearningAnimation**.

2. Replace the markup in Window1.xaml with the XAML supplied in Listing 23.1.

LISTING 23.1   Window1.xaml

```xaml
<Window x:Class="LearningAnimation.Window1"
        xmlns="http://schemas.microsoft.com/winfx/2006/xaml/presentation"
        xmlns:x="http://schemas.microsoft.com/winfx/2006/xaml"
        Title="Window1"
        Height="300" Width="300">
    <Window.Triggers>
        <EventTrigger RoutedEvent="Window.Loaded">
            <BeginStoryboard>
                <Storyboard Storyboard.TargetName="Ball"
                            Storyboard.TargetProperty="(Canvas.Left)">
                    <DoubleAnimation By="300"
                                     Duration="0:0:07.5"/>
                </Storyboard>
            </BeginStoryboard>
        </EventTrigger>
    </Window.Triggers>
    <Canvas>
        <Ellipse x:Name="Ball"
                 Width="20" Height="20"
                 Fill="Red"
                 Canvas.Top="50" Canvas.Left="0">
        </Ellipse>
    </Canvas>
</Window>
```

3. The animation will not play in the preview pane, so you need to run the application to see it.

We have a simple, red `Ellipse` that we have given the name `Ball`. We place `Ball` at 50px from the top. We want to animate it so that it moves all the way across the window.

The `Storyboard` element answers two of our questions. It says that we are targeting `Ball` and that we want to animate the attached property, `Canvas.Left`. We want the animation to start when the `Loaded` event for the `Window` executes. The `EventTrigger` takes a `BeginStoryboard`, which derives from `TriggerAction`. We'll discuss `BeginStoryboard` in more detail later; for now you can read the XAML as "when the window is loaded begin the storyboard."

The `Storyboard` has a single child. It's a `DoubleAnimation` because `Canvas.Left` is of type `double`. It also answers our remaining questions. The animation will last for 7.5 seconds, and at the end of the duration the targeted property should be increased by 300. `DoubleAnimation` increases the value linearly, which results in a very mechanical animation.

Making an Animation Tick

The `Clock` class (also located in the `System.Windows.Media.Animation` namespace) performs the actual work of the animation. You don't handle clocks directly in XAML (though you might do so in code). Every timeline instance has a related clock instance. I like to think of a timeline as a set of instructions for a clock. The timeline merely describes what should happen. The clock handles updating the property that we are animating, and it keeps track of the current state of the animation.

A clock behaves like a timer, updating its target at intervals. The intervals are very small, but the actual size and regularity is dependent on the system resources.

By the Way

> We are focusing on how to create animations in XAML and so we're not going to go through any examples that show you how to use clocks in code. There are lots of resources and tutorials available on MSDN. Search for the `Clock` class, as well as "Animation and Timing System Overview."
>
> You might benefit from using a clock in code if you have demanding animations and need to optimize for performance.

Timelines as Easing Equations

If you have a background with Adobe Flash, you may be familiar with the term *easing*. Easing refers to how an animated value changes with time. To talk about this mathematically, we are changing some value *v* with respect to time *t*. If we are changing `Canvas.Left` for an element, and we are moving from 50 to 250 over the course of 5 seconds, we could express it as the following equation:

$$v = 50 + \frac{t}{5}(200)$$

More generically, if we call the starting value *A*, the ending value *B*, and the duration *d*, we could express it as

$$v = A + \frac{t}{d(B - A)}$$

You might recognize that this can be simplified to a linear equation of the form

$$y = mx + b$$

The graph of a linear equation is a straight line, as shown in Figure 23.1.

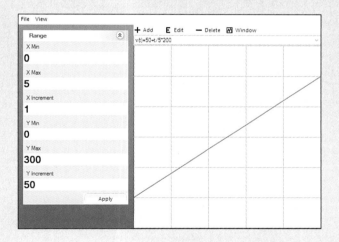

FIGURE 23.1
The graph of a linear equation: x axis is time; y axis is the value.

The timeline classes in WPF named with pattern XAnimation use linear equations. They will plug in the values that you provide into a linear equation. The clock supplies *t*, and then sets targeted property to resulting *v*. If we use the property names as variables, the equation would look like

$$v = From + \frac{t}{Duration}(To - From)$$

(Using the property By is just short for (*To–From*).)

Visually, a linear equation produces change at a constant speed. If you are animating position, the element will not speed up nor slow down as it moves. There is no acceleration.

Linear equations result in animations that look stiff and mechanical, especially when we are animating motion. For motion to look natural, we expect it to speed up and slow down. This speeding up and slowing down is where the term *easing* comes from—in the sense of lessening or abating.

If you want to achieve nonlinear easing in WPF you have two options. The first is to use any of the classes named with pattern XAnimationUsingPath. They allow you to define the curve used to interpolate values over time using the PathGeometry class that we covered in Hour 18, "Drawing with Shapes." The second option is to create your own custom timeline classes using whatever equations you like.

For more information on these concepts, check out http://thewpfblog.com. Specifically, look for the posts regarding Robert Penner and porting his easing equations from ActionScript to C#.

Animations in the Media Viewer

In the previous hours, we added animations for fancyButtonStyle in DefaultStyles.xaml. Specifically, we added two animations to the control template embedded in that style. Let's take a moment to examine them. The following snippet has the two EventTrigger from the template.

```
<EventTrigger RoutedEvent="UIElement.MouseEnter">
    <BeginStoryboard>
        <Storyboard Storyboard.TargetName="chromeEdge"
            Storyboard.TargetProperty="RenderTransform.Angle">
            <DoubleAnimation To="90" Duration="0:0:0.10" />
        </Storyboard>
    </BeginStoryboard>
</EventTrigger>
<EventTrigger RoutedEvent="UIElement.MouseLeave">
    <BeginStoryboard>
        <Storyboard Storyboard.TargetName="chromeEdge"
            Storyboard.TargetProperty="RenderTransform.Angle">
            <DoubleAnimation To="0" Duration="0:0:0.10" />
        </Storyboard>
    </BeginStoryboard>
</EventTrigger>
```

Both of these animations should make more sense to you now. We can read the first animation as "when the mouse enters the UIElement, animate the angle on the RenderTransform for the element named chromeEdge, beginning from its current value to the value of 90, over the course of 0.10 seconds." The second animation is merely the inverse of this.

There are a few things to note about these animations. By default, an Ellipse will have a null value for RenderTransform. In the markup for our control template, we explicitly set RenderTransform to an instance of RotateTransform. The default value of `Angle` on a new instance of `RotateTransform` is 0. If we had not provided a `RotateTransform`, the animation would have thrown an exception when it was triggered. Additionally, `RenderTransform` isn't guaranteed to be an instance of `RotateTransform`; it might have been any derivative of `Transform`. If so, the animation could not have resolved the `Angle` property, and again it would have thrown an exception.

We purposefully did not set the `From` values on either animation. If we set `From`, the target property will snap to that value when the animation is triggered. If we moved the mouse over and off of the element repeatedly, this would result in very jumpy motion. If you change the `Duration` to a longer value, such as 3 seconds, you can easily see how the animation transitions smoothly.

Let's add a new animation to the Media Viewer. We want to make images on the picture view grow when we mouse over them, and revert to their default size when we mouse out.

1. Open the MediaViewer project.

2. Open `PictureView.xaml`, and locate the `Image` element. It's located in the `DataTemplate`.

3. We need to add a couple of `EventTrigger` elements, one for the `Image.MouseEnter` event and another for `Image.MouseLeave`. Add the following markup inside the `Image` element:

```
<Image.Triggers>
    <EventTrigger RoutedEvent="Image.MouseEnter">
        <BeginStoryboard>
            <Storyboard>
                <DoubleAnimation By="25" Duration="0:0:0.25"
                                 Storyboard.TargetProperty="Width" />
            </Storyboard>
        </BeginStoryboard>
    </EventTrigger>
    <EventTrigger RoutedEvent="Image.MouseLeave">
        <BeginStoryboard>
            <Storyboard>
                <DoubleAnimation To="{TemplateBinding Width}"
                                 Duration="0:0:0.25"
                                 Storyboard.TargetProperty="Width" />
            </Storyboard>
        </BeginStoryboard>
    </EventTrigger>
</Image.Triggers>
```

4. The only new thing we've introduced here is the use of the template binding. Because we are in a data template, we can use this kind of binding to see the `To` value from the animation. Run the application and examine the new animations.

The animation for `MouseEnter` uses the `By` property, and the `MouseLeave` animation is bound to the `Width`. This means that both animations are independent of the actual size of the image. The designer could change the image size and not need to worry about breaking the animations.

Also, notice that we are animating only the `Width`, but the `Height` of the images also changes. This is because the default value of `Image.Stretch` is `Uniform`, which keeps the `Width` and `Height` synchronized.

Resolving the Target Property

The target property for an animation can be any dependency property. This also includes properties that have no visual significance. As we have already seen, we can specify a path to the target property. This is similar to what we have seen with data binding.

There are a few cases in which the path to the property requires disambiguation. Consider this snippet from earlier in the hour:

```
<Storyboard Storyboard.TargetName="Ball"
            Storyboard.TargetProperty="(Canvas.Left)">
    <DoubleAnimation By="300" Duration="0:0:07.5"/>
</Storyboard>
```

Notice the parentheses around the target property. We use the parentheses to tell WPF that `Canvas.Left` is a single property. If we omit the parentheses, WPF would look for a property named `Canvas` on the `Ellipse`. This means that when animating an attached property, you will need to enclose it in parentheses.

If you are using a tool such as Blend, you might also encounter a target property that looks like this:

```
Storyboard.TargetProperty="(UIElement.RenderTransform).(RotateTransform.Angle)"
```

These are not attached properties. Instead, these are properties that are qualified by their types. This property path is equivalent to the one we used in `fancyButtonStyle`:

```
Storyboard.TargetProperty="RenderTransform.Angle"
```

You might also need a property path that references a specific index in a collection. Imagine that the `RenderTransform` from `chromeEdge` has this value:

```
<Ellipse.RenderTransform>
    <TransformGroup>
        <ScaleTransform/>
        <RotateTransform />
```

```
        <TranslateTransform/>
    </TransformGroup>
</Ellipse.RenderTransform>
```

We could still reference the `RotateTransform` using

```
Storyboard.TargetProperty="RenderTransform.Children[1].Angle"
```

Notice that we have to include the `Children` property, even though it is not present in the XAML.

For a thorough discussion of the syntax used for accessing properties, search for "PropertyPath XAML Syntax" on MSDN.

Where to Put Your Animations

There is a great deal of flexibility in where you can place an animation. `Storyboard` elements themselves are reusable, and they are frequently placed in a resource dictionary. This is also helpful for maintainability.

Storyboards can be triggered directly from an instance of an element. Our very first example this hour, the `LearningAnimation` project, triggered the animation directly from the instance of the window.

Any element can trigger an animation. Again, the animation in `LearningAnimation` could have been triggered from the `Canvas` element, or even the `Ellipse` that was the target of the animation.

In the official documentation, the practice of triggering an animation directly from an instance of an element is referred to as beginning an animation *per-instance*.

In addition to this technique, animations can be triggered from styles, control templates, and data templates. Animations can even be started by triggers other than event triggers, although the syntax is somewhat different.

You should be aware of some limitations when you place animations in a style or template.

Inside of a `Style`, you cannot use `Storyboard.TargetName`. When you create an animation in a style, it will always target the element that the style is applied to. Likewise, you cannot specify the `SourceName` on a trigger. On the whole, a storyboard inside a style cannot reference dynamic resources or data bind.

For animations within a control template and data templates, you may only reference elements that are children of the template. Just as with styles, you cannot reference dynamic resources or perform data binding.

Achieving the Desired Effect

A set of properties common to most timelines help you achieve certain effects with your animation that might otherwise be tedious. These are properties set directly on the animation elements in XAML.

Table 23.1 lists some of the more frequently used properties.

TABLE 23.1   Useful Properties on Timeline

Name	Description
AccelerationRatio	Percentage of Duration that the animation will speed up at the beginning. Values are between 0.0 and 1.0. We'll explain this in more detail in the following section.
AutoReverse	If true, the animation will play in reverse after its first forward playback.
BeginTime	This allows you to set an offset for when the animation will begin—for example, if you want the playback to start 2 seconds after the animation is triggered.
DecelerationRatio	Like AccelerationRatio, except it governs how the animation will slow down at the end.
FillBehavior	Determines what the animation will do after it's done.
RepeatBehavior	Allows you to control if and how an animation will repeat. For example, it might repeat just once or forever.
SpeedRatio	Changes the rate of playback relative to the parent timeline (which is most commonly the Storyboard). For example, even if the Duration is the same for both the parent and child, a SpeedRatio of 5 will result in the child playing 5× faster than the parent.

Acceleration and Deceleration

These two properties, AccelerationRatio and DecelerationRatio, allow you to change the easing of the animation. Both properties are percentages, ranging in value from 0.0 to 1.0. AccelerationRatio affects the beginning of the animation, and DecelerationRatio affects the end.

Suppose you have a simple animation, similar to the one we created in
LearningAnimation, and that it has a Duration of 10 seconds.

```
<DoubleAnimation By="300" Duration="0:0:10"/>
```

In this case, the ball would move at a constant rate of 30 pixels per second. Now
we'll add AccelerationRatio and DecelerationRatio, both with a value of 40%.

```
<DoubleAnimation By="300"
                AccelerationRatio="0.4"
                DecelerationRatio="0.4"
                Duration="0:0:10"/>
```

With this markup, the ball will start at a speed of 0 and accelerate for 4 seconds.
Then, beginning at the sixth second, it will slow down for 4 seconds.

This is an easy and useful way to achieve a more natural motion.

What Happens When an Animation Ends?

The *fill* is what the animation does after it has run its course. In our ball example,
the ball just stops and maintains its last position at the end of the animation. The
two possible values are Stop and HoldEnd. A FillBehavior of Stop will cause the
property being animated to revert to the initial value.

Fill is affected by the duration of the containing timeline. The behavior is only
applied if the child timeline is allowed to complete. This is really only noticeable
with Stop. In the following snippet, the ball will return to its original position at the
end of 10 seconds.

```
<Storyboard Storyboard.TargetName="Ball"
            Storyboard.TargetProperty="(Canvas.Left)">
    <DoubleAnimation By="300" Duration="0:0:10" FillBehavior="Stop"/>
</Storyboard>
```

However, if we explictly set the Duration of the Storyboard to 5 seconds, the
DoubleAnimation will never complete, and the FillBehavior has no effect.

```
<Storyboard Duration="0:0:5"
            Storyboard.TargetName="Ball"
            Storyboard.TargetProperty="(Canvas.Left)">
    <DoubleAnimation By="300" Duration="0:0:10" FillBehavior="Stop"/>
</Storyboard>
```

Making an Animation Repeat

RepeatBehavior also controls the behavior of the animation after it reaches the
end. Like FillBehavior, this is governed by its parent timeline. There are three

ways to set the behavior. The value `Forever` causes the animation to repeat forever. You can specify a specific number of iterations with a number followed by x. For example, 2x will repeat twice. Finally, you can specify a duration in the same format we've seen before, "`hh:mm:ss`." The animation will loop until this duration runs out. If the repeat duration is not a multiple of the animation's overall duration, the final loop will stop partway through the animation.

Animating with Key Frames

When people talk about animating with key frames in WPF, they usually mean using key frames explicitly to control the animation. Up to this point, I've used the term more loosely to mean significant values at specific points on the timeline. These values are what WPF uses to interpolate the intermediate values. These key frames are implied by the `From`, `To`, and `By` properties.

You can, however, use key frames explicitly. The classes that allow you to use key frames are named with pattern `XAnimationUsingKeyFrames`. Let's use one these classes to make our ball move in a square.

1. Open the project `LearningAnimation`.

2. Open Window1.xaml, and replace the Storyboard with this:

```
<Storyboard Storyboard.TargetName="Ball">
    <DoubleAnimationUsingKeyFrames
    ➡Storyboard.TargetProperty="(Canvas.Left)">
        <LinearDoubleKeyFrame Value="50" KeyTime="0:0:2" />
        <LinearDoubleKeyFrame Value="50" KeyTime="0:0:4" />
        <LinearDoubleKeyFrame Value="0" KeyTime="0:0:6" />
    </DoubleAnimationUsingKeyFrames>
    <DoubleAnimationUsingKeyFrames Storyboard.TargetProperty="(Canvas.Top)"
                                   BeginTime="0:0:2">
        <LinearDoubleKeyFrame Value="100" KeyTime="0:0:2"  />
        <LinearDoubleKeyFrame Value="100" KeyTime="0:0:4"  />
        <LinearDoubleKeyFrame Value="50" KeyTime="0:0:6" />
    </DoubleAnimationUsingKeyFrames>
</Storyboard>
```

3. Go ahead and run the application.

A few things to note: First we target `Ball` on the `Storyboard`, but we target the properties on the `DoubleAnimationUsingKeyFrame` instances. We are actually animating two properties at the same time. The `Storyboard` passes its targeting information to its children, but you can override it at the child.

Each of the `LinearDoubleKeyFrame` elements represents what the value for the property will be at a specific time.

The animation for `Canvas.Left` begins at a value of 0 and moves to 50 over the first two seconds. We want it to stay at 50 for another two seconds while we animate `Canvas.Top`. Finally, we want it to move back to 0 between the fourth and sixth seconds.

The animation for `Canvas.Top` begins with a value of 50. That is the value we set for the property on `Ball`. We used `BeginTime` to start the animation two seconds after the `Storyboard` is triggered. This means that all the `KeyTime` values are offset by two seconds. The `KeyTime`, `0:0:2` for `Canvas.Top`, is at the same moment as `0:0:4` for `Canvas.Left`. It was not necessary to use `BeginTime` here, but it demonstrates nicely how the property works.

`LinearDoubleKeyFrame` is one of several classes for representing key frames. The classes are all named using the pattern [InterpolationMethod][Type]KeyFrame. Thus, `LinearDoubleKeyFrame` represents a key frame for a double value that uses linear interpolation. There are three possible interpolation methods for the key frames classes. Table 23.2 describes them.

TABLE 23.2   Interpolation Methods for Key Frames

Name	Description
Discrete	The property snaps to the value at the KeyTime. In a sense, there is really no interpolation.
Linear	The value changes at a constant rate. This is the same behavior as using an XAnimation timeline.
Splined	This allows you to specify a set of points that represents a curve. It is not unlike using PathGeometry in an XAnimationUsingPath timeline.

One final thing to note about key frame classes is the options you have for setting the `KeyTime`. In our example, we have set `KeyTime` using hh:mm:ss. There are three alternatives to this.

You can express `KeyTime` as a percentage, such as 20%. This is interpreted as a percentage of the duration of the animation. (This means that Duration needs to be set to value.) If the duration of the timeline is `0:0:20`, and the `KeyTime` of a particular frame is 20%, the frame will be active at `0:0:04`.

If you set all `KeyTime` properties to `Uniform`, the duration of the animation is divided evenly between the key frames. For example, if we had an animation with a duration of 10 seconds, and it contained four key frames, equivalent `KeyTime` values would be 2.5, 5.0, 7.5, and 10.

When using a `KeyTime` value of `Paced`, WPF attempts to time the key frames in such a way as to create a constant velocity.

> The best way to understand the differences and nuances of these classes is to spend some time creating simple animations and then adjust. A plethora of examples are available online; just search MSDN for "`KeyTime.Paced`."

Animating with a Path

We can use path geometry to provide the values for our target property. It can sometimes be difficult to visualize how the values from a path will be used. Because we are dealing with geometry, we have both an X and a Y value for any given point on the path.

Let's imagine a very simple path such as the one in Figure 23.2. It consists of three equal segments; two horizontal and one vertical.

FIGURE 23.2
A path used for animation.

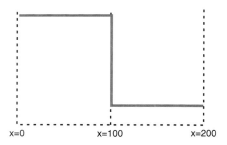

Now imagine a point moving along the path at a constant rate. If we wanted it to take 3 seconds total to traverse the path, it would take 1 second per segment. By default, our animated value corresponds to the position of the imaginary point on the X axis. This means that the value won't change at all between seconds 1 and 2.

Classes such as `DoubleAnimationUsingPath` have a property, `Source`, which allows us to say whether we want the X or the Y value. If we want to make an element trace a path, we can provide two animations, one using X and the other using Y.

Let's see how this works out in real XAML.

1. Open `LearningAnimation`.

2. We'll start using the path represented in Figure 23.2. Replace the markup in `Window1.xaml` with Listing 23.2.

LISTING 23.2 Window1.xaml Demonstrating Animation with a Path

```xaml
<Window x:Class="LearningAnimation.Window1"
        xmlns="http://schemas.microsoft.com/winfx/2006/xaml/presentation"
        xmlns:x="http://schemas.microsoft.com/winfx/2006/xaml"
        Title="Window1"
        Height="300" Width="300">
    <Window.Resources>
        <PathGeometry x:Key="path" Figures="M0,0 L100,0 100,100 200,100" />
    </Window.Resources>
    <Window.Triggers>
        <EventTrigger RoutedEvent="Window.Loaded">
            <BeginStoryboard>
                <Storyboard Storyboard.TargetName="Ball">
                    <DoubleAnimationUsingPath Duration="0:0:10"
                                              Storyboard.TargetProperty=
                                              ➥ "(Canvas.Left)"
                                              Source="X"
                                              PathGeometry=
                                              ➥ "{StaticResource path}" />
                    <DoubleAnimationUsingPath Duration="0:0:10"
                                              Storyboard.TargetProperty=
                                              ➥ "(Canvas.Top)"
                                              Source="Y"
                                              PathGeometry=
                                              ➥ "{StaticResource path}" />
                </Storyboard>
            </BeginStoryboard>
        </EventTrigger>
    </Window.Triggers>
    <Canvas>
        <Ellipse x:Name="Ball"
                 Width="20" Height="20"
                 Fill="Red"
                 Canvas.Top="50" Canvas.Left="0">
        </Ellipse>
        <Path Stroke="Red" StrokeThickness="2" Data="{StaticResource path}">

        </Path>
    </Canvas>
</Window>
```

3. Run the application and observe the animation.

4. Stop the program, and replace `Figures` on `PathGeometry` with

   ```
   M50,10 C100,10 0,90 50,100 C100,90 0,10 50,10 z
   ```

5. Run the application once more and observe the animation.

If you would like to make the center of the ball follow the path, instead of the upper left corner, you can use a transform. You would shift the ball's x and y position by half of its width and height. Thus the resulting `Ellipse` would look like this:

```
<Ellipse x:Name="Ball"
         Width="20" Height="20"
         Fill="Red"
         Canvas.Top="50" Canvas.Left="0">
    <Ellipse.RenderTransform>
        <TranslateTransform X="-10" Y="-10" />
    </Ellipse.RenderTransform>
</Ellipse>
```

We placed the `PathGeometry` in the resources so that we could use it both in the `Path` and the `DoubleAnimationUsingPath`. `Ball` doesn't quite stay on the path as it moves, because `Ball` is positioned using the upper-left corner of its bounding box. The corner is what is tracing the path exactly. Change the `Ellipse` to a `Rectangle` and you will be able to see this more clearly.

Controlling an Animation

In all our examples so far, we've used `BeginStoryboard`. This element was confusing to me when I first encountered it. The name "BeginStoryBoard" is meant to communicate that it is a trigger action for initiating a storyboard animation. However, the element also serves as a handle for manipulating the animation after it has begun.

First, you must provide a name for the `BeginStoryboard` element. After you do so, you can use a series of trigger actions to manipulate the animation. Table 23.3 lists the available actions.

TABLE 23.3   Trigger Actions for Controlling Animations

Name	Description
PauseStoryboard	Pauses the animation.
RemoveStoryboard	Removes the storyboard. (See the documentation regarding this.)
ResumeStoryboard	Resumes play for a paused storyboard.
SetStoryboardSpeedRatio	Allows you to change the speed of playback.
SkipStoryboardToFill	Jumps to the fill portion of the storyboard.
StopStoryboard	Stops playback.

In this context, the name BeginStoryboard makes a little more sense. However, note that all these derive from ControllableStoryboardAction, whereas BeginStoryboard is a direct descendant of TriggerAction.

Let's add some of these to our project:

1. Open the project LearningAnimation.

2. Modify the markup of Window1.xaml to match Listing 23.3.

LISTING 23.3   Window1.xaml Demonstrating a Controlled Animation

```
<Window x:Class="LearningAnimation.Window1"
        xmlns="http://schemas.microsoft.com/winfx/2006/xaml/presentation"
        xmlns:x="http://schemas.microsoft.com/winfx/2006/xaml"
        Title="Window1"
        Height="300" Width="300">
    <Window.Triggers>
        <EventTrigger RoutedEvent="Window.Loaded">
            <BeginStoryboard x:Name="BallStoryboard">
                <Storyboard Storyboard.TargetName="Ball"
                            Storyboard.TargetProperty="(Canvas.Left)">
                    <DoubleAnimation By="300"
                                     Duration="0:0:07.5"/>
                </Storyboard>
            </BeginStoryboard>
        </EventTrigger>
        <EventTrigger RoutedEvent="Button.Click"
                      SourceName="Pause">
            <PauseStoryboard BeginStoryboardName="BallStoryboard" />
        </EventTrigger>
        <EventTrigger RoutedEvent="Button.Click"
                      SourceName="Resume">
            <ResumeStoryboard BeginStoryboardName="BallStoryboard" />
        </EventTrigger>
    </Window.Triggers>
    <StackPanel>
        <StackPanel Orientation="Horizontal">
            <Button x:Name="Pause">Pause</Button>
            <Button x:Name="Resume">Resume</Button>
        </StackPanel>
        <Canvas>
            <Ellipse x:Name="Ball"
                Width="20" Height="20"
                Fill="Red"
                Canvas.Top="50" Canvas.Left="0">
            </Ellipse>
        </Canvas>
    </StackPanel>
</Window>
```

3. Notice that we named the Button elements, but we didn't need to wire the Click event. Instead, we capture it using the SourceName on EventTrigger. Run the application and click Pause and Resume.

An interesting item to note is that Storyboard, because it is a timeline, is really a set of instructions. Those instructions could be used in more than one location. The BeginStoryboard class is responsible for managing the objects that actually perform the animation. This is why we reference it, instead of referencing the Storyboard directly.

Alternative Animation Techniques

The technique we've been using this hour is called *storyboard animation*; however, there are a few other approaches to animation in WPF. Even though we are not going to cover them in this book, it's useful to know that they exist and when they are applicable. The alternative techniques are available only in code.

Local Animations

This approach can be used with any class that descends from AnimationTimeline. Most of the timeline classes we've discussed so far qualify. You can create an instance of the class in code, set its properties, and then call BeginAnimation on the target object passing in the target property and AnimationTimeline instance. The following snippet shows an example using C# 3.0:

```
var animation = new ColorAnimation
               {
                   From = Colors.Blue,
                   To = Colors.Yellow,
                   Duration = new Duration(TimeSpan.FromSeconds(2))
               };
var button = new Button();
button.BeginAnimation(Button.BackgroundProperty,animation);
```

This is a very simple and quick way to create an animation. The downside is that you are not able to control the animation interactively after it's triggered. Likewise, there is no way to use a local animation in styles and templates.

Clock Animations

Clock animations are very similar to local animations. You would use this approach if you need something more complex than a local animation, but you want more control than a storyboard provides (perhaps for tweaking performance).

With this approach you use CreateClock on AnimationTimeline to produce an instance of an AnimationClock. The object to animate then calls its

ApplyAnimationClock method passing in the dependency property and the clock. In C# 3.0, it would look like this:

```
var animation = new ColorAnimation
{
    From = Colors.Blue,
    To = Colors.Yellow,
    Duration = new Duration(TimeSpan.FromSeconds(2))
};
var clock = animation.CreateClock();
var button = new Button();
button.ApplyAnimationClock(Button.BackgroundProperty, clock);
```

Manual Animation

The final approach is to completely bypass the animation system. You should take this approach only in rare and special cases. WPF has a static class called CompositionTarget that represents the display surface of the application. It raises an event Rendering for every frame that it paints to the screen. In the handler for this event, you would need to manually update the properties you are interested in animating. You would also need to manually keep track of the time elapsed for your animation.

All these techniques are discussed, and examples are provided, on MSDN. Search for the subject "Property Animation Techniques Overview."

Applying Animations to Media Viewer

Using animations in your application may feel superfluous. However, there are a couple of ways of applying animations that can have a real and positive impact even on prosaic business applications.

In the Media Viewer, we have already demonstrated using animation to communicate the state of a control. For example, when we move the mouse over a button using the fancyButtonStyle, we use a subtle animation to draw attention to the button. Such visual cues might seem trivial, but they can have a profound effect on an application's usability.

Another exciting way to use animations is to provide tutorials or context-sensitive help within an application. A tutorial storyboard can actually interact with and change the state of the UI. Additionally, a user could pause, resume, or otherwise interrupt such a tutorial.

By the Way

> We posted a special XAML-only version of the Font Viewer from Part I at bluespire.com/wpf/FontViewer.xaml. In this online version, clicking on the help icon in the upper-right corner triggers an animated explanation of how to use the application.

Let's add a Help button that triggers some animated tool tips that explain the purpose of the controls in `MediaPlayer.xaml`. We'll use a story board that positions the tool tip over the various elements, and change the text to explain each element. We'll also use the same storyboard to temporarily turn off the progress bar so that it won't obscure the tips:

1. In the Media Viewer project, open `MediaPlayer.xaml`.

2. Locate the `Grid` with `DockPanel.Dock="Bottom"`. This should be the first `Grid` inside the `DockPanel`.

3. Inside this `Grid`, immediately after the `Grid.ColumnDefinitions` element, add the following markup:

```
<Canvas VerticalAlignment="Top"
        Margin="0 6 0 0">
    <StackPanel x:Name="tipBox"
                Canvas.Bottom="0">
        <Border CornerRadius="4"
                SnapsToDevicePixels="True"
                Width="100"
                Padding="4"
                Background="{StaticResource paleBrush}"
                BorderBrush="{StaticResource orangeBrush}"
                BorderThickness="1">
            <TextBlock TextWrapping="Wrap"
                       TextAlignment="Center"
                       Text="{Binding ElementName=tipBox,
                                      Path=Tag}" />
        </Border>
        <Path Margin="0 -1 0 0"
              SnapsToDevicePixels="True"
              Stroke="{StaticResource orangeBrush}"
              Fill="{StaticResource paleBrush}"
              Data="M40,0 L50,10 60,0" />
    </StackPanel>
</Canvas>
```

Let's examine this markup a bit before we go on. We're making use of a couple of layout tricks in order to achieve a specific effect. I wanted a tool tip box with a little arrow at the bottom, pointing to the element it is explaining. However, I wanted the tool tip box to resize vertically to fit its content. The `Border` with a set width containing a `TextBlock` with wrapping is very close to that. I placed the `Border` in `StackPanel` along with a `Path` to represent the arrow pointing down. The `Path` has a negative margin so that it will overlap with the `Border` and thus give the effect that they are a single element. The `StackPanel` takes care of making sure the `Border` and the `Path` are always stacked properly. We set `SnapsToDevicePixels` on `Border` and `Path` to ensure that there is not a seam between them.

The `Grid` that all this is located in is the same one that contains the media controls (play, stop, mute, and volume). We're using a `Canvas` as the container for the `StackPanel` (which is in turn the whole tool tip). Because the `Canvas` defaults to zero height, the bottom of the `Canvas` is located at the top of the `Grid`. This allows us to keep our tool tip snapped to the top of the `Grid` even when lengthy text causes it to resize. This is important because the tool tip won't be pushed down and hence obscure the controls it's describing. We also set a 6px margin on the top of the `Canvas` so that the arrow just slightly overlaps with the `Grid`.

4. We need to add a storyboard to control the tool tip. At the top of `MediaPlayer.xaml`, just under the opening tag, add this:

```
<UserControl.Resources>
    <Storyboard x:Key="tipStoryboard"
            Storyboard.TargetName="tipBox" >
        <DoubleAnimationUsingKeyFrames Storyboard.TargetProperty=
                            ➥ "(Canvas.Left)">
            <DiscreteDoubleKeyFrame KeyTime="00:00:00"
                            Value="115"/>
            <DiscreteDoubleKeyFrame KeyTime="00:00:02"
                            Value="150"/>
            <DiscreteDoubleKeyFrame KeyTime="00:00:04"
                            Value="185"/>
            <DiscreteDoubleKeyFrame KeyTime="00:00:06"
                            Value="280"/>
        </DoubleAnimationUsingKeyFrames>
        <StringAnimationUsingKeyFrames Storyboard.TargetProperty="Tag">
            <DiscreteStringKeyFrame KeyTime="00:00:00"
                            Value="Stops media when playing."/>
            <DiscreteStringKeyFrame KeyTime="00:00:02"
                            Value=
        ➥ "Plays media, or pauses currently playing media." />
            <DiscreteStringKeyFrame KeyTime="00:00:04"
                            Value="Toggles mute." />
            <DiscreteStringKeyFrame KeyTime="00:00:06"
                            Value="Controls the volume." />
        </StringAnimationUsingKeyFrames>
        <ParallelTimeline Storyboard.TargetProperty="Opacity">
            <DoubleAnimation BeginTime="00:00:00"
                        To="1"/>
            <DoubleAnimation BeginTime="00:00:08"
                        To="0"/>
        </ParallelTimeline>
        <ParallelTimeline Storyboard.TargetName="progressSlider"
                        Storyboard.TargetProperty="Opacity">
            <DoubleAnimation BeginTime="00:00:00"
                        To="0"/>
```

```
        <DoubleAnimation BeginTime="00:00:08"
                         To="1"/>
    </ParallelTimeline>
  </Storyboard>
</UserControl.Resources>
```

The storyboard targets the StackPanel, which we named tipBox. We named the storyboard tipStoryboard so that we can reference it in a button. The storyboard contains a series of timelines that execute in tandem. The DoubleAnimationUsingKeyFrames timeline is responsible for positioning the tipBox over each of the controls, whereas StringAnimationUsingKeyFrames simultaneously changes the text. (We are actually changing Tag on tipBox, but the TextBlock inside tipBox is bound to that property. This was to simplify the markup on the storyboard.)

By the Way

> You can manually set the Canvas.Left property on tipBox and see the result in the design pane. This is how I determined the values to use in the storyboard. Also, two seconds is probably too brief for displaying this sort of help, but it's almost too long when you are just interested in learning WPF.

We have two ParallelTimeline elements, which are just used to group some related timelines. The first one targets the Opacity of tipBox, causes it to fade in and fade out. The second is similar, except that it fades out the progressSlider control so that it won't be in the way of our tool tip.

5. Now we need a way to trigger the storyboard. We'll just add a quick help button inside the same Grid as the tipBox. Immediately beneath the Canvas element, add the following:

```
<Button Style="{StaticResource mediaButtonStyle}"
        Content="Help">
    <Button.Triggers>
        <EventTrigger RoutedEvent="Button.Click">
            <BeginStoryboard Storyboard="{StaticResource tipStoryboard}"/>
        </EventTrigger>
    </Button.Triggers>
</Button>
```

6. Finally, we want to set the Opacity to 0 on tipBox. This prevents the tool tip from being visible until we trigger the storyboard.

7. Run the application, switch to a view that displays the media player, and click our new Help button. The animation should resemble Figure 23.3.

FIGURE 23.3
Animated Help
for the Media
Controls.

Summary

Again we have only introduced the foundation for animating with WPF. However, you are now equipped to handle all kinds of animation scenarios, including animating by paths and key frames. If you encounter situations that we have covered, you now have enough understanding to research deeper into the possibilities that WPF has.

Q&A

Q. *What kinds of things can be animated?*

A. Virtually every element you have encountered in WPF so far can be animated. However, the technical answer is any class that descends from `Animatable`, `ContentElement`, or `UIElement`. On these classes only dependency properties can be targeted. Even a class such as `DoubleAnimation` can be animated.

Q. *How can I make an animation where an element fades in or out?*

A. You can animate the `Opacity` property for any `UIElement`. The value is a double ranging from 0.0 (completely transparent) to 1.0 (completely opaque).

Q. *What if I want to animate the position of something but I can't place it in a* Canvas*?*

A. Many properties affect position, and the answer depends on the layout context. Some options would be to animate the Margin property or a TranslateTransform.

Q. *Are these animation techniques applicable to 3D?*

A. Yes, you can employ the same techniques we've discussed here for 3D elements in WPF.

Workshop

Quiz

1. What properties can you use to prevent an animation from having a stiff or mechanical appearance?

2. Based just on the names, what are the differences between PointAnimation and StringAnimationUsingKeyFrames?

Answers

1. You can use AccelerationRatio and DecelerationRatio to modify the speed so that it does not move at a constant rate. This gives the appearance of the animation starting slowly and speeding up, and then slowing down at the end.

2. PointAnimation produces values of the type Point, and its interpolation is linear. StringAnimationUsingKeyFrames produces string values and requires the use of key frames for managing interpolation.

Activities

1. Read the various overview articles on MSDN regarding animation. Start by searching for "wpf animation overview," and then examine the additional links in the See Also section.

HOUR 24

Best Practices

What You'll Learn in This Hour:

▶ Application design and organization
▶ Layout practices
▶ Proper use of Styles, Templates and Resources
▶ Code and XAML conventions

If you've made it this far, you now have the knowledge and experience to tackle most WPF development projects. WPF is a huge framework, so you'll want to continue to seek out new information and techniques. As you do this, the one important thing you cannot do without is a firm foundation of good development practices. We've tried to provide this type of advice throughout the book, but this topic is so critical that we wanted to devote an entire hour to reviewing and expanding on these ideas.

Application Design

Writing high-quality software is hard—very hard. Often the vision you have at the beginning of a project does not exactly correspond with the product you end up with. Over the course of development, requirements often shift, either because of changes in corporate policies or new discoveries surrounding what users need to do their jobs more efficiently. These changes often leave developers with a hacked code base that is difficult to understand or maintain. Because the changing nature of an application is almost unavoidable, we'll make a few recommendations that will help mitigate the troubles and ensure a solid application design.

Orthogonality

Writing *orthogonal* code is the main goal of several of the principles we are going to mention. But what does this term mean? The term itself has origins in the geometric world, where it means "lying in right angles." Over time, however, this word has come to describe "things that are independent of one another." This latter definition more accurately applies to software design.

As you look over the code in a typical software solution, you'll find many different "categories" of code. You will typically have UI code (the primary subject of this book), business logic, data access, and other infrastructural concerns, such as logging and authentication. If you think over the previous list, you'll realize that these items are orthogonal. What does logging have to do with UI code? What does user application authentication have to do with your choice of data persistence (SQL Server vs. flat file)? Nothing. But often, over the course of developing an application, these unrelated bits of code end up mixed together. It happens as a matter of convenience, but what many a developer doesn't recognize is the pain that it will cause them later.

For example, consider this simple, common scenario: You are writing an application like the Contact Manager for your company. In the process of writing this program, you write code in each of the presenters to track errors by writing details to the application event log. This isn't a big deal, because there are only two presenters. Your program gets popular and users begin to ask for more features, causing you to create additional presenters and views, as well as extend those already in existence. You consider factoring the logging code out into its own class, but decide not to take the time right now. Several months pass and your application is being used by nearly every employee in your company. Things were fine for the first few versions, but lately users have been complaining of frequent crashes. Your boss is concerned and would like you to get to the bottom of this quickly. He asks you to add email-based error logging to the system. You're thinking this won't be a big deal, but then you look at the code base and are reminded that the application now has more than 30 presenters with corresponding views, as well as a number of other classes that are doing logging. Right now, you are wishing that you had refactored to a more orthogonal solution several months ago when it first occurred to you. Now you have five hours of work to do instead of five minutes.

Single Responsibility Principle/ Separation of Concerns

If you recognize the value of orthogonality, you'll want to apply two related principles to your coding: the *Single Responsibility Principle* (SRP) and *Separation of Concerns*

(SoC). An understanding of these concepts and an ability to practically apply them will go very far in helping you to achieve clean, maintainable code.

The Single Responsibility Principle states "there should never be more than one reason for a class to change." Taking our earlier example, the presenters in our Contact Manager are exhibiting multiple responsibilities. This is because any given presenter will require code changes if either its presentation logic changes *or* the logging policy changes. SRP is violated because the class has at least two reasons to change rather than one. To fix this problem, and make our code more orthogonal, we would apply Separation of Concerns (SoC).

SoC embodies a "divide and conquer" approach to programming. Rather than having huge, complex classes, our system should be built from smaller, more focused components that work together. One way to apply SoC to our Contact Manager example would be to create a new class, possibly called Logger. This class could have several overloaded Log methods that enable logging of various types of information. We would then refactor our presenters to use an instance of the Logger rather than writing directly to the event log. In the case that the logging policy changes, all you have to do is change the Logger. Now the Logger has only one reason to change, and so do the presenters, satisfying SRP.

Don't Repeat Yourself

One of the obvious things wrong with the logging code scenario is the simple, needless repetition of code. One of the most fundamental programming principles, Don't Repeat Yourself (DRY), says No! There are many ways to avoid repetitious code. You can factor out a helper method, derive a new base class, or apply SRP to factor out a completely new class. The key point is if you find yourself writing the same sort of code over and over again, there's something wrong. You're not producing DRY code.

Patterns

As you seek to write more orthogonal code by applying the preceding principles, you'll find some interesting challenges. It's not always easy. Fortunately, you're not stranded. Patterns are cataloged, tested solutions to common coding problems. Many of these patterns have already been implemented in .NET and WPF itself and can be used to improve your own code. If you have not studied design patterns or haven't been thoroughly exposed to refactoring, we heartily suggest you take a look. Becoming familiar with these tried techniques will improve your code and your ability to quickly create solid, proven solutions to even the most difficult problems.

There are many categories of patterns. You will frequently hear about design patterns, enterprise architecture patterns, refactoring patterns, and several others. These categories are pretty loose, and some patterns can be placed in multiple categories. The most popular category is design patterns. Design patterns are ones that are more applicable to a developer's everyday work. They address problems common to building object oriented systems.

> When I first began learning design patterns I went out of my way to look for places to use them. Be careful! Don't invent reasons to use design patterns that you like or are familiar/comfortable with. This adds unnecessary complexity. Instead, just write code. When you begin to see repetition or other "code smells," then and only then refactor. It is at this point that understanding the patterns helps you to *improve already working code.*

Inversion of Control/Dependency Injection

When you begin to apply the preceding principles and utilize some of the documented patterns, your code will be transformed. More often than not, instead of having a few monolithic classes, you'll end up with a lot of very small classes. Each of these classes will have a very specific purpose. To accomplish complex tasks, you will often end up with "manager" or "coordinator" classes that orchestrate the interactions between many smaller classes. These coordinating classes are *dependent* on the classes they use. Presenters are great examples of coordinating classes. To see a concrete example of this, look back at the Contact Manager application. Examine the ApplicationPresenter. The constructor signature is shown next:

```
public ApplicationPresenter(Shell view, ContactRepository contactRepository)
```

Notice that the presenter is dependent on both a Shell view and a ContactRepository. It cannot function without these other components, yet it doesn't take the responsibility of creating them. This is called *Inversion of Control*, often abbreviated IoC. The control of dependency creation is *inverted* because the presenter has given up its right to create the components it depends on. It is relying on some outside source to hand it the pieces it needs to work. These dependencies are then *injected* into the class via the constructor. This is known as *Dependency Injection*, or DI, and it adds a great deal of flexibility and extensibility to your software design. Some argue that code isn't truly object oriented unless its dependencies are inverted.

Dependency Injection Frameworks

In medium to large applications (and sometimes small ones, as well) it is very easy to wind up with a large number of classes, each having complex dependencies on other classes. For example, imagine that you have a Presenter class. The Presenter relies on a Security Provider, a Data Access class, and a Logging Provider. The Security Provider relies on a different Data Access class as well, and the Logging Provider relies on the file system and the email subsystem. This is *very* typical. A problem quickly arises: to create the original presenter, you have to also create a host of other classes and wire them all up. This is tedious and time consuming, not to mention that it creates very "noisy" code. Fortunately, there are several open source frameworks as well as a Microsoft supported solution to this problem. These *dependency injection containers* provide a way to declare your component dependencies. Then, in the case of the Presenter, you just say, "Hey container, give me a Presenter!" and the DI container determines all the dependencies, creates them, wires them, and hands you back a Presenter that is fully configured and ready for use. No hassle, no mess.

Ya Aren't Gonna Need It

Ya Aren't Gonna Need It, or YAGNI, is one of the simplest principles to understand, but very rarely followed. Simply put, YAGNI says that you should code only what you know you need right now, nothing more. Scores of programmers get carried away trying to think of every possible future need, and they go out of their way to work those things in before they have been demonstrated as necessary. This often causes overly complex code and a host of unused features. If you follow the principles discussed earlier, you end up writing code that is more flexible and easy to maintain and extend. When you do need to add new features, it will be a much easier task.

WPF as an Architecture Example

You shouldn't be surprised to hear that the architects of WPF used many of the techniques we've been discussing. So, understanding them will both help you develop your own software better and understand more deeply how WPF is put together and functions. Let's look at a few of the many examples:

▶ **Orthogonality**—To state the obvious, WPF is a UI framework. The designers have been careful to keep its implementation within the .NET Framework separate from other portions that are unrelated. It is therefore free to evolve separately from other pieces.

▶ **DRY**—The WPF architects employed many techniques to limit repetition. One of the easiest to spot is in its rich control hierarchy. Think back to Hour 16, "Visualizing Lists," when we looked at all the controls that are inherited from `ItemsControl` and `ContentControl`. Early on, the designers recognized some core features that many controls would posses, and factored them into these two important base classes. Furthermore, they recognized an even broader set of functionality expressed by types such as `FrameworkElement` and `Visual`. The application of DRY helped to eliminate a potentially massive amount of repetitive code.

▶ **Design Patterns**—WPF's architecture is based on many of the most common design patterns in use. To begin, the hierarchical nature in which a UI is built in WPF is a perfect example of the *Composite* pattern and the XAML parser is a very advanced *Factory* and *Interpreter*. The command system in WPF is an obvious implementation of the *Command* pattern and the `Decorator` base class is an equally apparent implementation of the *Decorator* pattern. The application object itself is a *Singleton*. The list goes on and on.

By the Way

Composite, Factory, Interpreter, Command, Decorator, and Singleton are popular design patterns. There is a wealth of information available about these patterns on the Web. Excellent descriptions of these individual patterns are available on Wikipedia.

▶ **SRP/SoC**—If you look at the templated nature of controls in WPF, you'll realize that a control's *behavior* has been separated from its *appearance*. The architects of WPF recognized this fundamental difference in concerns. They separated them by delegating the responsibility of behavior to the control and of appearance to the control template. Therefore, a control has only one reason to change (SRP)—if its behavior changes. If its appearance needs to change, you just change the control template.

UI Design and Architecture Concerns

The previous design principles can be applied to all aspects of an application. In the sections that follow, we'd also like to give some specific recommendations concerning the building of user interfaces.

Organization

Code organization is very important. You should have a meaningful overall structure to your solution. When it comes to a WPF project, you should think carefully about how you want to organize the various types of classes and resources. We have tried to demonstrate an appropriate WPF project structure of various levels of complexity over the course of this book. In general, if you are using an MVP pattern, you want to group your classes in folders/namespaces that indicate their role. If your project is large enough, the model classes will often be broken out into a separate assembly. You should also keep user controls and custom controls in a special namespace. These can also be put in their own assembly if you find yourself needing to use your custom controls across multiple projects. Generally, you will want to have a dedicated location for resources. Many real-world applications require some embedded graphics or other files. You may want to subdivide the resources folder if you find yourself with a large number of resources. Don't forget to add your XAML resource dictionaries here as well. Again, if the project is complex enough, you may want to break out your resource dictionaries based on the type of resource and merge them at runtime. Regardless of the organizational strategy you choose, you want your code base to be easily navigable. If you are looking for the `EditContactPresenter` or the `gradientBackgroundBrush`, you don't want to have to think to know where to find it. Strive to make the organization as intuitive as possible.

Model View Presenter (MVP)

It should be obvious by now that we favor the use of an MVP pattern for all but the most trivial of applications. One of the reasons is that it is one of the best examples of SRP/SoC. Designing your UI with this pattern in mind leads to a result that is much easier to maintain and extend than the alternatives. Also, if you want to use the principles of IoC/DI, it might be difficult if all your code is in a code-behind file. It requires a lot of extra work to figure out how to inject dependencies into classes whose construction you cannot control (instances that are created through XAML). These patterns work better with a presenter, where you have complete control over the classes, base classes, and constructors.

> Although we haven't mentioned Test Driven Development (TDD) explicitly in this book, many of the principles we have been discussing in this hour make this practice much easier. To that end, if you are writing unit tests for your code, you will find it nearly impossible to test code that exists in a UI code-behind file. This is yet another reason to use the MVP pattern. MVP allows you to more easily unit test the three components. In general, you'll find an emphasis on testability leads to good software design.

By the Way

Usability

With WPF as your toolset, you are virtually unlimited with regard to the types of UI you can create. Literally, almost anything you can imagine can be done. Nevertheless, this tremendous power and flexibility make it very easy to go wrong in your design decisions. Remember, the goal of a user interface is to help users get their jobs done quickly and painlessly. You want them to have increased productivity and actually enjoy what they are doing. Sticking with established UI patterns seen in popular software will help you to get a start in the right direction. Whenever you are building a user interface, you should be in constant communication with your users. In this way, they can give you feedback about the UI decisions you are making. If they are utterly bewildered by your design choices and can't relatively quickly figure out how to do what they need to do, you might want to reconsider the direction you are heading in. Here's one bit of advice we've found to be true in designing user interfaces: less is more.

Technical Considerations

So far, most of our recommendations have been concerned with higher level or more abstract notions about application design. Let's take a look at some more specific practices surrounding various areas of WPF that developers often have difficulty with.

UI Layout

Over the course of the book, we've taken a variety of approaches to handling UI layout. We hope that by now you are fairly comfortable with how to approach this issue. We'd like to restate a few earlier recommendations that may have more meaning to you now:

- ▶ Design your layout using the simplest and most explicit `Panel`.

- ▶ Do not be afraid to combine multiple `Panel`s to achieve the effect you desire. As you have seen in previous hours, this is the rule rather than the exception.

- ▶ Pay close attention to the runtime behavior of your layout. You may need to change your strategy to accommodate window resizing. Remember, some panels look the same at design time but behave differently at runtime.

- ▶ Choose layout options that allow for flexible sizing. Avoid setting hard-coded `Height` and `Width` properties when possible. Instead, if necessary, consider using `MinHeight`, `MinWidth`, `MaxHeight` and `MaxWidth`.

- If using a graphical UI tool such as the VS Designer or Expression Blend, keep a close eye on `Margin` and the other layout-related properties of your elements. Sometimes these tools get confused and alter these values in strange ways, resulting in unexpected layout behavior. It's often necessary to clean up your XAML after using one of these tools.

- Use `Canvas` only as a last resort. This panel was designed primarily for rendering `Drawings` (such as icons or logos), not UI. Using `Canvas` for ordinary layout scenarios can defeat the purpose of WPF's dynamic layout capabilities. If you want a similar effect, use a `Grid` control in combination with `Margin` set on its children. This creates a canvas effect in which the positioning is relative.

Resources

Traditional application resources, as well as those stored in a `ResourceDictionary`, are an important aspect of using WPF successfully. Here are a few bits of advice:

- Create a designated folder in your project for storing resources. We have mentioned this several times now because it is very important.

- If you have many resources, consider organizing them in subfolders. For example: Images, Fonts, Styles, ControlTemplates, and so on.

- Use `ResourceDictionary.MergedDictionaries` to combine the contents of multiple resource dictionaries into one. This is especially important in the `Application.Resources`.

- Pay attention to resources early on in the project. We recommend that you plan for this from the initial solution setup and rigorously enforce the organization. If you let it go by the wayside, you will quickly have an unmanageable solution on your hands.

Styles

Styles are one of the most powerful features of WPF. When used properly, they can greatly decrease repetitive XAML and improve the overall maintainability of the system. Here are a few thoughts:

- Factor out commonly used components of styles such as colors, brushes, and fonts into a central location. Then merge them into your style resources.

▶ Use BasedOn to help eliminate repetition across different styles whose targets share a common base class. Remember, you have to key your styles to use inheritance.

▶ If you want a consistent look to your app, regardless of operating system version, you will need to style all the basic controls explicitly. You can do this by creating styles with TargetType without specifying x:Key. Otherwise, the controls will pick up whatever the default control style is for that OS. Remember that a Button looks different on XP than on Vista.

▶ Stay on top of the organization of your styles. If you start to get a large resource dictionary, break things out into separate files and merge them at the appropriate places. For example, you may want to separate your default styles from the exceptions and styles for built-in controls from those of custom controls.

Templates

WPF's templating mechanism is perhaps its most innovative feature. Being able to reuse control behavior while changing the look of the control is a great example of SRP/SoC and is a boon for developers. Here are a few thoughts on how to work wisely with templates:

▶ Keep your control templates in a separate resource dictionary from your styles. Use styles to set the template, rather than setting the template on individual elements. This gives you more flexibility with the composition of styles and helps eliminate needless repetition.

▶ If you build a custom control, strive to place as much of its look as possible into a control template. This will give future users of your control the flexibility to change the look if they so desire.

▶ Remember that control templates and data templates can both be assigned by type or key. Additionally, they can be declared inline or in resources at various levels of the application. When choosing how to apply a template, consider issues of reuse as well as discoverability.

▶ Remember to use control templates specifically for changing the core composition of a control. A data template should be used to help a control properly render an unknown data type. Do not build specific data types into control templates.

▶ Use `TemplateBinding` as much as possible in your control templates, and then provide the desired default values in a style. This allows your templates to be more flexible, and other developers can use your controls without having to modify the templates.

Coding Conventions

Coding conventions vary from programmer to programmer. The important thing to remember is that if you are working on a team of two or more people you need to establish conventions about how you write your code so that there will be consistency across the code base, regardless of developer. We would like to make a few loose recommendations.

Code

▶ Be explicit in your naming of classes, methods, properties, and so on. Good naming is one of the most important aspects of code authorship. Code with well-named constructs is often self-documenting.

▶ Use Pascal casing for properties, methods, and types and Camel casing for other names. Do not use Hungarian notation.

▶ Use blank lines to improve readability. Format your code into visual blocks that convey intent.

▶ Use a little extra effort to keep your code neatly formatted. You can use the Ctrl+K+D shortcut in Visual Studio to autoformat your code. You can use the Tools, Options, Text Editor, [your language] to select formatting options in VS.

Naming Conventions

Several conventions are popular when it comes to naming items such as variables, classes, methods and so on.

In Pascal case, items have an uppercase letter at the beginning of each word. There is no separator between words. For example, PascalCase.

Camel case is similar to Pascal case, except that the first letter is lower case. For example, camelCase. The name "camel" refers to the humps that occur in the middle of the word.

Hungarian notation is the practice of prefixing names with an abbreviation of a type. For example, if you have a string that holds a person's first name you might call it `strFirstName`. This practice originated with programming languages that did not support static typing.

XAML

▶ Avoid naming elements without a reason and prefer the `x:Name` attribute over `Name` when you do.

▶ If you name elements, give them meaningful names. "ListBox1" is not a good name, but "FontList" is.

▶ Decide on a naming convention for control template parts and resources.

▶ Use a little extra effort to keep your XAML neatly formatted. You can use the Ctrl+K+D shortcut in Visual Studio to autoformat your code. Your team should decide on a XAML formatting convention. You can use the Tools, Options, Text Editor, XAML to select formatting options in VS.

Most of our recommendations about naming and formatting are useful in creating maintainable code. It is not our intent to wax on over this subject. There are entire documents devoted to coding conventions.

Summary

We've finally wrapped up our study of WPF. In this hour we took some time to look back over some of the techniques applied throughout the book. We've given several strong recommendations that should help you become a better software developer in general, and we tied in many WPF-specific tips and practices that should make your job easier. We hope you have enjoyed learning this new technology and building these applications along with us. You now have the knowledge, experience, and tools to succeed. We wish you the best in your WPF creations!

Q&A

Q. *You mentioned dependency injection containers. What are some of the most popular containers other developers are using?*

A. The three most common containers are Castle project's *Windsor* container, Jeremy Miller's *StructureMap*, and *Spring.NET* (a .NET port of the Java Spring framework). Microsoft has also recently developed a container called *Unity*.

Q. *What are some good resources I can use to learn more about design patterns and the other principles you mentioned?*

A. The classic C++/Smalltalk book on the subject is *Design Patterns*, written by Gamma, Helm, Johnson, and Vlissides (Addison-Wesley, 1994, 978-0-201-63361-0)—often referred to as the Gang of Four (GoF). There are plenty of .NET books on the same subject as well. Almost any one will do. A related book that examines a different set of patterns is *Patterns of Enterprise Application Architecture*, (PoEAA) by Martin Fowler (Addison-Wesley, 2002, 978-0-321-12742-6). Martin Fowler has several other books worth reading, as well as extensive materials on his website: www.martinfowler.com/. Finally, I would recommend *Agile Principles, Patterns, and Practices in C#* by Robert Martin and Micah Martin (Prentice Hall, 2006, 978-0-131-85725-4). This is perhaps the best overall look at these topics and related areas.

Workshop

Quiz

1. Briefly describe the MVP pattern and explain why it is important.

2. What is orthogonality and how is it beneficial to your code?

Answers

1. The MVP pattern is a GUI layer pattern generally composed of three types of objects: models, views, and presenters. The model objects represent business entities. If I were building an e-commerce application, the model might contain types such as customer, order, and product. The views are the actual visual representation of the user interface. In WPF this generally boils down to user controls and windows. Presenters are a special type of class that coordinates views and models. Sometimes they control other presenters as well. This pattern is important because it is a clear and practical application of SRP/SoC. Each class has a single responsibility and works with the other classes to achieve a goal. This separation of concerns keeps classes small and focused, making the UI easier to maintain and extend over time.

2. Orthogonal code is written in such a way that unrelated components can vary independently. For example, a data access component has nothing to do with a UI component, so a developer should be able to change either or both without affecting the other. Building systems in this way gives the code a longer lifespan because each of its individual components can adapt to changing business or technical needs without breaking the rest of the system.

Activities

1. Go out and build your own WPF applications!

PART V

Appendixes

APPENDIX A

Tools and Resources

When creating custom software, you want to do it as efficiently and painlessly as possible. To that end, we have included a brief listing of tools and other resources that we believe will help you in your work.

Developer Tools

A host of tools are available for developers to more effectively leverage WPF. Following is a list of the tools we think all WPF developers should have at their disposal.

Visual Studio 2008

This is the premier developer tool released by Microsoft for building .NET applications. You can find the trial versions at http://msdn2.microsoft.com/en-us/vstudio/products/aa700831.aspx.

Kaxaml

This tool was created by Robby Ingebretsen and is a fantastic, simple application for experimenting with XAML. Surprisingly, its preview mode rendering is better than Visual Studio. It can be found at www.kaxaml.com/.

Mole

Mole is a Visual Studio debugging visualizer created by Karl Shifflett, Andrew Smith, and Josh Smith. It allows you to better understand what is happening inside your WPF application at runtime by examining the effects of styles, properties, routed events, and so on. You can find the download and plenty of documentation at http://karlshifflett.wordpress.com/mole-for-visual-studio/.

Designer Tools

As WPF ages, more and more designer-centric products are becoming available. Following are a few of the most popular XAML designer applications.

Expression Blend

This is Microsoft's premier tool for designers who are creating user interfaces for WPF. We highly recommend this tool. More information can be found at www. microsoft.com/expression/products/overview.aspx?key=blend.

Mobiform's Aurora

Aurora is the leading third-party XAML design tool. It offers many of the same features as Blend, but has some of its own unique traits. The most notable trait is that it can be hosted inside your own applications. More information about this robust tool can be found at www.mobiform.com/products/Aurora/aurora.htm.

ZAM 3D

This tool is great for creating 3D content. There's no need to use any special converters or exporters; ZAM 3D works directly with XAML. The product's home page is found at www.erain.com/products/zam3d/.

XAML Converters

Designers and artists often have preferred tools that they use to create content. Allowing them to use these helps increase their productively and reduce frustration. Most of these tools are unaware of the existence of XAML. Fortunately a host of XAML exporters are available for the most common graphics and 3D applications.

2D

Adobe Illustrator: www.mikeswanson.com/XAMLExport/

Adobe Fireworks: www.infragistics.com/design/#VisualDesign

3D

Blender: www.codeplex.com/xamlexporter

Lightwave: www.shaxam.com/

Maya: www.highend3d.com/maya/downloads/tools/3d_converters/3782.html

3DS: www.wpf-graphics.com/Converter.aspx

Other Formats

SVG: www.wpf-graphics.com/ViewerSvg.aspx

Flash/SWF: www.mikeswanson.com/SWF2XAML/

Application Frameworks

Because building real applications can be quite difficult, a variety of frameworks can help you architect your solutions better. In many cases, these frameworks help to lessen the amount of tedious "boiler-plate" code that a developer has to write.

Caliburn

Caliburn is a WPF application framework written by the authors of this book. It has a wide range of features designed to make building WPF business applications easy and painless. It promotes best practices in software architecture by making it easy to use proven patterns such as MVC/MVP, and it aids in the development of complex composite applications by providing various forms of loose coupling. It is the most feature rich of the three frameworks listed here and is the first "from the ground up" WPF application framework to date. Caliburn is an open source project and its full source code, along with developer documentation, can be found at http://caliburn.tigris.org/.

WPF CAB

If you've worked previously with WinForms, you may have heard of the Composite Application Block (CAB). WPF CAB is an open source port of that technology to WPF. More information can be found at the Smart Client Contrib site: www.codeplex.com/scsfcontrib.

Prism

Prism is a new effort by the Microsoft Patterns and Practices team to attempt to create a WPF framework similar in function to its previous WinForms technology, CAB. At the time of this writing, it is too early to say whether this framework will be of any real use. Its features are not yet on par with Caliburn or WPF CAB. However, you can keep an eye on its progress at www.codeplex.com/prism.

Additional Resources

Icons

In Part II of the book, we built the Text Editor using a set of open source icons. The set is both high quality and versatile. They can be found at www.famfamfam.com/lab/icons/silk/.

APPENDIX B

3D Tutorial Using ZAM 3D

3D is one of the *really* cool features of WPF. It's something that we all get very excited about. Unlike most of the other features in WPF, though, learning how to make use of 3D can be somewhat challenging. In the 3D world, you will encounter terms and concepts that are likely to be unfamiliar to many developers. Things like diffusion, materials, meshes, normals, field of view, and orthographic project.

Even so, you can do a lot given the proper tools. One such tool is ZAM 3D from Electric Rain. Although everything that we produce in this tutorial could be written by hand directly in XAML, we have found that it is very impractical. (This is coming from someone who often prefers to hand write XAML.)

Unfortunately, a trial edition of ZAM 3D isn't available at the time of this writing. However, you can still follow along using a trial of ZAM 3D's sister product, Swift 3D. The trial edition can be found at www.erain.com/downloads/Trials/.

(There is a 30-day money back guarantee for ZAM 3D as well.)

You can also use Blender and the XAML Exporter for Blender, both of which are free. However, there is a very steep learning curve for Blender, especially if you have no prior experience in creating 3D content.

Understanding the Interface

Let's very quickly examine the interface for ZAM 3D. When you open the application for the first time, it will look like Figure B.1.

Our description here is by no means exhaustive. The documentation that comes with ZAM 3D covers this in much more detail.

1. **Viewports**—Here we can examine the 3D scene that we are creating.

2. **Hierarchy Toolbar**—Displays all of the models in our scene.

3. **Animation Toolbar**—Contains the timeline and key frames for any animations.

4. **Rotation Trackball**—Displays the currently selected model and allows us to rotate it.

5. **Gallery Toolbar**—Allows us to easily apply animations and textures to the models in our scene.

6. **Property Toolbar**—Various properties for adjusting your scene or selected item.

7. **Editor Tabs**—Used for switching to the various editors ZAM 3D has available.

FIGURE B.1
ZAM 3D's interface.

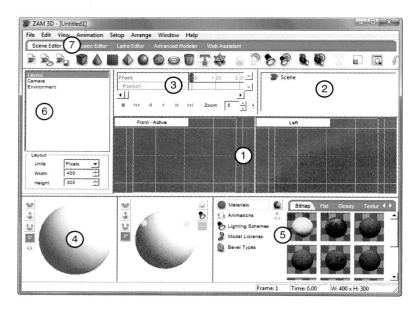

Creating a Carrot

In this sweeping overview of ZAM 3D, we're going to create a cartoonish carrot like the one shown in Figure B.2.

We'll be able to export the 3D scene and the animation as XAML, and then place it into a real WPF application:

1. Open ZAM 3D. By default, you should have a brand new project.

2. Select the Lathe Editor tab at the top. We'll use this editor to create the main body of our carrot. The idea behind a *lathe* is that you create a 2D path that can be spun on an axis to produce the surface of your 3D model. I like to think of this 2D path as half of a silhouette. This technique is very useful for modeling objects such as wine glasses, candlesticks, and lamps.

3. By default, the Add Point Tool is selected. This is the second icon on the toolbar, and can be selected by pressing A. Notice that we can see the X and Y position of our cursor in the status bar.

4. Using this tool create five points, as shown in Figure B.3. Don't worry about being precise. Just for reference, my points were located at (0,–0.2), (0.04,–0.12), (0.07,0), (0.07,0.09), and (0,0.11).

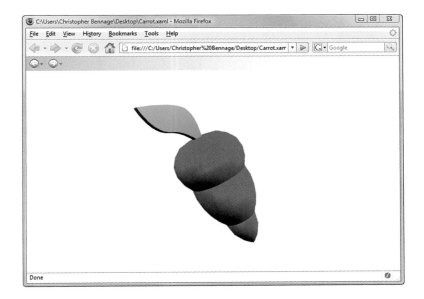

FIGURE B.2
Rotating carrot.

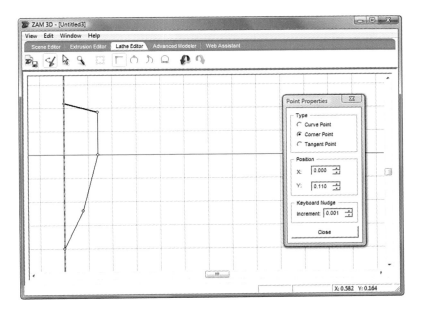

FIGURE B.3
Adding points in the Lathe Editor.

5. The path we drew will rotate around the Y axis. Select the Scene Editor tab at the top, and you'll see that our "carrot" looks very angular at the moment. Switch back to the Lathe Editor.

6. Our carrot needs some curve. Choose the Shape Tool by pressing S on the keyboard. The third icon on the toolbar is now selected.

7. Drag a selection around the three middle points on the point. You can tell that a point is selected when the circle representing it is filled in.

8. With those three points selected, press T on the keyboard. This converts the selected points from *corner points* to *tangent points*. Each tangent point now has two *handles* that we can use to adjust the curvature of the path.

9. Still using the Shape Tool, adjust the handles by clicking and dragging them until the path looks something like Figure B.4. You can use Ctrl+Z to undo any adjustments, and remember that you don't need to worry about being precise.

FIGURE B.4
Adjusting tangent points.

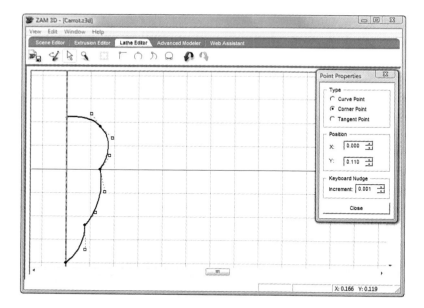

10. Switch back to the Scene Editor. Our carrot is visible in the viewports. We are viewing it from the front and the left. Notice an item called "Lathe" in the Hierarchy Toolbar. This is the carrot model we just created.

11. Examine the Gallery Toolbar in the lower right. Select the tab labeled Flat. You'll see a series of spheres displaying the available flat materials. Flat means "not shiny."

12. Scroll down through the materials until you find a color that is sufficiently orange. If you hover your mouse over a material, a ToolTip appears, displaying its name. I chose "ER – Flat 68."

13. Click and drag your selected material and drop it onto the carrot in the viewport. The material will be immediately applied to the model.

14. Now let's create the leafy bit to go on top of our carrot. Select the Extrusion Editor tab from the top.

15. Using the Add Point tool (A), create a shape similar to the one in Figure B.5. After adding the four points, click the first point again to close the shape. The cursor displays a + when you are over the first point. For reference, my points are located at (–0.05,0.05), (0.05,0.1), (0.06,0.015), and (–0.05,–0.05).

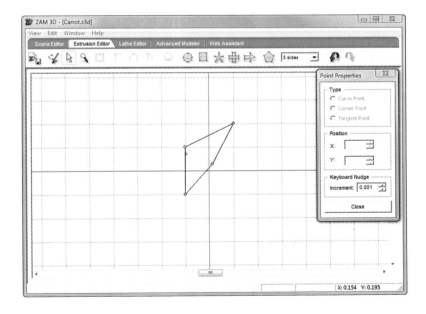

FIGURE B.5
Creating a leaf with the Extrusion Editor.

16. Select the upper-left and the lower-right points using the Shape tool (S). You can hold down Shift and drag+select them individually, but don't hold Shift and click them.

17. With the two points selected, press U to convert the corner points to *curve points*. Adjust the handles until the path resembles Figure B.6.

FIGURE B.6
Making the leaf
curvy.

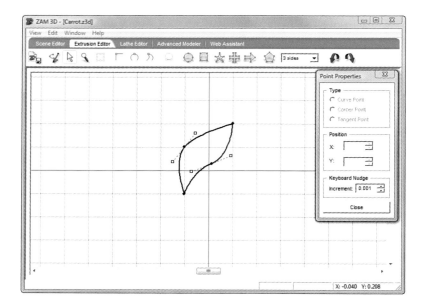

18. Switch back the Scene Editor. In the Front viewport, you can see that the leaf is too low. We need to move it upward. In the Left viewport, you can see that the leaf is wider than the carrot. Also notice that the new model is now in the Hierarchy Toolbar under the name Extrusion.

19. Click the leaf in the Front viewport and drag it toward the top. The movement is restricted to the X and Y axes. If the top of your carrot is outside the viewport, click the third from the last icon on the main toolbar. Its ToolTip reads Frame All Objects. The icon is circled in Figure B.7.

20. With the leaf still selected, click Sizing in the Properties Toolbar. Underneath the Properties Toolbar, controls appear for adjusting the size.

21. Change the Depth from 0.2 to 0.02.

22. Let's make our leaf a glossy, shiny green. Go to the Gallery Toolbar and click the icon between the word Materials and the tabs. Its ToolTip reads Toggle Material Drop Surface. If we don't toggle it, we have to drop a material on each of the four sides of the leaf.

The icon is circled in Figure B.8.

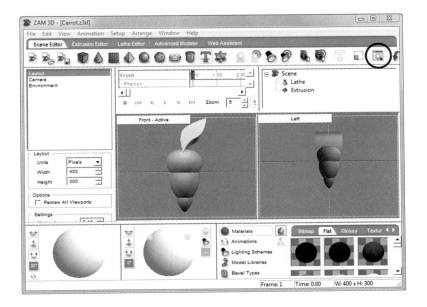

FIGURE B.7
Framing all the
objects.

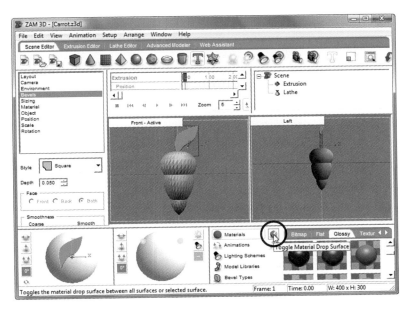

FIGURE B.8
Toggling the
material drop
surface.

23. Locate a nice glossy green; I used "ER – Glossy 21." Drag it onto the leaf model
in one of the viewports.

24. Hold down Shift and select both the leaf and the carrot. When they are both selected, you will see Group of 2 Objects appear in the Hierarchy Toolbar. On the left, just under the Properties Toolbar, change the name of the group to **Carrot**.

25. Now we can treat the two models as a single object. We're going to tilt the carrot so that the animation will be more pronounced. In the Rotation Toolbar, click the icon labeled 0°, then select 30°. This means that we can rotate the selection only in 30° increments.

26. Click the icon just above 30°. Its ToolTip reads Lock Spin. This restricts the rotation to just the X,Y plane.

27. Click and drag the carrot in the Rotation Toolbar until it resembles Figure B.9.

FIGURE B.9
Rotating the carrot.

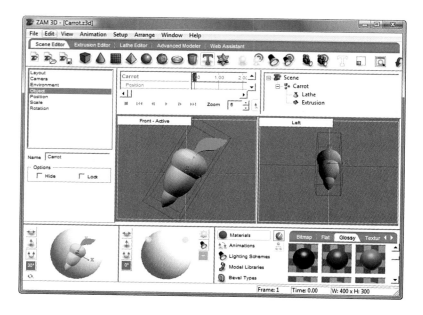

28. Back in the Gallery Toolbar, select Animations.

29. Underneath the first tab, Common Spins, you will see a number of readymade spin animations. Click and drag the first one, Horizontal Left, onto the carrot in one of the viewports.

30. Examine the Animation Toolbar and you will see that timeline controls are now available. Click the play icon to preview the animation.

31. Now we are ready to move our animated 3D carrot into a WPF application! From the menu select File, Export Scene to XAML.

32. There are lots of options here. For simplicity, we'll accept the default options. This will create a single, standalone XAML file that will begin playing our animation as soon as it loads.

33. Open the XAML file we just exported in a text editor, such as Notepad. You can now copy and paste the XAML directly into a Visual Studio project. Some of the namespace declarations are redundant, but it won't hurt anything if you create a Button and paste this markup inside of it!

APPENDIX C

Project Source (downloadable)

Creating a real world WPF application often requires large amounts of XAML and code. We realize that you may be hesitant to spend the required time to enter the source from this book into Visual Studio, so we have made it available to you online.

The code is divided into the following files:

- ▶ FontViewer.zip

- ▶ TextEditor.zip

- ▶ ContactManager.zip

- ▶ MediaViewer.zip

Regarding the Media Viewer, you will need to replace the icons referenced in the `MenuView.xaml` file with your own. The design is built for images sized at 256x256.

 By the Way

The code can be downloaded from the book website:

1. Go to www.informit.com/title/9780672329715.

2. Click Downloads.

3. Click one of links that appear, and the download should start automatically.

Index

SearchBar, 215

Contact Manager, adding to, 214-215

SearchBar.xaml listing (14.2), 214

SearchBar.xaml.cs listing (14.3), 214-215

secondary colors, 317

SeekStoryboard inheritor (TriggerAction), 379

Selection Range (Slider), 361

Selector class, 260-261

separation of concerns (SoC), 199

Separation of Concerns principle, 178

SetStoryboardSpeedRatio inheritor (TriggerAction), 379

Setter, 381

setting properties, 20-21

Several Lines in Window1.xaml listing (18.1), 294-295

shapes, 291

ellipses, drawing, 299

headers, drawing, 299-302

lines, drawing, 292-295

media controls, styling, 303-306

path geometry, 306-310

polygons, drawing, 296-298

polylines, drawing, 295, 297-298

rectangles, drawing, 299

stream geometry, 310-311

strokes, drawing, 292-295

SharpDevelop, 13

Shell.xaml listing (12.1), 180-181

shells

application shells, creating, 179-182

enhancing, 200-201

solution shells, creating, 179-182

Shifflett, Karl, 423

SideBar.xaml.cs, 200

signatures, 68

Silverlight, WPF, compared, 14-15

Simple Button in XAML listing (2.1), 19-20

Simple Contact Form XAML listing (5.1), 62-63

Simple Grid Layout listing (4.1), 48-49

SkewTransform, 333

SkipStoryboardTo Fill inheritor (TriggerAction), 379

Slider, 182

functional parts, 360

Slider named part (controls), 359

sliders, templates, creating for, 360-362

Smith, Andrew, 423

Smith, Josh, 423

SoC (separation of concerns), 199

SoC (Separation of Concerns), applications, designing, 408, 412

SolidColorBrush, 319

solution shell, creating, 179-182

solutions, applications, setting up, 268-271

SoundPlayerAction inheritor (TriggerAction), 379

Source property (RoutedEventArgs), 123

Span inline element (TextBlock), 61

SpeedRatio property, 392

splined interpolation, key frames, 395

split pane, Visual Studio 2008, 29

SRP (Single Responsibility Principal), applications, designing, 408-409, 412

StackPanel function, 45-47

standard executable files, 93

States.cs listing (12.4), 188

StaticResource markup extension, 23

DynamicResource markup extension, compared, 216

StickyNoteControl named part (controls), 359

benefits, 10-11

data binding, 9

declarative UI, 7

layout, 7

markup extensions, 23

scalable graphics, 7-8

sibling libraries, 6

Silverlight, compared, 14-15

styling, 9

templates, 8-9

tools, 13-14

triggers, 9

WPF CAB, 425

WrapPanel function, 52-54

X-Z

X:Array markup extension, 23

x:Null markup extension, 23

x:Type markup extension, 23

XAML, 7, 14, 17-18, 24

application design, 418

collection views, 248-249

markup extensions, 22-23

properties

Content property, 21-22

setting, 20-21

syntax, 19-23

XAML converters, 424-425

XAML files, 94

applications, converting to, 94-95

renaming, 30-32

XAML-only Font Viewer, 402

XBAP files, 93

applications, converting to, 96-97

publishing, 97-98

XML namespaces, 19

YAGNI (Ya Aren't Gonna Need It), 131

application design, 411

ZAM 3D, 424, 427

carrot animation, creating, 428-435

Extrusion Editor, 431

interface, 427-428

Lathe Editor, 429

Sams **Teach Yourself**

When you only have time
for the answers™

Whatever your need and whatever your time frame, there's a Sams **Teach Yourself** book for you. With a Sams **Teach Yourself** book as your guide, you can quickly get up to speed on just about any new product or technology—in the absolute shortest period of time possible. Guaranteed.

Learning how to do new things with your computer shouldn't be tedious or time-consuming. Sams **Teach Yourself** makes learning anything quick, easy, and even a little bit fun.

Visual Basic 2008 in 24 Hours

James Foxall

ISBN-13: 978-0-672-32984-5

C++ in One Hour a Day

Jesse Liberty
Bradley Jones
Siddhartha Rao

ISBN-13: 978-0-672-32941-8

SQL in 24 Hours, Fourth Edition

Ryan Stephens
Ron Plew
Arie Jones

ISBN-13: 978-0-672-33018-6

ASP.NET 3.5 in 24 Hours

Scott Mitchell

ISBN-13: 978-0-672-32997-5

WPF in 24 Hours

Rob Eisenberg
Christopher Bennage

ISBN-13: 978-0-672-32985-2

Sams Teach Yourself books are available at most retail and online bookstores, in both print and e-book versions. For more information or to order direct visit our online bookstore at **www.informit.com/sams**

Online editions of all Sams Teach Yourself titles are available by subscription from Safari Books Online at **safari.samspublishing.com**

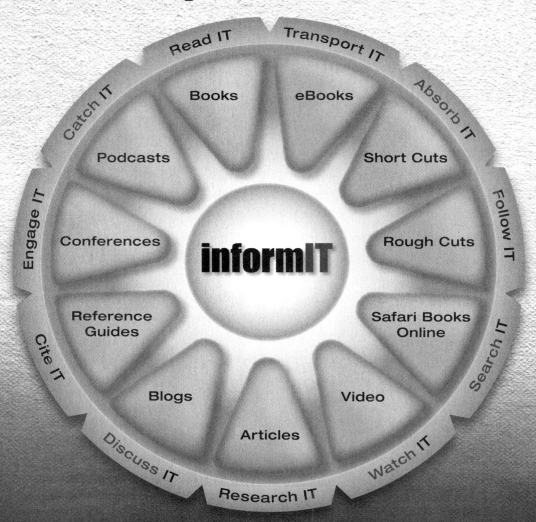